POETICS OF LOVE IN THE ARABIC NOVEL

Nation-State, Modernity and Tradition

Wen-chin Ouyang

EDINBURGH
University Press

For my mother
林艷芳

and my brother
文怡

Transferred to digital print 2015

Edinburgh University Press Ltd
22 George Square, Edinburgh EH8 9LF
www.euppublishing.com

Typeset in 11/13 JaghbUni by
Servis Filmsetting Ltd, Stockport, Cheshire, and
printed and bound in Great Britain by
CPI Group (UK) Ltd, Croydon CR0 4YY

A CIP record for this book is available from the
British Library

ISBN 978 0 7486 4273 1 (hardback)
ISBN 978 0 7486 5505 2 (webready PDF)
ISBN 978 0 7486 5507 6 (epub)
ISBN 978 0 7486 5506 9 (Amazon ebook)

CONTENTS

ACKNOWLEDGEMENTS

In the ten years since I began working on intertextuality and the intersection between classical and modern poetics and prosaics in modern Arabic literature, I have incurred innumerable professional and personal debts. Colleagues, friends and students listened to me patiently, at conferences or social gatherings, in living rooms or classrooms, and gave me invaluable feedback and support. Many colleagues even published some of the material I wrote on the subject in articles and book chapters. Those early contemplations are not always recognisable in *Poetics of Love in the Arabic Novel* or its companion volume, *Politics of Nostalgia in the Arabic Novel*, but they remain the kernel of the vision that gave shape to my books. I am particularly grateful to Roger Allen, Giovanni Canova, Aboubakr Chraïbi, Marshall Brown, Sabry Hafez, Marlé Hammond, Philip Kennedy, Haida Liang, Tim Matthews, Robin Ostle, Paul Starkey, Geert Jan van Gelder and Robert Weninger. I thank AHRB (now AHRC) for giving me a research leave grant in 2002 that allowed me time off to write the first part of this book and to map the remainder of the project. Above all, I thank Michael Beard and Mohamed-Salah Omri for their friendship. They have been and will always be my truest intellectual interlocutors.

Prologue

PRESENTING THE PAST: THE ARABIC NOVEL AND THE DIALECTICS OF MODERNISATION

> Our Arabic novel continues to travel along the European path set by Balzac, and other realists of the nineteenth century, or by the writers of the New Novel like Robbe-Grillet and Nathalie Sarraute, by whom our new novelists have been influenced.
>
> Yūsuf Idrīs, *Islām bilā ḍifāf*, p. 131

In his assessment of the Arabic novel, Yūsuf Idrīs (1927–91) characteristically undermined the efforts of all contemporary Arab novelists. While writing about Mexican novelist Gabriel Garcia Marquez, Idrīs underscores the contrast between the success of *Autumn of the Patriarch* in 'Mexicanising' the novel, as well as his own in 'Egyptianising' drama, and the failure of all Arab novelists in 'Arabicising' the novel.[1] Idrīs, whose fame rests on his successful, bold experiments in the Arabic short story and drama, is clearly engaged in self-promotion. He is alluding to his success in creating an Egyptian theatre and authentic Egyptian plays (*riwāyāt miṣriyya aṣīla*), dealing with modern global, local Egyptian problems – *al-mushkila al-miṣriyya al-maḥaliyya al-ᶜālamiyya al-ḥadītha*.[2] His appraisal of the Arabic novel is, first, not atypical among Arab intellectuals, critics and historians of Arabic literature at the time, and second, symptomatic of the tensions prevalent in contemporary Arab culture – the tension between the deceptive polarity of the present-West-other-based 'modernity' and the past-tradition-self-oriented 'authenticity' in the post-colonial Arab world.

The colonial encounter of the nineteenth and twentieth centuries, which initiated accelerated cross-cultural exchanges between Europe and the Arab world, including Egypt, led to irrevocable changes in Arab culture. These changes have in turn provoked a new process of soul searching among the Arab intellectuals about the shape and future of their culture often in terms of polarities derived from the binary opposites of 'East' and 'West'.

The cluster of adjectives Idrīs uses to describe the purpose and function of theatre as he envisions it – Egyptian, modern, global and local – address and challenge a set of paradoxes proposed by cultural critics in their discussion of post-colonial conditions in the Arab world, and by writers and literary critics in their assessment of the predicament of modern Arabic literature. Locating his discourse in the central debate about the legitimacy of modern Arabic fiction (short story, drama and novel) as genres of cultural and literary expression, Idrīs brings up three interconnected dichotomies often articulated in the discourses on Arab culture and Arabic literature. The word 'Egyptian' decisively pleads for 'authenticity' – a concept rooted in the fundamental question of identity. In this instance, the 'self' is defined against the 'other', in this case, the non-Egyptian West and the rest of the Arab world. The second adjective, 'modern', intervenes in the dilemma between modernist aspirations and traditional tendencies to the benefit of the former, a dilemma pertinent to the problematic relationship to the 'past'. Finally, the pairing of 'global and local' betrays the impulses to simultaneously participate in shaping the civilisation of the world and maintain distinct characteristics, or to concomitantly move towards the 'centre' while maintaining the privileges of the 'margin'. The boundaries of these paradoxes are, however, collapsed. The clustering of these adjectives reveals that legitimacy– the crux of the matter – is founded on the dissolution of all three paradoxes. More importantly, they question at the same time the plausibility of the binary oppositions implied by the very idea of a paradox, and invite us to re-examine the way we read texts and write about them. It is the collapse of these critical categories in the discourse on text and the textual discourse presented by Idrīs that challenges and guides the ways we read contemporary Arabic literary texts. Reading the Arabic novel is complicated by its cross-cultural genealogy, problems of definition and post-colonial cultural and identity politics.

CROSS-CULTURAL GENEALOGY

Critics and historians of the Arabic novel agree that as a literary form, broadly defined as a form of storytelling with specific internal structures, or conventions, it came into being in Arabic culture and literature at the turn of the twentieth century. The rise of the Arabic novel, many historians of Arabic literature observe, is one of the fruits of the process of cultural exchange of the colonial period. They more specifically situate the birth of the genre in the cultural and literary renaissance of the nineteenth century in the Levant and, more importantly, Egypt, during the reign of Muḥammad ^{c}Alī and his family. Modern Arabic fiction in general and the novel in particular emerged and developed after a century of translating and imitating European works. There is, however, no agreement on its origins, on which any history of the genre is dependent. The Arabic novel may be traced to the European tradition alone, or to both European and pre-modern Arabic precursors.

Early historians of the genre ascribe to the notion that the Arabic novel is imported from the West and bears no relation to any form of pre-modern Arabic storytelling,[3] even as they acknowledge this tradition. Matti Moosa, for example, dismisses the *Arabian Nights* and the *Maqāma* as possible ancestors of modern Arabic fiction because '[t]hey are completely different not only from each other but also from the recent fiction, particularly the short story, in their scope, their relation to the environment, and their form'.[4] In fact, the contrary was the case, argues ^{c}Abd al-Muḥsin Ṭāhā Badr. In their eagerness to define distinct Egyptian characteristics against the might of European civilisation, Arab writers turned to emulating this aggressive, arrogant and powerful Western model, consequently rejecting their own cultural heritage.[5] The novel, *al-riwāya al-faniyya*, the product of the social transformations of the middle class during the rise of the modern city, appeared only around the 1919 revolution of Sa^{c}d Zaghlūl as a critical response to the revolution as well as the earlier types of storytelling.[6] Muḥsin J. al-Mūsawī, agrees,[7] asserting that the Arabic novel remains until today imprisoned in the purposes, structures and conventions appropriated from the Western novel, failing to establish an authentic, unique identity.[8]

A younger generation of historians contrarily trace the origins of the Arabic novel to pre-modern forms of Arabic storytelling. Ibrāhīm al-Sa^{c}āfīn, for example, refutes the Western origin of the Arabic novel and insists that it is rooted in the Arabic storytelling tradition and the cultural context of the Arab world, and has in the past few decades successfully achieved authenticity, or what he deems 'native characteristics' independent of the Western novel.[9] The influence of the Western novel on its Arabic counterpart during the colonial period, albeit undeniable, should be viewed in the broader context of the history of cultural exchanges between East and West. The emergence of the novel in Europe was indebted to Arabic storytelling, which travelled to Europe initially via Spain in the thirteenth century in the form of heroic tales and the *maqāmāt*, and later through translations of the *Thousand and One Nights* in the early eighteenth century.[10] The Western influence on the Arabic novel is then more the case of what goes around comes around. The novel, both European and Arabic, belongs to the Arabic family of storytelling rather than the Western one.

Problems of definition compound the confusion. The vagueness of the Arabic term used today to designate the novel is conveniently suitable for the purposes of a revisionist history. *Al-riwāya* at first denoted both story and drama during the Nahḍa, has historically meant narration and narrative in the corpus of classical Arabic literature, and its definition need not be confined to the parameters set by the type of Western novel circulating in the Arab context. The classical roots of the Arabic have been obscured to the critics until recently, Manṣūr Qaysūma argues, for two main reasons: the relative narrow definition of the novel on the basis of plot and character development in the Arabic context (here, clearly shorn of the problems of definition in the European context); and the superficial understanding of not only the early Arabic novels, what others consider 'prototypes' or 'forerunners', but also of the Arabic storytelling tradition. In the first instance, translations of the Western novel during the nineteenth century Nahḍa contributed in no small degree to the emphasis on the Western influence. The types of novels translated into Arabic shaped the perspectives of the critics in their assessment of the early Arabic novel, leading to the dominance of the West-based definition of the genre. And secondly, the critics saw only the tradition of the periods of decline of Arabic storytelling not the golden age. Their lack of understanding of this tradition inevitably prevented them from seeing the continuity between the Arabic novel and pre-modern Arabic storytelling.[11]

The ambivalence surrounding the origins of the Arabic novel is also traceable to the cultural politics relevant to definitions of modernity and identity politics of the post-colonial Arab world. The West undeniably played an instrumental role in stimulating modernisation in Arab culture, but it also participated in rupturing the Arabs' relationship with their past. The discourses on the Arabic novel are haunted by this perceived rupture with 'tradition', and the consequent problematic of an 'authentic' Arab identity. Even those who locate the Arabic novel in the Western tradition are not immune to the question of authenticity. 'Haikal's Zainab is the first Egyptian novel', proclaims Ali Jad, 'of literary merit to have been written in response to the concerted call for locally inspired literature'.[12] Ḥamdī Sakkūt concurs but terms it differently:

> The first work that can be considered a true novel, in the sense that it has a proper plot and characterization, and moreover endeavors

to depict Egyptian life in a realistic way instead of adapting some Western theme, was Muhammad Husain Haikal's *Zainab*.[13]

Arab modernists, challenged to provide their visions of modernity with 'authenticity', have had to mediate the two poles of various paradoxes: of 'self' versus the 'other'; 'past' versus 'present'; 'tradition'-'East' versus 'modern'-'West'; imitation versus originality; and cultural subordination versus 'authenticity', and negotiate among the pulls of these paradoxes for a conception of concomitantly modern and 'authentic' Arab identity. The title of al-Mūsawī's later book, *Thārāt Shahrazād*, conveys in one stroke these paradoxes in their fullness. It summarises the (hi)story of the Arabic novel: it is both narrative and counter narrative, traditional and original, borrowed and authentic; it is a narrative rooted in the Arabic storytelling tradition, as well as the Western novel; it tells the (hi)story of modern Arabs and resists the Western narrative of the Arabs; and it is distinctively Arab and modern despite its Western origins and traditional roots. The first word of this title, *thārāt*, evokes concurrently the revolt against tradition – represented by Shahrazād, who has become the symbol of Arabic tradition of storytelling that had previously been excluded from the Arabic literary corpus – and revenge against the externally imposed Western influence – invoked by the adjective *ḥadīth* (modern) used to describe contemporary Arabic narrative. His reference to Shahrazād, and his analysis of the significance of the incorporation of storytelling techniques of the *Thousand and One Nights* in the Arabic novel, bespeak the importance of tracing the Arabic novel to the classical Arabic genres of storytelling. The absence of this genre in the recognised traditional Arabic literary canon, or what al-Mūsawī calls absence of critical awareness of the pre-modern Arabic tradition of storytelling even among early modern Arab intellectuals and writers,[14] then, presents another complication. How may proponents of the Arabic novel legitimate the borrowing of a genre from the colonisers and argue for its potential centrality in the twinned process of decolonisation and modernisation? Histories and critical writings about the Arabic novel, as well as the subject of their contemplation, are – willy-nilly – parts of and participants in the cultural and identity politics surrounding decolonisation and modernisation.

POST-COLONIAL IDENTITY POLITICS

In an analysis of *Ḥadīth ᶜĪsā Ibn Hishām* (1898–1902; 1907) by Muḥammad al-Muwayliḥī (1858–1930), Asfour asserts that the Arabic novel tells its own story which in fact is the search for an identity.[15] The formulation of this identity needs to be located in the multi-layered tension between the 'self' and 'other' surrounding the birth of the Arabic novel

> in a society in the process of dividing itself. Its present is torn between the traditions of its past and the visions for its future in the same way that the identity of this society is being torn between its heritage, which propels it towards an utopian dream of its past golden age, and the civilisation of the foreign other, which pushes it towards a contradictory utopian dream of a promising future. This search for identity is what makes the Arabic novel begin from the premise of the paradox for change: the polarity between past and present on the one hand, and present and aspirations for the future on the other hand. In this paradox, the relation of the national/ist self with its (Arab) heritage intersected with its relation with the present of the (Western) other within the space of the Arabic novel. The rupture between present impulses to move forward to the future and the other impulses to return to the past has become pervasive in the Arabic novel. Parallel to this rupture is yet another rupture: the rupture between the national/ist self and the Western other, especially when the subordination to this other is juxtaposed to the self's subordination to the heritage of its past. The other haunts the national/ist self with its advanced technology and science and that insists on its (self's) alienation from its (other's) world.[16]

The tension between the 'self' and the 'other' is palpable in *Ḥadīth ᶜĪsā Ibn Hishām*, Asfour tells us. It combines the Western novel with the *Maqāma*[17] and delineates a space falling between 'Easterness' and 'Westerness', and between Arab and foreign. There is no longer any room for the antiquated protagonist Aḥmad Pasha, resurrected from his grave to witness the changes in society. He must therefore return to his grave because he belongs to the past.[18] The space, as well as the characters' movement, are in the narrator ᶜĪsā Ibn Hishām's summation, neither Eastern nor Western, or in Asfour's take, both Eastern and Western.[19]

Asfour describes here the discourse on and in the Arabic novel. This discourse is constructed on the notions that the 'self' is distinct from the 'other, and that the 'other' threatens to subsume the 'self', to render it non-distinct. His concern is not atypical in the post-colonial discourses on culture in which the integrity of the subjectivity of the previously colonised subject has become a matter of some urgency. How will these subjects decolonise, separate themselves from their colonisers, recover their selfhood, and prevent their identity from being taken over as their countries had been? The colonised subject/ivity, should we adopt a post-colonial framework for analysis of the notions the 'self' and the 'other', inevitably defines itself as the 'other' of the colonising subject/ivity, a hegemonic entity wilfully seeking to absorb all subjects/ivities into its singular subject/ivity. Asfour implement this very strategy and delineates the Arabic novel against the different, external, distant European. The preoccupation with examining, resisting and coming to terms with the intrusion of the 'other' on the 'self' is so prevalent in the discourses of Arab intellectuals today that other issues are relatively obscured, that literary history has unabashedly abandoned its habitual self-proclaimed objectivity and fashioned itself a complicit partner in fraught-with-tension massive discourses on culture. History provides varying stories of the development of, let us say, the Arabic novel, dependent on the historian and critic's position on the influence, or lack thereof, of the 'other' on shaping the 'self'. Even in a work that acknowledges the Western origin of the novel, the Arabic novel is placed in the context of the history of Arabic fiction. Moosa, by calling his book *The Origins of Modern Arabic Fiction*, is able to imply that the Arabic novel, despite its 'Western' garb, in fact represents the continuity of an indigenous tradition of fiction that has existed since before the advent of the Western influence. It is therefore possible to consider the revival of the classical *Maqāma* in the writings of nineteenth-century authors for the beginnings of modern Arabic fiction. What is tacit in Moosa's work is made explicit in al-Saᶜāfīn's.

Al-Saᶜāfīn roots the Arabic novel in the classical *Maqāma* genre, citing *Majmaᶜ al-baḥrayn* (1856; Confluence of two seas) by Nāṣif al-Yāzijī (1800–54) and *Al-sāq ᶜalā al-sāq* (1855; Leg over leg) by al-Shidyāq (1801–87) as evidence,[20] as well as in the vernacular *Nights* and epic cycles, giving Jurjī Zaydān's historical novels as examples.[21] Ṣabrī Muslim Ḥammādī similarly asserts that the local environment of Iraq, through the folklore of the country, played a most crucial role in the development of the novel in Iraq. This folk tradition, identified as pre-Islamic Mesopotamian myths, the Arabic-Islamic *Nights* and popular epic cycles, has shaped the Iraqi novel.[22] Qaysūma, in an even more radical approach, insists that the Arabic novel has its roots in the Arabic literary tradition and that the Western novel's role in the development of its Arabic counterpart is limited to that of lending a helping hand; under its influence the Arabic novel defined itself more clearly and delineated its form more precisely.[23] Embedded in the overall discourse on the 'self' and 'other', manifest in the debates about the origin of Arabic novel, are discourses on the 'self', sometimes in connection with the 'other' and others separate from it, and on the 'other' always in relation to the 'self'. The varying versions of the genesis of Arabic novel produced thus far embody these discourses, and actively participate in negotiating a modern identity for Arab culture in the twentieth century.[24]

At the outset, whether the Arabic novel is traced to pre-Islamic or Islamic historical, cultural contexts depends to a great extent on the significance of the geopolitical specificity the authors of its genealogy find in the current reality of the Arab world, a former world empire fragmented into a number of nation-states in the aftermath of colonialism. In this case, discourse on literary history intersects with discourse on nationalism – writing the history of literature is intricately connected with writing the history of nation – and the type of literary history produced is responsive to the concepts of nationalism, which has a story of its own that parallels the story of modern Arabic literature: it is as engaged in the discourses on post-colonial subjectivity. Whatever one may conclude about the origin, history and development of nationalist thought, and however one may assess – negatively or positively – the effects of nationalist movements in the world, which are the subject matter of extensive study and debate,[25] nationalist aspirations have had profound impact on the views of, as well as on the development of literature in the Arab world.[26] Narratives of modern Arabic literature, as well as modern Arabic literary narratives, read at times like narratives of Arab nation(s). The issue at heart is the legitimacy of both, for just like many genres of modern Arabic literature, nationalism and the formation of nation-states in the region are attributable to the West.[27]

Yet nationalism, with all the contradictory impulses and significations it implies, has been embraced by the Arabs, beginning in the nineteenth century when it was incorporated into the discourses on the future of Muslim *Umma*, and continuing into the twentieth century when it took on a secular garb and produced a variety of nationalist movements. It manifests itself in Arab nationalism that encompasses all Arab states, or in regional nationalisms concerned with a historical cohesive geographical area, for example, Levant as advocated by the Syrian Nationalist Party (*al-Ḥizb al-Qawmī al-Sūrī*), or in local nationalisms pertinent to the de facto nation-states. While these diverse paradigms of Arab nationalisms are all still alive, two trends have come to dominate all discourses on nationalism – Arab nationalism and local nationalisms – which exist side by side, though the prominence of each swings like a pendulum as we see in the histories of the Arabic novel. These histories internalise the dual discourses of Arab nationalism. To the extent that there is such an observable category as the Arabic novel, there is also a necessity, given the diversity of the Arab world and its divergent paths of development, to speak of the development of this genre in a more particular context of a region or country.

Roger Allen gives a brief account of the early developments of the Arabic novel tradition with an eye to the historical and contemporary mapping of the region. Geographical categories, such as 'Syria and Lebanon',[28] 'Iraq and the Arabian Gulf',[29] 'The Maghrib',[30] 'Egypt',[31] 'Syria, Lebanon and Palestine'[32] and 'Iraq',[33] appear as section headings that facilitate discussions of the divergent developments of the genre in Arabic. The reality of the nation-states has become a frame of reference in both histories and discourses of the genre. Under the broader loyalty to Arab nationalism is a competing loyalty to each nation-state. Egyptians, such as Moussa and Sakkūt, identify *Zaynab* as the true beginning of the Arabic novel, Levantines, such as Moosa and al-Saᶜāfīn, locate the point of departure in the works of Jurjī Zaydān. The Arabic novel is now often examined in the context of the history of a nation-state, each yielding its own tradition. One speaks easily of, for example, the Egyptian novel, the Palestinian novel,[34] the Lebanese novel, the Iraqi novel, the Moroccan novel, the Tunisian novel, the Libyan novel, and of their origins in the indigenous traditions of these countries. Ḥammādī, for example, deals with the modern Iraqi novel alone and by doing so reconstructs for it a genealogy that grows out of ancient Mesopotamian myths.

The discourses on Arabic literature in general and the Arabic novel in particular and Arab nationalism have in common the concern with coming to terms with colonialism. Nationalism, as a paradigm for the formation of modern state, as Chaterjee points out, was adopted almost lock, stock and barrel, including the very intellectual premises of modernity on which colonial domination was based, to challenge the colonial claim to political domination.[35] Nationalist discourses do two things at the same time. First, they demonstrate the falsity of the colonial claim that the backward peoples are culturally incapable of ruling themselves in the conditions of the modern world – they deny the alleged inferiority of the colonised people and assert that a backward nation could modernise itself while retaining its cultural identity.[36] And second, they struggle to overcome the 'otherness' of the 'other'. Similarly, discourses on the Arabic novel take for granted that the novel is here to stay, and make a case for its acceptance by constructing a genealogy for it located in the history of Arabic literature. On the basis of this genealogy, it is argued that the Arabic novel is a product of Arab culture, at least potentially, not an entirely alien genre bestowed upon it by the West. Here is where the 'self' begins to think of its 'self' in terms of its past, for its past, as Alfrīd Faraj says, is its 'self'.[37] This past derived from the 'self' is, according to Ḥammādī, what gives the Iraqi novel its 'authenticity' (*aṣāla*).[38] The word *aṣāla* is derived from *aṣl*, which means root and by extension, source, origin; cause, reason; descent, lineage, stock; foundation, fundament, basis. In his insistence on the crucial role of pre-Islamic Arabian and Arabic-Islamic folk traditions in shaping the Iraqi novel, with no mention of any Western influence, Ḥammādī marginalises Western influence in the development of the Arabic novel. He rather locates the novel in the heart of an Arabic literary tradition, the Arab past.

The centrality of the 'past' in the definition of the 'self' in this specific case poses theoretical, as well as practical, difficulties for intellectuals and artists active in shaping the vision for a modern Arab world. While having to deal with the integrity of the 'past', which has been violated by colonialism, Arab intellectuals must also come to terms with modernity. Without denying the possibility of deriving its definition conceptually and practically from the specificity of the Arab situation, the most recent Arab modernity is a by-product of the cultural exchange that has been taking place in the past two centuries since the beginning of the colonial penetration into the Arab world. The Arab aspirations to occupy a central place in the world, politically, economically and culturally and to relive the glory days of the Islamic civilisation (ninth to eighteenth centuries), as expressed by Idrīs in his critique of the Arabic novel, are confounded by the dichotomy of the 'self' and the 'other'. This dichotomy further takes the form of quarrels between 'ancient' and 'modern'.

CULTURAL POLITICS OF MODERNISATION

Unlike the earlier indigenous movements of modernity in Arabic-Islamic culture and, more recently, the European modernisation, the movement towards modernity in the contemporary Arab world is often perceived as Westernisation. The quarrels between 'ancient' and 'modern', which were the staples of earlier and Western modernisms, take on different meanings, as they now intersect with the dialectics of the 'self' and the 'other'. At stake is no longer simply the matter of originality, of transcending the accomplishments of the predecessors, but of 'authenticity' too, of continuity between past and present. In other words, how can modernity (*ḥadātha*) and modernisation (*taḥdīth*), often associated with the West (*gharb*) and Westernisation (*taghrīb*), by virtue of its genesis, overcome its alienation (*ightirāb*) in Arab culture, and achieve cultural rejuvenation (*tajdīd*) and world relevancy (*muᶜāṣara*), while maintaining its authenticity (*aṣāla*)? In the past two centuries Arab intellectuals have proposed a number of models for cultural modernity, which they have hoped would lead to the modernisation of the Arab world. These proposed projects of modernisation all seem to straddle the two poles of the paradox of 'past' and 'present', the 'past' being identified with the Arabic-Islamic tradition(s),[39] and the present defined by its most influential player – the West.[40] As Arab writers have observed, the discussion on Arab modernity has focused on the seemingly irreconcilable bipolar impulses towards either modernity, which aspires to world relevancy to be realised through integrating Arab culture into the dominant Western one, or 'authenticity', which is grounded in the 'past'.[41] As Alfrīd Faraj puts it:

> Our Arab cultural renaissance in Egypt began in the nineteenth century with two contradictory trends in the first half of the nineteenth century:
>
> Al-Shaykh Rifāᶜa al-Ṭahṭāwī originated a trend [that advocated] joining the Egyptian mind to the contemporary European mind at its best forms of democracy and technology . . .
>
> As for the second trend, which seems in contradiction with the first, it is the trend started by Maḥmūd Sāmī al-Bārūdī in the middle of the nineteenth century. It called for the revival of the ancient Arabic literary heritage, by collecting it, publishing it, and emulating it.
>
> Al-Bārūdī was accompanied by masters of the revival of the [Arabic-Islamic] heritage – who edited the [Arabic-Islamic] legal, literary and intellectual heritage – like Jamāl al-Dīn al-Afghānī and his disciples Muḥammad ᶜAbduh, al-Muwayliḥī, [ᶜAbdallāh] al-Nadīm, all the way to Ṭāhā Ḥusayn and his contemporaries, as well as tens of Arab intellectuals who attempted to link the past with the present, to revive classical Arabic literature and to renew it with modern sensibilities.[42]

Both trends, Faraj further observes, emerged as 'progressive' strategies for resisting colonisation, the first of which aimed at confirming Egypt's compatibility with the rest of the world, and its ability to resist the Ottoman occupation, and the second at consolidating the independent identity by the force of its 'past'.[43] Whichever trend an Arab intellectual chooses, it seems inevitable that the continuity of Arab history will be disrupted. To choose Western-based modernity, the indigenous past must be given up, and to elect 'authenticity' rooted in the 'past', the 'present' must be erased. The result, as Burhān Ghalyūn terms it, is rupture in the Arab history (*qaṭīʿa tārikhiyya*), making it impossible for the 'self' to cohere. The problem, as Ḥasan Ḥanafī explains, lies in the impossibility of choice: should the 'self' derive itself from Westernised modernity (*taghrīb*) imposed by the 'other', it exiles itself from its own past, and if it roots itself in the classical Arabic-Islamic tradition, it alienates itself from the 'present' (*ightirāb*). In order to restore the historical continuity of the 'self', the otherness of the 'other' must be overcome, never destroying it, or destroying the 'other' by redefining it, or even rejecting it, but by integrating it into the 'self', for example, giving nationalism and the culture that produced it a history rooted in the development of the 'self'. Occidentalism (*ʿilm al-istighrāb*), a response to Orientalism proposed by Ḥanafī, does not emulate Orientalism, the driving force of which is the subjugation of the (Eastern) 'other' by the (Western) 'self'; rather, it absorbs the (Western) 'other' into the (Eastern) 'self', making the former an integral part of the latter.[44]

In this context, the 'anxiety of influence', the theoretical paradigm devised by Harold Bloom for interpreting literary texts, takes on paradoxical meanings. It operates cross-culturally as Arab writers struggle to overcome, depart from, transcend and reject the influence of Western models. At the same time, it turns into anxiety of absence of influence, of not being grounded in the traditions of the past. Intertextuality, within the Arabic-Islamic culture or between East and West, becomes a deliberate enterprise, carefully calculated and executed by the authors of texts. By appropriating the forms, themes and techniques both from their classical heritage and the colonial legacy, Arab authors attempt to restore the wholeness of the 'self'. They try to remedy the schism inflicted on the Arab subjectivity – the disruption in the continuity between past and present – by integrating both its native and imported traditions, by concomitantly claiming authenticity (*aṣāla*) and contemporaneity, and therefore, world relevancy (*muʿāṣara*). Only the simultaneous presence of these two elements can assure the legitimacy of the newly envisioned culture, as well as its institutions, being formulated for an Arab modernity.

This simultaneity, however, creates tensions in both critical texts written on the subject of modernity in Arab culture and literary texts produced in this context. The Arabic novel, according to Asfour, continues to attempt to transcend the push-and-pull relation between the two poles of the paradoxes he names – 'self' and 'other', 'past' and 'present', 'East' and 'West', 'old' and 'new', and 'native' and 'foreign' – in order to find its unique identity.[45] The poles of these articulated paradoxes do not correspond in a systematic fashion. If authenticity is rooted in 'self', 'past', 'East', 'old' and 'native', then contemporaneity must necessarily be located in 'other', 'present', 'West', 'new' and 'foreign'. There is clearly a problem. Contemporaneity, as the Arabic word *muᶜāṣara* implies, means to be timely, to be in the 'present' and 'new'. Here, authenticity becomes simultaneously rooted in 'past' and 'present', 'old' and 'new' and 'tradition' and 'modernity'. What is considered authentic becomes then a matter of ideology, of competing visions for Arab modernity and the priorities and sources of these visions. The term, *aṣāla*, can suddenly imply the 'past' and 'present' dependent on the ideology of the critics.

For those who give more importance to the 'here' and 'now', 'authenticity' means to be located in the immediate problems of a nation-state struggling to overcome oppression, poverty, ignorance, sectarian conflicts, military occupation, all part of the legacy of the 'past'. Reality, *al-wāqiᶜ*, therefore, should be the source of 'authenticity'. In Marxist discourses on the Arabic novel, the 'past' is also the 'other'. Realism, not the return to the literary heritage of the 'past', marks the true beginning of the Arabic novel in the view of Badr, a Marxist, for only in realism does one find a treatment of conditions of the Arabs now. This is not to say that the 'West' is not the 'other', on the contrary, part of the reality of the nation-states is to defend themselves against the further encroachment of the West in the form of capitalism before the collapse of the Soviet Union, and globalisation now. Maḥmūd Amīn al-ᶜĀlam acknowledges that the world has become one, however, he warns of the danger of American-driven globalisation, which threatens to erase the cultural and national specificities and identities (*khuṣūṣiyyāt wa huwiyya qawmiyya wa thaqāfiyya*) of the various parts of this one world.[46] The solution is clearly not to give up specificity for the sake of universality or universality for the sake of specificity, for isolation (*ᶜuzla wa qaṭīᶜa*) from humanity is foolish and loss of specificity and identity is national and cultural suicide. Rather, the answer is to be part of the world while retaining distinction, to work towards a common humanity while resisting hegemonic attempts at obliterating national and cultural identities,[47] or, in his words, to defend the nation-state. Arabic literature, therefore, should detail the progress of the nation-states in achieving specificity, derived from lived experiences, as well as aspirations for contemporaneity and world relevancy.

For those who see the priority in the continuity of 'past' and 'present', the process of authentication, *taᶜṣīl*, does not simply mean finding the origin or root (*aṣl*) for modern Arab culture or Arabic literature in the intellectual heritage of the Arab world. It rather involves redefining this heritage so that it would accommodate the new cultural and literary phenomena that had historically been excluded from the classical canon: the traditional vision of the culture for itself. The stupendous revisionist projects undertaken by leading Muslim and Arab intellectuals – from the nineteenth-century Jamāl al-Dīn al-Afghānī and Muḥammad ᶜAbduh to the twentieth-century Ṭāhā Ḥusayn,[48] Adūnīs,[49] Ḥanafī,[50] al-Jābirī, Ṭayyib Tizīnī,[51] to name but a few, all internalise and externalise the pressure and urgency of the situation:

> The issue is not replacing the present with the past, or the old with the new, but it is first and foremost the reconstruction of our consciousness of the past and the present and their relationship. It is a process that requires simultaneous planning for the intellectual heritage of the past and of the future. Planning for the intellectual heritage of the past means rewriting its history, and by extension, re-establishing it in our consciousness, and reconstructing it as a heritage we embrace, not one that contains us. As for planning for the intellectual heritage for the future, it means furnishing it with conditions for synchrony and participation: synchrony with contemporary thought and participation in enriching and guiding it, and this is the meaning of *muᶜāṣara*.[52]

Contemporary Arab modernity, albeit of foreign genesis, is legitimated on the basis of the genealogy constructed for it, its precedence located in the movement of the eighth century, as the derivation of the contemporary term designating modernity in Arabic, *ḥadātha*, from the medieval term, *muḥdath*, clearly indicates. Likewise, Western genres integrated into Arabic literature in the nineteenth and twentieth centuries seek legitimacy in an imagined genealogy with its roots extending into the classical Arabic literary tradition. This kind of *taᶜṣīl* process can give new literary genres, such as the Arabic novel, authenticity in the form of a history derived primarily from the 'self', and authority to shape contemporary Arab culture. The legitimacy of this authorial voice is in turn avowed on the basis of how authentic this voice is, in other words, of how central literature is to the formulation of cultural modernity.[53]

QUEST FOR LEGITIMACY

In the introduction to *Zaman al-riwāya* (1992–6), Gaber Asfour begins by quoting the following passage from an article Naguib Mahfouz wrote for *al-Risāla* journal dated 3 September 1945:

> Poetry prevailed in periods of nature and myths. This era [in which we live], the age of science, industry and facts, however, definitely requires a new art that will, to the extent possible, reconcile between a modern person's interest in facts and his old nostalgia for fantasy. The era has found what it has been looking for in story. If poetry has by comparison fallen behind in popularity and reach, it is not because story is privileged by its age; rather, it is because poetry lacks certain elements that will make it suitable for this age. Story, in this sense, is the poetry of the modern world.[54]

Asfour then goes on to note in a celebratory tone the achievements of the Arabic novel in the years between the publication of this article and the awarding of the Nobel Prize to Mahfouz in 1988. Mahfouz, Asfour asserts,

> has given his creative life to the art which has gradually occupied the leading position in the map of Arabic writing, so that we, the critics, are able to describe our age, in relation to [literary] creativity, as the age of the novel. In fact, some of us speak of the Arabic novel as the registry of the modern Arabs.[55]

Asfour is clearly hinting at the ascendance of the Arabic novel at the expense of Arabic poetry, which has been known as the registry of Arabs (*dīwān al-ᶜarab*). By attributing the reformulated famous phrase, *dīwān al-ᶜarab al-muḥdathīn*, to the Arabic novel, he is in fact claiming for the Arabic novel a leading role in discourses on modern Arab culture. However, this elevated status accorded to the Arabic novel by Asfour is at best tenuous; in fact, many critics will disagree with this view. Asfour himself realises this.

> Since I realised that we lived in the age of the novel, it has occurred to me that the Arabic novel has been wronged; we do not celebrate it enough in comparison with poetry. It remains until today of lesser stature than poetry in the official Arab cultural festivals.[56]

The relative absence of the Arabic novel in literary festivals and prizes is not becoming of the Arabic novel, the leading Arabic literary art today, Asfour muses. The reasons for this slight, he explains, may have something to do with the traditionally inclined Arab culture today, which tends to view literary arts in a hierarchical order. Poetry has always been on the top of this hierarchy and drama and the novel towards the bottom until 1988, when Mahfouz received the Nobel Prize.[57] International recognition for an Arab novelist seems to have given the novel a boost and, more importantly, legitimacy that it has been seeking. These musings reveal, perhaps unintentionally, not only the contradictory responses to the West, but also the problematic place of the novel in contemporary Arab culture.

Since its inception in public life in the Arab world the Arabic novel has been linked to popular storytelling. The early link between the novel and popular storytelling paved the way for literary historians and critics to make a case for its authenticity by finding its roots in the tradition of classical Arabic storytelling, especially the stories of marvel and wonder (*ḥikāyāt gharība wa ᶜajība*), to which the stories of *Alf layla wa layla* (*Thousand and One Nights*) and the *siyar shaᶜbiyya* (popular epic cycles), among others, belong. The problem is, however, that storytelling has been perceived as marginal to the Arabic Islamic culture's view of itself. It was considered frivolous for the most part, and was occasionally condemned. Al-Ghazzāli, for instance, warned the Muslims against listening to storytellers. Stories (*qiṣaṣ*), he tells in *Iḥyāᵓ ᶜulūm al-dīn* (the revival of religious sciences), are an innovation (*bidᶜa*) not sanctioned by the Qurᵓān, the Prophetic Tradition, or the practice of the Companions. They ought to be prohibited unless they are accurately recounted stories about the prophets concerning religious matters.[58]

Authenticating the Arabic novel by linking it to pre-modern Arabic storytelling is paradoxically affirming and undermining, for the tradition on the basis of which their claim to the right to represent cultural 'authenticity' is made has always been considered nothing more than entertainment, inessential to the culture that produced it. Qaysūma assesses the predicament of the Arabic novel under the subject heading of 'disdain (*iḥtiqār*) for the novel and novelists during the Nahḍa era', and points to two sets of problems. Firstly, the novel was an imported art with no distinct features or clear foundations. Secondly, it was viewed from the negative perspective associated with pre-modern Arabic storytelling (folklore, myths and Arabic stories). This negative view allegedly condemned the various forms of storytelling for their less than elegant language and their lack of morality.

The Arab novelists did not have the respect enjoyed by their Western counterparts; on the contrary, they were looked down upon. They often wrote under pen names and distanced themselves from the art, notwithstanding their interest and faith in its potential role in reform.[59] The issue, in Badr's argument, is relevant to the legitimacy of pre-modern popular Arabic storytelling. The early forms of modern Arabic storytelling were despised, therefore, marginalised and excluded from the literary canon, precisely because of the link to the so-called 'vulgar' *Thousand and One Nights* and vernacular epic cycles (*al-sīra al-sha*ᶜ*biyya*) and the 'decadent' *Maqāma*. The 'prototypes' or 'forerunners' of the Arabic novel remained hostage to purposes of didacticism and entertainment, *al-ta*ᶜ*līm wa al-tasliya*.[60]

The early generation of fiction writers understandably turned against the Arabic storytelling tradition in its entirety – what Ghālī Shukrī calls '*mukhāṣamat al-ḥikāya*'[61] – including not only the so-called folk literature (*al-adab al-sha*ᶜ*bī*) but also the works of the earlier generation.[62] Rather than finding 'authenticity' in the 'past', they allied themselves with the nationalist project of decolonisation and devoted their artistry to portraying the reality of resistance and life in their respective countries.[63] The result was a reformulation of the novel in Shukrī's assessment: 'neither our history nor our literature echoes Western history or culture. We have indeed been inspired by the [Western] literary forms, such as the novel, play, short story and poetry, but the [inherent] thought, feelings, characters, language, situations, national, or local, events, contributed much to the reformulation of the novel and play'.[64] The truce with the West was possible, explains Shukrī, only during nationalist ascendance, especially in the 1940s and 1950s, when the interaction with the 'other' could be healthy.[65] The tension between 'tradition' and 'modernity', 'authenticity' and 'contemporaneity' seemed suspended during the period of nationalist fervour.[66] The truce was, however, temporary. It ended abruptly with the Arab defeat in the 1967 Arab–Israeli war.[67] In the aftermath of this defeat, authenticity came to be identified with the 'past', and the 'past' once again came to represent the 'self'.

The vicissitudes of Arabic literary tradition's fortune are not the doing of the historical accounts and critical assessments of the Arabic novel alone. The Arabic novel is implicated in the making and unmaking of this fortune as it plots its own rise to power. While al-Muwayliḥī, should we consider him the author of a novel, wrote in the style of the classical *Maqāma* at the turn of the century, Haykal, Ṭāhir Lāshīn, Tawfīq al-Ḥakīm and Suhayl Idrīs, who are quoted as vehemently denying any relation between the Arabic novel and pre-modern Arabic storytelling,[68] produced works modelled on the 'Western' novel in the five decades of the history of the genre since the appearance of Haykal's *Zaynab* in 1913. By the 1970s, beginning with the publication of Jamāl al-Ghīṭānī's *Al-Zaynī Barakāt* in 1974, tradition returned to the scene of legitimisation of the novel with a vengeance: it came to dominate the discourses on the culture and literature of the post-colonial nation-states. Yet, given its ebbs and flows, tradition alone seems precariously insufficient to fully provide the novel with legitimacy. The novel has intelligently sought other means as well.

The Arabic novel, albeit steeped in the tradition of entertainment, has always taken its own mission seriously. Its participation in the nationalist project, first in the service of decolonisation (between the two world wars) and later in the processes of nation-building (in the 1950s and 1960s), was in hindsight a consciously adopted strategy in a deliberate attempt to establish its own legitimacy in a culture in the process of transformation. Already in the nineteenth century, the pioneers of storytelling named by Asfour and Qaysūma took upon themselves the task of debating the shape as well as future of their nation. Writing under the pressures of the colonial encounter as well as the ensuing cultural exchange, their works, willy-nilly, internalise and externalise the changing sensibilities. The shift from addressing the court to the people is one indication of the reordering of the priorities of a modernising culture. The move from emphasising the culture of the pre-modern elite to that of the masses, is not only sanctioned by modern sensibilities, but makes it even more plausible for the Arabic novel to negotiate more effectively its centrality to shaping the emerging culture of modernity. Modernity, however many nuances this word may imply, meant primarily revolutionising the power structure in the Arab world, and in the nineteenth and the most part of the twentieth centuries from 'theocratic authoritarianism' to 'nationalist secular democracy'. Profane folk literature, by alleging to represent secularity and the masses, can be the voice of the new nationalist culture.

REVIVING TRADITION, REVISING HISTORY

The mechanisms Arab novelists employed for the legitimisation of the Arabic novel – partaking in the nationalist discourses through reviving tradition – in turn redefined the Arabic literary tradition. What this newly redefined tradition looks like is necessarily determined by its perceived role in the modern nation-states. Whatever shape this tradition takes in the dialectics of modernisation, the Arabic novel presents the 'past' in such a way that makes the 'past' a constant presence. It is impossible to ignore the presence of pre-modern Arabic storytelling tradition in the Arabic novel today. In a paper he presented at the first international conference on the Arabic novel[69] hosted by the High Council of Culture in Cairo, 22–8 February 1998, Maḥmūd Ṭarshūna begins his analysis of al-Ghīṭānī's triology, *Kitāb al-tajaliyyāt* (1990; Book of manifestations), by situating al-Ghīṭānī's works in one of the four trends of the Arabic novel at the end of the twentieth century. Attentive to the tenuous nature of categories, Ṭarshūna nevertheless speaks of the following trends (*tayyārāt*) of Arabic novels on the basis of some discernible dominant features: *tayyār al-waᶜy* (stream of consciousness); *al-riwāya al-jadīda* (new novel); *al-wāqiᶜiyya al-jadīda* (new realism); and *al-tayyār al-turāthī* in which *tawẓīf al-turāth* (employment of heritage) is its staple feature.[70] More importantly, he identifies the last as that which represents best the specificity of the Arabic novel (*khuṣūṣiyyat al-riwāya al-ᶜarabiyya*), which is also the theme of the conference. What is perhaps most significant, however, is the possibility of identifying for the first time in the history of the Arabic novel a trend known for its explicitly stated purposeful intertextuality with the Arabic literary tradition, what Ṭarshūna calls *madrasat tawẓīf al-turāth fī al-riwāya al-ᶜarabiyya al-muᶜāṣira* (school of employing heritage in the contemporary Arabic novel).[71] Between the early efforts of al-Ghīṭānī in the early 1970s and the 1998 conference on the Arabic novel, new literary and critical sensibilities seemed to have emerged, making it possible, if not desirable or urgent, to engage with tradition in novel ways. Rather than viewing the revival of tradition in contemporary narratives as a step backward, a retreat from modernity into traditionalism, the critics, some at least, seem to endorse the endeavour as a progressive measure that gives the Arabic novel its distinction. Al-Ghīṭānī, one of the most important writers of the genre, has won the day.

It is possible now, in a revisionist sort of way, to point to the first generation of novelists, such as Ṭāhā Ḥusayn (1889–1973) and Tawfīq al-Ḥakīm (1898–1987), as having done something similar. In his play, *Shahrazād* (1934), al-Ḥakīm tells the story of Shahrazād after one thousand and one nights. In response to his rendition, Ḥusayn wrote his own version, *Aḥlām Shahrazād* (1943; Dreams of Shahrazād). Prior to *Aḥlām Shahrazād*, al-Ḥakīm and Ḥusayn co-wrote a novel, *Al-qaṣr al-masḥūr* (1935; Enchanted palace), in which they give yet another version of the story of Shahrazād.[72] Here, they simply take a character from the frame tale of the *Nights* and recast her in a new work, abandoning the characteristics of storytelling in the *Nights*. Al-Ghīṭānī, quite contrarily, emulates pre-modern narratives in form, style and language, but tells stories of day-to-day living in contemporary Egypt. In other words, pre-modern Arabic narrative 'tradition', not characters from classical historical or fictional writings, is the subject of his rewritings. The narrative tradition thus evoked in his works exceeds the hitherto recognised genres of storytelling, primarily the *maqāmat*, the *Nights*, popular epic cycles and folklore, to encompass historical chronicles, epistles, Sufi manifestos, geographical literature, philosophical treatises as well as other forms of writing. Thanks to his writings and those of like-minded novelists across the Arab world, it has even become prudent today to consider, as Asfour and Qaysūma do, Rifāᶜa al-Ṭahṭāwī's (1801–73) *Takhlīṣ al-ibrīz fī talkhīṣ bārīz* (1834), even his translation of a French novel rendered as *Mawāqiᶜ al-aflāk fī waqāʾiᶜ Tillimāk* (1867), in which French narrative is married to Mamluk rhyme prose,[73] ᶜAlī Mubārak's (1823–93) *ᶜAlam al-Dīn*,[74] Aḥmad Fāris al-Shidyāq's (1801–87) *Al-sāq ᶜalā al-sāq* (1855), Nāṣif al-Yāzijī's (1800–71) *Majmaᶜ al-baḥrayn* (1856), Muḥammad al-Muwayliḥī's (1858–1930) *Ḥadīth ᶜĪsā Ibn Hishām* (1898–1902; 1907), Shihāb al-Dīn al-Ālūsī's (1802–54) *Al-maqāmāt al-ālūsiyya*,[75] even Ḥāfiẓ Ibrāhīm's (1871–1932) *Layālī Saṭīḥ* (1906), and Faransīs al-Marrāsh's (1836–73) *Ghābat al-ḥaqq* (1865) as precursors of the Arabic novel.

The recognition of this subgenre of the Arabic novel, critically and creatively, however, is comparatively recent. In fact, it continues to be controversial. In 1982, al-Ghīṭānī's way of writing was challenged. At a symposium held for *Fuṣūl* magazine on the novelists who began writing in the 1960s and became established in the 1970s, known as the generation of the sixties (*jīl al-sittīnāt*),[76] al-Ghīṭānī was asked bluntly: 'do you not think that the historical form has exhausted its purposes already?'[77] 'Historical form' here means not historical romance but classical Arabic-Islamic historiography. As al-Ghīṭānī tried to explain his method of writing, he is further challenged by another novelist, Ṣabrī Mūsā: 'how were you able to use a language the syntax of which is old and techniques of storytelling from another era without their inherent values?' Mūsā did not necessarily object to al-Ghīṭānī's contention that the current reality in Egypt (as he presents in *Al-Zaynī Barakāt*) is not very different from the condition of the country at the end of the Mamluk period (fifteenth century) portrayed by historian Ibn Iyās; however, he thought the responsibility of the artist lay elsewhere:

> [M]any generations [of writers] write from the perspective of immutability (*thabāt*) not change (*taḥawwul*).[78] As you have said, a social

> phenomenon during the period of Ibn Iyās may recur in ours, and writers remain preoccupied with such a [recurring] phenomenon. I do not object to the writers' preoccupation with such a phenomenon, but I think one of the main responsibilities of the writers is to look towards the future. Great scientific discoveries are knocking on our doors! An artist must be ahead of his time. We continue to deal with a number of values dealt with by a number of artists in the past century, even though values and social relations are changing in such a way that traditional institutions are being threatened. I have posed for questioning the notions of 'homeland' in *Fasād al-amkina* (corrupt places) and *Al-sayyid min ḥaql al-sabānikh* (a man from spinach fields). There, I also deal with many social institutions I expect to disappear, such as marriage and the relationship between father and son.[79]

Even in 2002, al-Ghīṭānī was taken to task for his preoccupation in finding ways of dealing with the 'present' and visions for the 'future' in the 'past'. At the Symposium on the Arab Novel: Visions of Social Reality, held at the Center for Contemporary Arab Studies, Georgetown University, between 12 and 14 April 2002, Elias Khoury, a novelist of a different ideology, argued that the Arabic novel did not need to seek 'authenticity' in the 'past', but should instead be based on its engagement with the present reality, especially now, because Mahfouz has given this genre a history firmly rooted in the indigenous culture of the Arab world. The real difference between Khoury and al-Ghīṭānī, despite their engagement with exactly the same issues of 'authenticity' and 'legitimacy', is whether the content of tradition should be the concern or its narrative techniques. If Khoury finds contentment in domesticating the Western form by establishing continuity in Arabic narrative techniques, which he employs extensively in his own writings, al-Ghīṭānī seems to need not just the presence of these narrative techniques but also the entire weight of tradition.

Despite some positive reception of his works, considered as part of the 'adventure in form'[80] undertaken by the sixties' generation, al-Ghīṭānī seemed to always have to explain himself early in his career. In a 1984 interview with *Alif*, he spoke of his desire to 'write something I have not read'[81] – and his readings of the Western novel are extensive – and of his realisation that the Arabic narrative tradition could be a source of inspiration for 'new forms of expression'.[82] Transcendence, not mimeses, of the forms of both the Western novel and Arabic narrative tradition was the objective. He was, however, tentative about what he had achieved:

> I do not say I am creating a new form; rather, I am trying to renew the form within the framework of the novel. The Western novel, or the novel written in the familiar framework since Don Quixote to the so-called new novel in Europe and America, has been the model to which the Arab novelists must adhere. What I am attempting is to give authenticity to the form by deriving its roots from tradition. Tradition, in the broad sense of the word, includes oral tradition, or folk heritage, which I have internalized to a great extent thanks to my upbringing in Upper Egypt and al-Jamāliyya, and the written tradition.[83]

This tentativeness is understandable. At the time he could think of only a few examples of what he meant. He mentioned for his purposes Imīl Ḥabībī's *Al-waqāʾiᶜ al-gharība fī ikhtifāʾ Saᶜīd Abī al-Naḥs al-mutashāʾil* (1974) and Mahfouz's *Malḥamat al-ḥarāfīsh* (1977), *Riḥlat Ibn Fattūma* (1979) *and Layālī alf layla* (1983). With the growth of the body of works now grouped as a new 'school' of writing the novel as well as the critical appreciation for it today, al-Ghīṭānī's confidence as a matter of course grew. He can now assert his instrumental role in 'creating' (*ibtikār*) a new, in fact, unique form of the Arabic novel.[84]

In the introduction to *Muntahā al-ṭalab ilā turāth al-ᶜarab: dirāsāt fī al-turāth* (1997), al-Ghīṭānī speaks of his 'desire and ambition since I started writing, in 1959 specifically, to invent new forms of expression'.[85] In returning to tradition, he found the 'best form' of writing, which allowed him all the freedom he needed to think, innovate and go beyond old forms of expression.[86] His success precipitated a trend and he can now sit on his laurels and think of himself as the master of the new trend. The title of his book is poignant. Notwithstanding its ambivalence, the message is clear. Whether it means the 'utmost limit of' or 'the end to' the search for the heritage of the Arabs, there is no doubt that the book is intended to define the Arabic tradition from which new forms of Arabic narrative may be derived. Tradition is given contours of al-Ghīṭānī's design. Defining cultural heritage as part of lived experience, al-Ghīṭānī speaks of Islamic architecture and city-planning, historical chronicles and geographical treatises, essays on magic and the hereafter, and Sufi literature as part of the Arabic-Islamic heritage that may also serve as the Arabic narrative tradition. His version of tradition goes beyond the scope of the *Nights*, popular epics, folk tales and *Maqāmāt*, the corpus of pre-modern storytelling identified by others as the Arabic tradition of storytelling.

Al-Ghīṭānī's definition of the tradition and the identification of the 'school of employing tradition in the contemporary Arabic novel' with him, especially in adhering to the date he points to – the 1967 defeat – as the catalyst for change, are problematic. Firstly, the scope of tradition delineated by al-Ghīṭānī is peculiarly Arabic-Islamic and leaves out the non-Arabic components: pre-Islamic (such as Babylonian, Phoenician and Phaoronic) or non-Arabic (such as Berber in the Maghreb) or non-Islamic (such as Coptic in Egypt). Secondly, the date may be more pertinent to the development of the novel in Egypt and Palestine, but not necessarily in other parts of the Arab world or Diaspora. Morocco and Iraq have seen a sudden surge in interest in Arab heritage in the last decade of the twentieth century. Moroccan Ben Salem Himmich's works, *Majnūn al-ḥukm* (1990), *Miḥan al-fatā Zayn al-Shāma* (1993) and *Al-ᶜallāma* (1997) seemed relevant to the more recent question of identity being debated in the country. Moroccan identity, as the proceedings of the first conference on the subject in 1997 show,[87] is said to be challenged and destabilised by the emerging Berber and Islamic discourses in Morocco as well as the country's changing relationship with France, one of its former colonisers. In Iraq, *Sābiᶜ ayyām al-khalq* (1994), the Gulf War and the subsequent siege of the country after Desert Storm, seem to have provoked such a reaction both at home and abroad. Selim Matar (Salīm Maṭar Kāmil), an Iraqi writer living in Switzerland, seems to have written two novels, *Imraᶜat al-Qārūra* (1990) and *Al-tawᵓam al-mafqūd* (2001), as a response to the effects of the recent events in Iraq that have led to identity problems he describes in his study, *Al-dhāt al-jarīḥa: ishkālāt al-huwiyya fī al-ᶜirāq wa al-ᶜālam al-ᶜarabī al-sharqānī* (1997).

Historians of the Arabic novel have thus far documented, albeit not systematically, the allusions to and at times explicit appropriations of pre-modern Arabic genres of storytelling and narration as an aspect of the Arabic novel without much analysis. Critics, those who have dealt with the subject, on the other hand, have focused on it in relation to specific issues, authors or works. Al-Ghīṭānī seems to have the lion's share of the critical attention. The works by Mahfouz, al-Masᶜadī,[88] Ḥabībī and Himmich[89] have attracted some attention as well. The *Nights*'s 'influence' on the Arabic novel seems to have had better luck; references to this influence are pervasive even though profound critical analyses remain sporadic. Shahrazād, the symbol, not fictional character, is examined in the context of contemporary Arab thought,[90] and Mahfouz[91] and Ḥabībī's[92] rewritings of the *Nights* are discussed in a number of articles. To the critics who have written on the subject, the Arabic literary tradition is a secondary character in the (hi)story of the Arabic novel, its role limited to providing the Arabic novel with alternative narrative strategies or voices. It is time, then, to respond to Roger Allen's call,[93] and look at this body of literature not simply as individual texts, each telling its own story of intertextuality with a tradition of its own making, but rather as a collective project that partakes not only in narrating a specific vision of modernity in Arab culture and Arabic literature but also in intervening in other discourses on this modernity.

TRIANGULATION OF NATION, MODERNITY AND TRADITION

All too often analyses of Arabic literature focus on the so-called modernity of the texts with no attention paid to their relations to tradition, or on the aspects and meanings of intertextuality with tradition without necessarily relating these textual strategies to the discourses on the nation-state and dialectics of modernisation. The rupture with the 'past' observed by Ghalyūn may seem to be the case to readers of critical discourses on Arabic literature and Arab culture today. The Arabic novel that 'employs the Arab cultural heritage' tells a different story. This story is told in its narrative of the triangular relationship, or love affair, of nation-state, modernity and tradition, all in the trajectory of its own longing for form. The story of the nation-state, of modernity or of tradition is incomplete and incomprehensible unless the three poles are examined together, when the three angles of the triangle are connected. Needless to say, the West, even when it only plays in the dark, as Toni Morrison would say, provides the backdrop for the unfolding of this triangular love affair, its presence acutely felt. The story the Arabic novel tells is necessarily shaped by its own search for a unique identity and indigenous roots. It too is driven by its own impulse to simply tell stories and write histories. The purpose of this book is, then, to let the Arabic novel tell its stories, to look at the ways in which it tells the stories and the consequences of its narrative strategies in the production of meaning, to trace the formulation of its aesthetics in the intersection between past and present and, more importantly, to track the histories of the nation and novel it writes.

My reading of the Arabic novel is inspired by my work on pre-modern Arabic narrative and storytelling. I was writing an article on *Sīrat ᶜUmar al-Nuᶜmān*, a mini epic cycle inserted into the *Nights* possibly in the nineteenth century, when the disparity between the abundant presence of love stories with happy endings in pre-modern Arabic storytelling and their poignant absence in modern Arabic fiction suddenly became significant in the understanding of the function of the cycle of love stories in the *Sīra*. *Sīrat ᶜUmar al-Nuᶜmān*, like a great majority of the Arabic novels, details the rise, fall and rise again of a nation, in this case, defined by the kingly genealogy of the family of ᶜUmar al-Nuᶜmān. The continuity of this genealogy depends to a great extent on the propriety, and therefore legitimacy, of royal marriages. The love stories are in effect discourses, in a metaphorical sort of way, on the fate of the nation. This destiny is written by the members of the family forming the nucleus of the nation in their conduct while in love: the nation rises when propriety in matters of love is observed, and falls when this propriety is violated, when legitimacy becomes questionable. When the love story observes all the requirements of propriety, the nation coheres. The love stories pervasive in the Arabic novel in contrast are about frustrated desires, disappointed hopes, broken promises, betrayals of confidence and tragic destinies. From a comparative perspective they read like a statement on the Arabic novel as well as modern Arab nation-states, which have been grappling with issues of legitimacy. At another level, the story of the Arabic novel that employs heritage is that of, among other things, the love affair with the nation-state. Its love for the nation-state is, however, haunted by the nation-state's problematic relationship with modernity and tradition, which bespeaks its anxiety about its own genealogy. With the West 'playing in the dark', nation-state and modernity become 'improper' strangers or illegitimate partners to tradition and the novel, and tradition becomes the 'proper' or complete stranger to nation-state, modernity and the novel. Any kind of liaison is by definition potentially alienating and of questionable legitimacy.

The love stories underpinning the politics of the Arabic novel are, upon close scrutiny, reincarnations of Arabic poetics of love, not only inherent in pre-modern Arabic storytelling but also in classical and modern Arabic poetry, which are expressive of the aesthetics, ethics and politics of writing in Arab culture past and present. The Arabic novel deploys familiar tropes of love pervasive in Arabic poetry and storytelling – love, desire, nostalgia and madness – to tell stories of Arab aspirations for the nation and modernity and disappointment in the state and modernisation from two different but interlacing perspectives locatable in the dialectics between past and present. It looks at the past through the prism of the present in its imagining of political community and will to the modern, but sees the present through the eye of the past in its allegorisation of the nation-state and interrogation of modernisation and the role of tradition in the process, all the while telling the story of its own search for form. The idea of this book, *Poetics of Love in the Arabic Novel*, and its companion volume, *Politics of Nostalgia in the Arabic Novel*, is informed by the alternative visions and differing dialectics of past and present, as well as the division of labour among familiar tropes of love inherent in the Arabic novel's expression of its longing for form, its discourses on the triangulated nation, modernity and tradition, and the history it writes for the Arab nation and the Arabic novel.

Poetics of Love in the Arabic Novel examines how the present mobilises the past in the processes of nation building and modernisation in the narratives focalised on the two tropes of love and desire. I take as my point of departure the site on which changing notions of space play out the dialectics of past and present. Part I, in two chapters, looks at the ways the Arabic novel partakes in shaping the present in the form of territorialising what will become known as the nation-state. Chapter 1 explores the ways in which the geographical imagining of nation give shape to the Arabic novel, and Chapter 2 examines the effect of statelessness on narrative trajectories. Part II, also in two chapters, then investigates the Arabic novel's take on the incomplete project of the nation-state at present in the form of an anxiety resembling that of unrequited love. Chapter 3 examines the ways in which the Arabic novel interrogates the inherited structures of political authority and wills to transform these structures into a democratic form of rule in the nation-state. Chapter 4 locates the failures of the nation-state in the incomplete process of modernisation, or of educating the nation into responsible citizens capable of ruling themselves. Part III, also in two chapters, picks up the thread and turns its attention to modernity and modernisation, scrutinising the Arabic novel's expressions of the desire for modernity, and the ways it intervenes in and mediates the discourses, in the Foucauldian sense of the word, on modernisation. Chapter 5 analyses the intersection between two impulses, one to decolonise and the other to modernise, and its impact on modernist Arabic literary expression. Chapter 6 looks closely at the nostalgic impulse in the Arabic novel that engages in allegorising the nation and unravelling its possession by the past.

Politics of Nostalgia in the Arabic Novel will continue the interrogation of the Arabic novel's discourses on modernisation but will shift focus onto the two tropes of nostalgia and madness to examine the ways in which the Arabic novel looks at the present through the prism of the past. It will pick up from the thread left off at the end of this volume and begin by looking at the ways it nostalgically revives tradition, argues with it and rewrites it, then inserts it as an important component of the equation that will lead to an Arab modernity. It will then assess the transformation of the past into a burden when nation-building and modernisation come face to face with insurmountable political realities. It will finally examine the Arabic novel's preoccupation with narrativising the nation and narrating history, locating the historical impulse of the Arabic novel in its will to interrogate the past in order to write the future, then showing how it tells the (hi) story of the nation-state as well as the Arabic novel from an entirely new perspective.

My ultimate purpose, however, is to provide close readings of a number of the Arabic novels that make tradition and argument with the past their central preoccupation. These novels restore tradition to the discourses on the nation-state, and intervene in the debates about modernity. Their intervention in these discourses problematises and complicates our understanding of notions of modernity and modernisation especially in the Arab world. My task, as I see it, is archaeological: to unearth as many layers as possible embedded in the texts and to let loose the stories they tell, to let as many genies as possible out of the bottle that is literary history. My choice of texts is necessarily informed by the story I wish to tell about the Arabic novel as well as my taste. There is, it seems, no escaping the hegemony of personal taste, especially where quality of writing is concerned. Needless to say, I have chosen only the novels I like and understand. I console myself with the realisation that my work is a step towards a better understanding of the Arabic novel and the culture that produced it and that I can only tell part, not the whole, of the story. I hope other like-minded scholars will pick up where I leave off, in terms of both approach and scope, and improve the quality of scholarship in the field (Arabic) and discipline (literary studies) that have thus far captivated my attention.

This is not to say that no criteria informed my choice of texts. In addition to what I deem to be their participation in the discourses on modernisation, the one dimension of the Arabic novel that concerns me in this book, they must engage in intertextual dialogism with pre-modern texts. Intertextuality entails that a text deliberately evokes and embodies pre-modern texts, not only by internalising their languages, styles, tropes and moods, but also by rewriting their characters, plots and, more importantly, story. More importantly, it involves interrogating the paradigm of knowledge inherent in forms of writing. References to characters and reworking of themes, which are at any rate too abundant in the Arabic novel to even document, fall outside the scope of this book. As for dialogism, clearly derived from Bakhtin's 'dialogic imagination', it denotes that pre-modern texts are not innocently integrated into modern texts and do not remain innocent. Rather, the discourse(s) produced by these texts engage dialogically with the modern text to produce new discourse(s). Another consideration went into my selection of texts. The Arabic novel, especially that which employs heritage, does have common generic features despite its divergent regional colours and diverse paths, and it seems more appropriate not to be limited to one country or region. There has been a somewhat narrow emphasis on Egypt and to a lesser extent Lebanon and Palestine, understandably because of relative accessibility of material and information from and about these countries, and its seems time that novels from some other Arab countries were incorporated into a study on the Arabic novel. The texts selected go beyond Egypt, Lebanon and Palestine, albeit it all too slightly for my own liking, to include Iraq and Morocco, and include a number of lesser-known Egyptian, Lebanese and Palestinian texts.

From the countries not included, I could not identify texts that fulfil my criteria. This should be taken as a statement of my ignorance not the literary or cultural poverty of these countries. This is not to say that the novels from these countries are not concerned with the issues I examine, on the contrary, there are many that exhibit similar preoccupations. Saudi novelist Ghāzī al-Quṣaybī's *Al-ᶜuṣfūriyya* (1996; Insane asylum) tackles in many ways the area of inquiry of my interest. Its narrative is the rambling of a madman lodged in an insane asylum about the crazed modern butchery of the classical Arabic literary tradition. Missing, however, is the evocation of the styles, moods and stories of this classical tradition. The same may be said about Syrian Hānī al-Rāhib's *Alf layla wa laylatān* (1988; One thousand and two nights). Despite its title, which clearly refers to the famous premodern tales of the *Thousand and One Nights*, the novel rather disdainfully approximates the current situation in the Arab world to the incredibility of the stories of the *Nights*, saying in effect that reality is more fantastic than fiction. In Lebanon, the situation looks a little different.[94] Khoury, in his talk at the Georgetown University Symposium on *Arab Novel: Visions of Social Reality* (12–14 April 2002), alluded to the impact of the civil wars on the development of the novel. These civil wars (1975–90) freed the Lebanese novel from a number of prevalent ideologies, including that which determined its accountability towards the 'past'. Even though his novels are informed by similar preoccupations with regard to the Arabic novel – its modernity, authenticity and legitimacy – the strategies he adopts are different. He borrows freely narrative techniques from the *Nights*, especially what he calls the 'open form', but does not engage with 'tradition' in his discourses on the 'present' reality. Otherwise, I have no defence for the choices I have made.

NOTES

1. Yūsuf Idrīs, '*Autumn of the Patriarch* . . . and our summer', *Islām bilā ḍifāf* (Cairo: al-Hayʾa al-Miṣriyya al-ʿĀmma li al-Kitāb, 1989), pp. 127–37; 131.
2. Yūsuf Idrīs, *Al-farāfīr* (Cairo, 1964), p. 4.
3. See, for example, ʿAbd al-Muḥsin Ṭāha Badr, *Taṭawwur al-riwāya al-ʿarabiyya al-ḥadītha* (Cairo: Dār al-Maʿārif, 1973); Hamdi Sakkut, *The Egyptian Novel and Its Main Trends From 1913–1952* (Cairo: The American University in Cairo Press, 1971); Fatma Moussa Mahmoud, *The Arabic Novel in Egypt* (Cairo: General Book Organisation, 1973); Roger Allen, *The Arabic Novel: An Historical and Critical Introduction* (Syracuse, NY: Syracuse University Press, 1982, 1995); Pierre Cachia, 'The narrative genres', *An Overview of Modern Arabic Literature* (Edinburgh: Edinburgh University Press, 1990), pp. 104–22; Ali B. Jad, *Form and Technique in the Egyptian Novel 1912–1971* (London: Ithaca Press, 1983); Matti Moosa, *The Origins of Modern Arabic Fiction* (New York, NY: Three Continents Press, 1997).
4. Moosa, *Origins*, p. 1.
5. Badr, *Taṭawwur al-riwāya*, p. 51.
6. Ibid. p. 217.
7. Muḥsin J. al-Mūsawī, *Al-riwāya al-ʿarabiyya: al-nashʾa wa al-taḥawwul* (Cairo: al-Hayʾa al-Miṣriyya al-ʿĀmma li al-Kitāb, 1988), p. 15–28.
8. Muḥsin J. al-Mūsawī, *Thārāt Shahrazād: fann al-sard al-ʿarabī al-ḥadīth* (Beirut: Dār al-Ādāb, 1993), p. 25.
9. Ibrāhīm al-Saʿāfin, *Taṭwwur al-riwāya al-ʿarabiyya al-ḥadītha fī bilād al-shām 1870–1967* (Baghdad: Dār al-Rashīd, 1980), pp. 15–16.
10. Ibid. pp. 15–21.
11. Manṣūr Qaysūma (Guissouma), *Al-riwāya al-ʿarabiyya: al-iskhāl wa al-tashakkul* (Tunis: Dār Saḥar, 1997), pp. 5–45.
12. Ali Jad, *Form and Technique*, p. 26.
13. Hamdi Sakkut concurs but terms it differently in *The Egyptian Novel and Its Main Trends*, p. 11.
14. Al-Mūsawī, *Al-riwāya al-ʿarabiyya*, pp. 12–28.
15. Jābir ʿUṣfūr, *Zaman al-riwāya* (Damascus: Dār al-Madā, 1999), p. 31.
16. Ibid. pp. 31–2.
17. Ibid. p. 32.
18. Ibid. pp. 32–3.
19. Ibid. p. 33.
20. Al-Saʿāfin, *Taṭwwur al-riwāya*, p. 31.
21. Ibid. p. 23.

22. Ṣabrī Muslim Ḥammādī, *Athar al-turāth al-shaʿbi fī al-riwāya al-ʿirāqiyya al-ḥadītha* (Beirut: al-Muʾssasa al-ʿArabiyya li al-Dirāsāt wa al-Nashr, 1980), p. 9.
23. Qaysūma, *Al-riwāya al-ʿarabiyya*, p. 14.
24. For a thematic survey, see Muhsin Jassim al-Musawi, *The Postcolonial Arabic Novel: Debating Ambivalence* (Leiden: E. J. Brill, 2003).
25. See, for example, J. Fishman (ed.), *Language Problems of Developing Countries* (New York, NY: John Wiley & Sons, 1968); J. Breuilly, *Nationalism and the State* (New York, NY: St. Martin's Press, 1982); Benedict Anderson, *Imagined Communities* (London: Verso, 1983, 1991); J. A. Armstrong, *Nations Before Nationalism* (Chapell Hill, NC: University of North Carolina Press, 1982); Ernest Gellner, *Nations and Nationalism* (Ithaca, NY: Cornell University Press, 1983); Anthony D. Smith, *Theories of Nationalism* (New York, NY: Holmes & Meier, 1983), *The Ethnic Origins of Nations* (Oxford: Blackwell, 1986), and *Nationalism and Modernism: a Critical Survey of Recent Theories of Nations and Nationalism* (London: Routledge, 1998); Miroslav Hroch, *Social Preconditions of National Revival in Europe* (Cambridge: Cambridge University Press, 1985); E. J. Hobsbawm and Terence Ranger (eds), *The Invention of Tradition* (Cambridge: Cambridge University Press, 1983); E. J. Hobsbawm, *Nation and Nationalism Since 1780: Programme, Myth, Reality* (Cambridge: Cambridge University Press, 1990); Partha Chaterjee, *Nationalist Thought and the Colonial World: A Derivative Discourse?* (Minneapolis, MN: University of Minnesota Press, 1986) and *The Nation and Its Fragments: Colonial and Postcolonial Histories* (Princeton, NJ: Princeton University Press, 1993); Liah Greenfeld, *Nationalism: Five Roads to Modernity* (Cambridge, MA: Harvard University Press, 1992); Umut Özkirimli, *Theories of Nationalism: A Critical Introduction* (Basingstoke: Macmillan, 2000).
26. See *Literature and Nation in the Middle East*, ed. Yasir Suleiman and Ibrahim Muhawi (Edinburgh: Edinburgh University Press, 2006).
27. See, for example, Albert Hourani, *Arabic Thought in the Liberal Age*, 1798–1939 (London: Oxford University Press, 1962) and *A History of the Arab Peoples* (Cambridge, MA: Belknap Press of Harvard University Press, 1991); Israel Gershoni and James Jankowski, *Egypt, Islam and the Arabs: the Search for Egyptian Nationhood 1900–1930* (Oxford: Oxford University Press, 1986), *Redefining the Egyptian Nation 1930–1945* (Cambridge: Cambridge University Press, 1995), and *Rethinking Nationalism in the Arab Middle East* (New York, NY: Columbia University Press, 1997); Bassam Tibi, *Arab Nationalism: A Critical Enquiry*, English translation by Marion Farouk-Sluglett and Peter Sluglett (New York, NY: St. Martin's Press, 1981, 1990); Rashid Khalidi, Lisa Anderson, Muhammad Muslih and Reeva S. Simon (eds), *The Origins of Arab Nationalism* (New York, NY: Columbia University

Press, 1991); Paul Salem, *Bitter Legacy: Ideology and Politics in the Arab World* (Syracuse, NY: Syracuse University Press, 1994).

28. Allen, *The Arabic Novel*, p. 13.
29. Ibid. p. 16.
30. Ibid. pp. 18, 48.
31. Ibid. p. 19.
32. Ibid. p. 45.
33. Ibid. p. 47.
34. See Ibrāhīm Ṭāhā, *The Palestinian Novel: a Study in Communication* (London: Routledge Curzon, 2002).
35. Chaterjee, *Nationalist Thought*, p. 30.
36. Ibid. p. 30
37. Alfrīd Faraj, *Dalīl al-mutafarrij al-dhakī ilā al-masraḥ* (1966), *Mu᾽allafāt Alfrīd Faraj* (Cairo: al-Hay᾽a al-Miṣriyya li al-Kitāb, 1990), vol. 8, p. 303.
38. Ḥammādī, *Athar al-turāth*, p. 5.
39. See *Tradition and Modernity in Arabic Literature*, eds Issa J. Boullata and Terri DeYoung (Fayetteville, AR: Arkansas University Press, 1997).
40. See Rasheed El-Enany, *Arab Representations of the Occident: East-West Encounters in Arabic Fiction* (London: Routledge, 2006); Kamran Rastegar, *Literary Modernity between Middle East and Europe: Textual Transactions in 19th century Arabic, English and Persian Literatures* (London: Routledge, 2007).
41. See also Burhān Ghalyūn, *Ightiyāl al-ᶜaql: miḥnat al-thaqāfa al-ᶜarabiyya bayn al-salafiyya wa al-tabaᶜiyya* (Beirut: Dār al-Tanwīr, 1985), *Mujatamaᶜ al-Nukhba* (Beirut: Maᶜhad al-Inmā᾽ al-ᶜArabī, 1986), *Al-waᶜy al-dhātī* (al-Dār al-Bayḍā': Manshūrāt ᶜUyūn, 1987); Ḥasan Ḥanafī, *Al-turāth wa al-tajdīd, mawqifunā min al-turāth al-qadīm* (Cairo: al-Markaz al-ᶜArabī li al-Baḥth wa al-Nashr, 1980), *Al-turāth wa al-tajdīd, mawqifunā min al-turāth al-gharbī: muqaddima fī ᶜilm al-istighrāb* (Cairo: al-Dār al-Faniyya li al-Nashr wa al-Tawzīᶜ, 1991); Muḥammad ᶜĀbid al-Jābirī, *Ishkāliyyat al-fikr al-ᶜarabī al-muᶜāṣir* (Beirut: Markaz Dirāsāt al-Waḥda al-ᶜArabiyya, 1989), *Al-turāth wa al-ḥadātha* (Beirut: Markaz Dirāsāt al-Waḥda al-ᶜArabiyya, 1991); Ḥasan Ḥanafī and Muḥammad ᶜĀbid al-Jābirī, *Ḥiwār al-mashriq wa al-maghrib* (Cairo: Maktabat Madbūlī, 1990); and Jūrj Ṭarābīshī, *Al-muthaqqafūn al-ᶜarab wa al-turāth: al-taḥlīl al-nafsī li ᶜuṣāb jamāᶜī* (London: Riad El-Rayyes, 1991), *Madhbaḥat al-turāth fī al-thaqāfa al-ᶜarabiyya al-muᶜāṣira* (London: Riad El-Rayyes, 1993).
42. Alfrīd Faraj, *Al-milāḥa fā biḥār ṣaᶜba* (Cairo: Dār al-Mustaqbal al-ᶜArabī, 1986) pp. 306–8.
43. Ibid. p. 309.
44. Ḥanafī, *ᶜIlm al-istighrāb*, p. 76
45. 'Uṣfūr, *Zaman al-riwāya*, p. 34.

46. Maḥmūd Amīn ^{c}Ālim, *Al-fikr al-^{c}arabī bayn al-khuṣuṣiyya wa al-kawniyya* (Cairo: Dār al-Mustaqbal al-^{c}Arabī, 1996), p. 71.
47. Ibid. p. 72.
48. See his controversial study on pre-Islamic poetry, *Fī al-shi^{c}r al-jāhilī* (Cairo, 1926), in which he attempted to re-evaluate the pre-Islamic Arabic poetic tradition by applying Cartesian methods.
49. See *Al-thābith wa al-mutaḥawwil: baḥth fī al-ibdā^{c} wa al-itbā^{c} ^{c}ind al-^{c}arab*, first published in 3 volumes in Beirut in 1973, and now available in a revised 4-volume edition (London: Dar Al Saqi, 1994).
50. See *Al-turāth wa al-tajdīd: Mawqifunā min al-turāth al-qadīm* (Cairo: al-Markaz al-^{c}Arabī li al-Baḥth wa al-Nashr, 1980), a critical introduction to his project in reassessing the cultural heritage of the Arabs, *Min al-^{c}aqīda ilā al-thawra*, 5 vols (Beirut: Dār al-Tanwīr li al-Ṭibā^{c}a wa al-Nashr, 1988).
51. See *Mashrū^{c} ruʾya jadīda li al-fikr al-^{c}arabī fi al-^{c}aṣr al-wasīṭ* (Damascus: Dār Dimashq, 1971); and *Mashrū^{c} ruʾya jadīda li al-fikr al-^{c}arabī min al-^{c}aṣr al-jāhilī ḥattā al-marḥala al-mu^{c}āṣira*: vol. 1, *Min al-turāth ilā al-thawra: Ḥawl naẓariyya muqtaraḥa fī qaḍiyyat al-turāth al-^{c}arabī* (Beirut: Dār Ibn Khaldūn, 1978), vol. 2, *Al-fikr al-^{c}arabī fī bawākīrihi wa āfāqihi al-ūlā* (Damascus: Dār Dimashq, 1982).
52. Muḥammad ^{c}Ābid al-Jābirī, *Ishkāliyyat al-fikr al-^{c}arabī al-mu^{c}āṣir* (Beirut: Markaz Dirāsāt al-Waḥda al-^{c}Arabiyya, 1989), p. 38.
53. See also Muḥammad Madyanī, *Ishkāliyyat taʾṣīl al-masraḥ al-^{c}arabī* (Qarṭāj: al-Majma^{c} al-Tūnisī li al-^{c}Ulūm wa al-Ādāb wa al-Funūn, 1993).
54. Qtd. ^{c}Uṣfūr, *Zaman al-riwāya*, p. 9.
55. Ibid. p. 10.
56. Ibid. p. 55.
57. Ibid. p. 56.
58. Al-Ghazzālī, *Iḥyāʾ ^{c}ulūm al-dīn*, 5 volumes (Beirut: Dār al-Qalam, 1st edn, n.d.), vol. 1, pp. 58–9.
59. Qaysūma, *Al-riwāya al-^{c}arabiyya*, p. 39.
60. Badr, *Taṭawwur al-riwāya*, p. 17.
61. Ghālī Shukrī, *Burj bābil: al-nqd wa al-ḥadātha al-sharīda* (London: Riad el-Reyyes, 1989), p. 52.
62. Badr, *Taṭawwur al-riwāya*, p. 211.
63. Ibid. pp. 210–16.
64. Shukrī, *Burj bābil*, p. 135.
65. Ibid. p. 135.
66. Ibid. pp. 107–8.
67. Ibid. p. 107.
68. Badr, *Taṭawwur al-riwāya*, pp. 212–15; al-Sa‘āfīn, *Taṭawwur al-riwāya*, pp. 22–3.
69. The conference proceedings are published in *Fuṣūl* 16: 3 (Winter 1997), 16:

4 (Spring 1998) and 17: 1 (Summer 1998). The publication of the journal seemed to have fallen behind and the dates do not correspond to real events.

70. Maḥmūd Ṭarshūna, 'Madrasat tawẓīf al-turāth fī al-riwāya al-ᶜarabiyya al-muᶜāṣira', *Fuṣūl* 17: 1 (Summer 1998), pp. 27–39.
71. Ibid. p. 28.
72. For a more detailed discussion, see Shukrī Muḥammad ᶜAyyād, 'Sharzazād bayn Ṭāhā wa al-Ḥakīm', *Fuṣūl* 13: 1 (Spring 1994), pp. 9–19.
73. ᶜUṣfūr, *Zaman al-riwāya*, pp. 33–4.
74. Jābir ᶜUṣfūr, 'Ghiwāyat al-taḥdīth', *Fuṣūl* 12: 1 (1993), pp. 9–21; 10–11.
75. Qaysūma, *Al-riwāya al-ᶜarabiyya*, p. 26.
76. Including names such as Ṣunᶜallāh Ibrāhīm, ᶜAbd al-Ḥakīm Qāsim, Yaḥya al-Ṭāhir ᶜAbdallāh, Yūsuf al-Qaᶜīd and Ṣabrī Mūsā, all Egyptians.
77. 'Mushkilat al-ibdāᶜ al-riwā'ī ᶜind al-jīl al-sittīnīyāt wa al-sabᶜīnīyāt', *Fuṣūl* 2: 2 (Spring 1982), pp. 208–14; 212.
78. Referring to Adūnīs's thesis on the two main principles the Arabic-Islamic tradition has evolved in history in *Al-thābit wa al-mutaḥawwil.*
79. 'Mushkilat al-ibdāᶜ al-riwā'ī ᶜind al-jīl al-sittīnīyāt wa al-sabᶜīnīyāt', *Fuṣūl* 2: 2 (Spring 1982), pp. 208–14; 213.
80. See Muḥammad Badawī, 'Mughāmarat al-shakl ᶜind riwāʾī al-sittīnāt', *Fuṣūl* 2: 2 (1982), pp. 125–42.
81. 'Intertextual dialectics: an interview with Gamal al-Ghitany', *Alif* 4 (1984), pp. 71–82; 75.
82. Ibid. p. 76.
83. Ibid. p. 87.
84. Jamāl al-Ghīṭānī, *Muntahā al-ṭalab ilā turāth al-ᶜarab: dirāsa fī al-turāth* (Cairo: Dār al-Shurūq, 1997), p. 5.
85. Ibid. p. 5.
86. Ibid. p. 5.
87. See *Mustaqbal al-huwiyya al-maghribiyaa amām al-taḥadiyyāt al-muᶜāṣira*, proceedings of the conference held in Tetwan, 6–7 January 1997 (Rabat: Akādimiyyat al-Mamlaka al-Maghribiyya, 1998).
88. The question of authenticity in Maḥmūd al-Masᶜadī's works is the subject of Khālid al-Gharībī's monograph, *Jadaliyyat al-aṣāla wa al-muᶜāṣara fi adab al-Masᶜadī* (Qayrawān: Ṣāmid, 1994). See also, Mohamad-Salah Omri, *Nationalism, Islam and World Literature: Sites of Confluence in the Writings of Maḥmūd al-Masᶜadī* (London: Routledge, 2006).
89. Ben Salem Himmich's *Majnūn al-ḥukm* is looked at as an example of achieving specificity in intertextuality with pre-modern Arabic narratives by Muṣṭafā ᶜAbd al-Ghanī in 'Khuṣuṣiyyat al-tanāṣṣ fī al-riwāya al-ᶜarabiyya: Majnūn al-ḥukm namūdajan taṭbīqīyyan', *Fuṣūl* 16: 4 (Spring 1998), pp. 270–89.
90. See Muṣṭafā ᶜAbd al-Ghanī, *Shahrazād fī al-fikr al-ᶜarabī al-ḥadīth* (Cairo: Dār al-Shurūq, 1995).

91. See Ṣabrī Ḥāfiẓ, 'Jadaliyyāt al-bunya al-saridyya al-murakkaba fī layālī Shahrazād wa Najīb Maḥfūẓ', *Fuṣūl* 13: 2 (Summer 1994), pp. 20–69; and Ferial Ghazoul, *Nocturnal Poetics: The Arabian Nights in Comparative Perspective* (Cairo: American University Press, 1996).
92. See Anna Zambelli Sessona, 'The rewriting of *The Arabian Nights* by Īmīl Ḥabībī, *Middle Eastern Literatures* 5: 1 (2002), pp. 29–48.
93. Roger Allen, 'Literary history and the Arabic novel', *World Literature Today* 75: 2 (Spring 2001), pp. 205–13.
94. The story of Sindbād is recast in Selim Matar's *Al-tawʾam al-mafqūd* (2001; the lost twin), ^{c}Abd al-Raḥmān Fahmī's *Raḥalāt al-Sindbād al-sab*^{c} (1966; the seven voyages of Sindbad) and Samīr ^{c}Aṭallāh's *Awrāq al-Sindbād* (1998; Sindbad's papers). 'The story of Qamar al-Zamān' also is rewritten in part 2 of Aḥmad Ibrāhīm al-Faqīh's trilogy (1990), translated into English as *Gardens of the Night* (1995), to provide a vision for an idealised community in the post-independence Libya. The titles of the three parts of the trilogy are: *Sa-ahibuki madīna ukhrā* (I shall offer you another city); *Hādhihi tukhūm mamlakatī* (these are the borders of my kingdom); and *Nafaq tuḍīʾuhu imraʾa wāḥida* (a tunnel lit by one woman). Algerian Wasīnā al-A^{c}raj's *Fāji*^{c}*at al-layla al-sābi*^{c}*a ba*^{c}*d al-alf* (1993; the tragedy of the thousand-and-seventh night), also rejects the vision of Arab history inherent in the *Nights* and rewrites a new version, making Dunyāzād rather than Shahrazād the originator and the source of the tales.

PART I

Mapping the Nation: Place, Space, Text

Chapter 1

NATION-STATE

TEXTUAL NATION

> I want to draw a map, so to speak, of a critical geography and use that map to open as much space for discovery, intellectual adventure, and close exploration as did the original charting of the New World – without the mandate for conquest.
>
> Toni Morrison, *Playing in the Dark*, p. 3

In 1990, Toni Morrison, already at the time a renowned Pulitzer-winning African-American writer and Robert F. Goheen Professor at Princeton University, was invited to deliver three William E. Massey Sr lectures in the history of American Civilisation at Harvard University. Morrison began her lectures on 'whiteness and the literary imagination' with the formulation of a desire: 'to put forth an argument for extending the study of American literature into what I hope will be a wider landscape'.[1] In these lectures, Morrison demonstrated how the seemingly 'white' landscape of American literature has been haunted by the unspoken presence of 'blackness'. The wilful absenting of 'blackness' in American literary texts indicates rather that 'black matters' and that any reading of American texts must take into consideration the silenced presence of 'blackness', a feature she describes as 'playing in the dark'. 'Playing in the dark' does not refer only to the discourses on race embedded in the written texts, but also to new strategies of reading texts. These strategies ought to bring to the surface the hitherto unarticulated history of 'blacks' in America and especially the role they, directly or indirectly, played in shaping the American civilisation.

That her discourse is counter discourse is hard to miss. Speaking at Harvard University, one of the oldest and foremost elite institutions of education centrally engaged in developing the core curriculum that forms 'educated men and women' in America since its founding in 1636, Morrison could not but be aware of the historical significance of the change of role. She is now playing the 'educator' at the reputedly leading centre of learning in America, if not the world, which has shaped the views of American civilisation, not to mention 'whiteness' and 'blackness' for hundreds of years. By accepting to be the first African-American woman to deliver William E. Massey Sr lectures, she made her brief presence at Harvard a site on which contradictory and problematic symbols of America converge and enter into a dialogue. Harvard University, located in Cambridge, New England, is named after John Harvard, its first donor and a colonist originally from England, which is implicated in the history of slavery in America. William E. Massey Sr, a businessman and philanthropist in whose honour an anonymous donor endowed the lecture series in 1984, was from West Virginia. West Virginia is part of the South, historically the home of plantations and advocates of slavery and remains presently the ground of racism. The first paragraph of the published text speaks to and contests the colonial legacy of Harvard University in silencing her 'people', the African-Americans who were brought to the 'New World' as slaves. She sees too an opportunity to speak through Harvard University and effect changes in the perception of American civilisation, and bring the African-Americans into the centre of any discourse on this civilisation. She unsurprisingly evokes the discovery of the 'New World' that brought waves of colonists who charted both its geographical and intellectual horizons. It is now her turn to expand the familiar landscape bequeathed to Americans by the past, and draw a new map; for only a new map could open up spaces for adventure, discovery and exploration of a new kind. However, the new spaces she speaks of are not of geography, but of critical geography fundamental to thinking.

In the short paragraph I quoted above, we see the relevance of notions of place and space to the ways we think and define ourselves. Geographical and cartographic terms are pervasive in her language, an indication of the ways in which the impulses driving geography and cartography are internalised by the literary imagination and critical thinking. Her co-opting of the language of geography and cartography betrays too a will to mastery, to have a place in the American history of civilisation and to carve out a cultural space for African-Americans – to own her history and have a say in the making of American history. Her discourse signals a desire and necessity for effecting changes in culture and history, and these changes, it seems, require a reformulation of place and space. Space, it seems, is central to any articulation of time, history. More importantly, notions of place and space are inextricably connected to the ways we form and formulate identity. The five motifs of place and space manifest in Morrison's text – the implication of notions of place and space in the literary imagination and critical thinking, in the expression of the will to power, in the explanation of change, in the articulation of time, and in the formulation of identity – are pervasive in modern Arabic literature in general and the Arabic novel in particular. The reasons for the recurrence of the geographical and cartographic motifs in specific but different garbs in modern Arabic literature are many and have to do with the geographical and historical contexts and contests in which modern Arabic texts are produced. Badr Shākir al-Sayyāb's poem, 'Unshūdat al-maṭar', speaks to the contexts and contests I refer to.

I begin my inquiry of the Arabic novel with an analysis of a poem because poetry has historically been the vehicle through which Arab culture has found expression. It has remained uncontested as the dominant literary genre until perhaps the last two decades of the twentieth century. Its history in the past two centuries has been as contentious as the literary genres (short story, drama, novel) born out of the cultural exchange and change preceding, during and following colonialism. It represents too another discourse, not all that different from that of the novel, on Arab cultural and literary modernisation; in fact, the Arabic novel often borrows motifs from the Arabic poetic tradition. More importantly, it can provide a broader framework for us to think about the Arabic novel. Modern Arabic poetry has in common with other literary genres preoccupations with the future of Arabic literature and Arab culture, and in fact, the Arab future. This future is shaped by the ways in which literature in general is able at present to work out the problems it has with the past, in whatever form this past may be cast. The cultural discourses externalised by Arabic poetry, however, take place on a literary landscape that is necessarily mimetic of a geographical place. As it attempts to carve out for itself a cultural space, it creates a textual space that shapes and is shaped by its notions of place. 'Unshūdat al-maṭar' captures and encapsulates, albeit only sketchily, in one text the issues I will be looking at throughout this book and particularly this chapter.

Since the publication of 'Unshūdat al-maṭar' in 1954 (1953?) in the Beiruti avant-garde literary magazine, *Al-Adāb*, this poem by al-Sayyāb (1926–64) has attracted the attention of critics and scholars of Arabic poetry in both the Arab world and the West. It is considered a representative work of not only al-Sayyāb but also of modernist free verse – *al-shiʿr al-ḥurr* – and regarded as a landmark of the maturity of both the poet and the poetry he pioneered, the all too well-known Tammuzi poetry, which pervaded the poetic scene in the middle of the twentieth century. No history of modern Arabic poetry and poetics can ignore this title poem of one of the volumes of al-Sayyāb's poetry. Elias Khoury sums up the importance of this poem and the *dīwān* that contains it in the development of modern Arabic poetry in one sentence:

> With the poetry of al-Sayyāb begins an entire era of transformation in Arabic *qaṣīda* . . . The accomplishments of the poet lies in his ability to take the Arabic poetry out of deep defeat of Arab culture and construct a complex, complete *qaṣīda* which, while remaining grounded in the language of the past, transcends the boundaries of its own classical conventions to embrace additionally the pre-Islamic mythology of the region as well as Western influence. 'Unshūdat al-maṭar', an exemplary new poem, ushers in a new epoch for modern Arabic poetry. It integrates the poet into poetry, lyricism into symbolism, symbolism into realism, political into literary and rhythm into imagery in such a way that the *qaṣīda* is now a complex world composed of images. These images are defined and shaped by the rhythm of the poem.[2]

Scholarship on 'Unshūdat al-maṭar'[3] has given much attention to what historians of literary criticism would term '*explication du texte*'. The focus is understandably on the ways 'Unshūdat al-maṭar', and therefore modern Arabic poetry, achieved modernity by simultaneously internalising and transcending its traditions, both classical Arabic and European during the process of decolonisation. In addition, 'Unshūdat al-maṭar', as I have demonstrated elsewhere,[4] may be read within the context of the emergence of national and nationalist consciousness in post-colonial Iraq during the first half of the twentieth century as a kind of epical narrative, narrative of the will to nation, or nationness, perhaps even as narrative of nation that partakes in post-colonial cultural and identity politics. It too is a statement on modernity and modernisation of both the geographical and literary landscape it draws. It imagines a political community with roots in the immemorial past and at the same time grounds al-Sayyāb's modernist poem in the tradition of Babylonian Ishtar-Tammuz myth and the pre-Islamic and Islamic *qaṣīda*. Text and space shape and are shaped by each other. More importantly, the individual who imagines his community draws the shape of both text and space as he narrates the nation.

'Unshūdat al-maṭar', as text, may be considered narrative of nation, where the text delineates the space, and the space defines the text. The text is framed by the voice of the narrator (situated inside the text) whose gaze delineates the space, Iraq (the narrator is situated outside space, in fact, across the gulf from it, looking at it from outside). The interior of the text becomes the exterior of the space – interior and exterior landscapes merge. The merging of these two landscapes places both the individual and his community in the course of the same destiny: transformation through the cycle of death and resurrection implied in the use of Ishtar-Tammuz myth, and the rite of passage inherent in the classical Arabic *qaṣīda*. The opening lines evoke both precursors.

> Your eyes are two palm tree forests in early light,
> Or two balconies from which the moonlight recedes
> When they smile, your eyes, the vines put forth their leaves,
> And lights dance . . . like moons in a river
> Ripples by the blade of an oar at break of day;
> As if stars were throbbing in the depths of them . . .[5]

The first two lines remind us of the opening lines of the love prelude in any *mu*ᶜ*allaqa* or classical Arabic *qaṣīda*, but the third line evokes Ishtar and her function as goddess of fertility in Babylonian myths. The 'beloved' in this poem, it quickly becomes clear, is not the 'beloved' of the classical *qaṣīda*, but the mother, both Ishtar and the narrator's mother.[6] These two mothers, the objects of desire in the narrative, become Iraq later in the poem.[7] Iraq, as the narrator stands gazing at it from the shores of Kuwait, becomes the object of desire. But the Iraq that is the object of desire is not any Iraq, but the Iraq that has a very specific history. The poem gives it this history.

The Iraq to which the poem alludes did not exist as a space with definitive borders prior to the 1916 Sykes-Picot agreement. It came into existence during the colonial period and its borders were arbitrarily drawn when the British and French empires divided the Middle East into British and French mandates. Iraq as a nation-state is the heir of the British colonial ambitions in the region. By the time 'Unshūdat al-maṭar' came out, Iraq as a nation-state was about a quarter of a century old. Yet, in 'Unshūdat al-maṭar', Iraq is imagined as 'sovereign' having a history extending to 'immemorial past', and is given 'limitless future'. Integrating the Ishtar-Tammuz myth and classical Arabic *qaṣīda* (structure, meter and motifs) into the story of contemporary desolation gives Iraq the history it needs, as an 'imagined community', a history that is both continuous and layered (pre-Islamic, Islamic and contemporary). The cyclical movement of time inherent in the Ishtar-Tammuz myth serves to give the notion of the limitless future of this newly imagined community. More importantly, the embrace of the pre-Islamic conceptualisation of time marks the departure from the more linear religious notion of time (birth, death, resurrection and paradise or hell). It signals the erosion of the certainty of the discourse that embodied this vision, and the adoption of, as Anderson calls it, the notion of 'harmonious, empty time' where the co-existence of competing religious discourses is purportedly made possible.

In addition to the tacit acceptance of the world views expressed in Babylonian myths, pre-Islamic *qaṣīda*, Islamic *qaṣīda*, and secularised Western long poems, there too is the integration of Christianity into this vision. Elsewhere, such as in 'Jaykūr and the City', the story of Jesus is synonymous with that of Tammuz. The effect is seemingly secularisation of religious discourses, which makes universality possible. The desired nation-state is the imagined community that possesses its unique history (authenticity) yet this history does not 'alienate' it from the rest of the world, which consists of other communities, each as uniquely imagined (contemporaneity). The Ishtar-Tammuz cycle is integrated too into Greek, Roman and Chinese myths, as well as modern European literary motifs. The effect is that 'present' is in a continuum with the 'past', not severed from it, and that the newly established nation is imagined as an integral part of the world, not isolated from it. More importantly, the individual is given a central role in the formation and formulation of this imagined community.

In *Imagined Communities: Reflections on the Origin and Spread of Nationalism*, Benedict Anderson describes the ways nation-states imagined themselves into existence worldwide, and the features of these imagined communities. However, Anderson does not focus on the strategies for realising these imagined communities on the ground, even though he alludes to the French Revolution as an early model that did not prevail. In 'Unshūdat al-maṭar', the aspiration to revolution is explicit; in fact, revolution is the mechanism of transformation for both individual and community. The poem is constructed around what ᶜAbbās calls duality,[8] derived from the key figures of the ancient Babylonian myth: Ishtar and Tammuz. Ishtar is clearly mother-goddess and mother, and Tammuz the son-god and the narrator-orphan. Iraq, like the text of the poem, straddles the poles of this structural duality. As object of desire in the narrative, it is both mother and son. It is the orphan's long lost mother and Ishtar's lost-to-the-netherworld-son Tammuz. Iraq plays a dual role, it is to transform itself first – from death to resurrection, and then to transform the narrator – from margin to centre, from homeless and exile to belonging and participation. The mechanism of this transformation is revolution, as the lines 53–7 allude to. These few lines mark the transition in the poem from what DeYoung describes as 'apocalyptic vision' to the more 'optimistic' one.[9] Lines 1–52 describe interconnected conditions/states of Iraq and the narrator. Iraq's destitution is a form of exile that corresponds to the Marxist notion of alienation and is similar to that of the narrator, who has been pushed out of Iraq, displaced, alienated and forced to gaze at Iraq from across the Gulf. Lines 58–95, while repeating the familiar sense of desolation, insist that Iraq will be revived in lines 88–9 and 95. Lines 96–120 is a refrain, a condensed version of lines 1–95. The return of the exile is predicated on the revival of Iraq. Both are possible, however, by means of revolution.

Here, the paradox of 'self' and 'other' intersects with another paradox noted in post-colonial theories: that of 'margin' and 'centre'. This intersection is, however, a source of trouble. If we imagine that one narrative of nation is 'self' willing itself towards the 'centre', then any competing narrative is inevitably looked upon as 'other' that threatens to push the 'self' towards the 'margin'. War, it seems, may be waged between any two or three communities imagined on the same space. The competition over space, however, is not simply a territorial contest but is rather a battle on subjectivity, the foundation of identity. Identity politics are meaningless unless subjectivity is at stake as it collides with other subjectivities in a race to territorialise the space it imagines as the home of its community. Definition, and redefinition, of space can only be effected on the basis of the change in subjectivity. By the same token, the loss, however one may understand the word, of space threatens to obliterate subjectivity. Reading 'Unshūdat al-maṭar' as narrative of nation exposes the interconnectedness between individual subjectivity and communal identity. Al-Sayyāb's narrative of nation – imagining of community – may be seen as the expression of his subjectivity. This subjectivity shapes and is in turn shaped by this imagined community. Simply put, the fates of the individual and of community are intertwined; it is impossible to imagine the individual in contradistinction to community.

What has become clear in my analysis of the poem is this impulse in narrative, and therefore text, to take the shape of a space it imagines on a concrete place, what Gaston Bachelard describes in *Poetics of Space*, that 'we dream over a map, like a geographer'.[10] This impulse is often spoken of as 'mapping', 'charting', 'territorialisation', 'deterritorialisation' and 'reterritorialisation' in the language of criticism of and theorising about literature, technical terms used in two disciplines of intellectual inquiry, geography and cartography, which have in turn become prevalent terms in speaking about literature. Geography and cartography are, however, not innocent sciences. They too are engaged in identity politics especially where mastery is concerned. Maps, as the recent exhibition at the British Library, *Lie of the Land: The Secret Life of Maps* (27 July 2001 to 7 April 2002), demonstrates, cannot be taken at face value, in fact, 'some deliberately set out to deceive and others show a selective view that reflects only the interest of the people who made them'.[11] The familiar map of the world, for example, privileges North America and Europe, the location and size of which in the map place them at the 'centre' of the world. In the world of representation, where location and size matter a great deal, positioning a place in the centre of the map and presenting it in a size larger than other places, especially when actual measurements tell a different story, betrays not only the will to master the place, but also the desire for power.

The will to power, to occupy a central place in the world, finds expression in maps of private estates too, which are quite often represented as both the centre and the towering mansion in their immediate neighbourhood. Mapping, like narrative, willy-nilly, tells the story of the will to power. Geography and cartography are inevitably an expression of both power and the desire for power. Maps of the early modern world, as Jerry Broton persuasively tells us, are in effect reflections of – among other things – the economic interests in the territories represented in these maps.[12] More importantly, geography is a discipline that makes explicit the tactics and strategies of power we deploy. At the end of a lengthy discussion with the editors of the journal *Hérodote*, Michel Foucault comes to the conclusion that geographical methods would become important in his inquiry into the triangular relationship of knowledge, power and discourse:

> The longer I continue, the more it seems to me that the formation of discourses and the genealogy of knowledge need to be analysed, not in terms of types of consciousness, modes of perception and forms of ideology, but in terms of tactics and strategies of power. Tactics and strategies deployed through implantations, distributions, demarcations, control of territories and organisation of domains which could well make up a sort of geopolitics where my preoccupations would link up with yours. One theme I would like to study in the next few

> years is that of the army as a matrix of organisation and knowledge; one would need to study the history of fortress, the 'campaign', the 'movement', the colony, the territory. Geography must indeed necessarily lie at the heart of my concerns.[13]

The text of 'Unshūdat al-maṭar' must be read like a map with its desire for power and the strategies it deploys to achieve this power in mind. Put differently, the poem details a geographer's will to mastery in the form of imagining a community on a map, organising in the process the categories of knowledge in such a way so as to privilege his position. The contested categories of knowledge, in this case 'past' and 'present', are re-articulated to insure the legitimacy of the new map and the individual drawing it.

This new map is itself a contested territory and is necessarily problematic in a number of ways. A map in the post-colonial imaginings of communities plays a paradoxical role. Even as the previously colonised subjects deterritorialise and reterritorialise their subjectivities, the site on which the processes of deterritorialisation and reterritorialisation take place comes to resemble the territory of the colonial making; the map brought in by the European colonisers, as Anderson points out in the Southeast Asian context, came to shape the imagination of the colonised.[14] Al-Sayyāb's mapping is then more of re-mapping; it maintains the contours of the European mapping of the territory that is Iraq now, but deterritorialises it from the dominant presence of the colonisers and reterritorialises it into a modern community in which he will occupy a position of power. His pre-occupation with and notions of modernity also informs his re-mapping of the space of his imagined community. The process of re-mapping takes the form of transformation in the poem, not only of the individual and community, but also of space and time; space that is the new community is defined by a new history given to it, a history that extends into time immemorial. Speaking of Western Enlightenment, Fredric Jameson argues in 'The Realist Floor-Plan'[15] that the emergence of a new space and a new temporality must be seen as 'at one with the whole philosophical programme of secularisation and modernisation'.[16] Without necessarily imposing the paradigm of transformation derived from the experience of Western Enlightenment, al-Sayybāb's imagining of a modern community is also, in a sense, his 'programme' for this community, not only of secularisation and modernisation but also of revolution. Modernity, however, is another area of complication; it is another contested territory. Any map of modernity in the Arab context is by definition a kind of mapping and open to re-mapping, as the relationship between 'past' and 'present', 'tradition' and 'modernity' are mediated and negotiated through the 'West', all in the long shadows it has cast on the Arab cultural, intellectual and literary landscapes.

Perhaps the most poignant statement this poem makes is the sense of profound powerlessness felt by the individual and the community he imagines. The movement from 'margin' to 'centre', to be effected by revolution, represents not a description of wish fulfilment but rather a formulation of desire; desire for power. The two parts of this formulation – power and desire – have each been articulated in quite specific terms. The power of the individual is premised on the right of the individual to take part in the political process and partake in political authority that is imagined to be both just and legitimate. The imagined community has come to take the shape of a modern nation-state and political authority has increasingly become the locus of narrative interrogation. Political authority is legitimised on the basis of its application of justice and, more importantly, its foundation in the tradition of political theories and its departures from historical practices of abuse. Principles of democracy are not necessarily imported from the West but have roots in indigenous traditions. 'Past' in this case is the source of authenticity, therefore, legitimacy. In the absence of the perfect nation-state and its perfect instrument of power, the individual is left powerless but full of dreams for a 'utopian' world. Any imagining of nation-state is understandably pulsating with desire; desire for all the components that will make the nation-state the Utopia imagined. In al-Sayyāb's poem, nation-state, modernity and tradition are all objects of desire. The formulation of this desire is, however, gendered. The objects of desire are feminised: nation-state, modernity and tradition, the mother and lover in the poem, are all inscribed on a woman's body – Ishtar. Mapping the nation is both geography of desire and cartography of the female body.

There are, obviously, consequences to this formulation of desire in the post-colonial discourses on nation and its culture. The impulses of post-colonial narratives of nation, and their consequences, not immediately apparent in al-Sayyāb's poem, become central to and the focus of the novelistic enterprise. The Arabic novel spells out in great detail the process of mapping the nation with all the complications and ambivalence this process entails. It tackles the central preoccupations of contemporary Arab culture – political authority, modernity and tradition – in diverse and divergent ways, revealing in its discourses the complex negotiations that go into defining the place of each in the space of the newly imagined community. It, moreover, contests, interrogates and intervenes in its own discourses, as well as other cultural discourses on nation, modernity and tradition. It scrutinises closely the impasses reached in these discourses. It deconstructs, to some extent, these discourses, especially the ways in which they formulate the issues in terms of simultaneous desire for nation, including its twin pillars of modernity and tradition, and the female body. It looks at the consequences of the gendering of nation, and provides, at times passionate, analyses of the reasons for the arrested development of both the nation and the discourses around it. These discourses of the novel take place in the textual world created by the novel itself and in its textualisation of space its textual politics come to correspond to politics of space. The politics of space is perhaps a good place to begin a study of the Arabic novel and its love affair with the nation-state.

IMAGININGS OF COMMUNITY AND POLITICS OF SPACE

Following the success of his earlier novels which one way or another rewrote pre-modern Arabic texts,[17] Jamāl al-Ghīṭānī (b. 1945) brought out *Khiṭaṭ al-Ghīṭānī* (1980), a novel that marks the end of his interest in historical narratives and the beginning of his preoccupation with Sufi writing.[18] As expected, this novel is another display of the intertextual narrative techniques and strategies for which he has become renowned, and yet another (hi)story of his beloved city Cairo.[19] The title, *khiṭaṭ*, clearly directs our attention to a tradition of geographical-historical writing about Egypt, more specifically, al-Maqrīzī's (1364–1442) *Al-khiṭaṭ al-Maqrīziyya* and ᶜAlī Mubārak's (1823/4–93) *Al-khiṭaṭ al-tawfīqiyya.* Samia Mehrez reads al-Ghīṭānī's works, much like Mahfouz's works, essentially as histories of Cairo. As they (al-Ghīṭānī and Mahfouz) reproduce the spatial and architectural signs of the city, Mehrez argues, 'they engage in writing and interpreting the history of a dynamic space. The city becomes a text that is constantly rewritten; a space that is continuously reconstructed/deconstructed through its ever-shifting, ever-changing sign'.[20] In her emphasis on al-Ghīṭānī's novel as narrative on history,[21] she reads *khiṭaṭ* as a genre of historiography[22] with strong affinities to the chronicle, another genre of historiography. The difference between these two genres is more a question of organisation. Topographical genres, which deal with the description of provinces, Mehrez explains, 'create, in a textual form, a space (i.e., the province) through time (i.e., history). The chronicle, on the other hand, creates time (i.e., a chronology of events) through space (i.e., textual space)'.[23]

As a genre premised on topographical accuracy, however, *khiṭaṭ* works must necessarily be constantly rewritten. Mubārak wrote his purported topographical description of new Cairo in order to provide a record of the changes occurring in a metropolis that grew beyond the boundaries and at the expense of Fatimid Cairo during the reign of Muḥammad ᶜAlī and his family. His *khiṭaṭ* was meant as an update of al-Maqrīzī, whose work could no longer serve as a guide to the revamped city.[24] That his new version of the Egyptian topography would be read as history was never in doubt; the genre he chose to cast his work in determined that it should also be read as a chronicle of the transformation of Cairo from a medieval city into a modern metropolis.[25] The topographical changes are, however, manifestation of something more profound and perhaps even sinister. The heart of the matter, as Mehrez insightfully points out about al-Ghīṭānī's novel, is 'another authority that is going to be responsible for the new socioeconomic and ideological organization of the city'.[26] The generic intertextual instances of al-Ghīṭānī's text with its two thus far identified pre-texts made possible an interpretation of the novel as history and counter history and, more importantly, as criticism of the practices of power in contemporary Egypt. I suggest that there is more to it than meets the historical eye. Geographical narratives need to be examined not simply as story of place (history) but also as discourses of power. Place is the contested site on which these discourses of power negotiate and create a space that is community. Al-Ghīṭānī's choice to write in the *khiṭaṭ* genre was not an innocent one. Whether he articulates the reasons for this choice, and whether we accept his rationale, we cannot ignore the consequences of this choice in the production of meaning, therefore, our reading of the text in the form he presents to us.

Speaking of the sources of pre-modern Arabic narrative in *Muntahā al-ṭalab*, al-Ghīṭānī identifies, among other genres, *khiṭaṭ* as an important corpus of works, which provide narrative techniques and strategies and, more importantly, a vision of the world unique to the Arabs. He mentions specifically three names: al-Maqrīzī, Mubārak, both Egyptians, and Muḥammad Kurd ᶜAlī, a Damascene intellectual, scholar and journalist,[27] who also authored a topographical survey and history of the Levant in 1925–8 known as *Khiṭaṭ al-shām*.[28] However, he has a particular axe to grind with Mubārak, whom he considers the architect of new Cairo. The new Cairo referred to here is, it seems, a symbol of Westernisation observable in Egyptian culture in the nineteenth century since the days of Muḥammad ᶜAlī (reigned 1805–48). Mubārak, minister of public works under Ismā^cīl (reigned 1863–79),[29] was responsible for the expansion of Cairo and, according to al-Ghīṭānī, 'laying the foundation for the modern European planning of the City, and for building straight avenues modelled on Parisian streets'. Boulevard Muhammad ᶜAli, for example, is an exact replica of Rue Rivoli in Paris. In the process of building this modern street, Mubarak destroyed more than thirty Islamic monuments, resulting in '*thaghrīb al-madīna*', the Westernisation of the city. The contention, however, is not the acceptance or rejection of Western influence per se; it is rather the question of striking a healthy balance so that what al-Ghīṭānī calls 'features of national character' (*khaṣāʾis} al-shakṣiyya al-qawmiyya*) are not threatened. The destruction of Islamic monuments and parts of old Cairo in the process of modernisation initiated by Mubārak is contrasted to the co-existence of new cities and intact old cities in Tunisia, Algeria and Morocco. It is possible to accept Western influence without obliterating the 'national' features of the Egyptian character.[30] At stake, then, are not only the historical monuments but also the identity these monuments give to the place.

The three pre-texts of al-Ghīṭānī's work – al-Maqrīzī, Mubārak, Kurd ᶜAlī – were interestingly written at a time of great changes for the regions they attempted to capture in words. Al-Maqrīzī's work, André Raymond points out, 'was written at a crucial period in Egypt's history, namely the period of transition between the Bahri (or Turkish) Mamluk dynasty (1250–1382) and the Circassian Mamluk dynasty'.[31] More particularly, he 'dwells on the negative aspects of the reign of Faraj (1399–1412)',[32] when Cairo was in great crisis and seen by al-Maqrīzī to be in ruins.[33] Mubārak's *Khiṭaṭ* was similarly written at the time when the city and country were experiencing great turmoil (1886–9). Mubārak's narrative is informed by the presence and active role of the French in destroying many of Cairo's features and monuments preceding Muḥammad ᶜAlī's accession to power,[34] and of the British in affecting the development of the city since the departure of the French[35] until their own withdrawal after World War II. Cairo developed into a Westernised metropolis, as al-Ghīṭānī points out, during this crucial period of pseudo and real colonisation of Egypt. Kurd ᶜAlī wrote *Khiṭaṭ al-shām* in the immediate aftermath of the Sykes-Picot partition of Levant, which was preceded and followed by continuous political, economic and social crises in the region, the effects of which are still felt today. The changes recorded in these works are linked to two things: the changing fortunes of the ruling power and the subsequent and consequent re-charting of place and reorganisation of space. Al-Ghīṭānī's work, a political allegory as Mehrez argues, must be read too with this aspect of *khiṭaṭ* writings in mind.

Khiṭaṭ, in addition to designating a genre of historiography, is a technical term referring to organisation of space. *Khaṭṭa*, in Arabic, means to write, to draw a line and to plan, and *khiṭṭa*, singular of *khiṭaṭ*, means a plan, in this instance, city planning. Planning, or 'to determine a plan',[36] as Timothy Mitchell shows, is part of 'construction of power' within the European framework of reference to the world as 'world-as-exhibit' and as periphery to its metropolis.[37] This framework, what Mitchell calls 'enframing', in effect produced strategies that subjected the colonised 'societies' to a kind of order and discipline that made managing them and 'understanding' them possible:

> The reorganisation of towns and the laying of new colonial quarters, every regulation of economic or social practice, the construction of country's new system of irrigation canals . . . the building of barracks, police stations and classrooms, the completion of a system of railways – this pervasive process of 'order' must be understood as more than mere improvement or 'reform'. Such projects were all undertaken as an enframing, and hence the effect of re-presenting a realm of the conceptual, conjuring up for the first time the prior abstractions of progress, reason, law, discipline, history, colonial authority and order.[38]

This colonial plan would 'create the appearance of objectness' in the colonised territories, and Egypt was to be ordered up as something object-like.[39] This ordering is part of the strategy to convert the colonised territory of the periphery to a series of 'plantations', as the reorganisation of the Egyptian villages shows, that would supply the metropolis with the raw material it coveted. Colonial romances reproduce this imperial impulse in its linear narrative of the colonised space, as Franco Moretti observes in his analysis of the ways European novels have mapped Africa:

> The European experience of African space begins with rim 'settlements', which are then quickly linked to those inland areas that are rich in those raw materials (including human beings) that the colonial power is eager to obtain. And, basically, this is it. A colonial regime may reach the next phase (development of lateral 'feeders' along the main line), but hardly much more. Colonialism aims at re-directing the

local economy *outwards*: towards the sea, the metropolis, the world market. A good internal distribution is literally none of its business.[40]

Khiṭaṭ, whether used by al-Maqrīzī, Mubārak, Kurd ᶜAlī or al-Ghīṭānī, it seems, conjures up epistemological and ontological contests across time and space, between 'past' and 'present' and 'East' and 'West', and provides a blueprint for new constructions of power and, more importantly, the articulation of the new tactics and strategies of control.

Khiṭaṭ al-Maqrīzī, written between 1415 and 1424, read in within this theoretical framework, becomes a historical statement of the ways in which pre-modern Arabic-Islamic constructions of power are manifest in the organisation of space in the geographical narratives of the time, notwithstanding its interest in geography. To borrow Runciman's terminology, the sources of power are located in access to and control of means of three things: production, coercion and persuasion.[41] The work unsurprisingly focuses on, besides its description of the Nile valley, which constituted Egypt of the day, the organisation of Egypt into tax districts (*aᶜmāl*), in fact, the coverage of cities and towns correspond to tax districts known to him.[42] The government offices responsible for running the country (*dīwān*) were of three kinds: those which administered the army (*juyūsh*), including lands allocated to them by the rulers as rewards for their services (*qaṭāʾiᶜ* or *iqṭāᶜāt*), tax revenues (*kharāj*), and official correspondence (*kitāba*). There is, as a matter of course, understandable focus on Cairo, which was the seat of power. Al-Maqrīzī's Cairo, according to Raymond, was governed directly by the sultan and his officials:[43] the judge (*qāḍī*) had a very broad jurisdiction that covered matters of civil law; the police prefect (*wālī*) maintained public order and security; and the overseer of the market (*muḥtasib*) supervised professional activities and levied monthly and weekly taxes on the shopkeepers.[44] The landscape of al-Maqrīzī's Cairo and text is dotted with and organised around rulers and their biographies, palaces, treasuries, royal stores and stables, government offices, and other arenas of royal activities, followed by houses of the notables and public places like baths and markets (in volumes two and three). Mosques (*jawāmiᶜ* and *masājid*), colleges (*madāris)* and Sufi establishments (*khawāniq*), where ideologies were manufactured and disseminated and jurists trained, take up the remainder of the space (the bulk of volume four). Like Cairo, which is the heart of Egypt, these monuments are the landmarks of the various quarters (*ḥārāt*), streets and alleys (*durūb* and *ᶜawāṭif*) and squares (*riḥāb*) of the city.

This is not to say that al-Maqrīzī's work is lacking in historical accuracy; rather, its narrative of facts is informed by an awareness of the role of power brokers in history making of his time. The historical vision is clearly an Islamic one. Real history begins with the establishment of Muslim communities in Fusṭāṭ in 641. Coverage of ancient Egyptian monuments, such as the Pyramids and the Sphinx, is inundated with legends and myths, mainly derived from Biblical stories, evocation of which is a familiar trope in Arabic-Islamic historiography. Histories of communities predating Islam are, of course, subsumed under the Islamic framework. Islamic history is in turn divided along ideological, or sectarian, lines. The Shi^{c}ite Fatimids are emphatically distinguished from the Sunnite Ayyubids. The Fatimids are the prominent inhabitants of volume two, whose organised public call to their cause (*da^{c}wa*) and ritual celebrations of Shi^{c}ite holidays are recounted. And the Ayyubids and their successors, the Mamluks, take over in volume three, not only in terms of building and residing in palaces, commanding the army, and appointing judges, tax collectors, market inspectors and government bureaucrats but also in the ways they controlled fabrication and dissemination of ideology. In volume four, the coverage of the *jawāmi^{c}* mosques, the platform of the Fatimid propaganda, is prefaced by an essay on the ways the Fatimids conducted the Friday congressional prayers. The survey of the *madāris* colleges, established by the Ayyubid to counter the Shi^{c}ite ideology,[45] is preceded by a treatise on the various Islamic sects and the eventual, perhaps even triumphant, spread of the Ash^{c}arite, or Sunnite ideology.

Mubārak does not repeat in *Al-khiṭaṭ al-tawfīqiyya* the tactics and strategies of control manifest in the organisation of space in al-Maqrīzī. His stupendous work rather reflected both his concerns and the concerns of his age. 'Streets and Schools were built as the expression and achievement of', Mitchell says of Mubārak's work, 'an intellectual orderliness, a social tidiness, a physical cleanliness, that was becoming to be considered the country's fundamental political requirement'.[46] The construction of Boulevard Muḥammad ^{c}Alī, and the destruction of historical monuments in its wake, about which al-Ghīṭānī quibbles with Mubārak, 'conformed with prevailing medical and political theory',[47] which targeted backwardness. 'The disorder and narrowness of the streets that open boulevards eliminated were considered a principal cause of physical disease and of crime', Mitchell points out, 'just as the indiscipline and lack of schooling among their inhabitants was the principal cause of the country backwardness'.[48] Mubārak's city planning and school building must be viewed in the context of the nineteenth-century politics of modern state. State, as defined by Mitchell on the basis of his study of the nineteenth-century constructions of power, is thought of as 'structural effect' resulting from modern techniques of functional specification, organisational control and social surveillance that are exercised within society by institutions such as armies, bureaucracies and schools.[49] 'The connection between street and school', as a matter of course, reveals the connection between 'new kinds of spatial framework and the means of coordinating and controlling those who move within them'.[50] Mitchell thus concludes:

> These means of coordination were something particular and physical, offering what Michel Foucault has called a micro-physical power; a power that worked by reordering material space in exact dimensions and acquiring continuous bodily hold upon its subjects. Yet at the same time, I have tried to show, this power was something meta-physical. It worked by creating and appearance of order, and appearance of structure as some sort of separate, non-material realm. The creation of this meta-physical realm was what made the education of the individual suddenly imperative – just as the micro-physical methods were what made such education possible. Power now sought to work not only upon the exterior of the body but also from the 'inside out' – by shaping the individual mind.[51]

Mitchell describes here the politics of modern state known in Western political thinking and practices, which were deployed in the process of *Colonising Egypt*, including organising the Egyptian villages in such a way as to control the agricultural wealth of the country.[52] These politics seemed to have worked their way into the minds of the Egyptian elite, who seemed to have embraced these politics during the ascendance of Westernisation. Al-Ṭahṭāwī, Muḥammad ᶜAbduh, Mubārak, al-Muwayliḥī, to name but a few of the architects of reform and modernisation in nineteenth-century Egypt quoted by Mitchell, were voluntary executors of Western thought, translating what they learned as students in Europe and through their readings into ideologies of reform or plans for modernisation. The picture from the perspective of the colonised is perhaps a bit more problematical.

Al-khiṭaṭ al-tawfīqiyya does confirm that education was part of the tactics and strategies deployed for social control that Mitchell speaks of: the landscape of the text is dominated by the institutions of learning, modern and traditional schools (*madāris*) as well as mosques (*jawāmi*ᶜ and *masājid*) and Sufi *khawāniq*, inside and outside Cairo, and by the biographies of a majority of religious scholars. There is no evidence in the text of the 'break down of the Islamic law profession' that 'was endemic to the kind of political authority which was breaking down' Mitchell refers to.[53] On the contrary, *Al-tawfīqiyya* projects Egypt as a vast, ordered network of knowledge whereby modern and traditional institutions of knowledge are integrated into a seemingly coherent, cohesive system. This is not to say that Mitchell is off base in his assessment of the waning fortunes of the Islamic law profession; the case is rather that the construction of power found in *Al-tawfīqiyya* is informed by an agenda that needs to be taken into consideration in our reading of the text. The text mediates between al-Maqrīzī and the colonial discourses. Its construction of power does replace that of al-Maqrīzī but not necessarily duplicate that of the colonial discourses and policies. More importantly, it interrogates colonial discourses and policies even as it absorbs parts of its tactics and strategies. The history of Cairo and Egypt it writes is full of subversive intent.

Cairo is the main protagonist of *Al-tawfīqiyya* and the history of Egypt is subordinated to the story of Cairo. The history of Cairo, with which the book begins, is distinctly Fatimid and takes up seven of the work's twenty volumes. The Islamic character of the rest of Egypt, highlighted by the Islamic institutions of learning and the biographies of the religious scholars, is emphasised.[54] Pre-Islamic history – Pharaonic, Greek and Coptic – is integrated into the Islamic history of both Cairo and Egypt. Unlike al-Maqrīzī, in which clear distinction is made of pre-Islamic, early Islamic, Fatimid, Ayyubid and Mamluk periods, *Al-tawfīqiyya* is driven by the impulse to integrate. Cairo, in spite of its Islamic character, is the locus of a history that extends from Pharaonic times to the present. Alexandria too is portrayed as a city of layered – Pharaonic, Greek and Islamic – but coherent history. The narrative of *Al-tawfīqiyya*, integrative of components thus far excluded, is in many ways counter-narrative, in fact, a two-pronged counter-narrative. Like his predecessor al-Ṭahṭāwī, Mubārak exploits the findings of Orientalist research and rewrites the history of Egypt. *Al-tawfīqiyya* has in common with *Anwār tawfīq al-jalīl fī akhbār Miṣr wa tawthīq banī Ismāᶜīl* (1868) the redefinition of al-Maqrīzī historiographical framework. The Pharaonic history, considered marvellous tales (*ᶜajāʾib*) in al-Maqrīzī, in fact, even in al-Jabartī's (1754–1822) *ᶜAjāʾib al-athār fī al-tarājim wa al-akhbār* (Marvellous traditions of biographies and histories), the famous nineteenth-century chronicles of Egypt, is incorporated into the history of Egypt, now that the language in which this history is written – hieroglyphic – has been deciphered.[55]

Egypt of *Al-tawfīqiyya*, however, is not the Egypt of *Description de l'Egypt*, one of Mubārak's sources,[56] or its spin-offs, the series of books on the discovery and rediscovery of Egypt,[57] or on the manners and customs of Egyptians.[58] In these books, Egypt comes across as a European archaeological site and anthropological curiosity, and its history begins only when the West turned its gaze towards it. The discovery and rediscovery books recount the history of European adventures into the country, military or otherwise, and describe the treasures found lying about, as if Egypt itself had nothing to do with these treasures, and as if the history of ancient Egypt was an extension of the military and intellectual history of Europe. The Western gaze often privileged Egypt's Pharaonic past at the expense of the living and the present. In a great number of the drawings of *Description de l'Egypt*, architectural monuments are represented in meticulous details while people, always dwarfed by the monuments and fuzzy, tend to look away from or have their backs towards the gaze. Mubārak, and al-Ṭahṭāwī shortly before him, rescue ancient Egypt from the West and restore it to modern Egypt, as Kurd ᶜAlī would later do for Levant in *Khiṭaṭ al-shām*. Its tireless accounts of the diverse social habits, traditional customs, religious rituals and daily practices of contemporary Egyptians across the towns and cities of the country seem to speak directly to the reductive Western gaze, and place the inhabitants of the contested space to centre stage. What emerges in *Al-tawfīqiyya* is a country with visible, clear contours and a distinct history. This country is delineated as a part of but separate from the Muslim Umma, understandable at the time when Egypt under the rule of the Muḥammad ᶜAlī dynasty enjoyed relative autonomy from the Ottoman Caliphate. It is further depicted as distinct from the West. It is distinguished from the rest of the Muslim community by its Pharaonic past and from the West by its Islamic character. More importantly, it is not the periphery of the European Empire; rather, Cairo, if we should draw a map of the cities, towns and villages mentioned in the work, is the metropolis to which all roads lead. Geography, in this case, drives historical narratives.

Seen in this light, that *Al-tawfīqiyya* is responsive to colonial politics of space, the focus of the text on indigenous institutions of learning becomes pregnant with significance. Both Egypt and Levant at the turn of the century were targets of missionary schools, which, as Kurd ᶜAlī points out in *Khiṭaṭ al-shām* with regard to the Levant, had their own agendas. 'The sectarian and missionary schools established by Americans, Jesuits, Germans,

English, Italians, Greeks, Russians, and other "nations" who have ambitions in the Holy Lands, made education very diverse in these lands'.[59] These schools necessarily engaged in forwarding their own agenda, creating differences among the members of one community. Students of these schools, given their education, serve the agenda of their schools rather than the 'national cause' of their homelands. These schools, in short, 'extract' from their students, 'their love for their nation and country (*yanza*ᶜ*u mina l-muta*ᶜ*allimi ḥubba qawmiyyatihi wa bilādihi*)'.[60] 'How many men and women have we seen', he continues, 'who studied at those schools and turned out neither Arab nor Western (*ifranj*). They speak at home a language that is not their own. The do not feel Levantine. On the contrary, they hate their customs and history and view their country with contempt (*taswaddu bilāduhum fī* ᶜ*uyūnihim*). It is, therefore, correct to say that those schools did not benefit the country adequately; rather, they benefited the companies, which founded them in that [the schools] provided for [the companies] allies in these lands'.[61] In its repossession of the institutions of learning, *Al-tawfīqiyya* tacitly engages in the counter-colonial discourses that *Khiṭaṭ al-shām* openly propagates. The learning institutions are the site on which contests over power-shaping and power-giving knowledge take place. Nationalism, a response to powerlessness and an attempt to regain power, inevitably becomes embroiled in the fight over the programmes of these learning institutions. It is not surprising then that education, seen by Kurd ᶜAlī as the culprit in snuffing the love for the homeland out of the Levantines,[62] is subordinated to his more explicit nationalist discourse.

Kurd ᶜAlī, who was also a student of the West and the Syrian-Egyptian Nahḍa, produces similar anti-Ottoman and counter colonial discourses in *Khiṭaṭ al-shām*. His is, however, a more straightforward historical narrative despite the apparent grounding in geography, but only in the sense that no alternative tactics and strategies of controlling the social space are devised. The politics of space are manifest in the ways the text borrows some of *Al-tawfīqiyya*'s spatial organisation and counter-narrative strategies. *Bilād al-Shām* is now clearly delineated as the area extending from the Mediterranean in the west to the Euphrates in the east, and from Alexandretta in the north to Aqaba in the south, in other words, the Eastern Mediterranean coast including primarily Syria, Lebanon and Palestine we know today. The region's pre-Islamic history – Pharaonic, Assyrian, Babylonian, Phoenician, Greek and Byzantine – distinguishes it from the Ottoman Empire, and its Arabic-Islamic (with emphasis on Arabic) history separates it not only from the Ottomans but also from the West. What is most significant is perhaps its insistence on the unity of the region historically and geographically even though it had by that time been carved and divided into French Syria (including Lebanon) and British Palestine. It too contests vehemently the ways in which France and Britain arbitrarily mapped the region. The borders of Bilād al-Shām, he exclaims, are 'all man made (*maṣnūᶜ*)'.[63] Kurd ᶜAlī's narrative is clearly informed by his ideology and its location in the competing ideologies operative in Bilād al-Shām, particularly Damascus, in the first two decades of the twentieth century. It reflects the early stirrings of Arab nationalism of which Kurd ᶜAlī was an important advocate.[64] *Khiṭaṭ al-Shām* repeats the nationalist politics Kurd ᶜAlī propagates in *Al-muqtabas*, a periodical he founded and edited between 1908 and 1914: that the region he maps ought to be autonomous from the direct rule of Istanbul as well as free from European control. There are, however, a number of unresolved ambiguities.

Unlike Egypt, which has historically had a more distinct perception of the Nile Valley as a relatively coherent region with Cairo as its centre of power, Bilād al-Shām is cartographically more problematic. Its mapping has always depended on the ways the rulers of the region – whoever they may be – devised strategies for its control throughout the history Kurd ᶜAlī himself writes. It has historically had more than one centre or power. Damascus, Aleppo, Hims, Hama, Tripoli, Beirut, Sidon, Acre, Haifa, Jerusalem, to mention just a few of the cities mentioned by Kurd ᶜAlī, were co-existing or alternating centres of power at one point or another in the history of the region. The ethnic and religious make-up and dynamics of Bilād al-Shām are more diverse and complex than those of Egypt as well. The unity of the region on which Kurd 'Alī's narrative insists, as a matter of course, demands new mapping. The resultant new map is in effect an expression of a new imagining of community taking place on the site of a historically contested geographical area. Despite the insistence on the autonomy of the Bilād al-Shām from the Ottomans and the rulers of the community defined as Islamic, there is a lingering ambivalence towards this larger Muslim community. Ottomanism and Arabism, as C. Ernest Dawn has shown, overlap.[65] Even as *Khiṭaṭ al-Shām* defines a community for itself against this Muslim community, it recognises Islamic history as its own, although in a secularised form. The emphasis on secularity, an inclination strengthened through contacts with the West, does not redefine this history unproblematically; on the contrary, it creates an additional tension that will have a lingering effect on all later imaginings of community. Anti-colonial narrative strategies polarise 'East' and 'West' further, and bequeath yet another source of trouble. Insistence on the independence of the 'East' cannot disguise the intellectual and cultural ties between the 'East' and the 'West', and the crucial role the 'West' played in the development of the notions of nationness and modernity in the 'East'. Bias towards the city throws up yet another area of contest. History, projected as that of cities as centres of power and civilisation,[66] with the 'countryside' as the periphery and the desert as no-place, will also leave its mark on the literary imagination. Al-Ghīṭānī, self-proclaimed heir to this tradition of writing, inherits its cartographic impulses, tactics and strategies of control, and unresolved ambiguities.

THE IMAGINED COMMUNITY THAT IS THE NATION-STATE

Khiṭaṭ al-Ghīṭānī, written in the post-colonial, post-independence era of Egypt, remains preoccupied with the concerns that went into earlier imaginings of community. The difference is that nation-state has become reality; Egypt is now a politically independent country with clearly defined borders as well as a 'sovereign' system of government. The competition with the West over territorialising the space that is Egypt has, it seems, come to an end. Al-Ghīṭānī's *Khiṭaṭ*, at one level, takes comfort in the clarity of the real borders of Egypt. The novel, as Anderson and others of the relation between the nation and the novel would say, makes the nation-state its fictional space. The nation-state *Khiṭaṭ* delineates has four clear borders, three with friends and one with the enemy in the north. Regardless of the other misleading set of definitions, that *Khiṭaṭ* is surrounded by water on one side and land on three sides, the country that is the subject of allegory here must look like Egypt with slight adjustments to our sense of direction. The enemy to the north refers specifically to Israel and generally to the West, which was responsible for installing Israel where it is now. The centre of power is, however, located in the city. *Khiṭaṭ*, at another level, is Cairo the capital city of Egypt where the central governing body of the country resides. The home of power in *Khiṭaṭ* is not the new Cairo of Western influence but the old Cairo of al-Maqrīzī. Its borders are drawn with walls, and its landscape marked by streets that branch into smaller lanes (*durūb*) that in turn fork into even narrower alleys (*aziqqa*) with bends (*ᶜawāṭif*) and squares (*riḥāb*) scattered here and there. *Khiṭaṭ* is, at a third level, the Fatimid part of the city, which gives Cairo and Egypt their non-Western identity.

Al-Ghīṭānī resumes but refines identity politics manifest in the politics of space inherent in the genre, the belonging to which he seeks for his novel. He picks up where his predecessors had left off. He valorises the Egyptian identity on the basis of authenticity, which is to be derived from the indigenous history and culture of Cairo and Egypt. Authenticity is set against the West in this case. The site of the novel is significant in this regard. New Cairo, modelled on the Western city and at one time home to Europeans and the base of British colonial rule (1882–1936),[67] is displaced. Old Cairo is placed in its stead as the centre of power and, as a matter of course, generator of history and civilisation. Anti-colonial discourse is evident in situating the examination of the sources and effects of power in a locality called *Khiṭaṭ*. *Khiṭaṭ*, as a topographical term, has meant different things over the centuries. While it means simply residential quarters *(ḥārāt)* in al-Maqrīzī,[68] it denotes the eight administrative districts the French devised during their three-year occupation (1798–1801) of old Cairo in order to control the city.[69] The tactics and strategies of control deployed by the French colonisers called for a compromise between their own 'modern' principles and the local customs. On his arrival in Cairo Napoleon 'formed a *dīwān* (council) comprising nine members drawn from the foremost shaykhs. He appointed an *agha* of the janissaries, who was in charge of the police, a *wālī* (night *agha*), a *muḥtasib* (supervisor of weights and measures) . . .'.[70] These local officials were to help the French 'director of trades', who supervised the occupational corporations, to maintain public order and ensure the collection of taxes levied on the corporations. The French also created a half-Muslim and half-Coptic court of commerce and an office of property records, which affected not only the material interests of the Egyptians but also their civil status.[71] Like its precursors, al-Ghīṭānī's *Khiṭaṭ* is a discourse on power.

It revises al-Maqrīzī, for the medieval structure of power is no longer recognisable in a modern nation-state. It rejects the colonial forms of power, of which *Al-tawfīqiyya*'s are implicated as part. Mubārak's objectives in transforming Egypt into a modern nation-state by means of education have been to some extent achieved, even though one may question the modernity of the recently founded Egyptian nation-state. The post-colonial structure of power, however, has its own problems. The project of modern nation-state that is *Al-tawfīqiyya* is, on hindsight, a naive dream; it did not anticipate the quagmire that is political authority in the post-independence era. National or nationalist forms of power did get rid of the colonisers but they also created their own kinds of hegemony. *Khiṭaṭ al-Ghīṭānī* interrogates one of the structures of hegemony in the post-independence nation-state. Its discourse on power takes the form of spatial politics too, just like the *Khiṭaṭ* of al-Maqrīzī, Mubārak and Kurd ᶜAlī. Taking a cue fromr the geographical-historical genre it claims to be its precursors, it begins by defining the borders of the area it wishes to describe. It then takes us through the area's walls, streets, lanes, alleys, bends, squares, sufi *zawāyā*, buildings and historical monuments, then its suburbs (*ḍawāḥī* and *nawāḥī*) and the desert (*khalāwī*). As the narrative seemingly meanders through the streets and alleys of Khiṭaṭ, the story of a powerful institution unfolds. The story, however, is not of a single protagonist, but of the numerous individuals who are intimately or remotely connected to this powerful institution. In the story of this institution and the rise to power of a number of individuals, the secrets of power and powerfulness are unveiled.

The novel comprises two main parts. The first part, given the title of 'Streets and Walls' (*al-shawāriᶜ wa l-aswār*), revolves around the mysterious figure known only as al-Ustādh, who runs a newspaper called *Al-anbā᾿* (the news). The newspaper, a century-old institution, is housed in a large century-old, seven-storey building located on the first street of the Khiṭaṭ. This edifice of power is run by al-Ustādh himself, who occupies the entire seventh flour. He maintains his power through his carefully selected entourage. The membership of this entourage is made up of al-Tanūkhī, al-Ṭanbūlī, al-Imbābī and Rawnaq. Al-Ṭanbūlī, a failed medical student, is the financial manager and seems to have a complete file on every resident of Khiṭaṭ. Al-Tanūkhī, of dubious past, is the second-in-command. Al-Imbābī, of keen hearing and memory, commands the telephone switchboard and seems to possess all the information imparted in phone conversations. And, Rawnaq, a talented daughter of a former diplomat who has mastered many foreign languages during her residence abroad with her father, is al-Ustādh's personal secretary. She holds the fort and no one gains access to al-Ustādh without her permission. The supporting cast is no less formidable. Ja᾿far, the courier, Burnuq, the security guard, al-ᶜInānī, the informant, al-Wātidī, the conference manager, al-Jaᶜīdī, former bouncer and now al-Ustādh's eyes and ears in the streets, all take active part in running and consolidating the *Al-anbā᾿* empire. They ensure that al-Ustādh is kept informed of all the goings-on in Khiṭaṭ: that his wishes are fulfilled and orders carried out to the letter.

The events recounted in this part of the novel take place under tense circumstances. The enemies, with whom Khiṭaṭ has thus far had three wars, at an average of one every seven years, are becoming an external threat again. In the meantime, the construction of the *khazzān*, an obvious euphemism for the High Dam (*al-sadd al-ᶜālī*) has divided the Khiṭaṭ from within.

ᶜAjam, originally meaning the Persians and later coming to denote foreigners in general, are now the opposition. They are the original inhabitants and current residents of the Khiṭaṭ who have turned against the ruling party and are now becoming a security concern for the authorities. The story of the reign of al-Ustādh and his mysterious sources of power tells the tale of the tactics and strategies of control implemented by those in power and felt by those subjected to it. The means of control known of, let us say, monarchy, such as those al-Maqrīzī describes, or colonisation, such as those Mubārak and Kurd ᶜAlī allude to, are no longer practical or legitimate in the republican era. In seeming deference to republican principles, such as democracy, civil liberty, freedom of expression and human rights, Khiṭaṭ, a republic now, is free of the presence of a hands-on ruler, his armies or guards. On the contrary, the most powerful institution in this republic is a newspaper, whose role in shaping the imagined community into a modern nation with democratic aspirations, as Anderson has demonstrated, is instrumental. The landscape of Khiṭaṭ is understandably dominated by the *Al-anbāʾ* building and dotted by its correspondents, who are stationed in every nook and cranny and allowed to roam freely from one corner to another. What would ensure the solvency and efficiency of the state and the civil rights and liberties of the individual more than the transparency of the instruments of power? Journalism, with its potential to uncover and disseminate information vital to shaping the public opinion, is central to the health of a republic, one would think.

Al-anbāʾ, as it turns out, is in fact an instrument of hegemonic power itself. It is implicated as a complicit partner of the police and the secret service, the two institutions charged with consolidating the power of the state in Khiṭaṭ. The stations of *Al-anbāʾ* correspondents effectively complement the security checkpoints situated at the end of every alley, lane and street. The three institutions together tighten the noose around democracy and the necks of the inhabitants of Khiṭaṭ, whose every move is watched, every word heard, recorded and used against them. *Al-anbāʾ*, like the police and secret service, is engaged in collecting, sorting, filing, deciphering, fabricating and exploiting information to the advantage of the powers that be. Information, of all kinds, is the means of control. *Al-anbāʾ* derives its own power from the support it gives the current form of political authority by providing the information it needs to take out every potential opponent. The residents of Khiṭaṭ live in apprehension and suspense: whispered remarks, even innocent ones, they make could lead to their imprisonment, disappearance or demise. Rather than questioning the practices of political authority,

Al-anbāʾ as a matter of fact mimics these practices: it is practically the police state it serves.

Al-Ustādh, who mysteriously rises to the most powerful position at the newspaper, resembles Gamal Abdel Nasser. He is charismatic and very involved in and in command of the day-to-day affairs of the newspaper. He controls his employees by making sure he is abreast of every detail of their lives. He himself, however, is an enigma. No one knows who or what he is, where he comes from or ends up. He has no name through which his origins may be traced. The title by which he is known, al-Ustādh, like the word *al-qāʾid* by which Nasser is known, can vaguely mean a number of things. *Ustādh* is mister, master, teacher or professor, while *qāʾid* denotes anyone possessing means of control, from police captain to movement leader and military commander. His life is shrouded in mystery and his mind impenetrable, like his office to which practically no one has access. No one knows his connections, whether he has family or whom among the elite is his friend, or what makes him tick. His famous appetite for sex with virgins is more an expression of his power than pleasure. Only two things are really known about him: he is a hands-on manager of the newspaper and is able to make and break anyone he wishes. Even the ways he manipulates his employees and sets them against one another are matters of conjecture and rumour, murmurs in darkened corridors and back alleys. No one has actually seen him in action. His unknowablity is paradoxically his power, like God. Information as means of power works in two interrelated ways: the source of power is concomitantly all knowing and utterly unknowable. Al-Ustādh is so powerful precisely because he is master of the power games that involve knowledge. By simultaneously withholding information about himself and learning everything about others he is able to control those around him. More importantly, he is not afraid to put his knowledge to use, necessarily to his advantage and the detriment of others.

This is not to say that al-Ustādh is immune to similar manoeuvres. His sudden fall from power and disappearance from Khiṭaṭ at the end of part one of al-Ghīṭānī's novel are explicable in similar terms. His entourage, in a way his disciples, eventually beat him to his game and in a race to power snared him, as part two tells us. The second part of the novel, titled al-Ḍawāḥī, al-Nawāḥī, al-Khalāwī, is organised around space, with the focus on three districts: al-Ḍāḥiya al-Ūlā (the First Suburb), al-Ḥayy al-Sābiʿ (the Seventh Quarter), and al-Khalāwī (the Desert). In this part of the novel, power games take on even more sinister proportions. With the fall of al-Ustādh, the centre of power also moves from the heart of Khiṭaṭ to the First Suburb. The entourage of al-Ustādh is now dispersed, with only al-Tanūkhī still in a position of relative power. He is running the Seventh Quarter, wondering why he is not in charge of *Al-anbā᾽* or Khiṭaṭ. The administration of Khiṭaṭ is in the hands of al-Hilālī who, like al-Ustādh, is an enigma. As the narrative moves from one district to another, it brings to the surface new tactics and strategies of controlling public opinion devised and implemented by al-Hilālī. Artists, poets and writers are no longer permitted to be freely creative and all their works must be commissioned. Public spaces, the cafés and hotels known for gatherings of intellectuals, are closed. Folk songs and epics expressive of 'genuine' public sentiments are banned. In addition, steps towards the destruction of Khiṭaṭ are taken. Artefacts and monuments *(athār)* from ancient Khiṭaṭ are seized and sold wholesale to Americans and Europeans. Trees are completely uprooted. Foreign workers are imported to replace the local labourers. These measures, combined with the disastrous consequences of the Khazzān, seem to augur an ominous future for Khiṭaṭ. And, finally, enemies are unconditionally invited into Khiṭaṭ. Surveillance, searches of houses and interrogation of persons are commonplace. Torture is used to extract information from and subdue members of the opposition, or anyone who dares criticise the government.

Egypt watchers will easily discern the main points of criticism levelled against Sadat's policies in the aftermath of the 1973 October War with Israel. The dead give away is, of course, the carte blanche invitation to the country given to the enemies. The story of the architect of this move is revealing. Ḥamdī Ramzī comes home to Khiṭaṭ from abroad with a doctorate in engineering, hoping to one day receive a Nobel Prize. His career develops in an utterly undistinguished fashion until he devises the plan to let the enemies in through the front door. He receives an international prize for his initiative and suddenly becomes famous and powerful. The reference to the 1978 Camp David Peace Accord with Israel and Sadat's subsequent receipt of the Nobel Peace Prize is difficult to miss. There too is the allusion to Sadat's 'open door policy'. This policy of *al-infitāḥ* invited foreign investments and encouraged trade of all kinds, including in Pharaonic artefacts, with America and Europe. The results for Cairo are changes perhaps not to the best advantage of the city and its residents. The influx into Cairo and Egypt and the dominance of foreigners and foreign corporations in the Egyptian economy aside, the gap between the rich and poor widened and, more importantly, further expansions led to the uncontrollable sprawling of the city's landscape. There too is the issue of political hegemony inside the country. Al-Sadat's rule was no less dark than that of his predecessor, Nasser, in terms of political oppression of the Egyptians, especially those who opposed his policies. Intellectuals, including al-Ghīṭānī, often landed in jail for opinions they expressed publicly, be they in writing or not.

The measures of tight control taken by the administration of al-Hilālī, like those of Sadat, fail to suppress resistance and opposition to the government policies. Folk songs continue to be heard throughout Khiṭaṭ, and despite the tireless efforts of the secret service, the singer cannot be identified and therefore captured and stopped. On the contrary, oppression pervasive initially in the old part of the Khiṭaṭ and presently in the new al-Ḍāḥiya al-Ūlā, precipitated resistance of equal vehemence. The opposition, against all odds, becomes stronger and its following grows bigger. Resistance to oppression, however, can take place only in spaces outside the control of the old and new regimes of power. The desert, al-Khalāwī, becomes the site onto which ideological conflicts and power struggles are deferred. The second part of the novel understandably deviates from the spatial organisation of the first part. The unilateral authority of al-Ustādh, reflected in the dominance of the landscape of the old city, is replaced by three forces competing for power, now mirrored in the tripartite structure of the latter part of the novel. The heir of al-Ustādh, al-Tanūkhī takes up residence in the Seventh Quarter and attempts to exert control over the entire Khiṭaṭ from there. Al-Tanūkhī's ambitions are often checked by the machinations of the new wizard of power games, al-Hilālī, who adopts the First Suburb as his base of operation. The opposition, as it gathers momentum and becomes the force to be reckoned with, comes to control the desert. It too devises subversive tactics and strategies to evade, escape, resist and counter government control. These subversive tactics and strategies take the shape of the topography of the desert.

The desert is a no-place that turns into a place of refuge and exile. It is a no-place only in the sense that it is out of reach of the state power housed in the old city or the new suburbs. Already in part one we hear of the opposition (*ᶜajam* and the *murābiṭūn*) fleeing to the desert from the brutal measures of the regime. In fact, the end of this part witnesses a massive exodus of the oppressed and the disenchanted from the old city to the desert.[72] Those who will become their leaders, al-Khiḍr, Ilyās and Sulaymān, survive intimidation, imprisonment and torture to reappear in al-Khalāwī and assume leadership of the resistance. Their leadership is interestingly esoteric and occult; subterfuge seems the only means to resist the mercurial overwhelming influence of al-Tanūkhī and al-Hilālī. The desert, where anything can disappear without leaving a trace, is then the ideal home for the persecuted and rebels. There, they cannot be found easily. Like mirages, they may seem real but are not necessarily so. The mystical turn of writing in this part of the novel makes sense; like the flickering sands of the desert mirage, mysticism destabilises any notion of certainty. Al-Khiḍr, Ilyās and Sulaymān, the potential saviours of the Khiṭaṭ who will never die[73] are, Mehrez points out, names of both prophets and mystical figures.[74] They are not necessarily naive or innocent. They too take necessary steps to ensure their own safety and build up mass support. They put to good practice the well-known Shiᶜite doctrine of *taqiyya*, a protective measure that requires dissimulation of one's religion under duress or in the face of threatening damage. The caves, where they seek refuge and transcendence, are known as *kuhūf al-taqiyya*. There, they are transformed from ordinary individuals to leaders. These caves become in time alternative centres of power. The reality of power in the desert is, paradoxically, as illusory as that in the city.

The city and the desert, despite their vast topographical differences, are of equally tricky terrain. This terrain at once conceals and reveals. The function of narrative in truth telling is interrogated here in addition to the nature and practices of power. *Khiṭaṭ al-Ghīṭānī*, Mehrez argues, is 'a discourse on a discourse: an alternative narrative on history that challenges and exposes the misrepresentations, the exclusions and the silences of the dominant record'.[75] It, however, more poignantly questions the possibility of deriving any truth from narrative, especially when it is implicated in power games. Narrative is steered by the labyrinthine topography of the Khiṭaṭ, of its old and new cities and of the desert; the movements of the narrative are as unpredictable as the twists and turns of the streets, lanes and alleys, or the abrupt appearance of their nooks and crannies. In this sense, narrative mirrors the unpredictability of the power games it narrativises, following in movement the labyrinthine topography that shapes and is shaped by it. Yet narrative movements in this novel, like the clearly marked streets and landmarks of its landscape, are deliberate and unmistakably leading to the only feasible climax: the inevitable birth of resistance to hegemony and their contest over the ownership of both power and truth.

The streets, lanes, alleys and, at times, corners are named after the players in the power games excluding al-Ustādh, who is in fact a symbol of power and who, despite his disappearance from the scene, is never really absent from the text. A title like 'Ḥārat Rawnaq'[76] signals that the story is that of the role of Rawnaq in the games. Digressions, such as those marked by the word 'Fāʾida', obviously a device borrowed from classical texts, impart information vital to the understanding of the story. The third of five avenues is logistically named 'Shāriᶜ al-Wishāyā' when malicious rumours are unveiled as one of the mechanisms of control.[77] 'Ḥārat al-Ḥisār'[78] conveys the sense of siege brought about by the tactics and strategies of control employed by *Al-anbāʾ*. The story begins with the order to arrest the opposition[79] then proceeds to recount details of the relentless pursuit of anyone suspected of harbouring less than flattering sentiments towards the regime. The pressure mounts rapidly and steadily, like air travelling speedily through alleys and streets, until it reaches a boiling point and explodes into the open space of *al-maydān al-kabīr* (the big square) at the end of part one of the novel, and into new sites of power and exile at the beginning of part two. In this latter part, the tension is diffused as the contests over power take place more openly in more open spaces.

The topography of Khiṭaṭ, both the city and the genre, drives narrative in and gives shape to this novel and the community it imagines. This topography paradoxically frees the narrative from the familiar novelistic enterprise and allows its strands to roam, digress, disperse and eventually converge into a uniquely new form without losing the thread of the story. The lines derived from this topography and drawn by the narrative delineate the imagined community as a nation-state. In fact, it is impossible to imagine nation without state, state being the system of political authority operative in the nation. The contrast between the role of the city and that of the desert in the text is instructive. The closed space of the city, like the tight grips of power, induces oppression, claustrophobia and exile, while the open space of the desert fosters freedom, empowerment and will to power. The city, it seems, is the site of power while the desert is the site of powerlessness. The back and forth movement between the city and the desert speaks to the push and pull relationship between power and powerlessness, which finds expression in the ways place is drawn and made relevant. Power, especially of the tyrannical type, leads to a sense of placelessness, homelessness or statelessness. The persecuted in the city turn to the desert for refuge. The desert becomes synonymous with displacement and statelessness. The absence of state paradoxically makes empowerment of the disempowered possible.

NOTES

1. Toni Morrison, *Playing in the Dark: Whiteness and the Literary Imagination* (New York, NY: Vintage Books, 1993), p. 3. Originally published in hardcover by Harvard University Press, 1992.

2. Ilyās Khūrī, *Dirāsāt fī naqd ak-shi^{c}r* (Beirut: Dār Ibn Rushd, 1981), pp. 28–31.
3. Although Khūrī makes no reference to other studies of 'Unshūdat al-maṭar', whether as a single poem or as a collection of poems published between 1950 and 1960, he in fact summarises not only the conclusions thus far reached about al-Sayyāb and his poetry but also anticipated those which followed suit. Regardless of their theoretical frameworks, critics seem to agree that 'Unshūdat al-maṭar', both the poem and the *dīwān*, signalled the transformation of the poet, his poetry and modern Arabic poetry: from individualistic expression to group aspirations, or lyricism to realism (Iliyyā Ḥāwī, *Badr Shākir al-Sayyāb* (Beirut: Dār al-Kitāb al-Lubnānī, 1973), vol. 2, p. 173; and Sabry Hafez, 'The Transformation of the Qaṣīda Form in Modern Arabic Poetry', in Stefan Sperl and Christopher Shackle (eds) *Qaṣīda Poetry in Islamic Asia and Africa* (Leiden: E. J. Brill, 1996), vol. 1, pp. 99–120; 108), and Arabic poetry's transformation from classicism to modernism (Iḥsān ^{c}Abbās, *Badr Shākir al-Sayyāb: dirāsa fī ḥayātihi was shi^{c}rihi* (Beirut: Dār al-Thaqāffa, 1969); Ḥāwī, Ibid; Hafez, Ibid; Ḥasan Tawfīq, *Shi^{c}r Badr Shākir al-Sayyāb: dirāsa faniyya wa fikriyya* (Beirut: al-Mu$^{\circ}$assasa al-^{c}Arabiyya li al-Dirāsāt wa al-Nashr, 1979); and Terri DeYoung, 'A new reading of Badr Shākir al-Sayyāb's "Hymn of the Rain"', *Journal of Arabic Literature* 22 (1994), pp. 40–61, and *Placing the Poet: Badr Shākir al-Sayyāb and Postcolonial Iraq* (Albany, NY: State University of New York Press,1998)). The difference is in the details of this transformation dependent on where emphasis is placed. ^{c}Abbās, for example, in the literary biography he wrote on al-Sayyāb considers this poem within the context of the development of the poet, traces the thread of alienation that links the poems written in the period of al-Sayyāb's exile in al-Kuwait, and regards the use of the myth of Ishtar as the symbol of both the poet's rejuvenation as well as Iraq's revival (pp. 206–13). Khūrī, on the other hand, discusses extensively the composition of the poem, such as the myth and its transmutations, the associations, the imagery, the paradoxes, and the rhythm derived from single units of language or complex compositions (pp. 27–59). Hafez looks at the ways the form of the classical Arabic *qaṣīda* is transformed in the post-colonial context, paying special attention to the dialectical relationship between self and other, and past and present (pp. 99–120). As for DeYoung ('A new reading'), she traces the rain imagery to mainly pre-Islamic *qaṣīda* and to a lesser extent to what she calls 'scripture' (Qur$^{\circ}$ān and Ḥadīth) and examines the paradoxical affects of rain, especially the mythical motif of creation and destruction (pp. 39–58).
4. See Wen-chin Ouyang, 'Text, Space and the Individual in the Poetry of Badr Shākir al-Sayyāb: an Essay on Nationalism, Revolution and Subjectivity', in Robin Ostle (ed.), *Sensibilities of the Islamic Mediterranean: Self-Expression in a Muslim Culture from Post-Classical Times to the Present* (London: I. B. Tauris, 2008), pp. 330–42.

5. Translated by Lena Jayyusi and Christopher Middleton as 'Rain Song', in Salma Khadra Jayyusi (ed.), *Modern Arabic Poetry: an Anthology* (New York, NY: Columbia University Press, 1987), pp. 427–30; 427. References are to the Arabic original in *Dīwān Badr Shākir al-Sayyāb*, 2 vols (Beirut: Dār al-ᶜAwda, 1971), pp. 474–81.
6. *Dīwān . . . al-Sayyāb*, lines 23–5.
7. Ibid. line 44.
8. ᶜAbbās, *Badr Shākir al-Sayyāb*, p. 106.
9. DeYoung, 'Anew reading', p. 49.
10. Gaston Bachelard, *Poetics of Space*, tr. Maria Jolas (Boston, MA: Beacon Press, 1964 [1969]), p. 204.
11. *TimeOut* 1644 (20–7 February 2002), p. 50.
12. See *Trading Territories: Mapping in Early Modern World* (London: Reaktion Books, 1997).
13. Michel Foucault, *Power/Knowledge: Selected Interviews and Other Writings 1972–1977*, ed. Colin Gordon, tr. Colin Gordon, Leo Marshall, John Mepham and Kate Soper (New York, NY: Pantheon Books, 1980), p. 77.
14. Benedict Anderson, *Imagined Communities: Reflections on the Origin and Spread of Nationalism* (London: Verso, 1991), p. 171.
15. In *On Signs*, ed. Marshall Blonsky (Baltimore, MD: Johns Hopkins University Press, 1985), pp. 373–83.
16. Ibid. p. 373.
17. *Al-Zuwayl* (Baghdad, 1974); *Al-Zaynī Barakāt* (Damascus, 1975); *Waqāᵓiᶜ Ḥārat al-Zaᶜfarānī* (Cairo, 1976); *Al-Rifāᶜī* (Cairo, 1978).
18. *Kitāb al-tajaliyyāt*, Part 1 (Cairo, 1983), Part II (Cairo, 1985), Part III (Cairo, 1987); *Risālat al-Ṣabāba wa al-wajd* (Cairo, 1987); *Risālat al-baṣāᵓir fī al-maṣāᵓir* (Cairo, 1989); *Shaṭḥ al-madīna* (Cairo, 1990).
19. For a survey of intertextual techniques in this novel, see al-Ḥabīb al-Dāᵓim Rabbī, *Al-kitāba wa al-tanāṣṣ fī al-riwāya al-ᶜarabiyya: dirāsa naṣṣiyya li-āliyāt al-intāj wa al-talaqqī fi* Khiṭaṭ al-Ghīṭanī (Rabat: Manshūrat Ittiḥād Kuttāb al-Maghrib, 2004).
20. Samia Mehrez, *Egyptian Writers between History and Fiction* (Cairo: American University Press, 1994), p. 61.
21. Ibid. p. 77.
22. Ibid. p. 66.
23. Ibid. p. 67.
24. ᶜAlī Mubarāk, *Al-khiṭaṭ al-tawfīqiyya* (Cairo: Bulaq, 1886–9), vol. 1, p. 2.
25. There is a large body of literature on the development and growth of Cairo since its foundation in the tenth century. Janet Abu-Lughod's *Cairo: 1001 Years of City Victorious* (Princeton, NJ: Princeton University Press, 1971) remains one of the most important sources of the history of the city. André Raymond provides more up-to-date scholarship on the subject in *Cairo:*

City of History, tr. Willard Wood (Cairo: American University Press, 2001). Appended bibliographies provide more details on the sources of the study of the history and growth of Cairo.

26. Mehrez, *Egyptian Writers*, p. 68.
27. For a brief biography, see C. Pellat, 'Kurd ^{c}Alī', *Encyclopaedia of Islam*, 2nd edn, pp. 437–8.
28. Jamāl al-Ghīṭānī, *Muntahā al-ṭalab ilā turāth al-^{c}arab: dirāsa fī al-turāth* (Cairo: Dār al-Shurūq, 1997), p. 7.
29. For his life, career and works, see Muḥammad ^{c}Abd al-Karīm, *^{c}Alī Mubārak: ḥayātuhu wa maʾāthirhu* (Cairo: Maṭba^{c}at al-Risāla, n.d.); Samīr Abū Ḥamdān, *^{c}Alī Mubārak al-mufakkir wa al-mu^{c}ammir* (Beirut: al-Sharika al-^{c}Ālamiyya li al-Kitāb, 1993); Aḥmad Amīn, *Zu^{c}amāʾ al-iṣlāḥ fī al-^{c}aṣr al-ḥadīth* (Cairo: al-Nahḍa al-Miṣriyya, 1949), pp. 184–201; J. A. Crabbs, *The Writing of History in Nineteenth-century Egypt* (Cairo: American University Press, 1984), pp. 109–29; Gilbert Delanoue, *Moralistes et Politiques Musulmans dans l'Egypte du XIXe Siècle (1798–1882)*, 2 vols (Cairo: IFAO, 1982), vol. 2, pp. 489–564; Darrell Ivan Dykstra, *A Biographical Study in Egyptian Modernisation: ^{c}Alī Mubārak (1823/4–1893)*, Ph.D. dissertation for the University of Michigan, 1977; Muḥammad ^{c}Imāra, *^{c}Alī Mubārak, muʾarrikh wa muhandis al-^{c}umrān* (Cairo: Dār al-Shurūq, 1988); Lorne Kenny, '^{c}Alī Mubārak: nineteenth century Egyptian educator and administrator', *Middle Eastern Journal* 21: 1 (Winter 1967), pp. 35–51; Muḥammad Aḥmad Khalafallāh, *^{c}Alī Mubārak wa āthāruhu* (Cairo: Anglo-Egyptian Library, 1957); Ḥusayn Fawzī al-Najjār, *^{c}Alī Mubārak Abū al-ta^{c}līm* (Cairo: Dār al-Kitāb al-^{c}Arabī, 1967); Maḥmūd al-Sharqāwī, *^{c}Alī Mubārak: ḥayātuhu wa da^{c}watuhu wa āthāruhu* (Cairo: Anglo-Egyptian Library, 1962); 'Mubārak, ^{c}Alī', *Encyclopaedia of Arabic Literature* (London: Routledge, 1998), vol. 2, pp. 535–6; K. Vollers, '^{c}Alī Pasha Mubārak', *Encyclopaedia of Islam*, 2nd edn, p. 396; Sa^{c}īd Zāyid, *^{c}Alī Mubārak wa a^{c}māluhu* (Cairo, 1958); Jurjī Zaydān, *Tarājim mashāhīr al-sharq fī al-qarn al-tāsi^{c} ^{c}ashr*, 2 vols (Cairo: Dār al-Hilāl, 1910), vol. 2, pp. 33–9.
30. Al-Ghīṭānī, *Muntahā al-ṭalab*, p. 14.
31. André Raymond, *Cairo: City of History*, original French, *Le Caire* (Paris: Librairie Arthème Fayrad, 1993), translated into English by Willard Wood (Cairo: American University Press, 2001). References are made to the English translation. This quote, p. 149.
32. Ibid. p. 149.
33. Ibid. pp. 138–48.
34. Mubārak, *Al-tawfīqiyya*, vol. 1, pp. 60–2.
35. Ibid. vol. 9, pp. 54–60.
36. Quoted by Mitchell from a letter by Jeremy Bentham to Muḥammad ^{c}Alī' in 1828. See Timothy Mitchell, *Colonising Egypt* (Cambridge: Cambridge University Press, 1988 [1991]), p. 33, note 95.

37. Ibid. p. 33.
38. Ibid. p. 179.
39. Ibid. p. 33.
40. Franco Moretti, *Atlas of the European Novel: 1800–1900* (London: Verso, 1998), pp. 60–1.
41. Qtd Nazih N. Ayubi, *Over-stating the Arab State: Politics and Society in the Middle East* (London: I. B. Tauris, 2001), p. 38.
42. References are made to al-Maqrīzī, *Al-khiṭaṭ al-Maqrīziyya* (Beirut: Dār al-Kutub al-ᶜIlmiyya, 1998), vol. 1, pp. 136–462.
43. Raymond, *Cairo*, p. 152.
44. Ibid. pp. 153–4.
45. Ibid. pp. 102–7.
46. Mitchell, *Colonising Egypt*, p. 63.
47. Ibid. p. 65.
48. Ibid. pp. 66–7.
49. Ibid. pp. 78–96, also qtd Nazih N.Ayubi, *Over-stating the Arab State*, p. 13.
50. Ibid. p. 93.
51. Ibid. pp. 93–4.
52. Ibid. p. 34.
53. Ibid. pp. 84–5.
54. *Al-khiṭaṭ*, Michael J. Reiner similarly argues in a close reading of Mubārak's 'description' of al-Azhar and its contemporary practices, harmonises and homogenises al-Azhar's history. Mubārak is, Reiner explains, transfixed by the European 'progress' of 'civilisation', being involved, as he was, in the diffusing of European technology started by Muḥammad ᶜAlī. Closer scrutiny shows that Mubārak is ambivalent towards al-Azhar, for it must make way for the kind of knowledge behind European modernity, now being disseminated in 'modern' schools. The progress Mubārak has in mind, Reiner asserts, 'is essentially technocratic, uncomplicated by an awareness of the unforeseen and disparate effects of state-sponsored reforms on different social groups and institutions' (*IJMES* 29: 1 (1997) pp. 53–69, 57). I am not sure I agree. I have discussed this issue in 'Fictive Mode, "Journey to the West", and Transformation of Space: Discourses of Modernization in ᶜAli Mubarak's *ᶜAlam al-Din*', *Comparative Critical Studies* 4: 3 (December 2007), pp. 331–58.
55. Mubārak, *Al-tawfīqiyya*, vol. 1, p. 3.
56. For further details, see Gabriel Baer, "ᶜAlī Mubārak's *Khiṭaṭ* as a source of the history of modern Egypt', in P. M. Holt (ed.), *Political and Social Change in Modern Egypt* (Oxford: Oxford University Press, 1968), pp. 13–27; and Darrell Ivan Dykstra, *A Biographical Study in Egyptian Modernization: ᶜAlī Mubārak*, vol. 2, pp. 418–39.
57. See, for example, Peter Arthur Clayton, *The Rediscovery of Ancient Egypt:*

Artists and Travellers in 19th Century (London: Thames and Hudson, 1982); and Fernand Beaucour, Yves Laissus, and Chantal Orgogozo, *The Discovery of Egypt*, tr. Bambi Ballard (Paris: Flammarion, 1990).

58. See, for example, Edward William Lane, *An Account of the Manners and Customs of Modern Egyptians* (London: Charles Knight & Co., 1836).
59. Muḥammad Kurd ᶜAlī, *Khiṭaṭ al-shām* (Beirut: Dār al-ᶜIlm li al-Malayīn, 1969–71), vol. 4, p. 80.
60. Ibid. vol. 4, p. 80.
61. Ibid. vol. 4, p. 80.
62. Ibid. vol. 4, pp. 80–2.
63. Ibid. vol. 1, p. 51.
64. See Philip Khoury, *Urban Notables and Arab Nationalism: the Politics of Damascus 1860–1920* (Cambridge: Cambridge University Press, 1983); and C. Ernest Dawn, 'The origins of Arab Nationalism', in Rashid Khalidi *et al.* (eds), *The Origins of Arab Nationalism* (New York, NY: Columbia University Press, 1991), pp. 3–30.
65. See C. Ernest Dawn, *From Ottomanism to Arabism: Essays on the Origins of Arab Nationalism* (Urbana, IL: Illinois University Press, 1973).
66. Volumes 3–6 of *Khiṭaṭ al-Shām* comprises of what Kurd ᶜAlī calls *al-tārīkh al-madanī*, what may be translated as 'history of civilisation'. The adjective, *madanī*, is derived from *madīna*, 'city' in Arabic. This notion of history has its roots in Ibn Khaldūn.
67. Raymond, *Cairo*, pp. 309–38.
68. Al-Maqrīzī, *Al-khiṭaṭ*, vol. 1, p. 86.
69. Raymond, *Cairo*, p. 294.
70. Ibid. p. 293.
71. Ibid. p. 293.
72. Jamāl al-Ghīṭānī, *Khiṭaṭ al-Ghīṭānī* (Beirut: Dār al-Masīra, 1981), pp. 221–41.
73. Ibid. p. 438.
74. Mehrez, *Egyptian Writers*, p. 70.
75. Ibid. p. 77.
76. Al-Ghīṭānī, *Khiṭaṭ*, p. 104.
77. Ibid. p. 93.
78. Ibid. p. 53.
79. Ibid. p. 49.

Chapter 2

NATION-WITHOUT-STATE

TOPOGRAPHY OF STATELESSNESS

It is only possible for the opposition to lay claim to the desert, a recurring theme in the Arabic novel, because the desert has often been thought of as 'no-man's-land' in the predominantly city-centred writings pretty much throughout Arabic literary history. The celebration of the desert in pre-Islamic poetry was quickly usurped and used as a metaphor of transformation of the individual and even the imagined community especially in the twentieth century. In al-Sayyāb's reworking of the *qaṣīda*, the desert disappears from his landscape but is replaced with the fertile lands of Mesopotamia. In the *Khiṭaṭ* works of Mubārak and Kurd ᶜAlī, who inherited Ibn Khaldūn's ambivalence, the desert is problematical. It does not fit in with the inherited notions of communal identity or the civilisational history of the new communities of their imagination. In the colonial mappings of these nation-states, lines are arbitrarily drawn on sand to create on the one hand countries such as Jordan, Libya and Saudi Arabia today, which are made up of primarily desert, and on the other countries with desert as part of their geography. Mubārak, an heir to the colonial mapping of Egypt in certain ways, puzzles over the oases of Egypt's Western desert, known also as the Libyan desert, now integrated into any map of Egypt, and their role in his imaginings of Egypt as a sovereign state. 'The land of oases (*bilād al-wāḥāt*)', referring to the Western desert, 'were not included in the provinces or tax districts of the Sultan's administration', he explains, 'but is independent and not attached to other areas (*qāʾima bi-nafsihā ghayr muttaṣila bi-ghayrihā*)'.[1] To Kurd ᶜAlī the Jordan and Sinai deserts provide eastern and southern borders for the greater Syria he defines but are not parts of it.[2] In fact, the civilisational history of the region, which he calls *al-tārīkh al-madanī*, is clearly centred in the city and its sedentary culture; *ḥaḍāra*, the word for civilisation in modern standard Arabic, is derived from *ḥaḍar*, a word denoting the people who live a relatively settled life around the cities and towns. The desert, where one-eighth or one-seventh of the population of Bilād al-Shām resides at the time, is the home of Bedouins and tribal customs and habits *(ᶜādāt)*, which are at best peripheral to the civilisation of the region.[3] This historical ambivalence towards the desert makes it possible for the Arabic novel to portray the desert as stateless and situate statelessness there. Al-Ghīṭānī is not alone in this; Palestinian novelists have a knack for making the desert the home of their strife too.

Since the founding of the State of Israel in 1948, the Palestinians have had to either live under military occupation and political siege, or leave their homeland and try to make a life elsewhere, migrating to other Arab countries, Africa, Europe and the Americas. Wherever they end up, they must contend with their choice, or lack thereof, and the consequences and implications of living away from their place of birth, their homeland. The Palestinian writers have since devoted their energies to documenting their plight, recording their contemporary tragic history in detail and charting the course for recovering their lost homeland. The recurring themes of the land left behind, harsh realities of life under occupation, diasporic fragmentation, social isolation, and return in Palestinian writings, seem to point to the ubiquitous preoccupation with statelessness. Notwithstanding a marked distinction between the expressions of those writing under occupation and of those writing away from it, statelessness comes to inform and drive Palestinian narratives. Statelessness, in this particular case, is dispossession of both place and power. In other words, the sense of powerlessness acutely felt by Palestinians is located in displacement and marginality. Whether living under occupation or in exile, Palestinians have no control over the place in which they live. The phrase, 'out of place', the title of Edward Said's autobiography, confirms the role of place in defining not only our notions of both home and exile, but also of self. In *Reflections on Exile*, Said speaks of exile as 'the unbearable rift forced between a human being and a native place, between the self and its true home; its essential sadness can never be surmounted'.[4] Displacement then, as Angelika Bammer defines the term, carries resonance of both Freud and Derrida: it is a form of 'pushing aside', a process in the course of which uncomfortable feelings and thoughts are repressed (Freud), and meanings are infinitely dispersed, indefinitely deferred (Derrida). In both cases, what is displaced – dispersed, deferred, repressed – is, significantly, still there: displaced but not replaced, it remains a source of trouble, the shifting ground of signification that makes meaning tremble.[5]

Palestinian statelessness is unique because it cannot be discussed in the lingua franca of exile, or of any political oppression and its subsequent, consequent marginalisation of an individual or a minority group from a majority group. Marginalisation here is not simply what David C. Gordon refers to as 'the situation or condition of a person or a group living within a society with which the individual or group feels only partial identification, while nourished and sustained by a culture that differs from that of the majority';[6] rather, it denotes a persistent process of isolating and disempowering Palestinians inside and outside the State of Israel. While the State of Israel lays siege to the Palestinians spatially, culturally and politically, the host countries of Palestinian refugees, including the Arab states, often explicitly espouse similar policies that make sure Palestinians do 'not enjoy the security and comfort of belonging to the mainstream or, often, the possibility of participating fully and freely in its political and cultural life'.[7] Where exile is both inner and outer, Palestinian resistance is never merely defiance against political hegemony exercised by the nation-state that is the imagined community gone awry, as in *Khiṭaṭ al-Ghīṭānī*, but resistance to a condition of being that is defined by total displacement and marginality, whereby the imagined community is constantly prevented from actualisation, and the imagining of community necessarily entails the separation of nation from state. The alienation, or estrangement, of the nation from the state in the age of nation-states adds a profoundly problematic dimension to understandings and articulations of nationness and nationalism, which ultimately come to be defined by displacement and marginality. Displacement and marginality, understandably, become a point of departure and site of inquiry in both Palestinian narratives and any criticism of them.

In Palestinian writings, statelessness is often depicted as the no-place between the sea and the desert, two voids of uncharted territories and dangerous terrains that threaten to obliterate the Palestinians from existence. Following the expulsion of Palestinians from Beirut in the aftermath of the 1982 Israeli invasion of Lebanon, Maḥmūd Darwīsh (1942–2008), the Palestinian national poet by then living in exile, ends his long poetic essay on the post-1982 Palestinian predicament, *Dhākira li l-nisyān* (Memory for forgetfulness),[8] with a painful declaration: 'I do not love the sea . . . I do not want the sea, because I do not see a shore; or a dove . . . I do not see in the sea but the sea. . .'[9] This outcry comes at the culmination of the sense of siege the Palestinians have been experiencing in the five decades since they were expunged from their homeland, or as he says to a fellow Palestinian poet Samīḥ al-Qāsim in their public correspondence: 'thrown into the sea'.[10] The sea, which had traditionally served as a source of fantastic adventures and military aspirations, has turned into a vast nothingness that surrounds the already beleaguered people, threatening to drown them, to erase any traces of them from the face of the earth. The Israeli attack launched from the sea turned the sea into a war machine in Darwīsh's writings. The sea became the complicit partner of war against Palestinians, holding them hostage to the Israeli military might as well as to an unmapped and unmappable destiny. The sea no longer evokes the adventures of Sindbād of *The Thousand and One Nights*, who always brings home riches from far away lands across the sea, or the glory days of Ṭāriq Ibn Ziyād, the Umayyad captain who, having strategically burnt his ships, led his soldiers into al-Andalus, conquering it for the emerging Arab-Islamic Empire in the eighth century. Instead, being swallowed by the sea, the fate Ibn Ziyād and his soldiers challenged and averted, is seemingly the Palestinian destiny today.

The sense of siege by the sea pervades the works of Darwīsh, even when he was still living 'inside'. He thus speaks of his homeland under occupation:

> We will not be separated,
> The seas are before us, and the jungles
> Are behind us; how may we be separated?[11]

The word 'jungles' (*ghābāt*) may easily be substituted with an equally evocative word, the 'desert' (*saḥrā'*). Standing at the harbour watching his beloved, Palestine, being sent away, he notices that he is flanked by the desert, 'and the desert was behind me (*wa khalfī kānati s-saḥrā'*)'.[12] In his exile, after he left the occupied territories in 1971, the sea turns into a prison made of water, *ḥisār al-mā'*,[13] and becomes synonymous with exile, where the idea of homeland is reduced to a distant dream, a mirage. The disappearance of this homeland is often expressed in terms of the meeting between the sea and the desert, one flowing into the other. The phrase 'sea of the desert (*baḥr al-saḥrā'*)' he constructs in *Dhākira li al-nisyān*[14] conveys poignantly the impossibility of imagining community when a viable site of such imagining, place, is absent. Between the sea and the desert, in this particular case, there is no room left for a mappable country. The reality of the Palestinian situation – being squeezed out of their homeland into the sea or the desert – in turn reconstitutes the sea and the desert as metaphors of displacement and marginality, and sites of nationness.

The evocative similarities between the sea and the desert – their seamless borders, perils and enthralling romantic inspirations – have always been noted in Arabic literature, classical and modern. Travelling across the desert is often compared to seafaring, and the rewards ahead are often enticing enough that the dangers encountered during the journey on a landscape where direction can hardly be discerned are worthwhile. The desert, however, has always been a more pervasive metaphor of exile, but not necessarily of exilic wanderings, perhaps because it is the more prevalent motif in Arabic literature, especially the pre-Islamic *qaṣīda*. The Palestinian novel appropriates, internalises and problematises the desert motif of the *qaṣīda* to make a statement about the Palestinian statelessness, exile and diaspora. In *Mā tabaqqā lakum* (1966; All that's left to you),[15] Ghassān Kanafānī (1936–72) tells the story of a journey from Gaza to the West Bank and casts the entire journey in the desert. Setting the site of the novel in the desert is, however, significantly curious because the landscape of the narrated journey from Gaza (under the administration of Egypt at the time) to the West Bank (under the jurisdiction of Jordan then) is not real desert but the State of Israel. In contrast to al-Sayyāb, Kanafānī retains the desert as the site of the journey of transformation he details in his reinterpretation of the pre-Islamic *qaṣīda*; for unlike the Iraqis who have found a home in a nation-state, the Palestinians are stateless. Israel's statehood is precisely Palestine's statelessness. Like al-Ghīṭānī's *al-Khalāwī*, Kanafānī's desert is a metaphor of displacement, homelessness and statelessness. *Mā tabaqqā lakum*, as well as *Barārī al-ḥummā* (1985; Prairies of fever),[16] a novel by another Palestinian, Ibrāhīm Naṣrallāh (b. 1954), map this statelessness.

The landscape in *Mā tabaqqā lakum* and *Barārī al-ḥummā* corresponds to what Khālida Saᶜīd calls 'geography of danger (*jughrāfiyyat al-khaṭar*)' in her analysis of Kanafānī's novel.[17] The textual space in the two novels is dominated by the dangerous landscape of the desert. The desert is a death trap. Kanafānī's desert is, not unlike Darwīsh's, an endless nothingness, while messengers of death inhabit Naṣrallāh's. The desert motif interestingly appears in an earlier novel by Kanafānī, though without the trappings of the *qaṣīda*. *Rijāl fī al-shams* (1962; Men in the sun),[18] tells the story of four Palestinian men crossing the desert from Palestine to Kuwait under the ineffectual leadership of Abū Khayzarān and who suffocate to death in the tank of a truck while waiting for the driver to clear the customs, leave the desert, and arrive in Kuwait.[19] *Mā tabaqqā lakum* is cast in the form of a desert journey as well. It begins with Ḥāmid, one of the protagonists of the novel, arriving at one edge of the desert and ends with him reaching the other edge, where he comes face to face with an Israeli soldier. The desert in Kanafānī's novel is a seamless, uncharted landscape overwhelmed by sunlight and heat, where death lies in ambushes ready to pounce without notice. Naṣrallāh's desert is as dangerous but in different ways. His is more like Darwīsh's sea; great walls isolating the Palestinians from the rest of the world. Set in al-Qunfudha, a desert town on the Red Sea south of Jeddah in today's Saudi Arabia, *Barārī al-ḥummā* describes the claustrophobic experience of a community of Palestinian teachers and their families living and working in exile. The Palestinians, farmers used to the greenery of their homeland transplanted to a land of immense whiteness, are under a state of siege. The desert spreads,[20] stretches endlessly,[21] covers everything[22] and swallows anything on its path.[23] It engulfs, like its night,[24] day[25] and silence,[26] leaving nothing and nobody immune to its overpowering hegemonic immensity. It cannot be cultivated, not even when it rains, for when it does, rain turns into gushing torrents that uproot everything in its wake.[27] It is the home of wolves, foxes, hyenas, snakes,[28] carnivorous vultures feasting on human remains,[29] and wild dogs barking incessantly.

Whatever the source of danger may be, however, the desert is the territory the Palestinians must conquer and traverse with clear direction and resolve. The desert can be a place of temporary respite rather than eternal exile or a one-way path to death. It is potentially a place of empowerment, of transformation from powerlessness to powerfulness. The Sinai Desert, known as the place of loss in Arabic (*al-tīh*, or *tīh banī Isrāʾīl*), is the site of the forty-year Jewish wandering in the famous biblical story retold by al-Maqrīzī[30] and Mubārak,[31] and referred to by Kurd ᶜAlī.[32] In the biblical story, Moses leads Jews from slavery in Egypt to nationness on the other side of the desert. Like the desert in pre-Islamic *qaṣīda*, the desert in the biblical story is the site on which the process of empowerment takes place. The forces of opposition in *Khiṭaṭ al-Ghīṭānī* find ways to turn the tides around in the desert then look toward returning to the city, now fully empowered. The process of transformation occurring in *al-Khalāwī* recalls that which is inscribed in the desert interlude in the pre-Islamic *qaṣīda*. The desert journey, al-Sayyāb demonstrates in his reinterpretation of the *qaṣīda*, is a metaphor of transformation from helplessness to revolution. Kanafānī's appropriation of the desert motif,[33] both site and metaphor in *Rijāl fī al-shams* and *Mā tabaqqā lakum*, is an expression of both powerlessness and will to power. If the journey through the desert leads to death in *Rijāl fī al-shams*, it forecasts the possibility of empowerment in *Mā tabaqqā lakum*. In fact, the fiction of Kanafānī in general depicts the development of Palestinian political consciousness,[34] and embodies the journey of the Palestinian individual and nation from powerlessness to empowerment. Kanafānī's novels, taken as a whole, detail the process of transformation that the Palestinians had to undergo in order to make sense of their past, to come to terms with their present, and map out the course of their future. They describe the Palestinian journey from despair in *Rijāl fī al-shams* (1962), to realisation of the necessity to take action in *Mā tabaqqā lakum* (1966), to resolution to take such action in *ᶜĀʾid ilā Ḥayfā* (1969; Returning to Haifa), and to action in *Umm Saᶜd* (1969).[35]

STATELESS NATION

Mā tabaqqā lakum, more particularly, details in its appropriation of the structural, thematic, narrative and semantic codes of the classical, or more particularly, pre-Islamic *qaṣīda*, as I have argued elsewhere,[36] the process through which the Palestinian statelessness may be reversed.[37] The two protagonists of the novel, Ḥāmid and his sister Maryam, begin their journey from a position of powerlessness. Fatherless and separated from their mother, they have no one to fend for them. At sixteen Ḥāmid is depicted as a child who has no control over his environment or destiny. His station is necessarily tied to that of his older sister, who too is powerless. At twenty-six Maryam has placed herself under the mercy of Zakariyyā, a villainous, treacherous man. She becomes pregnant during an illicit affair with this married man and is forced to become his second wife. As the breadwinner of the family (now including Maryam and her young brother Ḥāmid), Zakariyyā easily exerts authority over them. The dominance of the desert landscape corresponds to the pervasive sense of powerlessness. However, they soon see the impasse they have reached in their life, realise their need to action and indeed come to a clear resolution about what they ought to do.

This short novel of fifty-eight pages comprises a journey. The novel begins with Ḥāmid's departure – rather, his plunge – into the desert at dusk, and ends with events taking place at the edge of the desert at dawn. The events leading to this journey slowly unfold as the two protagonists, Ḥāmid and his sister Maryam, travel together and arrive at a resolution revealed at the end. The novel contains three major parts of pre-Islamic Arabic *qaṣīda*: departure, journey and arrival. These parts correspond to the paradigm of the rite of passage formulated by van Gennep in *The Rites of Passage* (1960) as separation, liminality and reaggregation,[38] as well as that of the adventure of the hero forwarded by Joseph Campbell in *The Hero With a Thousand Faces* (1973) as departure, initiation and return.[39] The protagonist of the pre-Islamic *qaṣīda* and its heirs, such as al-Sayyāb, must first leave the society by which he is forsaken, then enter the region of the unknown, the desert, and finally emerge from it a changed person, a hero, but only if he is able to overcome the dark powers in a final confrontation. When he emerges as a hero, he has already resolved on a course of action. He then returns to his society to claim his rightful place and declares war on the enemies who threaten its safety. In a similar but more complex fashion, *Mā tabaqqā lakum* depicts the journey of not one but three kinds: the journey from childhood (immaturity) to adulthood (maturity); the journey from ordinariness to heroism; and the journey from confusion and despair to clarity and action. The multiplicity of the journey is reflected in the plurality of the narrative voice. The four narrative voices in the novel, the (clock) time, the desert, Ḥāmid and Maryam, however, are united by the overwhelming 'I' throughout the narrative; all four of the voices speak in the first person that at time it is almost impossible to distinguish between them. The unity is further enforced by the overwhelming time element in the narrative, which serves to link the characters existing in and events taking place in various locales,[40] and the various journeys being completed.

At one level, the novel is about the process of individuation of Ḥāmid and Maryam. Ḥāmid emerges out of the desert journey as a mature and responsible man willing to confront his enemy, an Israeli soldier. Maryam realises that she must kill her husband Zakariyyā in order to save her unborn child. Ḥāmid and Maryam must reach individuation each on his or her own, and deal with their immaturity themselves. Their 'orphanhood' and separation from each other are necessary prerequisites of their journey. As in any hero's journey, D. Norman explains in *The Hero: Myth/Image/Symbol* (1990), all bonds of dependence must be cut away.[41] At a second level, the novel is about the transformation of the human psyche from despair to action. Ḥāmid and Maryam are two components of one and the same, male and female, animus and anima, and yang and yin counterparts of one psyche and their seemingly separate journeys are two faces of one journey of transformation. The consciousness conveyed in the narrative is one, that of the journey taking place. The desert narrative provides us with the context in which the journey must be completed, the clock-time narrative furnishes the time frame of this journey, and conveys the urgency for such undertaking as its ticking is echoed throughout the novel. And the Ḥāmid and Maryam narratives, one picking up where the other leaves off without interrupting the flow of the narrative or repeating what has already transpired, complement each other in providing the detailed background and progress of the journey. Ḥāmid and Maryam must undertake the journey together otherwise the rite of passage cannot be complete: the infant cannot emerge as an adult, and the ordinary a hero. If Ḥāmid is the one who actually leaves Gaza, crossing the 'desert' at night hoping to return to the West Bank and find his real mother, Maryam is with him every step of the way, accompanying him in the desert journey and sharing his yearning for their mother. At a third level, the novel details the process through which Palestinian national consciousness and aspirations are articulated.

The journey is set against a background of crisis in Ḥāmid and Maryam's life. This crisis is precipitated by Maryam's marriage. Ḥāmid feels 'betrayed' by his sister Maryam, who has against his wishes married Zakariyyā, a traitor to the Palestinian cause (symbolised by his betrayal of Sālim, a member of Palestinian resistance, to the Israeli military command). Ḥāmid leaves for the West Bank in search of their mother. Ḥāmid's departure and arrival at the edge of the desert, with which the novel begins, serve as his response to what Campbell speaks of as the 'call to adventure'. Crossing into the desert symbolises what Campbell calls 'crossing the threshold' into the unknown regions,[42] and penetrating deep into it symbolises stepping into 'the belly of the whale',[43] where darkness pervades. Ḥāmid undertakes his desert journey at night and the darkness of the night is precisely the darkness of 'the belly of the whale'. There are two deserts here: Ḥāmid's is an outer space created by nature and Maryam's is an inner space created by the emotional darkness in which she lives. The desert, likened to the womb in many places, is also the 'world womb'[44] out of which the hero is born. Before they are born 'again', however, they must pass the tests and trials of 'self-mastery',[45] and face anxiety, doubt, confusion and, most important, the dark powers obstructing their rite of passage. Like the wild cows in the pre-Islamic *qaṣīda* who must confront their hunters, so must Ḥāmid and Maryam face their demons. Ḥāmid must decide what to do with the Israeli soldier who appears suddenly in his path, and Maryam must make a decision regarding Zakariyyā, who stands in her way to a purposeful life.

The dark powers confronted, however, represent too the external and internal stumbling blocks facing psychic development. The Israeli soldier represents the external danger, whose removal is impossible unless the internal menace, Zakariyyā, is purged first. The dangers they pose are life threatening, and Ḥāmid and Maryam have no choice but to attempt to overcome their enemies. After all, choosing life over death is the ultimate message of the emergence of the hero.[46] Once the obstacle is removed from within, the danger from without can be faced. The actions leading to, and taking place at the two-level confrontation are fast and simultaneous. When Ḥāmid encounters the Israeli soldier in the desert,[47] Maryam senses the danger,[48] realising that hers and Ḥāmid's fates are inextricably linked. Coming face to face with Zakariyyā in the final scenes of the novel, she suddenly becomes aware that Zakariyyā's presence threatens to banish Ḥāmid and send him farther and farther away from her life. She is rendered helpless by her emotional attachment to Zakariyyā so that she muses, 'I cannot get rid of Zakariyyā yet, or he of me. I can only continue the journey on my destined path, my hands over my ears, and my teeth biting my lips'.[49] However, when Zakariyyā grabs her and shakes her, threatening divorce if she will not abort, she feels the urgency – as the ticking of the clock intensifies – to put a stop to her misery. She picks up a knife and sinks it into Zakariyyā's chest, killing him instantly.[50] Precisely at the moment Maryam kills Zakariyyā, Ḥāmid flashes the dagger before the Israeli soldier.[51] The parallel development in Maryam and Ḥāmid's stories suggests that Ḥāmid's resolution to confront the Israeli soldier is contingent upon Maryam's action in killing Zakariyyā. Ḥāmid and Maryam represent

> the tension of the opposites, or inseparable dualities, mirror the path that the hero must, of necessity tread. A way inexorably identified with the traditional and dangerous night journey – a journey, in truth, extending far beyond such brief duration – into the deepest reaches of ourselves: our most dire and tormented netherpoint of despair. So that as a result of what we confront, experience and must transcend, a fresh level of awareness or rebirth is achieved, as at the horizon of a new day, each battle forged by the hero, in his manifold manifestations, but leading to the next.[52]

The choice of the Israeli soldier and Zakariyyā to represent external and internal dangers respectively places the novel in the type of writing that Frederic Jameson would call 'national allegory', not in the sense that the novel is locked in the impulses, priorities and aesthetics of realism, but more in the literal sense of the words in that the novel is a political allegory. The Israeli solider clearly symbolises the State of Israel and its control over the territories the Palestinians would call Palestine, and by extension the Palestinian statelessness. They, both the soldier and the State of Israel, are the obstacles to the rise of a Palestinian nation-state. They are, however, not the only ones. Zakariyyā, the other oppressor, represents a face of Palestinian leadership complementary to that of the truck-driver, Abū Khayzarān, in the earlier *Rijāl fī al-shams*. Zakariyyā is tyranny to Abū Khayzarān's impotence. The ineffectual Palestinian leadership represents the twin obstacle to the formation of a Palestinian nation-state. The desert, the site on which the events of the novel are set, yields no nation-state. The rite of passage in the novel is by force of circumstance incomplete. Its completion requires that the Palestinian psyche, individual and nation undertake the threefold journey all at once in order to be able to find a way to deal with and perhaps reverse their homelessness and statelessness. The Palestinian psyche must rise above despair, the Palestinian individual must become a responsible adult right away, and the Palestinian nation must quickly transform itself into a community of heroes so as to take up the task of fighting for their survival and, more importantly, their statehood. There is no time to lose. The ticking of the clock and its increasing intensity point to the urgency of the Palestinian predicament. For a people who have lost their homeland and become stateless time means death; the ticking clock shrouded in a coffin[53] seems to beckon Ḥāmid and Maryam to surrender to its deadly power. Statelessness paradoxically means death too, just as the emptied, desolate desert landscape of the novel suggests.

Naṣrallah's *Barārī al-ḥummā*, which appropriates too the codes and paradigm of the desert journey in the classical *qaṣīda*, does not duplicate the projected success in transformation; rather, it sabotages the process. Instead of Ḥāmid and Maryam's clarity in direction and resolve, Naṣrallāh's two protagonists are feverish with sunstroke. *Barārī al-ḥummā* begins with five policemen knocking on the door of and rousing from his bed Muḥammad Ḥammād, a Palestinian teacher working in al-Qunfudha. They ask him to remit his funeral expenses now that he is dead and buried. As the story unfolds, he realises that the police should be looking for another Muḥammad Ḥammād, coincidentally his roommate, colleague and, more importantly, identical double, who has disappeared. When he goes searching for him, he suddenly finds himself accused of murder. Thus begins his search for the other Muḥammad Ḥammād across the desert landscape of al-Qunfudha. In his search he comes across the other members of the Palestinian community in this desert town, each with a story of barrenness, from hens refusing to lay eggs, to lands resisting cultivation and Aḥmad

Luṭfī's impotence. The desert and its barrenness are contrasted to homeland and its fertility. Exile, synonymous with desert, is the end of life, and can easily undermine dreams of nation-state. The isolation of the Palestinian community is accentuated by the desert forever encroaching on and dissolving every bit of territory carved out for generation of life of any form (bird, plant or human). Heat exacerbates claustrophobia, a deadly combination that leads to a confusing daze. At the end of the novel, we are disoriented by the 'I' and 'you' voices oscillating in dizzying spins, just as the two identical protagonists fail to discover who is who, and who is dead and who is alive in their star-crossed pursuit of each other. Madness, to which I will return in Chapter 5, becomes the name of the game. And, fear comes to give the text its contours.

Narrative in this novel, like *Mā tabaqqā lakum*, is driven by a similar fear, even though it recasts the paradigm of transformation in diametrical opposed fashion. The two texts are informed and shaped by the fear of obliteration that is statelessness. Statelessness, or the impossibility of imagining a community that is nation-state in this case, is a threat to both individual and community. The individual is rendered powerless of a peculiar kind, a kind that makes it impossible for him to speak of geography as tactics and strategies of control. Kanafānī and Naṣrallāh's desert does not look like al-Ghīṭānī's at all, even though it is the same site of exile. Al-Ghīṭānī's *al-Khalāwī* is the site of communal empowerment where alternative strategies are devised to counter those of the city, but Kanafānī and Naṣrallāh's desert is the place where control is lost. The moods pervading the two texts are, however, quite different. Kanafānī's becomes the site and narrative of individual transformation upon which communal transformation is seen to be dependent, whereas Naṣrallāh's embodies disappointed hopes and frustrated dreams. If Kanafānī expresses a will to power and imagines empowerment as not necessarily development of elaborate tactics and strategies of controlling space but psychic transcendence, Naṣrallāh finds it impossible to even think of empowerment. If Kanafānī predicts and urges Palestinian armed struggle as a means of regaining control over lost space, which in fact began in 1965, on the premise of expected success in transformation of both individual and community, Naṣrallāh embraces a more pessimistic vision in which no transformation of either individual or community is anticipated. In the aftermath of the devastating Arab defeat in the 1967 war during which the lands previously under the control of Egypt and Jordan (Gaza and the West Bank) were lost to Israel, all hopes seemed lost; the transformation inherent in the *qaṣīda*'s paradigm is muted in *Barārī al-ḥummā*, in fact, it is made impossible by the barren landscape of the desert.

The absence of state, in this case a system of political authority set up on a real, sovereign piece of land, does not necessarily prevent the rise of nationness. *Mā tabaqqā lakum* and *Barārī al-ḥummā* in fact articulate Palestinian nationness, which in their variant but similar reinterpretations of the pre-Islamic *qaṣīda* is defined, in contrast to al-Sayyāb's, by statelessness not statehood. Statelessness, it seems, defines the community to which the main members of the cast in both novels belong. Ḥāmid, Maryam and Zakariyyā of Kanafānī's fabrication operate, interact and antagonise each other within a community narrowly defined as the 'other' of what is perceived as the larger community that is the host country. Muḥammad Ḥammād, his object of desire Fāṭima, her father Abū Muḥammad, Aḥmad Luṭfī, and Ibnat Sa^cd of Naṣrallāh's concoction belong to a community isolated by both the desert and the host country and defined by the futility of their actions. Just as the desert gives shape to these Palestinian texts, statelessness paradoxically defines Palestinian nationness. In his autobiographical work, *Soul in Exile: Lives of a Palestinian Revolutionary* (1988), Fawaz Turki muses on the meaning of the Palestinian expulsion from their homeland: 'I just know that for my own generation of Palestinians our last day in Palestine was the first day that we began to define our Palestinian identity'.[54] Palestinian nationalism is, it seems, born out of statelessness too. In *Mā tabaqqā lakum,* the desert is not entirely barren; rather, it is the womb that carries Ḥāmid, as Maryam's carries her child, before he hopefully emerges as adult and hero. Palestinian nationness and nationalism are waiting to be born too, just like Maryam's child and Ḥāmid. Like the story of Maryam's foetus and Ḥāmid, wherein the birth of a child and emergence of a hero are projections of desire, Palestinian nationalism can only be formulation of a desire, desire for a Palestinian nation-state.

The wanderings to which Palestinians in exile are condemned can paradoxically be liberating for narrative and its movements. Regardless of their differing visions for the Palestinian future, both Kanafānī and Naṣrallāh achieve for their pieces a kind of narrative transcendence. These novels experiment with the form, and let loose the narratives, just like their protagonists, to wander in, map anew and territorialise differently the fictional space of the novel. Statelessness, or the absence of a state and its political programme, frees this space from the novel's familiar, if not ritualised, generic expectations; it is now an uncharted space, just like the desert that is its landscape, open to new ways of mapping. By inscribing into the novel the paradigm of transformation of the Arabic *qaṣīda*, these two works bring the novel in from the cold, so to speak, from a zone of unfamiliarity into the fold of the Arabic literary tradition and, more importantly, makes available to it the structural, thematic, narrative and semantic codes of the Arabic poetic tradition. The distribution of these codes in the landscape of the novel is in turn informed by the norms of the novel. Characterisation, plot, development of events and narrative are now imbued with Arabic poetic codes. The meaning of the text is contingent on an understanding of the function of these codes in the novel. The marriage between the two paradigms of transformation, one inherent in the novel and the other in the *qaṣīda*, redefines the Arabic novel and delineates its space in a new way. Mastery of space, the driving force behind narrative in *Khiṭaṭ al-Ghīṭānī*, is not possible in *Mā tabaqqā lakum* and *Barārī al-ḥummā* when power is not available to either the individual or the community. Desire for mastery is paradoxically heightened. Mastery is, however, located in the empowerment of the individual and community in an out-of-place fashion rather than devising new tactics and strategies of spatial control. Without a place, a site on which power is structured and disseminated, any discussion of tactics and strategies of control is moot. The purpose of empowerment is recovery of place and restoration to it the power of the self.

Mastery of self is plausible perhaps only when the intrusion of an 'other' is 'out of bounds'. Powerlessness for the exiled Palestinians means displacement in a physical sense, in that they are removed from their homelands and stripped of their rights to political participation of any kind anywhere. Statelessness, however, does not mean the same thing to the Palestinians living under occupation. If exile removes Palestinians to a place that is no-place, such as the desert, the sea, or the no-man's-land in-between, occupation imprisons them in a place that is out of their reach and under the control of those who do not belong in the same imagined community. Powerlessness in the case of what Paul Ilie calls inner exile,[55] a condition in which one is denied access to power of any kind while living in the homeland, is even more acutely felt because power seems so near but is in reality so far. Daily reminders of the absence of even self-mastery play havoc with the literary imagination, when a place that is supposedly homeland is no place at all and provides no viable space for negotiations over power. Narrative comes to display symptoms of 'cabin fever', of being under siege and having nowhere to go. *Al-waqāʾiʿ al-gharība fī ikhtifāʾ Saʿīd abī al-naḥs al-mutashāʾil* (1972–4; The Strange Events Leading to the Disappearance of Saʿīd, Father of Ill-fortune, the Pessoptimist),[56] the famous novel by Emile Habiby (Imīl Ḥabībī, 1919–96), invokes, among other things, the *maqāmāt*, but only to subvert the freedom of mobility that is at the heart of this classical genre.

POLITICS OF MOBILITY

For reasons no historian of Arabic literature will be able to fully articulate, the *maqāma* has been one of the most popular literary genres of writing during the nineteenth and early part of the twentieth centuries. In Sabry Hafez's assessment of what he calls 'revitalization' of the *maqāma*, 'the nineteenth century alone witnessed the writing and publication of more *maqāmāt* than in the preceding 800 years', since Badīᶜ al-Zamān al-Hamadhānī (956–1008), considered father of the genre, wrote his pieces in 990. In fact, 'there was hardly any significant writer of talent who did not try his hand at *maqāmāt* writing'.[57] This revitalisation eventually led to another equally, if not more important, process of 'rejuvenation' in the twentieth century, when the genre is 'liberate[d] . . . from its archaic style and prototypical concerns . . . [and] inject[ed] with a vigorous sense of individuality, intimacy, realism and interest in current and domestic concerns'.[58] The *maqāma* seems to have been reincarnated in a number of new genres of writing. Its staple features are found in early autobiographical writings, such as al-Ṭahṭāwī's *Talkhī bārīz*, al-Shidyāq's *Al-sāq ᶜalā al-sāq*, and Mubārak's *ᶜAlam al-Dīn*. Translations of European fiction, such as al-Ṭahṭāwī's *Télémaque*, seem to emulate its style too. And it has made a strong presence in fictionalised social commentary, such as 'Abdallāh al-Nadīm's (1845–96) *Al-masāmīr* (1894), al-Muwayliḥī's *Ḥadīth ᶜĪsā b. Hishām* and Ḥāfiẓ Ibrāhīm's *Layālī Saṭīḥ*.[59] Histories of modern Arabic literature, as I have discussed in the Prologue, often locate the beginning of modern Arabic fiction in the instances of 'revival', 'revitalisation' or 'rejuvenation' of the *maqāma*, identifying the successful transformation of this genre in the writings of Egyptian and Levantine pioneers of the Arabic literary Nahḍa at the turn of the twentieth century as the precursors of the Arabic short story[60] and novel.[61]

The competition between the short story and the novel to claim the *maqāma* as it precursor is understandable. The episodic structure of the genre allows the two famous works by al-Hamadhānī and al-Ḥarīrī (1054–1122) to be read as short stories or novels. Each piece can stand on its own as a story. The pieces can be read as one long story, with each piece as an episode and all episodes contributing to its coherence. Critics who have looked at the 'influence' of the *maqāma* on modern Arabic fiction point out the consistent features that run through the episodes. Each episode is constructed around a paradigmatic plot. The narrator, a financially independent and well-educated traveller, meets a stranger well versed in the arts of rhetoric in a different city in every episode only to recognise him as the protagonist at the end of the piece. Each piece provides biting social commentary as well as intricate construction of language. These four staple features of the *maqāma* – plot, characterisation (of narrator, protagonist and other characters), satire and style rich in rhetorical devices – are also the essential ingredients of modern fiction,[62] and with some adjustments, such as losing the excessive use of word play and obtuse imagery, the genre may easily be transformed into a modern short story or novel.

One dimension of the genre, however, may threaten the coherence of the novel. The genre's tendency to roam geographically, historically and intellectually, if transplanted to a novel, can easily undermine the integrity of the new fictional form. The strength of the *maqāma* – its freedom to parody or satirise any intellectual, social or religious issue[63] – is potentially the weakness of the novel in which the working out of the plot requires a focused narration of events employed for such a purpose. This perhaps explains the rare instances of success in reviving the *maqāma* in the Arabic novel despite the proliferation of the genre in the literary writings of the nineteenth and twentieth centuries. For the success of rewriting the *maqāma* into a novel, the wanderlust of the genre must be tamed, domesticated and muted. In the critical assessment of the genre in the known two cases of successful, albeit controversial, modern reincarnations, al-Muwayliḥī and Habiby, mobility is considered simply a parody of the mendicant lifestyle of medieval men of letters, or secular intellectuals, *udabāʾ*. Their need to travel far and wide in search of patronage in the classical genre can no longer serve as impulse for narrative in the drastically altered political, social and economical conditions today. I am not certain this should be the case.

Mobility is, to me, a vital component of the genre and its reincarnations in the contemporary novel. It evokes freedom of many kinds, and engages in cultural and identity politics of all sorts, more particularly, the kind of spatial politics I have been discussing in this chapter. *Maqām* and *muqām*, the singular nouns from which the name of the genre is derived, are nouns of place, the first denoting place of standing and the second residence. Place is never far from the heart of the matter in the *maqāmāt*; each *maqāma* is the story of and occurs in a real place. The field of vision of the collective episodes is larger but is always grounded in a place with identifiable contours. The archetypal *maqāmāt*, if one may thus describe the famous classics by al-Hamadhānī and al-Ḥarīrī, take for granted the liberty Muslim intellectuals enjoyed in a world where Islam pervades politically, socially and culturally. The *Maqāmāt* of al-Hamadhānī and al-Ḥarīrī, however, reflect at the same time the contemporary paradoxical reality of the world of Islam between the tenth and twelfth centuries. The political fragmentation of the world of Islam manifest in the organisation of what Albert Hourani would call dynastic powers around cities[64] informs and shapes the narrative of these works. However, the same narrative mirrors at the same time the unity of both the Muslim community and its culture. The *Maqāmāt* are woven around cities that were at the time the centres of patronage, and each *maqāma* takes place in a different city. ʿĪsā Ibn Hishām and Abū al-Fatḥ al-Iskandarī, al-Hamadhānī's narrator and protagonist, and their counterparts in al-Ḥarīrī, al-Ḥārith b. Humām and Abū Zayd al-Sarūjī, travel freely from one city to another in the Eastern part of the Muslim world, al-Mashriq. Their playground, in today's terms, stretches from Egypt in the west to Afghanistan in the east, from Turkey in the north to Yemen in the south, with the major cities in between as their stopovers.

It is, of course, possible and, indeed, sensible to regard the wanderings of both narrator and protagonist as an expression of alienation of the *udabāʾ* at the time from centres of power politically, economically and culturally, as Abdelfattah Kilito tends to do.[65] The *Maqāmāt*, seen in this light, are narratives of exile destined to tell the stories of the margin's longing for the centre and the consequent identity crisis.[66] Al-Iskandarī and al-Sarūjī are also deemed members of the medieval underworld known as the Banū Sāsān.[67] Identified as the Middle Eastern Gypsies in one instance,[68] the Banū Sāsān lived nomadically outside the cities and towns and on the fringes of society, relying on begging (*kudya*) and con tricks for livelihood. The pairing of the narrator, the literate merchant, with the protagonist, the eloquent mendicant, seems to imply that the *udabāʾ*, merchants at best and mendicants at worst, circumnavigate the centres of power, always leaving but never really arriving. They have at their disposal only their intellectual pursuits and achievements, *adab*, a commodity that does not necessarily bring them political fortune, material wealth or even societal recognition. They seemed damned to wander from place to place, looking for that one patron who will appreciate their talent and turn them from pauper to prince. Their talent paradoxically condemns them to see the absurdity of the trappings of the fantasy of power of any kind; power that resides in religion, tradition, convention, ritual, position, rhetoric, language, for example, is always unravelled even while narrative seems to weave its own web of deceit. Narrative, the story of power, is simultaneously constructive and deconstructive; it at once exhibits and undermines its own power. The protagonist's success in bending the ears of his audience and emptying their purse is always recognised at the end of each episode by the narrator as a successful con trick premised on deceit and conceit; deceit on the part of the protagonist and conceit on the part of the audience, that they could know the 'truth' of what they saw or heard.

The powerlessness of the *udabāʾ* is precisely their power. In fact, their marginality allows them the freedom to roam, physically from one city to another and intellectually from one topic to another, and to parody and satirise powerful cultural 'institutions' or 'traditions'. More importantly, it avails them of a space to fantasise about power and make fun of their own fantasies. There is, underneath the fantasy of power, a sense of security that is possible only when community, as it is imagined, is viable. The freedom of *Maqāmāt*'s narrative movements is premised on the notion that the Mashriq is 'home', to which access was never impeded by any political will. The textual space of the *Maqāmāt* is the place of the imaginary community. In one of the later works, the same sense of self-mastery and control over space is heightened. Al-Yāzijī's *Majmaᶜ al-baḥrayn* (1856; The confluence of the two seas), often criticised for its failure to modernise the genre,[69] contributes to the nationalist discourses Hafez speaks of not only for its 'educational and nationalistic value and innovative intent',[70] but also for the new ways it imagines community. Written at a time when Egypt and the Levant were practically one 'country' under the aegis of the Muḥammad ᶜAlī family, the playground of al-Yāzijī's narrator, Suhayl Ibn ᶜAbbād, and protagonist, Maymūn Ibn al-Khizām, comprises today's Egypt, the Levant, Iraq and Arabia. There is perhaps a double entendre in the title of the book. It may very well refer to the 'confluence of the sea of tradition with that of modern forms and concerns',[71] but it evokes too the region known in the nineteenth century as that which is surrounded by the Mediterranean and the Red seas. *Majmaᶜ*, a noun of place, is the site on which the traditional and modern forms and concerns are to meet, and lands between the Mediterranean and Red seas are to unite.

The size of this community is, however, reduced, especially in comparison with that of al-Hamadhānī and al-Ḥarīrī. In al-Yāzijī's text, the community is shorn of what would be known as Turkey, Persia, Central Asia and Afghanistan today, the non-Arabic speaking parts of the larger Eastern Muslim community. In contrast to Mubārak and Kurd ᶜAlī, whose *Khiṭaṭ* works appeared between forty and seventy years later, al-Yāzijī constructs a language-based national community that is not affected by the colonial mapping of the area – it is not confined to Egypt or the Levant. Whatever shape this imaginary community takes, the freedom of mobility within this community is never in doubt. This is true also of al-Muwayliḥī's *Ḥadīth ᶜĪsā Ibn Hishām*, clearly an intended revival of the genre al-Hamadhānī is known to have established, whose narrator and protagonist are free to roam in the narrativised community. The kind of freedom al-Muwayliḥī inherits from al-Hamadhānī and al-Ḥarīrī is, however, different from that of al-Yāzijī. While al-Yāzijī accentuates his dexterity in the Arabic language in an imagined Arab community before the age of nation-states, al-Muwayliḥī plays up the genre's potential for satire within the confines of Egypt and its 'other', Europe. However, the expression of these freedoms is the same; the physical wandering of the narrator and protagonist in both texts bespeaks the sense of self-mastery and control over space found in their medieval precursors. Intellectual liberty seems to work in tandem with physical freedom, at least at the level of narrative, and control over space seems a precondition for intellectual liberty in the literary imagination. *Hadīth ᶜĪsā Ibn Hishām* internalises and externalises the kind of spatial politics that are an integral part of identity politics in Egypt at the turn of the twentieth century.

Al-Muwayliḥī's work, Allen points out in his introduction to his translation of *Fatra min al-zaman*, presents a portrait of Egypt under British occupation (1883–1907), especially the second decade of Lord Cromer, English Consul-General's rule, when 'the relentless process of Westernization and the aping of European customs and mannerism were leaving their mark on middle- and upper-class Egyptian society'.[72] The work stands out, all its critics seem to agree, for its biting criticism of the social mores of the middle- and upper-class Egyptians,[73] who were caught between the 'Westernness' and 'Easternness'. The work, in addition to providing commentary on the conduct of a class of Egyptians lost in the waves of change, takes part in colonial identity politics of the time and the place. I discussed earlier in the Prologue Gaber Asfour's interpretation of *Ḥadīth ᶜĪsā Ibn Hishām* as the story of the Arabic novel's search for identity, and pointed out that the formulation of this identity needed to be located in the multi-layered tension between the 'self' and 'other', 'past' and 'present'. In combining the Western novel with the *Maqāma* and in pairing contemporary ᶜĪsā Ibn Hishām with a Pasha resurrected from the immediate past, it delineates a space falling between 'self' and 'other', 'past' and 'present'.

There is no more room for the Pasha in the 'present' because the world known to him has changed beyond recognition and the Pasha can no longer function properly in and belong to this new world.[74] This geographical and historical in-between place is the site on which the various tensions of cultural exchange and change are observed, interrogated, negotiated and dealt with. This textual site corresponds more particularly to what may be called the 'colonial civic order' where the state and citizens interact and negotiate their power relations.

In her study of the colonial rule in French Lebanon and Syria, Elizabeth Thompson speaks of colonialism as involving 'constant negotiations of power relationships and identities', resulting in a 'network of power relationships' that 'constitutes the colonial civic order'.[75] 'Colonial civic order', as a term used by Thompson, designates 'the broad arena in which states and citizens interact'. And it 'embodies norms and institutions that govern relations among citizens and the state'. More importantly, 'it is within the civic order that the terms of citizenship and state power are both expressed and continually renegotiated among agents of the formal state apparatus, its unofficial agents, and their clients'. Thompson argues,

> The term civic order is useful because it emphasizes the fluidity of interaction and negotiation, and deemphasizes the boundary between state and society. Indeed, in colonial contexts, clear boundaries rarely existed, as colonizers routinely depended upon indigenous intermediaries to exercise rule. Bargains struck between the state and its mediating agents set the terms of membership in the civic order, and consequently defined terms of citizenship variously for different groups within the population.[76]

'Citizenship is usually defined as', Thompson explains, 'a relationship between the state and individuals governed by legal rights'.[77] The civic order she speaks of is, in its most obvious manifestations, structured around and maintained by the legal institutions, where the rights and responsibilities of citizens are adjudicated. The courts of law are, however, not the only place where citizenship is defined. Negotiations of power relationships and identities, Thompson points out, 'often came across the barrels of guns, but it more routinely occurred across desks and tables, and in newspapers and telegrams'.[78]

This 'colonial civic order' may be thought of as a network of political, economical and social institutions mediated by the courts of law and media. They express themselves in what Jürgen Habermas would call the 'public sphere', a space outside but co-extensive of the 'private sphere' where individuals come together to interact amongst themselves and with the state, and discourse on issues of common concern. It is a sphere where political authority performs public propaganda and private citizens enter into debate about their needs and desires, whether in social gatherings, media or literature. Habermas' 'public sphere' is the product of a specific historic development in particular societies and cultures of Europe. It is, more particularly, an aspect of the European bourgeois society between the seventeenth and twentieth centuries. It cannot and should not be unilaterally transferred to other contexts. What would be equivalent to Habermas' 'public sphere' in the Egyptian colonial context is yet to be analysed and theorised. It is, however, a useful conceptual tool for asking questions of and about literature produced in the colonial context of Egypt. The reason is not the superficial resemblance of the Egyptian bourgeois society, its members including Egyptians and Europeans, to the European one during the accelerated process of 'Westernisation' starting with Muḥammad ᶜAlī's policies and continuing under the British colonial rule. Rather, the idea that literature has a functional element in the 'public sphere', expressing, challenging and reformulating the structures of this very 'public sphere', may help to find new ways of reading colonial texts. The idea of 'structural transformation of the public sphere', the title of Habermas' book, signals to me that transformation is the point of interest and departure for me to look at the ways literature and the 'public sphere' collide and collude, and subjectivity publicises itself.

Ḥadīth ᶜĪsā Ibn Hishām was originally published serially as articles in the newspaper *Miṣbāḥ al-sharq* under the title *Fatra min al-zaman* (A period of time) between 1898 and 1902. It only appeared in the form of a book after extensive revisions by the author in 1907.[79] The confluence of the *maqāma*, a literary genre, and *maqāla*, a journalistic form,[80] makes an interesting case of the alliance between literature and journalism in Arab culture since the beginning of the Nahḍa. Both literature and media were, and have since been, active in the 'public sphere', partaking in identity politics of the time. In *Ḥadīth ᶜĪsā Ibn Hishām*, a text produced during the British colonial rule in Egypt, identity politics are manifest in spatial politics. The characters move from one 'public space' to another and take part in the politics of this space. Coherence is only maintained through the consistent presence of narrator ᶜĪsā Ibn Hishām and the main protagonist the Pasha. They are the main characters in the courts of law and the

West, where their misadventures serve as the vehicle for the all-too-well-documented-and-analysed commentary on the effects of Westernisation on the practices and manners of the Cairenes. They are secondary characters, spies and eavesdroppers, in the new Cairene cultural institutions, where the ^{c}Umda and his entourage take centre stage. The cultural exchange and change experienced by Egyptians at the end of the nineteenth century could be tangibly seen in the ways the structures of the 'public sphere' transformed, and the ways Egyptians responded to these transformations and behaved in the now differently structured 'public sphere'. Strangers to the process can more easily detect the transformations. The Pasha and the ^{c}Umda, an official and notable from the countryside, fulfil the role of the strangers in the story. The Pasha, a decorated 'minister of defence' belonging to the elite of the era of the Muḥammad ^{c}Alī dynasty, plays the role of the outsider in two places. He is resurrected from the 'past' to 'witness' the changes that have affected the 'present' first. He is then sent to the 'West' to examine more closely the sources of change in the 'East'. The ^{c}Umda, on the other hand, plays the outsider from the countryside whose adventures, or misadventures, in the city of Cairo accentuate the changes occurring and their effects on Egyptian society. These effects are unveiled in the encounters between the outsiders and insiders.

The Pasha, who embodies the values and practices of another era, returns a stranger to the city he knew well. He is unable to find his way around in spite of the help of an apparent insider, 'Īsā Ibn Hishām, who occupies a precarious position. He is both insider and outsider. He is insider as an individual belonging to and knowing of the ways of the 'present', but an outsider as an intellectual displaced from the society of the new elite who make the 'public sphere' the stage of their power games. He is a keen observer of the goings-on but an ineffective power broker; in fact, he has no place in the network of power relations. In his company, the Pasha runs into one problem after another in the transformed public space. The Pasha's behaviour with the 'donkey-man' and subsequent trouble with the law only goes to show how profoundly society has changed. As a powerful man from the bygone days, he is now an ordinary citizen subject to the laws governing all. He is tried for his offence, beating both the 'donkey-man' and the 'police officer' as he would have his servants and soldiers, and must apply to the courts to find relief from fines and a prison sentence. He finds out through his dealings with the offices of the police, public prosecution, native court, court of appeals, Islamic Sharī^{c}a court and its records office, his 'past' standing in society availed him of none of the privileges he previously enjoyed. The power brokers in the new society are the judges, public prosecutors and the lawyers. The laws and courts of law borrowed from the French legal system have now replaced and displaced the Islamic Sharīᶜa court, which now adjudicates mainly personal status and endowment cases.

The Pasha's attempt to repossess the properties he bequeathed to his descendants serves as the pretext for the examination of the diminishing status of the former 'aristocracy' to which he belonged. Upon discovering his descendants' neglect of their inheritance, he makes an attempt to repossess his properties. His success or failure is beside the point. The purpose of the exercise is rather to show the ways the disempowered former royal family and notables try to reinsert themselves in the elite circles. The Pasha's grandson has abandoned his ancestral palatial residence and moved to a hotel to appear fashionable in society. The machinations of this class of people are contrasted to the conduct of the new elite in public who, in their relative political powerlessness – their power curtailed by the colonial rule – display their preoccupation with wealth. The wealthy are the power brokers of the colonial society. The misadventures of the ᶜUmda serves to confirm this observation. The ᶜUmda, another outsider representing the traditions of another place, comes to town and finds himself embroiled in the intrigues of the new Egyptian society. An entourage of two accompanies him: an outsider merchant from similar background and an insider playboy from Cairo. This insider seems only to want to take advantage of the ᶜUmda's 'naiveté' and con him into paying for their party expenses. As the ᶜUmda negotiates his way around the power brokers of the new society, with the Pasha and Īsā Ibn Hishām close by to provide on-the-scene commentary, the fabric and workings of the new elite are unravelled. The new middle- and upper-class Egyptians are participants in social climbing, a race to be on top at all cost to the detriment of the welfare of society and its moral values.

The text is haunted by standing, *maqām*, in society, *muqām*; the two words recur endlessly in the narrative. The private residence, however grand, of an individual is not sufficient to promote his social status. His standing is rather confirmed by the ways he is able to command attention and dictate behaviour towards him in public. The misadventures of the Pasha and ᶜUmda happen in the 'public sphere' where exhibitions of social standing take place. The 'novel' is in 'East' and 'West', with the 'East' taking up the lion's share of the narrative. The 'East' is in turn divided between the courts of law and places of public gatherings, be they the grand halls in traditional houses allocated for public functions, or the public spaces of new cultural institutions, such as clubs, restaurants, bars, opera houses, dance halls, theatres, parks, museums and tourist sites. The 'West', to which I shall return in Chapter 3, is Paris, the Muḥammad ᶜAlī family's inspiration for modernity, and is set in the Exposition Universelle (1900). In a place where the state is under the control of the 'other' – thanks to huge national debt, Egypt was de facto under the mercy of Europe – the space for a national community is the 'public sphere' where loud displays of power are evidence of powerlessness. Social standing comes to be defined by association with 'foreigners' who are welcome company everywhere. They are sought as dinner partners in restaurants. The curious European tourists who crash wedding parties are enthusiastically encouraged. More importantly, their culture, customs and habits are blindly imitated. When and where the 'West' is in charge, it is the source of inspiration. 'Westernisation', however, does not mean transplantation of the 'West' in the 'East', but rather interaction between the two that produce, in this case, troubling results. The 'East' is neither 'East' of the past or 'West' of the present, as the Pasha's travels in Paris demonstrate to him and the reader, and is both 'East' and 'West' where one spills over into the other. Chaos reigns supreme in this fuzzy zone between eras, cultures, statehood and statelessness, power and powerlessness.

In the introduction to his translation of *Ḥadīth ᶜĪsā Ibn Hishām*, Roger Allen gives a lengthy account of 'al-Muwayliḥī's Picture of Egyptian Society'[81] during the second decade of the British rule marked by what he calls 'open manipulation of power'.[82] He describes the changes in the role of the ᶜUmda in colonial Egypt. Formerly an 'autocrat in his own domain' with considerable administrative powers and the 'right to draft men in his village for the corvée . . . and military service',[83] the ᶜUmda was deprived of such power and right under British rule and was instead 'given a large number of new [functions], including the supervision of the census, electoral roll, and postal service, and the collection of debts'.[84] Nevertheless, his position afforded him prestige, privileges and opportunities for personal gain.[85] He may be answerable to his British rulers, but he is powerful among the Egyptians and as the indigenous mediator between the British ruler and the Egyptian ruled. In other words, he remains a power broker in the 'colonial civic order' Thompson speaks of. The juxtaposition of the Pasha and the ᶜUmda in al-Muwayliḥī's text is in this sense significant. The Pasha of the 'past' is replaced by the likes of the ᶜUmda in the colonial 'present'; when the ᶜUmda and his entourage take centre stage, the

Pasha and his companion retreat into the background. It is not impossible to interpret this narrative strategy as a reflection of the emerging Egyptian nationalist discourse, which often expressed hostile sentiments towards the former Turkish ruling class. The tension between the Egyptians and the Turks, as Allen observes, was palpable at the time.[86] The ᶜUrābī revolt that served as the pretext for British occupation of Egypt was in fact provoked by the unequal treatment of the Turks and Egyptians in the military. There is, however, no overt antagonism towards the Turks or, for that matter, the British in al-Muwayliḥī's text. The statement, to me, is more about the predicament of the powerless Pasha and the relative powerful status of the ᶜUmda, whom British colonisers eagerly wooed to consolidate their power base in Egypt.

Like the al-Hamadhānī and al-Ḥarīrī's narrators and protagonists, the Pasha and his voluntary companion ᶜĪsā Ibn Hishām, the ᶜUmda and his entourage, travel from place to place not in search of patronage, but on a journey of negotiations of power and identity. While the Pasha seeks to restore his social standing by repossessing his properties, the ᶜUmda works out his position among the colonial Egyptian elite. The Egyptians remained active players in the 'colonial civic order' under the British occupation despite their lack of certain political powers, such as the right and responsibility to define and autonomously run the state. Mobility in *Ḥadīth ᶜĪsā Ibn Hishām*, like the *Maqāmāt* of al-Hamadhānī and al-Ḥarīrī, is paradoxical; it is both powerlessness and power. The protagonists of *Ḥadīth ᶜĪsā Ibn Hishām* are forced to wander from one court of law to another, and from one cultural institution to another in search of 'social standing'. However, they are not, strictly speaking, the victims of state hegemony or statelessness as in the works of al-Ghīṭānī or Kanafānī. Rather, they are more like the anti-heroes of the *Maqāmāt* who, despite marginalisation, are free to take on the cultural institutions that are the cause of their marginalisation and make fun of the cultural and identity politics occurring in them. The 'public sphere' is no longer structured around the patron's court (the public hall of the residence of the ruling class), the market and the literary assemblies of the *Maqāmāt*, but is instead made up of the newly created spaces of the social clubs, restaurants, bars, hotel lobbies, theatres, opera houses, dance halls, parks, museums and tourist sites. The transformation of the structures of the 'public sphere' signals, among other things, changes in the existing networks of power. Power relationships are necessarily renegotiated. These renegotiations in turn take place in the 'public sphere', and become a display of laughable human follies and manipulations.

The 'public sphere', at least in this case, is structured around real places, each with an edifice attached to its name. The Pasha's first journey in Cairo is not simply the journey in time (*al-riḥla fī al-zaman*) al-Hawārī speaks of,[87] but also in place, just like his travels in Paris. The differences between the two historical eras, the Muḥammad ᶜAlī dynasty and the British occupation, are made tangible only in the textualisation of the organisation, or reorganisation, of place and space. This place is the textual space of *Ḥadīth ᶜĪsā Ibn Hishām*. Egypt, symbolised by Cairo, is the imagined community, where its members are free to move from one part to another or to leave then return. It is true that there is no such thing as the Egyptian nation-state yet, but it is still possible to imagine a community on the grounds of a place and in a distinctly delineated and organised space, where its citizens possess self-mastery and control over space, when there is room left for negotiations over power. *Ḥadīth ᶜĪsā Ibn Hishām* can thus unproblematically inherit the *Maqāmāt*'s freedom of mobility. The geographical, historical and intellectual wanderings of the narrator and protagonist are an expression of relative marginalisation not complete powerlessness. Where powerlessness is complete, freedom of mobility is lost too. In contrast to al-Muwayliḥī's narrator and protagonist, Habiby's are 'imprisoned' in a place and space disallowed of mobility of any kind. Is Habiby's novel another reincarnation of the *maqāmāt*? And what would be the point of resurrecting the genre if the mobility that lies at the heart of its matter is written out?

MOBILITY UNDER OCCUPATION

Since the publication of *Pessoptimist* first in the pages of *al-Ittiḥād* (Unity), the Israeli Communist Party's bi-weekly newspaper, between 1972 and 1974, and in book form in 1974, this first novel by Habiby has remained the critics' favourite among his works despite the controversy surrounding the politics of the author and his other works. Habiby was a founding member of the Israeli Communist Party and was elected three times to the Israeli Knesset, or Parliament, and accepted the 1992 Israeli Prize for Arabic Literature. To those who advocate armed resistance against the Israeli occupation of Palestine, his recognition of and willingness to work with the State of Israel were not always welcome. His other fictional works have not been received as favourably. His second novel, *Lukaᶜ Ibn Lukaᶜ* (1980), for example, is condemned by Palestinian critic Fayṣal Darrāj for its failure to transform a political vision into a coherent literary work. In the heated exchange in 1981 between Habiby and Darrāj on the pages of *al-Safīr*, a Beiruti newspaper, and *al-Ittiḥād*, of which Habiby was editor-in-chief, the novelist and his critic hurled 'political' accusations at each other. It seems, at least in Darrāj's response,[88] that Habiby felt that Darrāj's less than complementary assessment of his work was motivated by political ideology. The success of the *Pessoptimist*, Nancy Coffin argues,[89] lies in its ability to straddle the expectations of both acceptable politics and good literature and, perhaps even more important, the fine lines between military response and political solution. The work's political ambivalence permits it to be read from as many perspectives as there are ideologies. Whatever the political response to this work, or for that matter the other works by Habiby, there is a consensus regarding *Pessoptimist*: it represents one half of the Palestinian experience. 'Whilst Ghassān Kanafānī portrays the experience of the Palestinians in exile', Darrāj explains, 'Emile Habiby depicts the other half of this experience: inner exile (*sharṭ al-manfā fī al-waṭan*) and the struggles (of the Palestinians) in the occupied homeland'.[90]

The struggles that engaged Emily Habiby's attention, according to Darrāj, were defence of a Palestinian 'national cultural identity'.[91] Resistance to Israeli policies of oppression, suppression and integration is manifest, at one level, is his insistence on using the Arabic language in literary expressions, and wilfully grounding his works in the Arabic literary tradition, to which Palestinians living under occupation are often denied access. Intertextuality inevitably becomes the focus of analysis of Habiby's works.[92] The *Pessoptimist*, Muḥammad al-ᶜĀfiya tells us, engages in dialogue with texts from classical and modern Arabic literary heritage, from the more high-brow Qurᵓān, Ḥadīth, Arabic proverbs, Ikhwān al-Ṣafā's sufi writings, the poetry of Imruᵓ al-Qays, ᶜAntara, Abū Nuwās, Abū al-ᶜAlā' al-Maᶜarrī, al-Mutanabbī, Ibn ᶜArabī, Samīḥ al-Qāsim, Maḥmud Darwīsh, Tawfīq Zayyād and Sālim Jubrān, not to mention some Islamic religious and legal texts, to folk tales found in al-Jāḥiẓ, *The Thousand and One Nights* and the *Travels of Ibn Jubayr*.[93] The palimpsestic quality of Habiby's text is complicated further by intertextuality with European texts, such as Shakespeare's *Othello*,[94] Czech writer Jaroslav Hasek's *Good Soldier Schweik*,[95] and more particularly Voltaire's *Candide*.[96]

In this intertextual maze of the novel the *maqāma* makes an interesting appearance, noted even in Edward Said's short comment on the back cover of the second Arabic edition. 'Said notices, too', Jarrar begins his survey of the literature on the novel, 'that it reveals Kafkaesque elements, elements from the *maqāmah*, and from science fiction'.[97] What these elements from the *maqāma* are has proven elusive. Vague allusions to the art of comic,[98] satire,[99] biting social commentary,[100] playing with language[101] and lavish puns and word play[102] may all be construed as references to the *maqāma* in the abundant literature on *Pessoptimist.*[103] Akram F. Khater more succinctly links Habiby's style of writing to al-Ḥarīrī, but dismisses the resemblance as superficial.[104] '[T]he earlier genre has no overall tension or structure to hold the stories together', Khater insists, '[i]n comparison, Habiby's novels retain a central theme even when they divert into side-tales. Moreover, these tales are not incidental or groundwork for the exhibition of . . . rhetorical skill. Although they amuse, just as their distant relatives did, they also help to build the structure of the whole novel'.[105]

Allen, on the other hand, finds more significance in this particular type of intertextuality. He links the length and the construct of the title of *Pessoptimist* to medieval Arabic writings, 'whereby book titles were to be elaborate, more often than not consisting of two parts: a first which consisted of an attractive image of some kind, and a second which described the work's topic(s)'.[106] The lengthy title of the novel, 'The strange circumstances leading to the disappearance of Saᶜid, father of ill-fortune, the pessoptimist', is 'a conscious evocation of earlier genres in both its length and structure, and contains a good deal of information and allusion'.[107] The use of the word 'pessoptimist', *mutashāᵓil*, newly coined from a pair of antonyms, *mutashāᵓim* (pessimist) and *mutafāᵓil* (optimist), and the juxtaposition of another set of antonyms, Saᶜīd (fortunate) and Abū al-Naḥs (father of ill-fortune), create a double oxymoron immediately[108] and signal that playing with language will be the name of the game. The structuring of the text is revealing of features of medieval works too. The novel, like al-Muwahliḥī's *Ḥadīth ᶜĪsā Ibn Hishām*, was first published serially, and this shows in its composition. It comprises three parts: part one, named after protagonist Saᶜīd's first love Yuᶜād (she who will be returned), consists of twenty vignettes; part two, named after his wife Bāqiya (she who remains), is made up of thirteen vignettes; and part three, named after Yuᶜād's daughter also called Yuᶜād, is of twelve vignettes. Each part is in the form of a letter from Saᶜīd to an unnamed person disclosed at the end of the novel as a correspondent working for *al-Ittiḥād*. Like al-Hamadhānī and al-Ḥarīrī's *Maqāmāt*, *Pessoptimist* is an amalgamation of short vignettes, each may stand on its own as a story, and all can be parts of one story. The actual Arabic phrase, with which the first chapter opens, Allen argues, is especially evocative of the *Maqāmāt*:

'Sa^cīd, the father of ill-fortune, the pessoptimist, wrote to me and said . . .' This desire on the narrator's part to establish from the outset the source of his story serves in the Arabic context as a direct evocation of the tradition of classical Arabic narrative, a tradition in which the authenticity of the message being transmitted was of crucial importance for the verification of *Ḥadīth*, the accounts of the actions of Muḥammad, the Prophet of Islam, upon which the behavior of the Muslims was to be based in those circumstances where the Qur'ān itself did not provide instruction. The chain of transmission (*isnād*) thus became necessary prelude to any narrative that was to aspire to authenticity. This structural feature, deeply rooted in traditional Arabic narrative, was later imitated in the belles-lettrist genre of the *maqāmah*. The *maqāmāt* of Badī^c al-Zamān al-Hamadhānī (d. 1008), almost certainly the originator of the genre, begin thus: '^cĪsā Ibn Hishām [the name of the narrator] narrated and said.' The word for 'to narrate' used in this context is *ḥaddatha*, a verb associated with the technical term *ḥadīth* noted above. Like the opening of the *maqāmah*, Ḥabībī's first sentence establishes the name of the source and recipient of the narrative, but, as is the case in the classical *maqāmah* genre, the antics of the person so named call into question the 'authenticity' of his message.[109]

Samia Mehrez takes up where Allen leaves off and gives a reading of *Pessoptimist* based on a comparative analysis of the use of irony in Joyce's *Ulysses* and Habibi's *Pessoptimist*.[110] Irony is defined as 'a position vis-à-vis tradition that is manifest in the reformulation, interpretation and transformation of [this tradition]' and located in intertextuality, or what Gerard Genette calls 'transtextuality' in the text.[111] The two genres with which the two novels engage 'transtextually' to produce the irony it speaks of are the epic and the *maqāma*. *Pessoptimist* is structured like an epic. It is fundamentally a three-part journey: beginning of the journey, the journey itself, and the end of the journey.[112] This epic structure is, however, subordinated to the form of the *maqāma*.[113] Two features of *Pessoptimist* tip the balance toward the advantage of the *maqāma* and disadvantage of the epic: the abundance of its rhetorical devices and the casting of its protagonist as anti-hero. Even though the 'hero' of both the epic and the *maqāma*, Mehrez points out, must rely on their dazzling rhetorical skills and quick wits to survive their journey, the protagonist of the *Pessoptimist* is more like the hero of the *maqāma*, who is effectively an anti-hero. Sa^cīd resembles al-Hamadhānī's al-Iskandarī and al-Ḥarīrī's al-Sarūjī as well as the hero of the Spanish picaresque novel, a descendant of the *maqāma*, who is a 'mendicant living on the margin of a society that rejects him and his mendicancy'.[114] Irony in this novel is effected on the contradiction the protagonist must live with and in: 'He lives in society but remains marginal to it and is thus able to provide us with two perspectives: one from the perspective of insider, a member of society, and another from that of the outsider, a spectator'.[115] The protagonist, fully aware of his contradictory predicament, inevitably falls victim to this irony, not being able to belong or not belong to society.

The predicament of Saᶜīd, a Palestinian Arab living in the State of Israel, is in fact absurd. He is at best a third-class citizen, subject to the authority of a second-class citizen, Jacob, a Sephardic (Oriental Jew), and of a first-class citizen, 'Big Man', an Ashkenazi (European) Jew. He works for the State as informer, spying and reporting on his comrades in the Communist Party as well as the Union of Palestinian Workers. His efforts are rarely rewarded and he never becomes an insider, or an 'important member of the Zionist secret service', as Jayyusi would say.[116] On the contrary, he lands in jail for nothing other than obeying instructions during an Israeli raid and raises a white flag to identify himself as a defeated Arab. He ends up losing everything he holds dear, from his first love, to his wife and son and finally his other love and, more importantly, his mind. He was prisoner of an insane asylum in Acre prior to his disappearance, the nameless narrator tells us at the end of the novel. Madness, to which I will return in *Politics of Nostalgia in the Arabic Novel*, seems an unavoidable fate when self-mastery is denied. As a dispossessed Palestinian Saᶜīd faces statelessness whether he chooses exile or remains in the 'homeland'. To remain at 'home' is to be in danger of either revolting and getting killed, like his son, Walāᵓ (loyalty), and wife, Bāqiya, or suppressing his 'self' and subsuming it to the 'other', the State of Israel. Neither is an acceptable, tolerable alternative. The novel details, at a more profound level, the journey of 'self' discovery and recovery. Whether we think of the novel as an epical journey, as Mehrez does, or an inverted three-stage quest narrative found in the Arabic poetic tradition – departure, time away, return – as Allen does,[117] the message is the same. From 1948 to 1956 and finally 1967, years that mark the defining moments in Palestinian history and the beginning of each of the three parts of the novel, the Palestinian must haphazardly come to the realisation that subjugation of the 'self' to the oppressive state established by the 'other' on the very ground of his 'homeland' cannot substitute for the statehood of the 'self'. Statelessness at home can be a fate worse than death. Saᶜīd can neither have a full life nor die; he is virtually imprisoned between life and death. He finds himself perched on a stake at the end of the novel, and ponders the predicament he is in:

> The end came when I awoke after one interminable night and found myself not in my bed . . . I realized I was sitting on the top of a blunt stake.
>
> I shouted, 'Help!' But only an echo responded, its every letter clear. I then realized that I was sitting at a dizzy height. I tried to alleviate my anxiety by chatting with the echo. This conversation was quite entertaining and finally the chasm beneath me gave a smile of dawn, even if it looked somewhat stern with all the dust.
>
> What was I to do? . . .
>
> So why am I still sitting here on this stake, being bumped and buffeted by the cold, without a cover, back support, or company. Why don't I go down? This stake business must be a nightmare. If I descend from the stake I will no doubt shake off the dream completely and get back to bed, where I'll be able to cover myself up and feel warm. Why hesitate? For fear of falling from my enormous height down into the depths below, like a duck killed by a hunter, to suffer pain and to die?
>
> It is all clearly imaginary, both my position and the stake too. It is all a typical dream, a contradiction of the laws of nature and the rules of logic. Come now, grip the stake with your legs and arms and, with all the strength, fortitude and will power you can muster under pressure, descend slowly, like a squirrel.
>
> So I dropped my dangling legs over, feeling the surface of the stake. But it was smooth and cold, like the skin of a snake, and I realized that I would not be able to grip on it. I was sure that if I tried to climb down, I would fall into the pit, break my neck, suffer pain, and die. I therefore stopped.
>
> Then I remembered those Indian magicians who send up a rope far into the air until its end disappears into the clouds. The magician climbs it until he too is lost to sight. Then he climbs down, not only without any harm befalling him but making his fortune in the process. However, I was no Indian magician, just an Arab who had remained, by some magic, in Israel.[118]

Many forms of imprisonment pervade Habiby's text. Saᶜīd is placed in prison in part three of the novel. He is unable to get out of the role of 'informer' he plays for the State secret service. He is haunted by his unrequited love for Yuᶜād. He is imprisoned in the insane asylum at the end. More importantly, he is confined to either Haifa, the city of his birth, or Acre, where the prison and insane asylum is located. Like all Palestinians living in Israel, he is prisoner in his own 'house', a new domicile assigned to him that makes his old family house unavailable to him. He is finally stranded on top of a stake, unable to descend. His mobility is severely curtailed. There is in fact very little traffic between Acre and Haifa. Since his return from Lebanon in 1948, his movements have been confined to mainly Haifa and, to a lesser extent, Acre. He is in effect a prisoner of the State. Haifa is synonymous with the State of Israel, *Madīnat Isrā'īl*,[119] *madīna* meaning state rather than city in Hebrew. The State of Israel is prison. This is how Saᶜīd describes his meeting with Yuᶜād II: 'I met Yuad where meetings in Israel often occur – in prison'.[120] This sentence in Arabic, as those familiar with al-Ḥarīrī would readily spot, contains a visual trick. The parallel prepositional phrases separated by a hyphen at the end of the sentence, '*iltaqaytu Yuᶜāda fīmā yakūnu fīhi l-liqā'u fī Isrā'īl – fī sijnī*',[121] may be read as apposition, whereby Isrā'īl may be substituted by *al-sijn*. As a resident of this state, he is denied any relationship with the other Palestinians who have become exiles. Yuᶜād and her daughter, Yuᶜād II, who sneak back to their 'homeland', are deported and forcefully separated from him. His immobility is accentuated by the mobility of his ancestors, who come from everywhere in the Arab world,[122] and other Palestinian refugees dispersed and wandering across the world, who occasionally return only to be sent away again.

This sense of siege, conveyed by the various motifs of imprisonment, arrests narrative movements in the text too. The journey the novel details is an emotional and intellectual one not accompanied by the physical travel that is part of the journey of the epic or classical Arabic *qaṣīda*. The protagonist of the epic and the *qaṣīda* take his body and mind on a ritualised journey of initiation, transformation and return, subjecting the body to physical hardships, trials and labyrinths, from mounting a boat, horse or camel to crossing the sea or the desert, finding a way out of a maze, taking up arms and literally slaying the dragon, and the mind to riddles, in the solution of which lies the beginning of the end of the journey and the morale of the undertaking. Saᶜīd rather sits still and lets his mind meander here and there and nowhere in particular, from one vignette to another, to and fro, past and present. The paradigmatic plot of the *qaṣīda* is bent out of shape in another way too. Memories of the places left behind in the *qaṣīda*, the ruins of former abodes and sites of past happy loves, are strung together in the mind's eye by the backward gaze the protagonist casts as he moves forward on his mount. Memories of villages destroyed by the State of Israel in the novel contrarily hover around Saᶜīd's consciousness. While Saᶜīd stays put in al-Jazzār Mosque in Acre, he hears the Palestinian villagers arrested and temporarily housed in the mosque for the night utter the names of the villages they come from, which are all in ruins now.[123] Narrativised movement does not match narrativised gaze in this instance.

The halted narrative movement in the novel goes against the grain of the *maqāma*, circumscribing the field of play, and vision, to the imprisoned space. Where and when place is inaccessible, the horizon of an imagined community is extraordinarily narrow, sealed in by the freedom of the 'other', the forces of oppressive occupation. Unlike the protagonists of the *Maqāmāt*, whose reach goes far beyond their place of birth, Saᶜīd's playground is confined to Haifa, his birthplace, or/and Acre, where the insane asylum he is in is located. He is alone in his imprisonment, with no one to take part in his games, bear witness to his dazzling rhetoric, admire and laugh at his deceit and conceit, unravel his absurd discourse, unveil his disguise, recognise his madness, to share his burdens. The narrator, the partner in crime in the *Maqāmāt*, is textualised. He is what Jarrar calls narratee, frozen in his textualisation and denied his role in the play. Saᶜīd must be both protagonist and narrator until the very end, when he disappears, then the narratee can be narrator for a brief moment, not to unmask the protagonist but to put another mask on his face. No, Saᶜīd is not rescued by an alien from out of space, his hurried investigations reveal, but is rather a madman who has disappeared without a trace. Who is the trickster here, Saᶜīd or narratee/narrator? And whose story is it? Is it autobiographical? Does it matter?

What matters, it seems to me, is the mounting despair Saᶜīd feels as narrative tighten its noose around his neck, as the space open to his movements shrinks from the northern tip of Palestine (when he returns from Lebanon, and when he makes another trip to Lebanon but returns), to Haifa and Acre, Haifa alone, Acre alone, Acre prison, and finally the tip of a stake. The textual space seems delineated by the size of Saᶜīd's room in the insane asylum, and narrative driven by immobility. Where horizontal movement, essential to any imaginings of community as nation-state in Anderson's formulation, is impossible, there is only one way to go – vertically. The up and down movements compensate for the absence of a horizon for mobility. Gaze and movement coincide in the vertical movement of Saᶜīd who, deciding not to bow his head and look at the earth, or land, as his ancestors did, looks for a saviour, al-Mahdī, al-Imām, al-Munqidh,[124] up there in outer space, the space above his 'prison'. Like a genie bursting out of a bottle, Saᶜīd climbs out of the Acre catacombs, where he regularly meets the alien from out of space, rides the tip of a stake, and flies away with the alien. His flight, like the story of the genie, is at best a flight of fantasy, a dream of self-mastery and control of space not available to him. Fantasy of mobility is the product of deprivation of place; when one is displaced in place, one is no longer in control of space. Control of space comes hand in hand with self-mastery, it seems; where one possesses no control over space, one loses the sense of self-mastery as well. In the absence of self-mastery, spatial politics are irrelevant and passivity comes to pervade literary imagination and discourse. Saᶜīd is lacking will of any kind. Those who have a will die, like Bāqiya and Walāᵓ, are imprisoned and tortured, like Yuᶜād's son Saᶜīd, or deported, like Yuᶜād and Yuᶜād II. Imagining a community is stifled, and the imagined community is deformed. In Saᶜīd's total powerlessness, the nation is either killed (Bāqiya) or exiled (Yuᶜād and Yuᶜād II). The exiled nation is stripped of agency – *yuᶜād* is the passive voice of the verb *yaᶜūd*, to return – when state (Saᶜīd) is denied its potential, when dreams of statehood are shattered day in day out. Nevertheless, desire for nation-state, and desire of nation and state for each other, like Saᶜīd and Yuᶜād's love, remain alive and continue to drive narrative.

CARTOGRAPHY OF WOMAN'S BODY

Desire works in narratives of nation only when nation is feminised and eroticised, a motif that is all-too-familiar to theorists of 'nationalisms and sexualities' and feminist critics of nationalist discourses. The eroticisation of the nation, I have shown, is new to modern Arabic narrative found in the contemporary novel but not in its precursors or pre-modern pretexts. It is premised on gendered binary dualities, whereby culture, mind, power, state and agency are masculinised and nature, soul, powerlessness, nation and passivity are feminised. Habiby's novel partakes in this kind of gendered discourse on nation, and inscribes the nation (-state) on a woman's body, displaying all the symptoms of masculinist objectification of woman's body and formulation of female subjectivity that feminists, in fact, most women, find objectionable. Habiby's projection of male desire on the female body, expressed in Saᶜīd's undying love for Yuᶜād, commits all the sins of 'misogyny' deconstructed in feminist analyses of the motif of eroticised nation. Saᶜīd, despite his empowerment, remains the potential source of power, while Yuᶜād, Bāqiya and Yuᶜād II, despite their strong will, continue to rely on men for their empowerment. Bāqiya, an obedient wife to Saᶜīd for the most part of her story, revolts against the status quo only when her son, Walāᵓ, takes up arms and fights, and Yuᶜād and Yuᶜād II are the exiled nation waiting for the empowered state to bring them home. Beside the implications of this kind of gendered thinking on the status of women and their agency in general, there are other equally problematic consequences in the 'imagined community', which finds itself divided into nation and state along gender polarities held together by desire, male desire for the female. The problem is that not all forms of male desire for the female are proper or legitimate.

This problematic motif of the 'idealised, iconographic woman' in modern Arabic literature has not escaped critical attention.[125] Jūrj Ṭarābīshī, a critic with a Freudian eye, has linked this motif, so pervasive in the Arabic novel, to the identity crisis of Arab intellectuals today. The sense of frustration felt by the Arabs at present finds expression in the depiction of a son's relationship with the mother, what he calls the 'Oedipal Complex',[126] and a man's unrequited love for a woman, whether this woman symbolises the nation[127] or the West.[128] What he observes of the Arabic novel in general applies to the Arabic novel that employs Arab cultural heritage as well. The problem, however, does not lie in the twin-forked desire for both 'self' and 'other', the 'nation' and the 'West'; but rather in inscribing the 'nation' on the female body. Woman, as mother, sister and lover, comes to symbolise the nation, and the female body the place that is home of the nation-state. Like Ishtar in al-Sayyāb's epical poem, the 'imagined community' in Kanafānī's novel is the mother, the sister and the lover. The journey in the novel is precipitated by the male protagonist Ḥāmid's longing for his mother upon his sister Maryam's marriage to Zakariyyā. This longing is, however, born out of Ḥāmid's sense of betrayal. In the absence of their parents since 1948, Maryam has been mother to her younger sibling, who is more than ten years her junior. If the mother represents the exiled Palestinian nation, Maryam then symbolises the Palestinian nation under occupation and the land on which the Palestinian nation-state ought to be built. Ḥāmid's disappointment is the flip side of his desire. Upon his sister's marriage his desire is stopped dead in its tracks. His relationship with his sister is almost incestuous and his conflict with Zakariyyā is the right to Maryam's body, the place that will be the home of the Palestinian nation-state.

In a perverse twist, Maryam's body becomes the desert that serves as the landscape on which Ḥāmid must map his destiny and the womb that will give birth to him as hero. The desert is likened to the womb in many places in the novel. Zakariyyā thus addresses Maryam upon hearing she is pregnant, 'you are a fertile land (*arḍ khiṣba*)',[129] referring to Maryam's womb, which is bearing the foetus. This sentence serves as the transition from Maryam narrative to Ḥāmid narrative. Ḥāmid, quickening his steps on the desert sand, thinks to himself that the desert is an illusory 'fertile land (*arḍ khiṣba fī al-tawahhum*)'.[130] The movements of the foetus in Maryam's womb and Ḥāmid in the middle of the desert are linked. Toward the middle of the journey, Maryam decides to name her child Ḥāmid when she feels the child pulsate for the first time like the nervous movements of a bird trapped between two palms.[131] At the mention of the name Ḥāmid, the narrative takes another turn and refocuses on Ḥāmid who is now in the heart of the desert. At this juncture of the narrative, Ḥāmid's nerves, muscles and limbs, as if gripped by fear, begin to tremble like those of a 'caged animal'.[132] The desert is like a womb, and Ḥāmid is like the child in Maryam, both waiting to be born. Maryam is virtually Ḥāmid's mother, sister and lover. The convergence of the three female roles in one body may be explained as plot requirement, borrowed from a variety of familiar paradigms, of a complex narrative of nation. Maryam is like the beloved in the classical *qaṣīda* who, in leaving the protagonist, pushes him to depart and travel across the desert. She is at the same time the mother/sister of the Ishtar-Tammuz myth. The role of the mother in the novel is paradoxical. Her presence and absence are required in the narrative, for she must serve as the temptation that sends the heroes to their journeys as well as the necessary ingredient in the making of the hero. As in any hero's journey, bonds of dependence must be cut away,[133] and like in any story of a hero's journey, Ḥāmid and Maryam must reach individuation on their own and must therefore be orphans. The mother understandably remains a romantic illusion in the novel; for in real terms, she has been as far removed from the two protagonists' lives as her dead husband has been. She has been away in Jordan, her fate unknown since 1948, and Ḥamid and Maryam are practically parentless. Without this romantic illusion, however, there will be no journey, no story to tell.

But perhaps the ambivalence generated by gender thinking in Kanafānī's novel is exceptional in its complexity and relatively unique to *Mā tabaqqā lakum*. There is only a slight hint of incestuous desire in Habiby's novel: in Sa^c^īd's desire for Yu^c^ād first, then her daughter Yu^c^ād II. More common to the Arabic novel is the motif of unrequited love, love frustrated by extraneous circumstances, or impropriety and illegitimacy. Sa^c^īd's love is necessarily disappointed. As metaphors of state and nation, Saᶜīd and the two Yuᶜāds cannot be united until the Palestinian State comes into being and the Palestinian nation goes home. Similarly, Fāṭima in Naṣrallāh's *Barārī al-ḥummā*, the protagonist's object of desire, cannot be united with her suitor. As a symbol of Palestinian nation and land, she is necessarily portrayed as a rape victim, spoilt goods, so to speak, who can no longer be a partner in a perfect love match. She is perversely the perfect match for the equally traumatised Muḥammad Ḥammād. There is alas no union for the lovers. Where there is union of one form or another, it is often marred by impropriety or illegitimacy. In al-Ghīṭānī's *Khiṭaṭ*, the female characters serve as symbols of various facets of the nation, a compromised nation haunted by the question of legitimacy. These female characters operate against a background of the disappearance of the legitimate daughter and her losing her way, '*bint tāhat ya awlād al-ḥalāl*',[134] another way of saying she has lost her perceived feminine virtues. Instead, women of ill repute, victims of powerful men, and ambitious social climbers dominate the love field. Film star, Hudā al-Maḥallāwī, who disappears at the beginning of the novel, turns out to be al-Ustādh's lover, and his complicit partner in conspiracy to discredit his opponents. Athīl, a young journalist who becomes pregnant by al-Ustādh, is forced to marry bouncer al-Wātidī in order to cover up al-Ustādh's indiscretion. Īthār marries Majdī, the womanising architect of peace with the enemies, and refuses to be disheartened by his cruel treatment, hoping that she too will become a prominent member of society when he receives his Nobel Prize. Rawnaq, perhaps the most memorable and powerful female character in the novel, is powerful only by association. She is at first mistress to al-Ustādh, and when he falls from grace, she turns to al-Hilālī and in time becomes his mistress in order to remain in power.

Absence of love marks the five sets of male-female sexual liaisons in *Khiṭaṭ*, whether inside or outside the framework of marriage. Sex is a matter of power and convenience. Al-Ustādh's womanising is his expression of power, and the compliance of the women, Rawnaq, Athīl and Hudā, is manifestation of their powerlessness and their desire for power. These women are able to achieve power by playing to the sexual desire of al-Ustādh. None of al-Ustādh's sexual liaisons leads to marriage and cannot be considered proper or legitimate. The lack of propriety of such sexual liaisons is accentuated by Athīl's marriage to al-Wātidī. Despite the legitimacy provided by the marriage contract, there is no love lost between the two. The same may be said of Īthār and Majdī. In spite of the legality of their union, love between them is poignantly absent. Majdī, like al-Ustādh, displays his power through womanising, and Īthār plays along in order to gain social recognition by association. The propriety of their union is always questionable. Under the circumstances, the unions can never lead to harmony. The various forms of union portrayed in *Khiṭaṭ* tell the same story as those of disappointed love in the Palestinian novel. The unions are either improper and illegitimate or impossible. Taken as a statement on the predicament and fate of the nation-state, the nation and state polarised along gender lines cannot cohere. They are linked only by misplaced desire or unrequited love, which in effect cause rather than solve problems.

The history of the nation-state in the Arabic novel, often cast in the form of love story in the typically gendered nationalist discourse, speaks to, among other things, three major preoccupations of the post-colonial Arab culture and the contemporary Arabic novel. At the outset, the sense of self, or subjectivity, continues to experience division and the nationalist response to colonialism, the formation of nation-states, does not seem to have brought coherence to post-colonial subjectivity. In his discussion of the role of desire in *Gender Thinking*,[135] Steven G. Smith points out that gender thinking inevitably entails 'othering', whether in the original or revisionist Freudian account of the development of selfhood or subjectivity. This 'othering' is the realisation of the gap between 'self' and 'other' and the impossibility of their integration, despite the desire to do so and for the 'other'. In the Arabic novel's rendition of the nation-state, the interior 'othering' of the nation is a statement of profound alienation of the Arab intellectuals from political authority. They are, like the women they portray in their novels, and feel powerless and must play the complicit partner to the tyrannical political authority in order to gain a modicum of the sense of self-mastery. The failure of political authority, therefore the disappointment in the nation-state, is explicable in terms of the other two concerns: first, the legitimacy of the state and the propriety of the union between the state and nation; and second, the problematic genealogy of the nation-state. These issues are in turn addressed in the love stories that permeate the Arabic novel. These concerns, as I shall demonstrate in the following chapters, pertain too to the Arabic novel's anxiety about its genealogy, legitimacy and centrality in Arab culture – its identity. The marriage, let us say, of the history of the nation-state to the story of the Arabic novel in nationalist discourses will exert its own brand of ideological hegemony, as we shall see, and will have consequences in the identity politics in the national culture and the novel. It will elicit ideological as well as literary responses from those excluded from and denied agency in the nationalist discourse internalised and externalised by the Arabic novel.

NOTES

1. ᶜAlī Mubārak, *Al-khiṭaṭ al-tawfīqiyya* (Cairo: Bulaq, 1886–9), vol. 17, p. 29.
2. Kurd ᶜAlī, *Khiṭaṭ al-shām* (Beirut: Dār al-ᶜIlm li al-Malāyīn, 1969–71), vol. 1, p. 49.
3. Ibid. vol. 6, pp. 314–22.
4. Edward Said, *Reflections on Exile and Other Essays* (Cambridge, MA: Harvard University Press, 2000), p. 173.
5. Angelia Bammer, 'Introduction', in A. Bammer (ed.), *Displacement: Cultural Identities in Questions* (Bloomington, IL: Indiana University Press, 1994), pp. xi–xx; xiii.
6. David C. Gordon, *Lebanon: The Fragmented Nation* (London: Croom Helm, 1980), p. 17.
7. Ibid. p. 18.
8. The work originally appeared in 1986, under the title *Al-zamān: Beirut/ Al-makān: August*, in *Al Karmel*, the literary quarterly Darwīsh had edited since 1981. It was later published under its present title in Beirut and Rabat, the Beirut edition using the original title as subtitle. English translation by Ibrahim Muhawi (Berkeley, CA: California University Press, 1995).
9. Maḥmūd Darwīsh, *Dhākira li al-nisyān*, p. 96; Muhawi, *Memory for Forgetfulness*, p. 182.
10. Maḥmūd Darwīsh and Samḥ al-Qāsim are two of the first generation of Palestinian poets who came to be known and respected not only inside the occupied territories but also in the Arab world. They, together with Tawfīq Zayyād, were introduced to Arab readers as the poets of resistance by Ghassān Kanafānī in *Adab al-muqāwama* (1946–68; Resistance literature). The trajectories of Darwīsh and al-Qāsim's lives and careers, however, have diverged since Darwīsh left Israel in 1971. In the 1980s, the two poets discussed the meanings of choosing to leave or stay in public correspondence in the pages of newspapers and magazines. These letters are now available in book form known as *Al-rasāʾil: Maḥmūd Darwīsh wa Samīḥ al-Qāsim* (Beirut: Dār al-ᶜAwda, 1990). This quote is from p. 169.
11. Maḥmūd Darwīsh, *Dīwān*, 2 vols (Beirut: Dār al-ᶜAwda, 1977), vol. 1, pp. 195–6.
12. Ibid. vol. 1, p. 256.
13. Ibid. vol. 2, p. 418.
14. Muhawi, *Memory for Forgetfulness*, p. 62.
15. Translated into English by May Jayyusi and Jeremy Reed (Austin, TX: Texas University Press, 1990).

16. Translated into English by May Jayyusi and Jeremy Reed (New York, NY: Interlink Books, 1993).
17. Khālida Sa^{c}īd, *Ḥarakiyyat al-ibdā^{c}: dirāsa fī al-adab al-^{c}arabī al-ḥadīth* (Beirut: Dār al-^{c}Awda, 1979), p. 240.
18. Translated into English by Hilary Kilpatrick (London: Heinemann, 1978).
19. For analyses of the novel, see Douglas Magrath, 'A study of *Rijāl fī al-shams* by Ghassān Kanafānī', *Journal of Arabic Literature* 10 (1979), pp. 95–108; and C. F. Audebert, 'Choice and responsibility in *Rijāl fī al-shams*', *Journal of Arabic Literature* 15 (1984), pp. 76–93.
20. Ibrāhīm Naṣrallāh, *Barārī al-ḥummā* (Beirut: Dār al-Shurūq, 1992), pp. 6, 40, 41, 69.
21. Ibid. p. 13.
22. Ibid. p. 68.
23. Ibid. p. 8.
24. Ibid. pp. 40, 69.
25. Ibid. p. 35.
26. Ibid. p. 65.
27. Ibid. p. 105.
28. Ibid. p. 4.
29. Ibid. pp. 56, 101.
30. Al-Maqrīzī, *Khiṭaṭ*, vol. 1, pp. 393–4.
31. Mubārak, *Al-tawfīqiyya*, vol. 14, pp. 107–8.
32. Kurd ^{c}Ali, *Khiṭaṭ al-shām*, vol. 1, p. 51.
33. Many critics allude to the importance of the desert journey in the novel but without meaningful analyses. See Roger Allen, *The Arabic Novel: an historical and critical introduction* (Syracuse, NY: Syracuse University Press, 1982), p. 109; Hilary Kilpatrick, 'Tradition and innovation in the fiction of Ghassān Kanafānī', *Journal of Arabic Literature* 7 (1976), p. 58; Raḍwā ^{c}Āshūr, *Al-Ṭarīq ilā al-khayma al-ukhrā: dirāsa fī a^{c}māl Ghassān Kanafānī* (Beirut: Dār al-Ādāb, 1977), pp. 59–91. However, Kilpatrick intimates its resemblance to a pre-Islamic Arabic ode (p. 60), and Khālida Sa^{c}īd suggests its structural correspondence to a modern Arabic ode (Sa^{c}īd, *Ḥarakiyyat al-ibdā^{c}*, p. 241).
34. See M. Siddiq, *Man is a Cause*: *Political Consciousness and the Fiction of Ghassān Kanafānī* (Seattle, WA: Washington University Press, 1984).
35. Although *^{c}Āʾid ilā Ḥayfa* and *Umm Sa^{c}d* were published in the same year, the events taking place in *^{c}Āʾid* precede those in *Umm Sa^{c}d*. See also Fārūq Wādī, *Thalāt ^{c}alāmāt fī al-riwāya al-filasflīniyya: Ghassān Kanafānī, Imīl Ḥabībī, Jabrā Ibrāhīm Jabrā* (Acre: al-Aswār, 1985), p. 66. Therefore I disagree with Ilyās Khūrī's view that *^{c}Āʾid ilā Ḥayfa* represents the last phase of a Palestinian action against the Israeli occupation, which is that of boycott. See Ilyās Khūrā, 'Al-baṭal al-filasṭīnī fī qiṣaṣ Ghassān Kanafānī', *Ghassān*

Kanafānī insānan wa-adīban wa-munāḍilan (Beirut: Manshūrāt al-Ittiḥād, 1974), pp. 92–129.

36. The details are found in my earlier article on the novel. See, 'A novel in the form of an ode: the power of Ghassān Kanafānī's narrative in *Mā tabaqqā lakum*', *Arabic and Middle Eastern Literatures* 1: 2 (1998), pp. 223–31.
37. Analyses of this novel focused on the development of the events that led to the catharsis – Ḥāmid flashing his dagger in the face of the Israeli soldier he encounters in the desert, and Maryam sinking her knife into Zakariyyā – concluding that running home (toward mother-land), not running away (as in *Rijāl fī al-shams)*, was the first step toward finding the solution for the homeless and stateless Palestinians (Aḥmad Abī Maṭar, *Al-riwāya fī al-adab al-filasṭīnī* (Beirut: al-Muᵓassasa al-ᶜArabiyya li al-Dirāsāt wa al-Nashr, 1980), p. 247), perhaps in the form of revolution (Fakhrī Ṣāliḥ, *Fī al-riwāya al-filasṭīniyya* (Beirut: Muᵓassasat Dār al-Kitāb al-Ḥadīth, 1985), p. 31; and Khūrī, 'Al-baṭal al-filasṭīnī', p. 118).
38. See Suzanne Stetkevych, 'Structuralist interpretations of pre-Islamic poetry: critique and new directions', *Journal of Near Eastern Studies* 42: 2 (1983), pp. 98–107; and 'The Ṣuᶜlūk and his poem: a paradigm of passage manqué', *Journal of the American Oriental Society* 104: 4 (1984), pp. 661–78); and Michael Sells, *Desert Tracings: Six Classical Arabian Odes* (Middletown, CT: Wesleyan University Press, 1989).
39. See Joseph Campbell, *The Hero with a Thousand Faces*, Bollington Series XVII (Princeton, NJ: Princeton University Press, 1973), pp. 149–244.
40. See Iḥsān ᶜAbbās, 'Al-mabnā al-ramzī fī qiṣaṣ Ghassān Kanafānī', Introduction to Ghassān Kanafānī, *Al-aᶜmāl al-kāmila* (Beirut: Dār al-Ṭalīᶜa 1972–3) vol. 1, pp. 11–27; 23.
41. D. Norman explains in *The Hero: Myth/Image/Symbol* (New York, NY: Doubleday Anchor Books, 1990), p. 124.
42. Campbell, *The Hero*, pp. 77–9.
43. Ibid. p. 90.
44. Ibid. p. 92.
45. Norman, *The Hero*, p. 56.
46. Ibid. p. 11.
47. Ghassān Kanafānī, *Mā tabaqqā lakum* (Beirut: Muᵓassasat al-Abḥāth al-ᶜArabiyya, 1986), pp. 48–56. Original published in 1966.
48. Ibid. p. 56.
49. Ibid. p. 64.
50. Ibid. p. 69.
51. Ibid. p. 67.
52. Norman, *The Hero*, p. 9.
53. Kanafānī, *Mā tabaqqā* , p. 19.

54. Fawaz Turki, *Soul in Exile: Lives of a Palestinian Revolutionary* (New York, NY: Monthly Review Press, 1988), p. 18.
55. See Paul Ilie, *Literature and Inner Exile: Authoritarian Spain, 1939–75* (Baltimore, MD: Johns Hopkins University Press, 1980).
56. Translated into English by Salma Khadra Jayyusi and Trevor LeGassick as *The Secret Life of Saeed the Pessoptimist* (London: Zed Books, 1985). Alternatively rendered as *The Strange Circumstances of the Disappearance of Saʿīd the Luckless Pessoptimist* by Nancy Coffin in 'Reading inside and out: a look at Habībī's Pessoptimist', *Arab Studies Journal* 8: 2 and 9: 1 (Fall 2000 and Spring 2001), pp. 25–46.
57. Sabry Hafez, *The Genesis of Arabic Narrative Discourse* (London: Saqi Books, 1993), p. 109. See also Yūsuf Nūr ʿAwaḍ, *Fann al-maqāmāt bayn al-mashriq wa al-maghrib* (Beirut: Dār al-Qalam, 1979); and Muḥammad Sullamī, *Fann al-maqāma bi al-maghrib fī al-ʿaṣr al-ʿalawī: dirāsa wa nuṣūṣ* (Rabat: al-ʿUkāẓ, 1992).
58. Hafez, *Genesis*, p. 129.
59. For a more complete list of the works emulating the pre-modern *maqāma* genre in the nineteenth century, see ibid. pp. 108–11; and at the turn of the twentieth century, pp. 129–36.
60. See, for example, ibid. pp. 129–36; and Muṣṭafā al-Shakʿa, *Badīʿ al-Zamān al-Hamadhānī: Rāʾid al-qiṣṣa al-ʿarabiyya wa al-maqāla al-ṣāḥāfiyya* (Beirut: Dār al-Rāʾid al-ʿArabī, 1979).
61. Already discussed in detail in the Prologue.
62. See, for example, Jamāl Sulṭān, *Fann al-qiṣṣa wa al-maqāma* (Beirut: Dār al-Anwār, 1967); and Muḥammad Rushdī Ḥasan, *Athar al-maqāma fī nashʾat al-qiṣṣa al-miṣriyya al-Ḥadītha* (Cairo: al-Hayʾa al-Miṣriyya al-ʿĀmma li al-Kitāb, 1974).
63. See, for example, Jaako Hȧmeen-Anttila, *Maqama: a History of a Genre* (Wiesbaden: Harrassowitz Verlag, 2002); Abdelfattah Kilito, *Les Séances: Récits et code culturels chez Hamadhanî et Harîrî* (Paris: Sindbad, 1983); and James T. Monroe, *The Art of Badīʿ az-Zamān al-Hamadhānī as Picaresque Narrative* (Beirut: American University of Beirut, 1983).
64. In *A History of the Arab Peoples* (Cambridge, MA: Harvard University Press, 1991), pp. 109–46.
65. See, for example, *Al-adab wa al-gharāba: dirāsāt bunyawiyya fī al-adab al-ʿarabī* (Beirut: Dār al-Ṭalīʿa, 1982); and *Al-ghāʾib: dirāsa fī maqāma li al-Ḥarīrī* (al-Dār al-Bayḍāʾ, 1987).
66. See al-Munṣif Shaʿrāna, *Azmat al-dhāt fī maqāmāt al-Hamadhānī* (Sūsa: Dār al-Maʿārif li al-Ṭibāʿa wa al-Nashr, 1996).
67. For a survey of the phenomenon, see Clifford Edmund Bosworth, *The Medieval Islamic Underworld: the Banū Sāsān in Arabic society and literature* (Leiden: E. J. Brill, 1976).

68. See Sulṭān, *Fann al-qiṣṣa*, pp. 34–63.
69. Hafez, *Genesis*, p. 110; Ḥasan, *Athar*, p. 95.
70. Hafez, *Genesis*, p. 110.
71. Ibid. p. 110; Ḥasan, *Athar*, p. 95.
72. Roger Allen, 'Introduction', *A Period of Time* (Reading: Ithaca Press, 1992), pp. 1–97; 72.
73. Ibid. pp. 1–97; ᶜAbdallāh ᶜAbd al-Muṭṭalib Aḥmad, *Al-Muwayliḥī al-Ṣaghīr: Ḥayātuhu wa adabuhu* (Cairo: al-Hayʾa al-Miṣriyya al-ᶜĀmma li al-Kitāb, 1985); and Aḥmad Ibrāhīm al-Hawārī, *Naqd al-mujtamaᶜ fī Ḥadīth ᶜĪsā Ibn Hishām li al-Muwayliḥī* (Cairo: Dār al-Maᶜārif, 1986).
74. Jābir ᶜUsfūr, *Zaman al-riwāya* (Damascus: Dār al-Madā, 1999), p. 11.
75. Elizabeth Thompson, *Colonial Citizens: Republican Rights, Paternal Privilege, and Gender in French Syria and Lebanon* (New York, NY: Columbia University Press, 2000), p. 1.
76. Ibid. p. 1.
77. Ibid. p. 2.
78. Ibid. p. 1.
79. For details of the genesis of this work, see Roger Allen's lengthy critical introduction to his translation of the work into English in *A Period of Time: Ḥadīth ᶜĪsā Ibn Hishām* (Reading: Ithaca Press, 1992), pp. 1–93.
80. In *Badīᶜ al-Zamān al-Hamadhānī: Rāʾid al-qiṣṣa al-ᶜarabiyya wa al-maqāla al-ṣaḥāfiyya*, Muṣṭafā al-Shakᶜa argues that the modern Arabic journalistic article is too inspired by al-Hamadhānī's epistles (*rasāʾil*). The evidence seems to point to a more complex genesis of the Arabic journalistic article. The *maqāma* is in fact the form that was more frequently used.
81. Allen, *A Period of Time*, p. 71.
82. Ibid. p. 72.
83. Ibid. p. 81.
84. Ibid. p. 82.
85. Ibid. p. 82.
86. Ibid. p. 73.
87. Al-Hawārī, *Naqd al-mujtamaᶜ*, p. 131.
88. Republished as a chapter of a book in Fayṣal Darrāj, *Hiwār fī ᶜalāqāt al-thaqāfa wa al-siyāsa* (Damascus: Dāʾirat al-Iᶜlām wa al-Thaqāfa, 1984), pp. 119–28.
89. Coffin, 'Reading inside and out', pp. 25–46.
90. Darrāj, *Hiwār*, p. 121. Quoted from his own article in French, 'On experiencing confiscated homeland', in *Palestinian Cultural Heritage* (Paris: Sicamore, 1980), pp. 125–59.
91. Ibid. pp. 125–59.
92. In 'The rewriting of *The Arabian Nights* by Īmīl Ḥabībī', Anna Zambelli Sessona looks at the ways Habiby rewrites 'The City of Brass', 'The Fifth

Voyage of Sindbad' and the story of king Shahryar in *Pessoptimist, Luka*^{c} *Ibn Luka*^{c} and *Ikhṭayya* (1986) respectively (*Middle Eastern Literatures* 5: 1 (2002), pp. 29–48). In *The Experimental Arabic Novel: Postcolonial Literary Modernism in the Levant* (Albany, NY: State University of New York Press, 2001), a deeply flawed book, Stefan G. Meyer deals with the use of Palestinian folk tale (*khurāfiyya*) in *Sarāyā bint al-ghūl* (1991; Saraya, daughter of demon), pp. 100–6.

93. Muḥammad al-^{c}Āfiya, *Al-khitāb al-riwāʾī* ^{c}*inda Īmīl Ḥabībī* (al-Dār al-Bayḍāʾ: Maṭba^{c}at al-Najāḥ al-Jadīda, 1997), pp. 69–106.
94. Ibid. p. 73.
95. Mentioned by Salma Khadra Jayyusi in her 'Introduction' to the 1985 English translation of the novel, p. xiv.
96. Al-'Āfiya, *Al-khitāb*, p. 73; Roger Allen, *The Arabic Novel: an Historical and Critical Introduction*, 2nd edn (Syracuse, NY: Syracuse University Press, 1995), p. 217; Jayyusi, 'Introduction', p. xiv; and Maher Jarrar, 'A Narration of "Deterritorialization": Īmīl Ḥabībī's *The Pessoptimist*', *Middle Eastern Literatures* 5: 1 (2002), pp. 15–28; 20–22.
97. Jarrar, 'A Narration', p. 15.
98. Jayyusi, 'Introduction', p. viii.
99. Ibid. p. xviii.
100. Coffin, 'Reading inside/out', p. 25.
101. Allen, *The Arabic Novel*, p. 209.
102. Coffin, 'Reading inside/out', p. 25.
103. Jarrar provides a useful survey of this material in his article mentioned above, 'A Narration', pp. 15–19.
104. Akram F. Khater, 'Emile Habibi: the mirror of irony in Palestinian literature', *Journal of Arabic Literature* 24 (1993), pp. 75–94.
105. Ibid. p. 84.
106. Allen, *The Arabic Novel*, p. 209.
107. Ibid. p. 209.
108. Ibid. p. 209.
109. Ibid. p. 213.
110. Samia Mehrez, 'Irony in Joyce's *Ulysses* and Habibi's *Pessoptimist*', *Alif: Journal of Comparative Poetics* 4 (Spring 1984), pp. 33–54.
111. Ibid. p. 43.
112. Ibid. p. 44.
113. Ibid. p. 45.
114. Ibid. p. 48.
115. Ibid. p. 48.
116. Jayyusi, 'Introduction', p. xii.
117. Allen, *The Arabic Novel*, p. 211.
118. Jayyusi and LeGassick, *The Secret Life*, pp. 117–18.

119. References in Arabic are made to Īmīl Ḥabībī, *Al-waqāʾiʿ al-gharība fī ikhtifāʾ Saʿīd Abī al-Naḥs al-mutashāʾil* (Dār Shuhdā, n.d.). This quote. p. 92.
120. Jayyusi and LeGassick, *The Secret Life*, p. 120.
121. Ḥabībī, *Al-waqāʾiʿ*, p. 161.
122. Ibid. pp. 62–3.
123. Ibid. pp. 73–4.
124. Ibid. pp. 88–99.
125. See, for example, *Love and Sexuality in Modern Arabic Literature*, (eds) Roger Allen, Hilary Kilpatrick and Ed de Moor (London: Saqi Books, 1995).
126. See Jūrj Ṭarābīshī, *ʿUqdat Ūdīb fī al-riwāya al-ʿarabiyya* (Beirut: Dār al-Ṭalīʿa li al-Ṭibāʿa wa al-Nashr, 1982).
127. See Jūrj Ṭarābīshī, *Ramziyyat al-marʾa fī al-riwāya al-ʿarabiyya* (Beirut: Dār al-Ṭalīʿa li al-Ṭibāʿa wa al-Nashr, 1981).
128. See *Sharq wa gharb, rujūla wa unūtha* (Beirut: Dār al-Ṭalāʿa li al-Ṭibāʿa wa al-Nashr, 1977).
129. Kanafānī, *Mā tabaqqā lakum*, p. 27.
130. Ibid. p. 27.
131. Ibid. p. 46.
132. Ibid. p. 47.
133. Norman, *Hero*, p. 124.
134. Al-Ghīṭānī, *Khiṭaṭ*, p. 124.

PART II

Love: Legitimacy of the Nation, Authenticity of the Novel

Chapter 3

LEGITIMACY OF THE NATION

FOR THE LOVE OF A NATION

Matilde: the name of a plant, or a rock, or a wine,
Of things that begin in the earth, and last:
Word in whose growth the dawn first opens,
In whose summer the light of the lemons bursts.

Wooden ships sail through that name,
And the fire-blue waves surround them:
Its letters are the waters of a river
That pours through my parched heart.

O name that lies uncovered among tangling vines
Like the door to a secret tunnel
Toward the fragrance of the world!

Invade me with your hot mouth: interrogate me
With your night-eyes, if you want – only let me
Steer like a ship through your name; let me rest there.

Pablo Neruda, *100 Love Sonnets*, p.7

Il Postino (1995; The postman), an Italian film constructed around Pablo Neruda's sojourn, or exile, in Italy, brought to the attention of the world many of Neruda's love poems. The film's Oscar contentions popularised further his love story with Matilde and, more importantly, it accentuated the relationship between poetry, love and politics. There is another dimension of Neruda's poetry that is equally poignant though not necessarily meaningful to those who have not experienced living away from home. Here, Matilde is synonymous with Chile. Neruda in effect re-imagines and inscribes the homeland he remembers on the body of his beloved. In the *100 Love Sonnets*,[1] as elsewhere in his poetry, Neruda 'transport[s] the physical contours of Chile to the printed page'[2] via the medium of a woman's body. In other words, a woman's body becomes a map of homeland, on which the geography of this homeland is reconstructed. Matilde is a plant, rock, sea, river, in fact, the earth itself. However, homeland is not only a matter of geography – place and space – but is also a question of belonging to a community – nation and nationness. A place becomes home only when 'earth' is transformed into 'world'. 'O name that lies uncovered among tangling vines/lie the door to a secret tunnel/toward the fragrance of the world', Neruda says. This transformation, Benedict Anderson explains in *Imagined Communities*, occurs when place is located in time – when a history is 'invented' for this place.[3] Time, in our notions of nation and nationness, is place's twin and is of equal importance in Neruda's love sonnets that, imbued with allusions to seasons aside, are arranged on the basis of the themes of morning, afternoon, evening and night. Put differently, these love sonnets are not simply about homeland the place, but are also about homeland the imagined community, the nation in the twentieth century. Geography becomes an expression of nation. So is woman's body. And, cartography, the discipline of territorial mapping, comes to be the metaphor of nation-building grounded in a clearly delineated place.

PROBLEMATIQUE OF NATION AND STATE

Inscribing the geography of a nation on a woman's body is a pervasive motif in literature and the arts. When I was a small child growing up in Libya, I lived for a few years in Gharyān, a mountain town situated on Jibāl Naffūsa less than a hundred kilometres south of Tripoli. To get there from Tripoli, my father drove through al-ᶜAzīziyya, at one time the hottest spot on earth, went up and came down one mountain then went up another mountain to take us home. On the top of this first mountain is another small town, whose name I forget, and in this small town is a villa that was a tourist attraction, and the first stop of our friends who came to visit us. I have no idea of who built the villa, when it was built or what has happened to it since we saw it last. However, I still remember vividly its white walls and the large sketches of nude women in various poses in brown on these walls. The real interest in these sketches, one may or may not be surprised to learn, was not the nude women but what they – the sketches – revealed about the relationship between geography and woman's body in our imagination. One of these sketches is a map of North Africa (cover). In literary and artistic expressions of our hopes, aspirations and fears for the imagined political community, I have shown in the preceding chapters that gender and geography seem inextricably linked.[4]

Current scholarship on gender, especially of its relationship to nation, has to a great extent focused on gender as a part of nationalist discourses. It explains the consequences of this linkage on discourses on women, pointing out the ways in which womanhood is defined and subordinated to the national cause and agenda. This line of inquiry and its conclusions have become all too familiar to us by now and I have no intention of conforming to this line of inquiry, of 'joining the crowd', so to speak. Rather, I would like to turn the familiar issue of gender and nation on its head and look instead at the consequences of gender thinking on the imagination of nation in Arabic literature in general and the Arabic novel in particular. Ṣalāḥ ᶜAbd al-Ṣabūr's (1931–81) poetry, especially plays, is a good, though not the only, place to start. I begin my discussion of Arabic novel's love affair with the nation-state with ᶜAbd al-Ṣabūr because his works, like al-Sayyāb's, provide a broader framework for the issues I will be discussing throughout this chapter and the following one. Like the Arab intellectuals and writers of his generation, ᶜAbd al-Ṣabūr, a nationalist committed to nation-building in the period immediately following independence, partook in the discourses on nation especially during the era of nationalist fervour in the aftermath of Gamal Abdel Nasser's 23 July 1952 revolution. Gender duality plays a crucial role in the imaginings of community and the articulations of aspirations and reservations about the future of the nation in these nationalist discourses. The kind of gender thinking that goes into nationalist discourses has implications on the imaginings of community, and tells us a great deal about the projected destiny of the nation, of the imagined community.

ᶜAbd al-Ṣabūr came to the attention of the Arab literary circles with the publication of his first *dīwān, Al-nās fī bilādī* (1957; People in my country). He has since been associated with the Tammuzi 'school' of modern Arabic poetry. Like most of the leading poets of his generation, ᶜAbd al-Ṣabūr made his main concern the plight of his fellow countrymen, as the title of his *dīwān* and poem shows, and the fate of his nation. It would not be difficult, in fact, it would be easy to trace the process through which ᶜAbd al-Ṣabūr participates in 'imagining an authentic, modern, democratic, national Arab Egyptian community' in his works along the lines of the model devised by Benedict Anderson. However, this modern national community never resembles an ideal community, a perfect nation, a utopian world free of problems and conflicts. Rather, this community remains a work-in-progress and is full of oppression, or *al-qahr*.[5] This is especially the case in his plays in verse, *Maʾsāt Ḥallāj* (1964; The tragedy of Hallaj), *Musāfir layl* (1969; Night traveller), *Al-amīra tantaẓir* (1969; The princess awaits), *Laylā wa al-Majnūn* (1970; Layla and the madman) and *Baʾd an yamūt al-malik* (1973; After the king dies).

In all these plays, the source of this oppression (*al-qahr*) is traced to power, especially political authority, and its accompanying systems of government, and the consequent political oppressions, especially those affecting the intellectuals (often represented by poets), are probed. In his two earliest plays, *Maʾsāt Ḥallāj* and *Musāfir layl*, the power struggle between tyranny and aspirations for fear-free life, freedom and justice is examined through a dramatised encounter between the title characters of the plays and symbolic figures of authority. Al-Ḥallāj's fate hinges on the whims of the ᶜAbbasid caliphate in the first play and the night traveller relies on the graces of the train conductor for his safe passage in the second. In the other three plays, this struggle is played out over the contested territory of a woman's body. In *Al-amīra tantaẓir*, a play full of allusions to the *The Thousand and One Nights*, the nameless princess is the means to power. She is fought over by the vizier al-Samandal (who seduces the princess, assassinates the king, marries the princess, and obtains power) and the poet al-Qarandal (who kills al-Samandal and helps to restore the princess's power). In *Laylā wa l-majnūn*, another play constructed around a well-known classical Arabic love story, Laylā too is the hotly contested object of desire, her body the battle ground for power politics. The same may be said of the Queen in *Baʾd an yamūt al-malik*. The course of the power struggle in these three plays is presented as a territorialisation of the female body, which is drawn as the geography of the nation. *Baʾd an yamūt al-malik*, the last of ᶜAbd al-Ṣabūr's plays, encapsulates his vision of the nation and encompasses all the themes, motifs and discourses inherent in his imaginings of an ideal community.

The play consists of three acts. Act One in one long scene takes place in the King's palace located in the city. Like the nameless characters, which must be taken to represent types, the temporal setting is abstract, not located in any historical era, although there are hints that the present may be meant. This act sets up the characters of both the King and the Queen and the circumstances that lead to the 'crisis of the play'. The King is depicted as a tyrant surrounded by a power-sensitive entourage, including his vizier, judge, historian, tailor, executioner, ladies-in-waiting and poet. At the end of the act, the Queen confronts the King with her desire to have a child and the King's failure to fulfil this wish. The King then dies. Act Two is in four short scenes. In scene one, the Queen leaves the palace and takes up residence in a hut (*kūkh*) by the river with the Poet outside the city. In scene two the Queen and the Poet are in love and living happily as a couple and the Tailor, whose tongue had been cut by the King in Act One, insinuates himself into their life. In scene three, which is set in the palace, the King's entourage decides that the Queen should be brought back and laid next to the King and the Executioner is dispatched to fetch the Queen. In scene four, the Executioner arrives at the Queen's hut. There is a scuffle between the Poet and the Executioner and the Executioner is dead and the Poet is injured. Act Three is again in one long scene. Three possible endings to the play are given. In the first version, *al-shakwā ilā l-qadar* (complaint to fate), the Queen is taken back to the palace by force and when the King and the Queen are not revived they both are sent to the underworld. The Poet then goes to the underworld to 'retrieve' the Queen and gives her up when faced with the choice of dividing her physically between the dead King and himself. The second solution requires waiting, *al-intaẓār*. The Poet and the Queen stay away until their son turns twenty, then they bring him back to the palace to take his rightful place. Seeing the dilapidation of the palace, the young king decides to rebuild but only to find that they are imprisoned in one room and that the rest of the palace has been taken over by enemies. The third alternative rests on the Poet and the Queen's resolve to fight the tyranny of the King's entourage. As the resolution crystallises, the Poet transforms into a knight and disempowers the King's entourage and begins a new era with the Queen in which the downtrodden, *al-maqhūrūn*, become the entourage.

The story is an obvious one. It is the story of the struggle between two forms of political authority, one symbolised by the King and his entourage, and the other by the Poet. The differences between these two forms of power are conveyed in three dualities. First: the duality of the man-made city, where the palace is located, and the country, where nature remains relatively unspoiled by the human hand. The incompatibility of these two forms of power becomes evident when the Poet is subordinated to the King (i.e. when the Poet has to serve at the court and pretend to be the King's voice). His voice emerges only when the King dies and upon his return to nature. Nature, it seems, is the catalyst of his transformation, of his self-empowerment, from speaking for others to speaking for himself, from poet to knight. Second: the duality of state and nation, which we see in the conflict between the King and the Poet. The conflict between the two forms of power they represent is depicted as a contest for the Queen's body. Despite the proclamations of love for the Queen by the King and the Poet, the body of the Queen (not her soul or love, let alone mind, for example) is the contested territory. To both the King and the Poet, this body is the vehicle of birth, the soil from which their future line will spring. In his death, the King, through the medium of his entourage, desires the body of the Queen, dead or alive. The Queen's body obviously is meant to symbolise the nation. But what is the shape of this nation? From the very beginning of the play, the Queen is depicted as part of the natural world. In fact, she may be taken to be, like Ishtar and Isis, the goddess of fertility in the ancient Mesopotamian and Egyptian mythology. It is, however, plausible to read her body as the earth upon which the nation is to be imagined and mapped. The geography of this nation is defined by the competing desires for the Queen's body, the third duality, whether it is love (*ḥubb*, *ᶜishq*) or desire (*shawq*, *raghbah*).

There are two sets of desires at work in this play. Firstly, there is the Queen's desire. She desires a child by any means. The King's death is in fact precipitated by her request to find and permit any man to impregnate her. Even when she is supposed to be in love with the Poet, her happiness comes from the realisation that he, like her coming from the earth, would be the most suitable to be the father of her child. There too is the King and the Poet's love for the Queen and their desire for her body. The motor driving their desire is not different from the Queen's. They too desire the Queen to provide them with offspring. In Act One, the King and Queen pretend to be nursing a child and when the illusion is shattered and the King further realises that he will not be able to have a child through the Queen he dies; gives up the ghost, so to speak. The Poet meets with better results. Whatever the ending may be, the Poet does have a child, a son for that matter, unborn (first and third endings) and grown-up (second ending). Desire for an offspring must be, of course, taken metaphorically. 'Love', through the voice of the Queen, 'is the yearning to create future not the desire to forget the past'.[6] The contest is then not over only geography but also history and over the right to write this history. In fact, history more particularly defines geography. The fate, or destiny, of the Queen's body, whether she remains with the King or goes away with the Poet, depends on who can impregnate her and give her a future, a new history that is more appropriate to her – a history more appropriate to the geography of the nation. Here, we find a third duality, that of past and future. The contest is between the palace – the edifice of a tyrannical history of power, and the hut – the home of a new national future. For the hut to displace and replace the palace, its residents must return to the city and rebuild the palace – the seat of political power. However, these residents must choose their own course of action, like the audience who must choose their preferred ending for the play – they possess their destiny, even though they must bear the consequences of their choice. Choice implies desire. Desire is, then, what drives the motor of nation-building, and therefore, national discourses.

There is, however, a problem. The national discourse inherent in ᶜAbd al-Ṣabūr's play presents us with a problematic of individual and collective selfhood. It can be identified and analysed by looking closely at gender thinking in the play. Gender thinking, I have discussed at the end of the preceding chapter, inevitably entails a kind of othering, which points to the realisation of the gap between self and other and the impossibility of their integration, despite the desire to do so and for the other.[7] In ᶜAbd al-Ṣabūr's play, the gender duality reflects the following sets of male-female dualities: city and country, past and future, state and nation. These dualities are the poles around which the geography, history and political authority of the nation-state are articulated. Nation is always imagined as state, the crux of the matter of which is political authority, on a newly mapped space with its own invented history. In gendering these three components of the nation-state and inscribing desire into the relationship between the two poles of the dualities, country is alienated from city, past from future, and nation from state. The integrity of selfhood, individual and communal, is compromised. Is it a Freudian slip that the masses play no part in the process of negotiating their own empowerment in the play? They are invited to 'populate' the palace only after the Queen and the Poet take over the machinery of power. The 'imagined community' in this play is a state without nation, past without future, city without country. This play, even as it imagines a national community, betrays an uncanny ambivalence towards its own imaginings.

The ambivalence in this play may be contrasted to the optimism of Yūsuf Idrīs's earlier play on the same subject, *Al-farāfīr* (1964). *Al-farāfīr*, as I have demonstrated elsewhere,[8] narrates Egypt's emergence as a nation-state. It portrays the attempt to establish a sovereign, secular, democratic state, in which individuals hold the key to their fate, as the traditional, divinely ordained dynastic systems crumble and fade away. Despite the gloomy prospects for a permanent solution to the question of political authority, all citizens of Idrīs's 'imagined community' may, indeed ought, to take part in the political process. Whatever one may conclude about the origin, history and development of nationalist thought, and however one may assess the effects of nationalist movements in the world, nationalist aspirations have had a profound impact on views of and on literary development in the Arab world. During the heyday of Arab nationalism between 1952 and 1967, there were genuine hopes for nationalism to transform the Arab countries into modern nation-states. Modernity is, in one sense, the reordering of political authority and society. In promoting secularity and democracy it would be possible, ideally, to guarantee the rights of the individual to liberty, justice, equality and pursuit of happiness, regardless of religion, class, ethnicity, race or gender. These rights would also insure that the individual has free access to political participation, equal opportunities to livelihood or, simply, a happy life. The failure to secularise or democratise political authority in the Arab world, a glimpse of which we caught in my discussion of *Khiṭaṭ al-Ghīṭānī* in Chapter 1, is deemed symptomatic of the lack of success in modernising the region and its culture and, more importantly, in failing to decolonise. This failure is accentuated by the Arab defeat in the 1967 war with Israel and the echoes of disappointment would reverberate in all post-1967 Arab writings. The pessimistic forecast for the nation-state inherent in ᶜAbd al-Ṣabūr's plays is an expression of a profound sense of defeat shared by Arab intellectuals even today.

AUTHENTICITY OF THE NOVEL

The Arabic novel, like contemporary Arabic poetry, short story and drama, has since been embroiled in the painful processes of self-examination. It has taken to heart the task of identifying and analysing the causes and effects of the failings of the nation-state since independence, focusing understandably on the question of political authority. In assessing its failures, questions are raised with regards to its legitimacy. Arabic novel's discourses are, however, not only pertinent to the fate of the nation-state but also to the identity of the Arabic novel and its status in modern Arab culture. The nation-state and the novel have one thing in common: they have their origins in the West. More important, as a genre that has allied itself with the nation-state, any question raised with regards to the former's legitimacy would have a haunting effect on the Arabic novel's view of itself. The Arabic novel, responsive to the problems of political authority operative in the nation-state, returns to pre-modern literary tradition in search for roots, and turns ways from realism to the fantastic to critique oppressive political regimes incognito. The story of the rewriting of the *Nights* in the Arabic novel is symbolic and symptomatic not only of the ways in which the destiny of the nation-state and the Arabic novel are tied, but also of their preoccupations with the questions of their legitimacy. Even Naguib Mahfouz has resorted to the fantastic in the classical Arabic literary tradition in his later works to write about the legitimacy of the nation-state, and contemplate the authenticity of the Arabic novel. In this endeavour, the *Nights* has become both the symbol of the classical Arabic tradition of storytelling and the material source for the Arabic novel.[9]

Layālī alf layla (1979; Arabian nights and days, 1995)[10] may not signal the beginning of Mahfouz's interest in or his return to the classical literary tradition – for this tradition has never been very far from the heart of the matter in all his works – it marks an entirely novel way of Arabic novel's intertextuality with the *Nights*. Mahfouz's interest in the *Nights* is in fact relatively late. Arabic novel, like Arabic poetry, short story and play, is pervaded with references to the *Nights*. These references have been a part of the strategies adopted in the Arabic novel to overcome its 'foreignness' since the beginning of its history in Arabic literature. The Arabic novel's rewritings of the *Nights* are a crucial part, though not all, of the story of Arab cultural heritage's participation in cultural and identity politics. The ways in which the *Nights* has worked itself into modern texts can encapsulate the history of the presence and the dialogical engagement of Arabic literary tradition in and with modern Arabic fiction. Mahfouz's rewriting of the *Nights*, *Layālī*, tells the story of the Arabic novel as it negotiates for its authenticity, legitimacy and centrality, all within another story it tells of the nation-state trying to find its way around secularity, democracy and modernity.

Since its publication, *Layālī* has attracted prodigious critical attention. Two of its distinctive features are highlighted: intertextuality with the *Nights* and the use of the fantastic.[11] Interpretations of this novel as political allegory are situated in the interplay between the *Nights*' fantastic and the novel's realism.[12] These divergent yet similar interpretations of the novel are interestingly not effected on reading Mahfouz's text against its intertexts despite the prodigious references to intertextuality with and narrative strategies inspired by the *Nights*. Beside the frame-within-frame technique and the frame tale, these interpretations do not depend on the token references to the *Nights* stories; in fact, they are straightforward readings of a story in a contemporary context as a political allegory with emphasis on narrative strategies 'exotic' to the European novel, especially the fantastic.

The interpretation of the novel must clearly be grounded in the political context of the contemporary Arab world, particularly Egypt, and the preoccupations of the author, whether the intertextual instances are identified or not. Mahfouz's novel, he says in an interview with *Fuṣūl*, is at once contemplation on the 'political reality' of the Arab world, as well as 'metaphysical' or 'Sufi' meditation on the human condition,[13] primarily on the paradoxical relations governing wisdom, or knowledge, salvation and power. It is, to a certain extent, unsatisfying to read the novel only as a political allegory of the kind Enany,[14] Ghazoul,[15] Hafez,[16] al-Mūsawī,[17] and Yaqṭīn[18] speak of. The disappointment in political authority, therefore, the nation-state, a theme picked up by his critics, has textual and narrative consequences that go beyond those identified, and entails more than irony, parody or satire of the current political reality. What would be the expression of disappointed hopes when the dreams, and visions, of modernity, which have been so heavily invested in the idea of nation-state, are seemingly irrevocably shattered? Perhaps the dialectics of forms Hafez alludes to merit closer scrutiny.[19] These dialectics do make ideological statements about political authority and the form of the novel, but they also provide diagnosis and prognosis of the ailing nation-state in which the future of the novel is invested. The novel is an expression and analysis of loss when the almost proverbial 'we could have been something' poignantly becomes the only possible articulated response to the situation plaguing the nation-state.

The question is also about the fate of the novel, as I have already mentioned. The selection of and the ways in which the *Nights* stories have been rewritten are part of the 'vision of the world' Mahfouz speaks of in the interview with *Fuṣūl*, a vision inspired by the famous corpus of pre-modern Arabic storytelling. 'I discovered on this mature second reading', he explains, 'that the *Nights* has managed to signify a world in its entirety, expressing its mentality, beliefs, imaginings and dreams. I discovered that it was indeed a unique work to be ranked among the great works of humanity'.[20] This vision is 'modernised' and employed by Mahfouz in the novel to delineate a new vision that is at once optimistic and pessimistic, political and philosophical, grounded in history and looking forward to the future, real and fantastic. It is paradoxically caught between the two poles of these dualities, both 'here' and 'there', neither 'here' nor 'there'. *Layālī* is at one level, according to Mahfouz, a concoction of themes he picked out from the *Nights* and wove into a cohesive novelistic world,[21] and at another, an experiment in form that brings together, as *Nights* does, divergent modes of expression.[22] The 'past' inherent in the Arabic narrative tradition spills over into the 'present'. The fantastic, the staple feature of the *Nights*, comes to cohabit with realism in the world of the novel.

The 'unholy' marriage between the fantastic world of the *Nights* and the contemporary political allegory in Mahfouz's novel, symptomatic and symbolic of the relationship governing the novel and pre-modern Arabic narrative tradition and storytelling, I will show, makes a statement about the nation-state and the Arabic novel at a crossroads. As Mahfouz returns to themes, narrative strategies and techniques, and vision contained in the Arabic literary tradition after a long sojourn in realism originated in the European novel, he looks back on the path Egypt has taken in its transformation from one kind of community to another. The novel imagines a community as a nation-state and at once subverts this imagining, producing a fantastic national allegory that simultaneously depicts and problematises the process through which the 'past' developed into the 'present' as well as both the 'past' and the 'present'. In his probing of the destiny of the nation-state there is an inherent discourse on the novel and the modernity, legitimacy and centrality of storytelling in contemporary Arab culture. Similarly, his exploration of the place of the novel in Arab culture is an investigation of the fate of the nation-state; for the history of the nation-state and the novel have been intertwined since their birth in the Arab world in the first half of the twentieth century. The nation-state and the novel have in common the questions of modernity and legitimacy; however, they diverge in one issue. While the novel concerns itself with its centrality in Arab culture as the foundation of its legitimacy, the nation-state is plagued with its propriety as a form of political organisation. The novel internalises and externalises these preoccupations in its rewriting of the *Nights*.

I suggest that it would be entirely productive to read closely the instances of intertextuality between Mahfouz's *Layālī* and the *Nights*. But where does one begin when it is not always possible to pin down the exact interlocutions of intertextuality in Mahfouz's rewriting of the *Nights*? This is not because Mahfouz's reading of the *Nights* is less than meticulous; on the contrary, Mahfouz takes advantage of the nebulous delineation of one story from another in the *Nights*. Overlapping names, seemingly hackneyed plots, repeated themes and storylines, familiar narrative devices, near symmetrical textual patterns, and anticipated resolutions of *Nights* stories open up Mahfouz's text for infinite ways of engagement and, more important, multiple layers of ambiguity. This ambiguity has an inherent capacity to allow not only indefinite possible readings of the novel but also to hint at potential manifold distribution of a pre-text in the text. Instead of exhausting all the possibilities, I will pursue a line of inquiry that allows me to unravel Mahfouz's double discourse on the nation-state and the novel embedded in his rewriting of what Northrop Frye would call 'naïve and sentimental romance', which bifurcates into what Andras Hamori identifies as 'patrimonial romance' and 'erotic romance' found in a majority of *Nights* stories.

In the following analysis of Mahfouz's *Layālī*, I look at transvaluation of the ideology, or world view, giving shape to both 'patrimonial romance' and 'erotic romance' and framing in their intersection the genre of 'love story' so pervasive in the *Nights*. Mahfouz tinkers with this 'ideology of genre', simultaneously evoking and distorting it with such an alienating effect that his text, a semilogical system, is at once familiar and unfamiliar to readers of the *Nights* and the novel. He takes the familiar signs of *Nights* story, which fulfil important roles in the system of knowledge underpinning this very different semiological system in its production of meaning, and reconfigures these signs into a new network of relations, a new system of knowledge, producing a set of meanings that are immediately relevant to our understanding of the political allegory his critics speak of, as well as going beyond this very allegorisation of the nation-state. Mahfouz brings the diverse and complex discourses embedded in *Nights* 'romance' into Bakhtinian dialogism with the contemporary nationalist discourse. Mahfouz's discourse on the nation-state is produced in the interstices of the dialogues between the *Nights* 'romance' and the 'novel'. His text is concomitantly embodiment and subversion of the two genres – *Nights*' romance and the novel – he brings together in the story he tells about the nation-state.

The textual space of the novel becomes the site on which the divergent discourses on community converge to tell not only the heart-breaking story of humanity's yearning, search for and failure in finding the utopian 'state of fantasy' rooted in the incompatibility between wisdom and power, set up as the dialectics between love and desire, but also the individual's despair in transcending the tyranny of the self-centred human desire to control and own destiny, as well the community's failure to overcome this tyranny manifest in social and political organisation and interaction.[23] There are multiple layers of intertextuality in *Layālī*. At the outset, the nation-state is set in the realm of the fantastic world of the *Nights* not the contemporary reality in Mahfouz's novel. The fantastic in the novel is not merely the interplay between humans and genies, good and evil, wisdom and power, transcendence and desire, contradictory impulses for letting go and possessing; rather, it lies also in exposing the nation-state as a flight of fantasy, a fantastic world that does not and cannot exist in reality.

ALLEGORISING THE IMAGINING OF NATION

Layālī reads like a 'sequel' but it is also a rewriting in more ways than one. The story Mahfouz tells begins on the 1002nd night but the trajectory of his narrative is bifurcated. It is simultaneously forward and backward looking. At one level, the narrative follows Shahrayār's development as king and man in the post-*1001 Nights* era. Shahrayār has internalised the stories Shahrazād has been telling him over a period of three years and takes an interest in the running of his kingdom and, above all, justice. Shahrayār now emulates Hārūn al-Rashīd of Shahrazād's tales, and often disguises himself as a merchant, accompanied only by his vizier and chamberlain, and tours his kingdom at night. He inspects the affairs of his subjects and brings relief to them from the miseries unjustly meted out against them. At another level, the narrative returns to the stories of the *Nights*, most of which are identified by Aboubakr Chraïbi,[24] Saᶜīd Shawqī Muḥammad Sulaymān,[25] revisits them, then rewrites them.

In recreating the world in these *Nights* stories, Mahfouz formulates a Cairene Quarter, of which he is famous, fleshing it out as a nation-state in the making, then allegorising the very nationalist discourse that partakes in the imagining of this nation. The novel mimics the nationalist discourses and imagines a community that secularises and democratises in a painfully bloody experience, all in the shadow of the 'religious community' and 'dynastic realm' the nation-state aims to displace and replace. It begins with humanising power and ends with popularising it. Power, more particularly, political authority, follows the movement of two inter-counter narratives: one of Shahrayār's descent from power, and the other of the people's ascent to positions of authority. These two narrative movements are in turn mediated by the story of Jamaṣa al-Bulṭī's metamorphosis from instrument of tyranny to means of justice. By choosing political power as his subject, Mahfouz creates a world akin to Anderson's 'political community' imagined 'both as inherently limited and sovereign'.[26] The community is defined by the all-too-well-known realist Mahfouzian *ḥāra* located in the heart of old Cairo, and its members are all citizens of this *ḥāra* who, like the characters of his realist novels, congregate for evenings in the Café of the Emirs. The feel of this 'imagined' community is, however, rather medieval.

The membership of the *ḥāra* is made up of the categories of urban population the fifteenth-century historian of Egypt, al-Maqrīzī, identifies in *Ighāthat al-umma bi kashf al-ghumma*.[27] Al-Maqrīzī speaks of seven categories of Egyptians at his time:

> Know . . . that the population of Egypt is divided on the whole into seven categories. This first category embraces those who hold the reins of power. The second [is formed of] the rich merchants and the wealthy who lead a life of affluence. The third [encompasses] the retailers who are merchants of average means, as are the cloth merchants. This also includes the small shopkeepers. The fourth category embraces the peasants, those who cultivate and plow the land. These are the inhabitants of the villages and of the countryside. The fifth category is made up of those who receive a stipend . . . and includes most legists, students of theology, and most of the *ajnād al-ḥalqa* and the like. The sixth category [corresponds to] the artisans and the salaried persons who possess a skill. The seventh category [consists of] the needy and the paupers; and these are the beggars who live off the [charities of] others.[28]

With the exception of the peasants, the categories of citizens al-Maqrīzī's identifies all inhabit the world of *Layālī*.

There are two tiers of political authority in Mahfouz's novel. The reign of the Sulṭān Shahrayār and his entourage made up of vizier Dandān and his executioner Shabīb Rāma extends beyond the boundaries of the *ḥāra*. And the governor, his chief of police and private secretary, under the aegis of Shahrayar, are involved in the day-to-day affairs of the Quarter. Among the citizens of the Quarter are two classes of merchants, the super rich like Karam al-Aṣīl who possesses the means to replenish Shahrayar's treasury, and relatively wealthy retailers like Sanᶜān al-Jamālī who owns a shop in the Quarter. ᶜAbdallāh al-Balkhī and his students, Fāḍil, son of Sanᶜān al-Jamālī, and Nūr al-Dīn and ᶜAlāᵓ al-Dīn, make up the class of students of religious studies. ᶜAbd al-Qādir al-Mahīnī the Physician, ᶜUjr the Barber, Maᶜrūf the Cobbler and others belong to the skilled professionals. There are then the unskilled peddlers and porters, such as Fāḍil al-Jamālī, Sindbād the Porter turned Sailor, and ᶜAbdallāh the Porter, and the vagabonds and outcasts, who constitute the poor sector of the population.

The decidedly medieval texture of the novel, derived from its attenuation to the *Nights* and al-Maqrīzī, cannot disguise the allusions to the nationalist discourse accompanying the emergence of Egypt as a nation-state as theorised by Anderson. The erosion of dynastic realm and religious certainty as well as the marginalisation of kingship and religious authority are conveyed through the stories of Shahrayār and ᶜAbdallāh al-Balkhī. Shahrayār's illusion of his God-like power al-Mūsawī speaks of[29] is shattered by the events recounted in the novel. It begins with his descent from the frame tale into the enframed tales and his integration into the historical character of Hārūn al-Rashīd, followed by his exit from his earthly palace, and ends with his fall from his utopian bliss. He is reduced from an omnipotent ruler to a griever mourning the loss of his paradise and happiness by the end of the novel. Despite the seemingly Sunni identity given to the community, in which the Shiᶜites and Kharajites are persecuted, religion in fact plays a minimal role in the running of the affairs of the community. ᶜAbdallāh al-Balkhī, the revered but remote religious scholar and teacher of the community, utters not political or social theories but esoteric and philosophical principles that have no immediate practical applications.

The emergence of the *ḥāra* as a nation-state is instead cast in the stories of a number of members of the community as they struggle to deal with various forms of power. The story of power starts with Sanᶜān al-Jamālī, goes through Jamaṣa al-Bulṭī, ᶜUjr the Barber, Fādil al-Jamālī, and ends with Maᶜrūf the Cobbler. The story imparts one lesson, that only those who are able to handle themselves responsibly should have power. Maᶜrūf the Cobbler attains power only when he successfully demonstrates his immunity to its corruptive effects. What is portrayed here is the attempt at establishing a sovereign, free, secular, democratic state as the perceived outdated, traditional, divinely ordained, hierarchical dynastic systems fall apart. In this newly 'imagined community', the individual holds the key to his own fate. Unlike the Greek tragedies, external powers or extraneous circumstances do not determine the fate of the main characters, or the heroes; rather, the choices they make, as Hafez points out,[30] are the decisive factors.

As a new 'imagined community', the world of *Layālī* is given 'immemorial past', and 'limitless future'. Time conveyed here is unlimited at both ends. Timelessness and placelessness are the setting of the novel. The novel is given a history grounded in the ancient tradition of Arabic storytelling, the roots of which extend to time immemorial. It is impossible to date the frame tale, the story of Shahrayār, which, now given a new lease on life in the novel, points to a 'limitless future'. The place in which the novel is set possesses generic features of any historical Islamic city today despite the obvious allusions to the old Cairo of the real world and realist Mahfouz being famous for the Cairo trilogy. The subject matter of the novel, the eternally insoluble question of power, further emphasises this sense of timelessness. The events of the novel can take place at any time in the past, present or future and, more importantly, they repeat themselves. Shahrayār's fall from his Utopia at the end of the novel is not his fate alone. He instead joins a plurality of grievers who have experienced the very same rise and fall. The novel is, paradoxically, historical; it displays history of political power from ancient times to the modern times and is grounded in Islamic history as allusions to Hārūn al-Rashīd and Ja^{c}far al-Barmakī, for example, imply. History as conceived in the novel may be likened to events that occur in what Anderson describes as 'homogeneous, empty time' marked by 'temporal coincidence, and measured by clock and calendar',[31] while its world 'is . . . a solid community moving steadily down or up history'.[32] Narrative moves along a linear progression, beginning with the frame tale and punctuated by the stories selected for rewriting from the *Nights* in twelve chapters, each contributing a piece to the overall puzzle of the overarching story of a relationship with power until the end is reached. The two processes of humanising and popularising power come hand in hand. Shahrayār's voluntary fall from power is premised on, precipitated by and accomplished in his impersonation of historical Hārūn al-Rashīd and living vicariously the experience of his subjects. The rise of his subjects to power is in turn conditioned on their direct experience of it and Shahrayār's descent from his throne.

This surface optimism of nationalist discourse is, however, undermined by an undercurrent of ambivalence explicit and implicit in the details of the novel's intertextuality with the *Nights*. All is not well, it seems, especially when the text is read against its pre-texts. Something has gone horribly wrong in the process of transforming the *Nights* stories into a national allegory. The narrative paradigms inherent in the *Nights* stories, upon closer scrutiny, have all lost pieces of themselves in their modern reincarnations. These missing pieces speak volumes of the lack of faith in the nation-state and of the fragility of the Arabic novel's self regard. In the reincarnated stories, the familiar patterns of the relationship between love and power, marriage and politics are distorted. The happy endings of *Nights* love stories are mercilessly sabotaged in the rewritten versions. The new unhappy endings may be part of the ploy to transform romance into novel, to transcend the universe of 'naïve and sentimental' romantic fantasy and enter into the real world. But perhaps there is something more than meets the realistic eye. Stories of love in the *Nights*, as Hamori has shown, are made up of the twining of 'erotic romance' and 'patrimonial romance'. A

Nights love story is rarely only about the meeting of a handsome young boy with a beautiful maiden that leads to lasting married bliss. It is more often than not, I have discussed at length elsewhere,[33] about the processes and consequences of a proper and appropriate union in cementing the legitimacy and continuity of a house of power, and the preservation and prosperity of a nation. The frame tale of the *Nights*, the story of Shahrayār and Shahrazād, is the story of a nation's return to health after a major trauma told in the form of a tale of marital betrayal healed eventually by storytelling and stories of love and loyalty. What, then, would be the point in changing the happy ending of familiar love stories in a narrative imagining of nation? Why is Shahrayār suddenly separated from Shahrazād? What does that and the persistent omnipotence of Shahrayar say about the nation-state?

REHABILITATION OF POWER

Shahrayār, as a symbol of the despotic form of political authority, is an indispensable protagonist in Mahfouz's narrative of the demise of kingship and emergence of democracy. He, as a character in the novel, is the most convenient site on which the rise of the nation-state may be articulated as the demise of kingship, or democracy as the taming of tyranny, and as the community's rise to power. This story is told as Shahrayār's journey towards wisdom and the community's aspirations for justice. Shahrayār's attempts at redeeming his own acts of tyranny and bloodshed in the three years preceding his union with Shahrazād poignantly brings him no respite. In his enlightened state of mind, he has become aware that his past sins have disqualified him to be the ruler of his kingdom. Upon his return from his last nocturnal journey Shahrayār calls Shahrazād to him and informs her of his decision to leave the palace. He will now give up his kingdom and kingship, in order to give way to just, pure rule (*aftaḥ lahā* [i.e. the City] *bāb al-naqāʾ*), and to find his personal redemption (*khalāṣ* in Arabic: deliverance).[34] Shahrayār leaves, and on his journey he comes upon an ethereal city in which he is able to find happiness – he marries its queen and discovers love for the first time in his life.[35] He spends a hundred years with his new wife, loving, meditating and worshipping.[36] His sojourn in this heaven-like world, however, does not last forever. Like Adam, his curiosity leads him to the forbidden door. As soon as he opens it, he falls back down to earth. Wisdom, for which a fire has been ignited in his heart, remains elusive. A brighter future for the community is equally illusory. Indeed, how would it be possible to envision a future basking in the light of justice when the present, the starting point of this future, is forever haunted by the 'darkness' of its past. Lessons of the past, though illuminating in more ways than one, provide no alternative courses of action.

This disappointment is phrased in the form of the reversal of the ending of the *Nights*' frame tale. In Mahfouz's sequel, just like all the rewritings of the *Nights*, the now universally expected happy ending is drastically altered, almost falling prey to the contemporary cliché that there is no such thing as happily ever after. The trajectory of Shahrayār and Shahrazād's romance moves in the opposite direction from its *Nights* counterpart. Mahfouz tells the story of the disintegration of their marriage rather than their falling in love and settling into a familial bliss. The story of Shahrazād and Shahrayār as rendered by Mahfouz reads more like the tragedy of a pair of star-crossed lovers fated to live apart in a state of unrequited love. Like wisdom, love has slipped through his fingers. In the wake of the completion of *Nights* stories, Mahfouz's Shahrazād, upon receiving Shahrayār's pardon and indeed having saved the nation, openly admits to her father Dandān that she lives in misery (*ta*ᶜ*īsa*) in the absence of love between herself and Shahrayār. His love for her is declared to be impossible at the beginning of the novel. In response to her father's entreaty, 'He loves you Shahrazād (*innahu* ***yuḥibbuki*** *yā Shahrazād*)!'[37] Shahrazād proclaims, 'Arrogance and love cannot co-exist in one heart; he loves himself first and foremost'.[38] Her repugnance for the king is obvious even to him. His knowledge of her indifference pushes him to often leave the palace and wander the streets of the *Salṭana*, or the city, at night, and to finally leave her. In their last conversation, Shahrayār thus confronts his queen, '"The truth", he said with resolute roughness, "is that your body approaches while your heart turns away"'.[39] He then conveys his intention to leave their son in charge of the palace and the city.

Paradoxically, as he explains his reasons for leaving her,

> For the space of ten years I have lived torn between temptation and duty: I remember and I pretend to have forgotten; I show myself as refined and I lead a dissolute life: I proceed and I regret; I advance and I retreat; and in all circumstances I am tormented. The time has come for me to listen to the call of salvation, the call of wisdom

she realises that she is finally falling in love with him, '"Your are spurning me as my heart opens to you", she said in a tone of avowal'.[40] Alas, it is all too late for their marriage:

'I no longer look to the hearts of human kind,' he said sternly.

'It is an opposing destiny that is mocking us.'

'We must be satisfied with what has been fated for us.'

'My natural place is as your shadow,' she said bitterly.

'The sultan,' he said with a calm unaffected by emotions, 'must depart once he has lost competence; as for the ordinary man, he must find his salvation.'

'You are exposing the city to horrors.'

'Rather am I opening to it the door of purity, while I wander about aimlessly seeking my salvation.'

She stretched out her hand towards his in the darkness, but he withdrew his own with the words, 'Get up and proceed to your task. You have disciplined the father and you must prepare the son for a better outcome.'[41]

The disintegration of their marriage signals the beginning of his family's loss of power; his abdication is paralleled by the rise of the people to power.

The allegorical aspect of profane love in the story of Shahrayār and Shahrazād is often overlooked in modern rewriting and criticism; rather, the story is interpreted symbolically with emphasis on the role of Shahrazād as storyteller and educator.[42] Mahfouz himself falls into the trap of the conventional reduction of the character of Shahrazād to an idealised symbol found in male writings in general. Stripped of her role as storyteller aside, his Shahrazād is, like ᶜAbd al-Ṣabūr's queens and princesses, symbolically the heart and soul of the nation, whose happiness is vested in the well-being of Shahrayār, the state. The absence of love between them and in all the reincarnated *Nights* stories makes a curious statement about the nation-state. The radical departure from the familiar, accepted ending of the *Nights* is especially significant in the context of the absence of stories of enduring love in modern Arabic storytelling in contrast to the abundance of tales of sex and sexuality. It is not sufficient, I have argued elsewhere,[43] to find the explanation of this absence in the possible nineteenth-century fabrication of the ending of the *Night*;[44] contemporary gendered pre-occupation with questions of power;[45] 'diaglossia' in pre-modern Arabic literature and culture, whereby popular love stories[46] and canonical *adab*[47] and religious[48] treatises on profane or sacred[49] love fall by the wayside in the process of modernisation; or dialectics of 'East' and 'West' in the process of assimilating the novel into modern Arabic literature. The absence of stories of enduring love in the Arabic novel, whether the end is happy or tragic, must be contrasted to the wealth of these stories in the pre-modern context and to the pervading modern tales of frustrated desires, disappointed hopes, broken promises, betrayals of confidence and tragic destinies. Understanding the function of the paradigmatic stories of enduring love, to which stories of desire found in the *Nights* are subordinated, may pave the way for a rich interpretation of Mahfouz's novel and of contemporary Arabic literary narratives.

The *Nights* love stories, sabotaged, subverted and distorted in Mahfouz's versions, are more often than not part of a vision of the 'nation', or 'imagined political community', which is the subject of the narrative. Romance in the *Nights*, Hamori shows in his analysis *Qamar al-Zamān*, one of Mahfouz's pre-texts, is divisible into 'patrimonial romance' and 'erotic romance'.[50] 'Patrimonial romance', the impulse of which I have related to that of the epic, details the ebbs and flows of the political fortunes of a kingly family and is centred more particularly on the cohesion of a kingdom.[51] 'Erotic romance' on the other hand follows the adventures of a pair of lovers; from the time they fall in love and become separated until they finally reunite. These two types of 'romance' are more often than not intricately, inextricably intertwined in *Nights* stories; the fate of the kingdom that is the heart of the matter in 'patrimonial romance' is often dependent on the resolution of the love story in 'erotic romance'. The legitimacy of the kingdom of the 'patrimonial romance' is determined by the propriety of the union of the lovers in the 'erotic romance'. The propriety of the 'erotic romance' leads to triumph and cohesion of empire, epic, and its impropriety results in disintegration of empire and wandering, romance.[52]

The *Nights*' frame tale follows this narrative logic. Shahrayār's healing and his kingdom's survival are entirely invested in his lasting union with Shahrazād and the continuity of his family line in the form of their three sons. The frame tale is, however, only a very small part of the picture. In fact, this interpretation of the frame tale is based on the ways in which the enframed stories, one by one, add a piece at a time to the overall vision of the survival, continuity and prosperity of the kingdom. Even though Mahfouz rewrites the frame tale and many of the enframed tales, he does not necessarily reconfigure the relationship between the frame and the enframed or the vision of the nation, fundamental to the *Nights* 'romance', constructed on the basis of a coherent, cohesive genealogy. On the contrary, he seems to have inherited the 'epical' vision inherent in the *Nights* 'romances' and put it to use in his narration of nation. The instances of intertextuality, once identified, lead us to a world of 'romances', in which 'patrimonial' or 'erotic' tales converge to discourse on the future of the lovers and the nation. The disruption of the narrative paradigms of *Nights* 'romances' in Mahfouz's novel is, then, a narrative device, a way of signalling to readers that in the story he is telling a familiar 'vision of the world' may be turned upside down, inside out. The novel's convenient amnesia of Shāhzamān, whose story is parallel to that of Shahrayār, the reversal of the ending of the frame tale, and the insertion of ᶜAbdallāh al-Balkhī into the main story line, are some of the obvious signs of difference. These, as well as the less visible markers, point the way to the potential archaeological sites where textual, and intertextual, treasures may be unearthed.

LEGITIMACY OF POLITICAL AUTHORITY

Mahfouz's fantastic national allegory is, upon close scrutiny, a modern empire of signs constructed on the ashes of an ancient empire of signs premised on both will to and anxiety of influence. A sign, even in the form of a proper name, may trigger an avalanche of memories and meanings located in complex intersections of the *Nights* and Mahfouz's novel, from the ideological narratives of a utopian community to existential meditations on the purpose of life. An exhaustive exploration of all the possible implications of intertextuality is, for my purposes, beside the point. It seems more appropriate to focus on what is immediately relevant to the topic at hand and leave the other equally important issues for future projects. I begin, then, my discovery, or recovery, of the layers of the palimpsestic text with the name Dandān who, in Mahfouz's novel, replaces Shahrazād's nameless father in the *Nights*, vizier to King Shahrayār. Dandān is, of course, not a creature of Mahfouz's imagination: he exists in the *Nights*. The Dandān in the *Nights* is also a vizier, though not to Shahrayār but rather to the ᶜUmar al-Nuᶜmān family in *The Story of ᶜUmar al-Nuᶜmān and His Two Sons*. More importantly, he is also Shahrazād's counterpart. He is the storyteller in *ᶜUmar al-Nuᶜmān*. His presence at the outset and centrality in Mahfouz's novel serve as a reminder of a bygone world that continues to exert influence on the nation-state. Dandān, a semiotic trace, opens up the novel to the world of the *Nights*, the novelistic nation-state to the *Nights* kingdom, and the modern symbolic order struggling to take shape to the pressures of an ancient one refusing to breathe its last. The love stories he tells in *ᶜUmar al-Nuᶜmān* serve as the foil to both Shahrazād and Mahfouz's tales.

ᶜUmar al-Nuᶜmān, a mini-epic cycle incorporated into the *Nights*, exhibits the features of both genres of epic, what Hamori calls 'patrimonial romance', and romance, or 'erotic romance'. The dual personality of this *sīra*, in its combination of romance – what Ferial Ghazoul would call anti-*sīra*[53] and I epic[54] – is as pertinent to the function of narrative in this story as that of empowerment. The *sīra* begins as what David Quint calls in *Epic and Empire* romance, the narrative of the defeated, which consists of a series of aimless wanderings of the 'heroes' whose potentials remain unrealised, as the family, and therefore, nation falls apart. However, it ends as epic, the narrative of the victors, which comprises the story of the emergence of the 'hero', who unites his family and nation, and leads them to triumph, repossessing the lands taken by the Christians. The epical turn of romance is conditioned on the reunion and unity of the members of the kingly family, the return to cohesion of the royal genealogy. More importantly, the cycle of love stories in *ᶜUmar al-Nuᶜmān* functions as the mechanism of turning defeat into victory, romance into epic. The contrasts between the two parts of the *sīra*, the first preceding and the second following the cycle of love stories, I have also argued, are relevant to the paradigms of love imparted in the love stories.[55]

The first part of the *sīra* recounts the beginning of the end of the ᶜUmar al-Nuᶜmān kingdom. It details the deadly sins committed by ᶜUmar al-Nuᶜmān and his sons: lust, jealousy, greed, rape, incest, and treachery. The excesses of ᶜUmar al-Nuᶜmān and his first-born, Sharrkān (or Shirkān), lead to the collapse of the kingdom. Ḍaww al-Makān and Nuzhat al-Zamān, ᶜUmar al-Nuᶜmān's children from a slave-girl, are doomed to leave home and wander. Soon, both ᶜUmar al-Nuᶜmān and Sharrkān die, leaving Ḍaww al-Makān a king under siege, facing the army of the rival king whose daughter his father raped. In the second part of the *sīra*, Ḍaww al-Makān dies and leaves the kingdom of ᶜUmar al-Nuᶜmān in the hands of outsiders. The narrative takes a drastic turn when it begins to tell the story of Kān-Mā-Kān, Ḍaww al-Makān's son. Orphaned, reduced to poverty, his kingdom usurped by Sāsān, and his union with his intended Quḍiya-Fa-Kān, daughter of the incestuous marriage between Sharrkān and Nuzhat al-Zamān, prevented by the pretender king, Kān-Mā-Kān leaves to seek his fortune in the desert. In this journey, he is transformed from child to adult, victim to hero, and returns to Baghdad triumphantly. There he escapes the assassination attempt cooked up by Sāsān, amasses the support of all the Muslims with the help of the family's loyal vizier Dandān, and marries his cousin Quḍiya-Fa-Kān. He further unites the Muslims, leads the newly assembled Muslim army towards the Christian lands. More importantly, he finds his lost family, his uncle Rūmzān, ᶜUmar al-Nuᶜmān's son with

Ibrīza, his rape victim, and together they restore cohesion to the kingdom bequeathed by ^{c}Umar al-Nu^{c}mān.

It is between the two parts of the *sīra* that the cycle of love stories is inserted. Like all the *Nights* stories, this cycle of love stories are stories within stories, similar to the way they are enframed in the narrative of *^{c}Umar al-Nu^{c}mān*, which is in turn enframed in the narrative of Shahrazād and Shahrayār. There are two love stories, one framing the other. At the outset, there is the story of Tāj al-Mulūk and Lady Dunyā, and at the inset, the story of ^{c}Azīz and ^{c}Azīza. The frame tale is the story of a king and his son and their quest for a suitable bride. King Sulaymān, king of the green city (*al-madīna al-khaḍrā'*), marries late in life a suitable bride, the daughter of the king of the white land (*al-arḍ al-bayḍāʾ*). They have a son of kingly qualities, Tāj al-Mulūk, who is more enamoured with hunting than maidens. When King Sulaymān exerts pressure on him to marry, to continue the family line, Tāj al-Mulūk runs away and goes on a hunting trip from which he does not intend to return. He meets a melancholic ^{c}Azīz, who tells him about Lady Dunyā, with whom ^{c}Azīz is in love but is no longer able to pursue with her a meaningful relationship. As Tāj al-Mulūk falls instantly in love with Lady Dunya, he is intrigued by ^{c}Azīz's condition and persists until ^{c}Azīz tells him the story of his ill-fated love with his cousin and intended bride, ^{c}Azīza. ^{c}Azīz had abandoned ^{c}Azīza on their wedding night, and with the help of ^{c}Azīza, was able to secure the favours of Dalīla Bint al-Muḥtāla, and move in with her. ^{c}Azīza then died of a broken heart. ^{c}Azīz then fell in love with Dalīla's nemesis and moved in with her. When Dalīla found him again, she castrated him and left him for dead. Upon hearing ^{c}Azīz's story, Tāj al-Mulūk embarks on a journey to secure Lady Dunyā's love.

The two inset love stories, *Tāj al-Mulūk* and *^{c}Azīz and ^{c}Azīza*, mirror the two parts of the *^{c}Umar al-Nu^{c}mān* in a reverse order. While *^{c}Azīz and ^{c}Azīza* reflects the first, *Tāj al-Mulūk* parallels the second. They represent an important instance of the intersection between 'patrimonial romance' and 'erotic romance' in the *Nights*. However, the pairing of *^{c}Azīz and ^{c}Azīza* with the first half of *^{c}Umar al-Nu^{c}mān* is structured round the trope of desire gone awry, while the coupling of *Tāj al-Mulūk* with the second half is driven by the trope of educating desire into love. Love, in the vocabulary of pre-modern Arabic-Islamic theory of love, is the right combination of reciprocal sexual desire, commitment and loyalty (what binds Tāj al-Mulūk and Dunyā, and Kān-Mā-Kān and Quḍiya-Fa-Kān), not the pursuit of unbridled passion alone (what ails ^{c}Umar al-Nu^{c}mān and ᶜAzīz). ᶜAzīz realises the true meaning of love when he has lost everything, and remembers ᶜAzīza's words: 'Loyalty is beautiful and treachery is ugly' (*al-wafāʾ malīḥ wa al-ghadr qabīḥ*).[56] Love can disable the workings of reason, *ᶜaql*, in its excessive form, *ᶜishq*, unbridled passion born of and driven by sexual desire, and lead to madness, *junūn*. Madness in this case means that love veils reason, therefore, the lover no longer comprehends what is beneficial or harmful to him. What is at stake for the pre-modern theorist of love is the future of the Muslim in this life and hereafter; for love can be his ruination in this life when he becomes a danger to himself and his community, and his displacement from Heaven when he becomes mindless to the teachings of Islam. Love then must not remain unbridled passion; rather, it must be guided and developed by reason into a something more.[57] But what is reasonable love?

COHERENCE OF COMMUNITY

In the first instance, propriety must be observed. Love must follow the law of nature – it can only occur between man and woman – and lead to social cohesion in the form of marriage. Marriage is a social responsibility and legal measure and good match, or proper love, must observe the compatibility in looks and manners (*khalq* and *khuluq*), as well as equivalence in social standing, *munāsaba*. Second, taxonomy of love between man and woman, as Hamori persuasively argues in 'Notes on Two Love Stories from the *Thousand and One Nights*', is important too. The couple must behave in a fashion appropriate to lovers and generating of reciprocal desire. Third, the union must take place lawfully. And fourth, more importantly, love must be vigilantly maintained through loyalty and endurance (*wafāʾ* and *ṣabr*), as Ibn Ḥazm explains in *Ṭawq al-ḥamāma*, in order to prevent betrayal and impatience, or weakness (*ghadr* and *jazaᶜ*) from breaking down the union.

The story of King Sulaymān's marriage serves as the basic model for a proper love match. The king patiently waits until a compatible princess (the daughter of an equal king) is found, and properly falls in love with her on their wedding night when he comes face to face with her, his equal. *Tāj al-Mulūk* follows this pattern but fleshes out the protocol of proper love. It is the story of prince-meets-princess deserving a happy ending for observing all the protocol of proper love. Tāj al-Mulūk, upon falling in love with Dunyā, pursues her in marriage in a single-minded fashion. He conducts himself properly as lover. He pines for his beloved, loses his appetite for food, becomes insomniac, and weeps whenever his beloved is remembered. He loyally pursues his beloved, and endures his heartache and patiently woos her until she falls in love with him too. He waits until it is both appropriate and legal for him to consummate his desire. More importantly, he is able to generate desire in Dunyā. Dunyā in turn behaves properly. When she falls in love with him, she does not give in to her desire immediately but waits for the right moment for their union, when they are legally married. She too displays loyalty towards her beloved and puts his well-being above her own. When her father raises his sword intent on killing Tāj al-Mulūk, she throws herself in front of her father's sword, crying 'kill me before you kill him!'[58] Theirs is a story of desire that leads to love, and love that leads to desire. The happy ending of their story should then be taken for granted, for what could go wrong in a story that observes all the proper requirements of reasonable love? The moral of their story is highlighted by its counter-story, *ᶜAzīz and ᶜAzīza*, the story of innocent devotion wasted on a self-indulgent young man who comes to a bad end, in which love is sabotaged by *ghadr* and *jazaᶜ* (ᶜAzīz mindlessly pursues his improper desire for and sex with Bint al-Dalīla al-Muḥtāla and her nemesis), and ᶜAzīza dies of unrequited love, unable to generate desire for her on ᶜAzīz's part.

The moral of a love story might end here but that of an epic could not, for in an epic it is not the fate of the lovers that is at stake but rather that of a nation, a fate determined by the vibrant continuity of kingly genealogy and kingship. The successful union of the lovers is only the first step towards the preservation of the nation. The maintenance of kingship requires more than requited love. The reasons for the insertion of this cycle of stories at this point in the narrative of *ᶜUmar al-Nuᶜmān* are suddenly clear. The possible love stories contained in the first half of the *sīra*, the part I call romance, appear improper, illegitimate and incomplete. The potentials of a love story between Sharrkān and Ibrīza, a seemingly well-matched couple, are never fully realised in the absence of desire. Ibrīza, the daughter of a rival king, is suddenly paired with ᶜUmar al-Nuᶜmān through rape at a point where we are still haunted by the promise of love between Ibrīza and Sharrkān, the son. This is a case of passion gone awry and the rape – improper, illegal and almost incest – generates life as well as death: Ibrīza dies while giving birth to a son. There is, moreover, the incestuous love affair between Nuzhat al-Zamān and her half-brother Sharrkān, a *maḥram* whom she is forbidden to marry by law. The liaison, despite the birth of a child, Quḍiya-Fa-Kān, ends unhappily as soon as their blood relationships is revealed: Nuzhat al-Zamān is hastily married off to Sharrkān's chamberlain to conceal the incest from King ^{c}Umar al-Nu^{c}mān. In contrast, the love story in the second half of the *sīra*, the part I call epic, develops differently. Kān-Mā-Kān, now orphaned and his throne usurped by Quḍiya-Fa-Kān's pretender father, is prevented from seeing his beloved. He pines as befitting a lover, then leaves in search for his fortune, transforms into a hero, then returns to reclaim his throne, defeat his enemies, reunite his family, and marry Quḍiya-Fa-Kān. This love story, like that of Tāj al-Mulūk and Dunyā, is proper, legitimate and perfect.

Where *^{c}Azīz and ^{c}Azīza* is situated in the *Nights* – within *Tāj al-Mulūk*, which is in turn inserted in *^{c}Umar al-Nu^{c}mān*, which is further framed by the story of Shahrayār and Shahrazād – is thus instructive. The story of ^{c}Azīz reminds Tāj al-Mulūk that he needs to find love in order to generate life. ^{c}Azīz's story, together with Tāj al-Mulūk's, counsel Ḍaww al-Makān that *jaza^{c}* alone would not turn defeat into triumph, and that in time – with persistence and patience – his kingdom will be restored. Tāj al-Mulūk indeed falls in love with Dunyā, and through *ṣabr*, guided by ^{c}Azīz, is able to eventually marry Dunyā, and Tāj al-Mulūk's kingdom is anticipated to continue. These stories together instruct Shahrayār that *ghadr* and *jaza^{c}* – both in terms of what has been inflicted upon him and what he has been meting out against his people – will lead to the annihilation of his entire 'nation'. The story of ^{c}Azīza teaches the meaning of 'true love': loyalty and patience. Through her love, during her life and after her death, ^{c}Aziz comes to understand the meaning of love, and is enabled to know his true heart (^{c}Azīza), and go on living, in fact, even fall in love. Here, the three characters of the three stories, ^{c}Azīza, Dandān and Shahrazād, merge into one. They instruct through their stories and by setting themselves as examples. While Shahrazād tells Shahrayār endless tales one night after another at the peak of his crisis, Dandān is telling Ḍaww al-Makān the story of another kingly family, when the latter is near despair for the survival of his kingdom, and ^{c}Azīza is telling ^{c}Azīz love stories when he is desperately pining after Bint Dalīla. These stories are the means by which the tides of misfortune are turned around; romance takes a turn towards epic. Tāj al-Mulūk finds his mate and starts a family. Ḍaww al-Makān returns to Baghdad and his offspring do unite his kingdom and restore its cohesion. And Shahrayār pardons Shahrazād as well as his nation. More importantly, life is generated again.

The absence of reciprocal desire and love between Shahrayār and Shahrazād in Mahfouz's novel, then, seems poignant, especially when seen from the perspective of the absented stories of Dandān, which continue to haunt the rewritten frame tale. With the disappearance of Shahrazād and Dandān as storytellers from the novel, there is no one to teach Shahrayār about love, patience and endurance. 'Patrimonial romance' cannot turn into epic without 'erotic romance', it seems, and in the absence of love between the king and the queen, the kingdom is on the verge of extinction. The union between Shahrayār and Shahrazād, a desperate measure taken in the middle of a dire predicament, is from the perspective of the enframed 'patrimonial romance' a marriage of convenience shorn of the prerequisite rituals of 'erotic romance' essential in the rise and longevity of a nation. The happy ending of the frame tale 'fabricated' in the nineteenth century, as the contemporary novelistic interpretations of the tale go to show, only highlights the impropriety of the union. Mahoufz's novel is haunted by this impropriety. Impropriety of royal marriage, as the *Nights* stories tell us, has consequences detrimental not only to the royal family but also the kingdom. More importantly, impropriety of any marriage threatens to undo the fabric of the kingdom. The nation-state in Mahfouz's novel is, however, a 'political community' newly imagined on the ruins of kingship, on the by-now inappropriate, improper form of political community. This nation-state is paradoxically modelled on the kingship it is meant to replace. The political allegory that it is works precisely because the boundaries between the two forms of political community are blurred. The story of the rise of nation-state in the shadow of kingdom is not a straightforward one, for the remnants of the latter easily contaminate the former, leaving behind a legacy of impropriety that threatens to sabotage the nation-state and erode its legitimacy.

The propriety of other love matches in the class-conscious *Nights* stories complement that of the royal love in the health of the kingdom and the longevity of kingship. Mahfouz revives the politics of love situated in the overlapping of 'patrimonial romance' and 'erotic romance' in the *Nights*, as well as of the instances of transgression committed against its inherent code of conduct in some of the stories of the *Nights*, and more importantly, in the stories he writes of modern Egyptian nation-state. Kings must marry queens, princes princesses, sons of viziers daughters of viziers, and sons of merchant daughters of merchants. Transgressions of such a code of conduct will lead to tragedies and disasters. However, the stories of desire gone awry are not simply about a man falling in love with or marrying a woman from the 'wrong' side of propriety, but also about man's inability to master and manage his conduct which, I have already explained, must follow a trajectory of propriety. The story of desire is paradoxically about power in both the *Nights* and Mahfouz's novel. It is about the ability to master desire, educate it into love, and behave responsibly, as king, his officer and subject and, above all, as man. Here too Mahfouz evokes *Nights*' discourses on the ethics of rule that govern kingship and that ensure the happiness of a kingdom.

ETHICS OF RULE

In the first chapter of his novel, 'San^c^ān al-Jamālī', Mahfouz sets up more than just the context in which the kingdom falls and the nation-state rises. He partakes in the *Nights*' interrogation of ethics of power. Al-Jamālī, a well-to-do merchant in *Layālī*, kills the governor of the *ḥāra*, ^c^Alī al-Salūlī, when the latter summons him to his palace and asks for the hand of his daughter and his intercession with his cousin, a contractor, to build a road around the quarter to his specification and, more importantly, profit. 'San^c^ān al-Jamālī' is the first *Nights*' enframed tale Mahfouz rewrites in *Layālī*. It provides the first glimpse of the intertwined movements of power: the downward spiral of the kingdom and the upward mobility of the nation-state. The nation-state's rise to power is, however, necessitated by and born out of the pervasive 'moral' decay of the kingdom. 'Al-Jamālī', the novel's initiation into the revolutionary process of re-imagining of community, is the story of political assassination. Al-Jamālī's encounter with Qumqām is a reminder of 'The Merchant and the Genie'. There are, however, some crucial differences. While the *Nights* merchant, who accidentally kills the genie's son and incurs the wrath of the genie, is saved by the stories of the three old men, al-Jamālī loses his life, even though he pays for his misstep. He is charged with killing al-Salūlī as ransom for stepping on the head of Qumqām, a demon serving as one of the quarter's two guardian angels, and does. Before he does, he commits an unspeakable act. In a moment of confusion, he rapes and strangles a ten-year old girl, Basma, a crime Qumqām conceals, allowing him time to accomplish his task. He then lets al-Jamālī get caught, be tried, then beheaded. His fulfilling his promise ironically does not save his life, perhaps because of his transgressions.

His story is followed by 'Jamaṣa al-Bulṭī' and 'The Porter', both of which detail the circumstances surrounding al-Bulṭī and his first reincarnation's successful political assassinations. Al-Bulṭī, chief of police, is charged with quashing the rebellions breaking out in the *ḥāra*. By order from the new governor Khalīl al-Hamadhānī he rounds up the Shi^c^ites, Kharajites and outcasts even though he knows well that they are not the culprits. Things come to a head when the governor, upon the theft of precious jewels from his home (compliments of Sinjām and Qumqām), accuses him of not doing his job, in fact, of being a thief, al-Bulṭī kills him. He then develops a taste for political assassination and, for the rest of the novel, he takes charge of killing or exposing the corrupt in the *ḥāra*, including Shahrayār's appointees. Al-Bulṭī's relationship with Sinjām is reminiscent of *The Fisherman and the Demon*. He, like the fisherman in the *Nights*' story, fishes Sinjām out of deep waters and frees him from the bottle then finds his fate bound to the genie's will. The difference is that the *Nights*' fisherman manages to save a kingdom without shedding blood, while al-Bulṭī must kill in order to save the *ḥāra*. His reincarnation, ᶜAbadallāh the porter, who is transformed into ᶜAbdallāh the landman at the end of 'The Porter', uses his accessibility to 'spy' on the houses he frequents. His freedom to roam from one house to another, like the porter in *The Porter and Three Ladies*, avails him of the innermost secrets of the powerful. Instead of enjoying their stories or banquets, he kills them.

These assassinations, as the story of the nation unfolds, lie at the heart of the first three enframed tales of the novel: 'Sanᶜān al-Jamālī', 'Jamaṣa al-Bulṭī' and 'The Porter'. These seemingly straightforward stories of political assassination are complicated by allusions to the *Nights* stories, which serve as a ready-made canvas of a 'decadent' universe upon which revolt paints the finishing touches in blood. The three *Nights*' stories evoked in these scene-setting chapters in Mahfouz's novel are the first three cycles of stories Shaharzād tells Shahrayār. They form the 'core' of the *Nights*, and delineate the contours of a world pervaded with betrayal and requiring intervention from its supreme authority. In *The Merchant and Genie* we hear stories of three forms of betrayal. The first of the three old men (all merchants) who come to the aid of the merchant condemned to death by the genie tells the story of how his barren wife transforms his second wife into a cow and the son he has with the latter into a calf. She causes him to kill the cow, the mother of his son. Fortunately, she is found out before she can cause the death of the son and is herself turned into a gazelle. The second old man then recounts his brothers' attempt at drowning him – with his demon wife – even though he has come to their aid and saved them from a life of destitution when they failed in their trade. As their punishment, the demon-wife turns them into dogs. The third old man speaks of returning home from a journey to find his wife in bed with a black slave. When she realises that she is exposed, she turns her husband into a dog. Thankfully, a butcher's daughter recognises the human in him, turns him back and transforms his wife into a mule.

The 'demonic' intervention that dispenses with justice in the stories found in *The Merchant and the Genie* comes down to earth in *The Fisherman and Demon*. Tragedies, personal in the first cycle of stories, take on communal proportions. The stories the fisherman tells the genie, of King Yūnān who, at the instigation of his jealous vizier, kills the physician Dūbān who cures him of leprosy, make up the narrative of the disintegration of a kingdom. When Dūbān realises that Yūnān will definitely kill him, he poisons a book he gives the King at the time of execution, and both die. *The Story of the Enchanted Prince*, enframed within *Fisherman and the Demon*, is another story of an adulteress queen betraying her king and enchanting his kingdom into a lake. *The Porter and Three Ladies* picks up this theme of betrayal and weaves another cycle of kindred stories about the downfall of man and break up of family and nation. Incest in the first dervish's tale, adultery in the second dervish's tale, sisterly betrayal in the first lady's story (a female version of the second old man's tale in *The Merchant and the Genie*), and the second lady's breaking her promise to her husband (never to set eyes upon another man) by kissing another man, are yet another litany of betrayals.

In his study of *The Porter and the Three Ladies of Baghdad*, Hamori observes very astutely that in this tale 'there is a structural coherence that ultimately speaks for a morally random universe'.[59] Hamori has in mind the slight asymmetry in the structure of this cycle of stories, for example, that the three stories of the three old men are countered by only two stories from the three ladies, and more importantly, the ending does not seem to meet our expectations of justice. Hārūn al-Rashīd, upon hearing all the stories of woe, can with a word he utters pardon all for their misdeeds and restore harmony to the universe. His resolution is more an act of magnanimity than justice; it provides no real justice in that a crime is not necessarily met with equal punishment or retribution. The atmosphere of 'a morally random universe' that Hamori speaks of pervades the world of the *Nights*; stories inevitably end with an all powerful Sulṭān holding court and portioning out justice as he deems fit, perhaps because the *Nights* is primarily about ransoming life and postponing death. What is a better antidote to death, known as the destroyer of happiness (*hādim al-ladhdhāt*) in the *Nights*, than living joyously? This is the certain outcome readers of the *Nights* can be trusted to find at the end of practically every story. Justice, seen in this light, is necessarily random, subject to the whims of the ruler, just like desire, whose movements are embroiled in the plots designed to unravel the workings of justice in the *Nights*. I am not convinced. The story of desire in the *Nights* has more to tell us.

The story of desire in Arabic narrative is a wily one, and amidst its wayward trajectories hints are dropped on the ways in which justice is defined in a paradigm of knowledge structuring the world and the stories about this world. The intertextual signs posted by the story of al-Bulṭī point to the importance of the notion of justice inferable from its inter-texts: *The Fisherman and the Demon*, *Jullanār* and *ᶜAbdallāh the Landman and ᶜAbdallāh the Seaman*. The story of desire, as it overwhelms love and is in turn tamed, is not only one of an epical transformation of romance, but also a morality tale in the vein of the 'mirror for princes' intended to provide instructions on the protocol of justice in a kingdom. The *Nights* tales, on whose skeletons Mahfouz fleshes out his story of the nation's rise to power, are mapped by desire's to-and-fro movements between two worlds, let us say, Utopia and dystopia, each with a system of justice upheld or undone by their kings and citizens. As Mahfouz simultaneously revives and subverts the *Nights* stories, he draws a road map for the nation's initiation into and education in the responsibility of power. The interplay between love and desire, on the theatre of power games, comes to take centre stage, yet again, in a play intended to teach the ruler and ruled the proper rites of political authority. These rites, as the revived stories instruct, must be guided by a workable system of justice.

In an earlier exploration of the trajectories of desire in the three *Nights* stories Mahfouz evokes in his novel, *The Fisherman and the Demon*, *Jullanār* and *ᶜAbdallāh the Landman and ᶜAbdallāh the Seaman*, I discussed at length the ways in which desire functions as a narrative trope around which a discourse on community is structured in pre-modern Arabic writings. There are two discourses on community embedded in these stories. The discourse on proper love frames another discourse on an ideal community emergent in the polarisation between Utopia and dystopia. Utopia is the world in which royal love is proper, and dystopia, as *The Enchanted Kingdom* enframed in *The Fisherman and Demon* shows, is a world ruled by improper desire. These polarised visions of community are traceable to the juxtaposition of two carefully patterned worlds in these *Nights* stories, one of the land ruled by reason, a by-product of which is the management of desire, and the other of the sea run amok with unchecked desire. Legitimate kingship in these stories is not only the conclusion of a proper royal love match, but also an appropriate code of conduct.

The prosperity of kingship now rests additionally on the king's ability to manage desires of all kinds in his kingdom. As we see in *The Fisherman and the Demon*, the king must personify reason (*^{c}aql*) and dispenses justice (*^{c}adl*) accordingly, rewarding the 'good' (*jamīl*) and punishing the 'bad' (*qabīḥ*), and 'righting' the 'wrong'.[60] The king's authority, *sulṭān*, is only legitimate and operative when desire is transformed by reason into proper conduct, into love. Love comes to be the equivalent of reason in *Jullānar*, and justice in *The Fisherman and the Demon*.

Kingship in the *Nights* stories, as I have already explained, is often spoken of in the language of love. Its legitimacy and effectiveness are premised on educating desire into love, self-interest into loyalty to king, wife, subject, or community. Marriage in this context is a metaphor for the contract that binds the king to his officers, subjects and, above all, kingship and kingdom. It is a contract based on *^{c}aql* that, when allowed to be the operative word in a story, ensures harmony, prosperity and continuity of the kingdom of the story. Love is commitment, not only of a king to a queen, but also of kingship to *^{c}aql*. Love, *ḥubb* or *maḥabba*, as Arabic theories of love tell us, may be founded on *^{c}aql*, in fact, it is best when it is what develops among the *^{c}āqilūn* – between king and vizier, friend and friend, or man and woman. When in charge, *^{c}aql*, as in *al-^{c}aql ^{c}an al-jimā^{c}* (refrain from sexual intercourse) in Arabic lexicography, stops love from turning into a kind of excessive *^{c}ishq* driven by sexual desire (*shahwat jimā^{c}*) and that results in madness or mortal peril.[61] *The Fisherman and the Demon* gives a glimpse of the workings of the triad of power, justice and reason in an ideal community following a bottom-up trajectory. The fisherman is model citizen who embodies the principles of a proper kingship overseen and maintained by the king. He is, in a crucial sense, the representative of the king and kingship. He is honest, kind, generous, upright and free of greed, or 'unreasonable' will. The demon's initial desire to kill him is unreasonable, improper and illegitimate, for it violates the code of conduct appropriate to a saved towards his saviour, as we learn in the enframed tale of *King Yūnān and Physician Dūbān*. Rewarding 'good' with 'bad' does not sit well with the logic of an ideal community.

The conduct of the fisherman follows the example of his king. When his catch, the fabulous set of four-colour fishes, is presented to the king and burnt in the royal kitchen time and again, the king sets out for the lake where the fishes originate. He scours the area and comes upon a great palace where he finds a young king whose lower half has been turned into stone. He tells the older king he was betrayed by his queen, his cousin.

She was a sorceress forced into the royal marriage but was in love with a demon from the Qāf Mountain. She drugged him every night then went to her lover. When he found out, followed her to her love nest, and struck the demon lover and left his wife untouched, his wife turned him into a half statue, his kingdom into a lake and his subjects into the fishes in the lake. The visiting king promises the enchanted king to right the wrong. And he does. He kills the demon lover, impersonates him, tricks the sorceress into breaking the spell, and kills her. Normal life and harmony do return but all is not the same. This kingdom becomes ransom for its own eventual good fortune. The saved kingdom is swallowed up by the saviour's kingdom. The young king follows the gallant older king home and remains there as a grateful boon companion. The vizier of his rescuer now rules his former kingdom. This ending makes sense in accordance with the logic of *Nights*. The marital betrayal in *The Enchanted Kingdom*, combined with the young king's inability to manage it, results in the disintegration of his kingdom. The older king's efficacy in righting the wrong, in restoring justice, guarantees the expansion and longevity of his own kingdom.

The king and the fisherman are two faces of the same coin; they both are the manifestation of the code of conduct appropriate to an ideal community. The *Nights* discourses on ideal community are binarised into Utopia and dystopia that, as I have alluded to, are represented respectively by one world constructed on land and the other on water. The land is home of domesticated desire and the sea is the playground of untamed desire. The juxtaposition and overlapping of these two polarised worlds provide us with an entry into its discourses on ideal community structured around the interplay between love and desire, while allowing for a certain ambiguity regarding this ideal community. If the taming of desire, or educating desire into love in *The Fisherman and the Demon* and *Jullanār* leads to legitimate kingship and ideal kingdom, the rejection of the world on land by *ᶜAbdallāh the Landman and ᶜAbdallāh the Seaman* points to a profound ambivalence towards a world where there is no room for desire to run a rampant path. Mahfouz's political allegory taps into and plays with these *Nights* discourses on ideal community. However, he turns the paradigms of knowledge structuring these stories upside down, disabling the workings of reason and allowing desire to wreak havoc in the world.

There is a reversal of fortune in the worlds of the land and the sea in Mahfouz's novel. The world of the land is, in the absence of justice, the playground for demons who, seizing the day, drive human desire to the point of no return from unbridled passion and obsession. Madness, *junūn*, comes to be the order of the day. Desire, planted in the hearts by good Sinjām and Qumqām or evil Sakhrabūṭ and Zarambāḥa, drive the citizens of the *ḥāra* to commit treacherous acts of all kinds: murder, adultery, theft, cheating, lying, blackmail, back-stabbing, sabotage, and the list goes on. Jullanār may be a paradoxical figure in the *Nights*. She is a paragon of reason and wisdom in the way she tests her husband for a year before she confesses that she returns his love and is with child, and how she handles herself when her son goes missing. She does not panic but instead, patient and steadfast, she returns to watch over his kingdom on his behalf. And when at last she learns of her son's whereabouts, she rescues him and restores him to the throne. She is equally personification of desire. She it is who unleashes desire from and on those around her. Mahfouz's Jullanār, making her presence first felt in 'The Porter'[62] then taking centre stage in 'The Adventures of 'Ujr the Barber',[63] unlike her *Nights* persona, is the epitome of desire gone mad. Sister to governor Yūsuf al-Ṭāhir, she takes advantage of her rank in the *ḥāra*'s hierarchy of power, and lives a life of ill repute, filled with clandestine nocturnal parties and illicit sexual liaisons. Her end comes, when she kills her own sister, Zahrayār, in a jealous rage, exposing her brother, as well as his entourage, as unfit officers of the state. This is precisely the world of the land in *Layālī*. The nation-state of Mahfouz's novel, not the kingdom of the *Nights*, is arguably 'a morally random universe' Hamori speaks of in the context of *The Porter and the Three Ladies of Baghdad*.

Mahfouz's sea is, in contrast to that of the *Nights*, a source of grace and home to reason and justice familiar to the *Nights* discourse on kingship and justice. The genie al-Bulṭī rescues from the sea is a good-doer: 'good' being what it means in the *Nights*: justice. He pushes al-Bulṭī to 'right wrong' and protects him from fatal consequences. The sea is, moreover, a refuge from the rampage of desire on land. When the porter, al-Bulṭī's reincarnation, runs to the sea after a killing, ᶜAbdallāh the seaman saves him by dipping him in the water and transforming him into ᶜAbdallāh the landman. ᶜAlāᵓ al-Dīn and Dunyazād turn to the sea at a critical moment until ᶜAbdallāh the landman intercedes and resolves their crisis. Most importantly, ᶜAbdallāh the landman is transformed into first the madman, *al-majnūn*, and finally the wise man, *al-ᶜāqil*, who will assume the governorship of the *ḥāra* at the end of the novel.

In reversing the roles of the land and the sea in the imaginings of the 'perfect state', Mahfouz also rewrites the roles of the Sulṭān, Shahrayār, and his governor, al-Bulṭī, who enters the arena of political authority as the former exits. The contemporary revision of the function of storytelling, let us say, from postponing death to narrating the nation, necessarily problematises the role of the authority figure, the sultan, whether in the form of Shahrayār or Hārūn al-Rashīd. The Sulṭān, inheritor of power by virtue of birth, can no longer be the sole arbitrator of justice, however charismatic or moral he may be. What worked for a kingdom is not good enough for a nation-state. The novel is, in its intertextuality with the *Nights*, an enquiry into the kind of political authority that would suit the nation-state but that will continue to uphold the kind of justice prescribed in the *Nights*. The triad of legitimacy – authority (*sulṭān*), justice (*ᶜadl*) and reason (*ᶜaql*) – appearing as early as the initial set-up, looms large over the horizon of the novel and informs the novel's quest for the responsible system of government not the 'rightful' ruler. The quest for a suitable ruler takes the power games from the Sulṭān to his officers and down to practically every member of the community. Having a just sultan (*sulṭān ᶜādil*)[64] is, alas, not sufficient to keep the genies at bay. The genies will stop interfering in human affairs only when the governor (*al-wālī*)[65] makes sure justice is upheld from the outset.[66] The *Nights*' atmosphere of moral randomness that permeates the first three chapters of Mahfouz's novel exposes the mishandling of power by those who have it and maps at the same time a path towards responsible management of power.

There is no monopoly on abuse of power. These first chapters, sculpted from and on *Nights*' paradigm of knowledge, made up of the triad of power, reason and justice, and cast in its language of love and desire, confirm the intimate relationship between sex and power, love and nation. Propriety of love and control of desire remain the dominant metaphor for the legitimacy of political authority and continue to haunt the nation-state at both the macro and micro levels. At one level, improper sexual conduct leads to communal and personal tragedies. Does his rape of Basma necessitate al-Jamālī's death? What, after all, distinguishes him from political assassin al-Bulṭī, to whose rescue the genies rush one political assassination after another? Al-Jamālī's liability to commit sexual violence is a sign that he will be irresponsible with power. He is ruled by his desire. Al-Bulṭī is contrarily in command of his desire. As much as he desires al-Jamālī's daughter, Ḥusniyya, he refrains from doing anything about it, not even legally. In fact, as he progresses in his reincarnations, he steadily divorces himself from the world of desire, sex and love. At another level of linking sex to power in literary representations, as conventional wisdom today would have us know, desire lying at the heart of sexual behaviour drives power politics. Conversely, sexual aberrations become symbolic of abuses of power. This perhaps explains why the landscape of Mahfouz's text is littered with debris of illicit sexual liaisons. Transgression, of all sorts, is the name of the game in Mahfouz's political allegory. Paradoxically, it is through the various experiences of transgression that power may be tamed and educated into the kind of desired political authority that is informed by reason and driven by justice.

NOTES

1. Translated by Stephen Tapscott (Austin, TX: Texas University Press, 1986), p. 7.
2. Margaret Sayers Peden, 'Translator's Introduction', *Selected Odes of Pablo Neruda* (Berkeley, CA: University of California Press, 1990), p. 4.
3. See Benedict Anderson, *Imagined Communities: Reflections on the Origin and Spread of Nationalism* (London: Verso, 1983, 1991).
4. For further discussions of the link between gender and nation in the Egyptian context, see Beth Baron, *Egypt as Woman: Nationalism, Gender and Politics* (Berkeley, CA: University of California Press, 2005), and Lila Abu-Lughod, *Dramas of Nationhood: the Politics of Television in Egypt* (Chicago, IL: University of Chicago Press, 2005).
5. Thurayyā al-ᶜUsaylī, *Al-masraḥ al-shiʾrī ᶜinda Ṣalāḥ ᶜAbd al-Ṣabūr* (Cairo: al-Ha'ya al-Miṣriyya al-ᶜĀmma li al-Kitāb, 1995).
6. *Dīwān Ṣalāḥ ᶜAbd al-Ṣabūr*, 2 vols (Beirut: Dar al-ᶜAwdah, 1977), vol. 2, p. 374.
7. See Steven G. Smith, 'Psychic Duality', *Gender Thinking* (Philadelphia, PA: Temple University Press, 1992), pp. 230–47.
8. See Wen-chin Ouyang, 'The imagined modern nation in Yūsuf Idrīs's *Al-farāfīr*', *Modern Language Quarterly: a Journal of Literary History* 60: 3 (September 1999), pp. 379–408.
9. In the expanded version of *The Arabic Novel: an Historical and Critical Introduction* (1995), Roger Allen alludes to Mahfouz's break with the familiar pattern of his oeuvres, his preoccupation with the particular problems of his society, in some of his more recent novels. 'For example', Allen explains, 'Maḥfūẓ has returned to the classical literary tradition, following perhaps the example of his young colleague, Jamāl al-Ghīṭānī, invoking the 'characters' of *A Thousand and One Nights* in *Layālī alf layla . . .*' (p. 118).
10. English translation by Denys Johnson-Davies, *Arabian Nights and Days* (Cairo: American University in Cairo Press, 1995).
11. In his new seven-volume compendium on the Arabic novel, *al-riwāya al-ᶜarabiyya: bibliyūghrāfiyā wa-madkhal naqdī, 1865–1995* (Cairo: American

University in Cairo Press, 2000), Hamdi al-Sakkut has identified a number of newspaper reviews of the novel as well as books that deal with the use of classical Arabic literary heritage in the Arabic novel including Mahfouz's works (1382–3). Except for Sa[c]īd Yaqṭīn's work, *Al-riwāya wa al-turāth al-sardī* (Beirut: al-Markaz al-Thaqāfī al-[c]Arabī, 1992), I have not been able to gain access to the items identified. The critical articles on Mahfouz's novel referred to in my writing are, it seems, unknown to al-Sakkut.

12. The reading of Mahfouz's *Layālī* as a political allegory is very much in tune with Fredric Jameson's view of third-world literature. Jameson has keenly noted the allegorical quality of third-world literature in his infamous article on 'Third-World Literature in the Era of Multinational Capitalism', in *Social Text* 15 (Fall, 1986). He may be misguided in his generalisation that third-world literature is a protracted response to colonialism and imperialism, as Aijaz Ahmad has discussed in detail in 'Jameson's Rhetoric of Otherness and the "National Allegory"', also in *Social Text* 17 (Fall, 1987). However, Jameson has unwittingly identified a distinct marker of the Arabic novel today. The Arabic novel reads like a 'national allegory', perhaps not in the Jamesonian sense – that it is imprisoned in its obsession with colonialism and realism – but rather in the sense that it is primarily concerned with the history, development and destiny of the nation-state. In an environment of political oppression, political criticism inevitably dons a mask, and speaks through the fantastic. Mafhouz's rewriting of the *Nights* clearly fits the bill of a 'fantastic national allegory'.
13. In *Fuṣūl* 13: 2 (Summer 1994), p. 380.
14. Rashed El-Enany, *Naguib Mahfouz: the Pursuit of Meaning* (London: Routledge, 1993), pp. 159–60.
15. Ferial Ghazoul, *Nocturnal Poetics: the Arabian Nights in Comparative Context* (Cairo: American University in Cairo Press, 1996), pp. 138–48.
16. Sabry Hafez, 'Jadaliyyat al-bunya al-saridyya al-murakkaba fī layālī Shahrazād wa Najīb Maḥfūẓ', *Fuṣūl* 13: 2 (Summer 1994), pp. 20–69.
17. Muḥsin J. al-Mūsawī, *Thārāt Shahrazād: fann al-sard al-[c]arabī al-ḥadīth* (Beirut: Dā al-Ādāb, 1993), pp. 109–39.
18. Sa[c]īd Yaqṭīn, *Al-riwāya wa al-turāth al-sardī* (Beirut: al-Markaz al-Thaqāfī al-[c]Arabī, 1992), pp. 33–47.
19. Hafez, 'Jadaliyya', p. 29.
20. *Fuṣūl*, 13: 2, p. 378.
21. Ibid. pp. 379–80.
22. Ibid. p. 380.
23. Fawzī al-Zumurrulī, *Shi[c]riyyat al-riwāya al-[c]arabiyya: baḥth fī ashkāl ta[ɔ]ṣīl al-riwāya al-[c]arabiyya wa dalālatihā* (Tunis: Markaz al-Nashr al-Jāmi[c]ī, 2002), pp. 31–89.
24. Aboubakr Chraïbi has identified in 'Les jinns penseurs de Naguib Mahfouz'

the *Nights* stories that make a cameo appearance in Mahfouz's novel. The plot in 'The Merchant and the Demon' drives the story of San^{c}ān al-Jamālī. Hints of the 'The Fisherman and the Demon' are found in the chapter on Jamasa al-Bulṭī. 'The Porter and the Three Ladies of Baghdad' provides a background canvas for the story of ^{c}Abdallāh the Porter, the first incarnation of Jamasa al-Bulṭī. The story of Dunyazād and Nūr al-Dīn alludes to 'The Story of Qamar al-Zamān'. The story of ^{c}Ujr the Barber is seemingly inspired by 'The Jewish Doctor', 'The Story of the Hunchback' and 'The Story of the Barber' in the 'Hunchback' cycle. The story of Anīs al-Jalīs may be linked to 'The Story of the Seven Viziers' as well as the *Nights* story of the same title. The story of Qūt al-Qulūb is derived from 'The Story of Ghānim Ibn Ayyūb'. And the stories of ^{c}Alā$^{\circ}$ al-Dīn with Moles on his Cheeks, Sindbād, Ma'rūf the Cobbler and the pretender Sulṭān all have their counterparts in the *Nights*. In F. Sanagustin *et al.* (eds) *L'Orient au coeur, en l'honneur d'André Miquel* (Paris: Maisonneuve et Larose, 2001), pp. 171–83.

25. Sa^{c}īd Shawqī Muḥammad Sulaymān identify two forms of *Layālī*'s intertextuality with the *Nights* in their comprehensive survey of 'traditional' elements in all Mahfouz's novels and show the ways in which *Nights*'s form and content and chronotope are redeployed in *Layālī*. See *Tawẓīf al-turāth fī riwāyāt Najīb Maḥfūẓ* (Cairo: Ītrāk li al-Nashr wa al-Tawzī^{c}, 2000), pp. 95–108, 241–62.
26. Anderson, *Imagined Communities*, p. 6.
27. Translated into English by Adel Allouche as *Mamluk Economics: a Study and Translation of al-Maqrīzī's Ighāthah* (Salt Lake City, UT: University of Utah Press, 1994).
28. Al-Maqrīzī, *Ighāthat al-umma bi kashf al-ghumma* (Cairo: Dār Taḥqīq al-Turāth, 2002), p. 73.
29. Al-Mūsawī, *Thārāt Shahrazād*, p. 114.
30. Hafez, 'Jadaliyya', p. 54.
31. Anderson, *Imagined Communities: Reflections on the Origin and Spread of Nationalism* (London: Verso, 1991), p. 24.
32. Ibid, p. 26.
33. Wen-chin Ouyang, 'The epical turn of romance: love in the narrative of ^{c}Umar al-Nu^{c}mān', *Oriente Moderno* XXII n.s. (LXXXIII), 2, (2003), pp. 485–504.
34. Maḥfūẓ, *Layālī*, p. 259.
35. Ibid. pp. 289–90.
36. Ibid. p. 289.
37. Maḥfūẓ, *Layālī*, p. 6; Johnson-Davies, *Arabian Nights*, p. 8.
38. Maḥfūẓ, *Layālī*, p. 6; Johnson-Davies, *Arabian Nights*, p. 8.
39. Maḥfūẓ, *Layālī*, p. 257; Johnson-Davies, *Arabian Nights*, p. 217.
40. Maḥfūẓ, *Layālī*, pp. 258–9; Johnson-Davies, *Arabian Nights*, pp. 217–18.
41. Maḥfūẓ, *Layālī*, p. 259; Johnson-Davies, *Arabian* Nights, p. 218.

42. In his play, *Shahrazād* (1934), Tawfīq al-Ḥakīm portrays Shahrazād not only as being in love with the vizier Qamar, but, more importantly, defiantly staging her own exposure in an adulterous situation with a black slave in order to test her success in taming the king. In response to al-Ḥakīm's rendition, Ṭāhā Ḥusayn wrote his own novel, *Aḥlām Shahrazād* (1943), in which he sees Shahrazād not as a symbol of nature as al-Ḥakīm does but of freedom. Prior to *Aḥlām Shahrazād*, Tawfīq al-Ḥakīm and Ṭāhā Ḥusayn co-wrote a novel, *Al-qaṣr al-masḥūr* (1935), in which they tell another version of the story of Shahrazād. Writing the chapters alternately, they debate their views on the relationship between power (Shahrayār) and nature or freedom (Shahrazād). For a more detailed discussion, see Shukrī Muḥammad ᶜAyyād, 'Sharzazād bayn Ṭāhā wa al-Ḥakīm', *Fuṣūl*, 13: 1 (Spring 1994), pp. 9–19.
43. Wen-chin Ouyang, 'The epical turn of romance' pp. 485–504.
44. For a discussion of other possible endings of the frame tale, see Heinz Grotzfeld, 'Neglected conclusions of the Arabian Nights: gleanings in forgotten and overlooked recensions', *Journal of Arabic Literature* 14 (1983), pp. 73–87.
45. A good example is Fedwa Malti-Douglas, 'Narration and desire', *Woman's Body, Woman's Word: Gender and Discourse in Arabo-Islamic Writing* (Princeton, NJ: Princeton University Press, 1991), pp. 11–28. There is a reference to gender dynamics in the frame tale in Hafez, 'Jadaliyya', pp. 20–69. Otherwise, there are simply too many references to document here.
46. For a survey and general structural analysis of the loves stories in the *Nights*, see Peter Heath, 'Romance as Genre in *The Thousand and One Nights*, Part I', *Journal of Arabic Literature*, 18 (1987), pp. 1–21, and 'Part II', *Journal of Arabic Literature* 19 (1988), pp. 1–26; and Muḥammad Rajab al-Najjār, 'Qiṣaṣ al-ḥubb fī l-layālī: al-binā᾽ wa al-waẓā᾽if', *Fuṣūl* 13: 1 (Spring 1994), pp. 251–68.
47. For a general survey of the works on profane love in Arabic, see Lois Anita Giffin, *Theory of Profane Love Among the Arabs: the Development of the Genre* (New York, NY: New York University Press, 1972).
48. For a survey and analysis of this genre of works on love, see Joseph Norment Bell, *Love Theory in Later Hanbalite Islam* (Albany, NY: State University of New York Press, 1979).
49. See, for example, Asᶜad Khairallah, *Love, Madness, and Poetry: an Interpretation of the Mağnūn Legend* (Beirut: Orient-Institut der Deutschen Morgenlandischen Gesellschaft, 1980).
50. Andras Hamori, 'The Magian and the Whore: Readings of Qamar al-Zaman', *The 1001 Nights: Critical Essays and Annotated Bibliography, Mundus Arabicus 3* (Cambridge, MA: Dar Mahjar, 1983), pp. 25–40
51. Wen-chin Ouyang, 'Romancing the epic: *ᶜUmar al-Nuᶜman* as narrative of empowerment', *Arabic and Middle Eastern Literatures* 3: 1 (January 2000), pp. 5–18.

52. See Ouyang, 'The epical turn of romance'.
53. Ghazoul, *Nocturnal Poetics*, p. 46.
54. See Ouyang, 'Romancing the epic'.
55. See Ouyang, 'The epical turn of romance'.
56. Bulaq text: Muḥammad Qiṭṭa al-ᶜAdawī (ed.), *Alfa layla wa layla*, 2 vols (Bulaq: 1252 AH), vol. 1, pp. 250, 252; W. H. Macnaghten, *Alf Layla wa-Layla: The Alif Laila or Book of the Thousand Nights and One Night, Commonly Known as ᶜThe Arabian Nights' Entertainment'*, 4 vols (Calcutta, 1839–42), vol. 1, pp. 592, 604.
57. Wen-chin Ouyang, 'Utopian Fantasy or dystopian nightmare: trajectories of desire in classical Arabic and Chinese fiction', in Aboubakr Chraïbi, Fredéric Bauden and Antonella Ghersetti (eds) *Le repertoire narrative arabe medieval: transmission et ouverture* (Geneve: Droz, 2008), pp. 323–51.
58. Bulaq, vol. 1, p. 269; Macnaghten, vol. 1, p. 643.
59. Andras Hamori, *On the Art of Medieval Arabic Literature* (Princeton, NJ: Princeton University Press, 1974), p. 164.
60. See Ouyang, 'Utopian fantasy or dystopian nightmare'.
61. See, for example, Muḥammad b. Dāwūd (d. 297/910), *Kitāb al-zahra*, ed. Ibrāhīm al-Samarrāᵓī (al-Zarqāᵓ: Maktabat al-Manṣūr, 1985), pp. 55–7, 58–9; Ibn Ḥazm (d. 456/1064), *Ṭawq al-ḥamāma*, ed. Ṣalāḥ al-Dīn al-Qāsimī (Tunis: Dār Ibn Salāma, n.d.), pp. 27–35; Ibn al-Jawzī (d. 597/1200), *Dhamm al-hawā*, ed. Muṣṭafā ᶜAbd al-Wāḥid and rev. Muḥammad al-Ghazālī (Cairo: Dār al-Kutub al-Ḥadītha, 1962), pp. 289–95; Ibn Qayyim al-Jawziyya (d. 751/1350), *Rawḍat al-muḥibbīn wa nuzhat al-mushtāqīn*, ed. Samīr Rabāb (Beriut: al-Maktaba al-ᶜAṣriyya, 2000), pp. 20–40, 49–64; Ibn Abī Ḥajla (d. 776/1375), *Dīwān al-ṣabāba* (Beirut: Dār wa Maktabat al-Hilāl, 1984), pp. 11–13; and al-Nuwayrī (d. 732/1332), *Nihāyat al-arab fī funūn al-adab* (Cairo: al-Muᵓassasa al-Miṣriyya al-ᶜĀmma, n.d.), vol. 2, pp. 125–31.
62. Maḥfūẓ, *Layālī*, p. 86.
63. Ibid. pp. 127–55.
64. Ibid. p. 77.
65. Ibid. p. 76.
66. Ibid. pp. 127–55.

Chapter 4

IMPROPRIETY OF THE STATE

CODE OF CONDUCT FOR THE RULER AND RULED

Mahfouz's novel, *Layālī alf layla*, is more than just a political allegory; rather, it is also a piece of 'mirror for princes' that partakes in the education not only of the ruler but also of the ruled. The cautionary tales he tells are precisely the didactic lessons that lie at the heart of a workable blueprint for the rise of the nation-state. 'Nūr al-Dīn and Dunyazād', a condensed, dense morality tale recreated from intertexuality with multiple cycles of stories from the *Nights*, begins the instructions on power. The lessons continue for the rest of the novel, as the chapters each rewrite a *Nights*' story, chronicle the learning outcome of the lessons and its impact on the rise of the nation-state. 'Nūr al-Dīn and Dunyazād', the story of a commoner who marries into royalty in Mahfouz's rendition, is curiously sandwiched between two types of stories about desire, let us say, the first of which are told from the perspective of the desire of the ruling class (especially men in power) and the second from that of the ruled (men or women). This shift in perspective is enabled by the marriage of Nūr al-Dīn and Dunyazād. This marriage reorders the social and gender hierarchy underpinning the *Nights* stories, making it important that we follow the trajectory of the desire of characters not from the powerful male elite (Shahrayār, al-Jamālī, Karam al-Aṣīl or al-Bulṭī) but from the middle and working classes as well as women in our understanding of Mahfouz's political allegory.

'Nūr al-Dīn and Dunyazād', the title of Mahfouz's tale, evokes at first glance the *Nights* frame tale. Here, Mahfouz rewrites Dunyazād's fate. Her story in the *Nights* signals the return of the kingdom to health. She marries Shāhzamān and is anticipated to perform a miracle similar to Shahrazād's in healing a parallel king and nation. In *Layālī*, however, she does not marry Shāhzamān, a king and brother to King Shahrayār, like her sister, or a vizier or son of a vizier as expected, but a merchant, son of a merchant. More importantly, she falls prey to the machinations of two naughty genies and descends from royalty to commonness. She has no role beyond domesticity. Mahfouz's tale is, of course, more than such a rewriting of Dunyazād's destiny. Nūr al-Dīn, a recurring name in three *Nights* stories, signals *Layālī*'s possible intertextuality with *The Two Viziers Nūr al-Dīn [ᶜAlī] and his Brother Shams al-Dīn [Muḥammad],*[1] *ᶜAlī Nūr al-Dīn and Slave-Girl Anīs al-Jalīs*[2] and *ᶜAlī Nūr al-Dīn and Christian Slave-Girl Maryam.*[3] The familiarity of Mafhouz's story is not necessarily derived from the name of the protagonist. The titles of these *Nights* stories all contain the name and each story has Nūr al-Dīn as one of its lead characters, though each has another name attached to their nick name – Ḥasan in the first, and ᶜAlī in the other two, but none resembles completely Mahfouz's protagonist, who has seemingly borrowed features from all his *Nights* namesakes. He impersonates these *Nights* characters and re-enacts eclectically their stories.

Mahfouz's tale has the plot and mechanisms used in unravelling this plot in common with *The Two Viziers*. In this it crosses over into *Qamar al-Zamān*. Hamori points this out from the outset in his discussion of *Qamar al-Zamān*: '[a]t first the matter promises to unfold as much as it does in the tale of Shams al-Dīn and Nur al-Dīn';[4] the stories are indeed constructed around the same central motif: 'To settle an esthetic debate, a pair of irresponsible demons contrive an intoxicating but brief encounter between two beautiful young people from far-flung lands. The demons quit the tale and various incidents occur before the young people find each other gain'.[5] The naming of these two 'irresponsible demons' (Maymūna for Zarambāḥa and Dahnāsh for Sakhrabūṭ), their returning Nūr al-Dīn to where they take him, and having an intermediary effecting the reunion (Marzuwān in the *Nights* and Shahrayār in *Layālī*), perhaps bring *Qamar al-Zamān* equally close to 'Nūr al-Dīn and Dunyazād'. It at the same time evokes the atmosphere of the omnipresence and fear of the Sulṭān in both *The Two Viziers* and *ᶜAlī Nūr al-Dīn and Anīs al-Jalīs*. Nūr al-Dīn's marriage to Dunyazād in Mahfouz's tale of unwitting social climbing, however, refers as fittingly to *ᶜAlī Nūr al-Dīn and Maryam*, which recounts how the son of a merchant ends up marrying the daughter of a king. The similarity between Mahfouz's 'Nūr al-Dīn and Dunyazād' and *Nights*' *ᶜAlī Nūr al-Dīn and Anīs al-Jalīs* is, however, atmospheric at most. The real engagement with this *Nights* story is deferred for two more chapters, when Anīs al-Jalīs finally takes centre stage. For now, her story, though anticipated, provides reinforcement for what is brought into play in the other two Nūr al-Dīn stories: what is it like to live with and work around the omniscient tyranny of a king? Here Mahfouz scrambles further the already complex crossings of *Nights* stories, evoking their transgressions, as well as observing, interrogating and subverting their implicit ideologies, particularly those relevant to class, genealogy and gender.

The nation in Mahfouz's class-conscious novel is made up of more than just the kingly family. Like the complex world of the composite *Nights*, Mahfouz's imagined nation-state is populated and operated by the various classes that constitute the society of this nation-state. The powerful class, whether the ruling elite or wealthy merchants, the middle class, including retail traders and professionals, the labourers and the have-nots, as well as the dissidents and rebels, all have a role in determining the fate of the nation-state. The making and unmaking of the nation-state are located in its quotidian adherence to or transgression of the paradigm of proper and legitimate love, whether this adherence or transgression is effected through resurrection or reincarnation of *Nights* stories. In Mahfouz's rewritings of these stories, the consequences of incompatibility of a love match, betrayal of confidence, unbridled passion and lack of endurance in the faltering of the nation-state, drawn in bold brush strokes, affect all sectors of society. The breakdown of the royal marriage is only a part of the story. There is more to the nation-state than the fate of the king and queen. Even though the narrative of *Layālī* is driven by its gendered imagining of the nation-state, in fact, the community of Mahfouz's imagining is divisible into state, symbolised by a male authority figure, and nation, represented by a female object of desire, the fate of the nation-state is staked most emphatically in the participation of each and every social class in defining, exercising and redefining political authority. The story of Shahrayār and Shahrazād in *Layālī*, as in the *Nights*, frames all the stories, of love or otherwise. The echoes of the impropriety of the frame tale similarly reverberate in the enframed tales.

The impropriety of Shahrayār and Shahrazād's union is highlighted in Mahfouz's version of the story. The reason for this impropriety is, however, explicable less in terms of genealogy but more of responsibility in power. As an irresponsible ruler – that he should shed so much innocent blood in response to his personal pain, his queen's adultery – he is not a suitable husband to Shahrazād. A tyrannical state is not deserving of the nation it governs. Here, Shahrayār is an improper stranger to Shahrazād, proper stranger being a non-*maḥram* male permitted to marry a female within the prescription of religious law and societal edict. Mahfouz's understanding of the impropriety of the match is in part a kind of misreading. Here he turns the paradigm of epical 'national' emergence and survival on its head. The happy ending of 'erotic romance' now depends on the triumph of 'patrimonial romance'. Instead of investing the fate of the nation in the royal match and the consequent, subsequent cohering genealogy, he locates the propriety and legitimacy of the royal match in the Sulṭān's right to rule, and makes his responsibility in power a test of and testimony to this right. Even though Shahrayār learns that power is responsibility, he also realises that his tyrannical past disqualifies him from holding political office. This said, Mahfouz's misreading is in another way a penetrating reading between and beyond the lines. The love story of Shahrayār and Shahrazād's in the *Nights* in fact deviates from the pervasive paradigm of love found in the 'patrimonial romance' and 'erotic romance' it has absorbed.

There are two kinds of proper strangers who are perfectly suited for matrimony in *Nights* epics and romances as we see in the cycle of love stories incorporated into *ᶜUmar al-Nuᶜmān*: first cousins like Kān-Mā-Kān and Quḍiya-Fa-Kān and ᶜAzīz and ᶜAzīza, and complete strangers like Tāj al-Mulūk and Dunyā. The difference is, however, deceptive. The pairing of cousins in popular epics or romances is not very different from the pairing of kings and queens or princes and princesses. Both are, above all, statements of the centrality of the compatibility of any love match in the coherence of community. The pairing of first cousins is the most straightforward way of conveying what this compatibility entails. It sums up in one stroke the elaborations necessary in the pairing of, let us say, a prince from one kingdom with a princess from another. There must be symmetry in social class and societal status, upbringing and education, looks and manners, and intelligence and temperament (the *khalq* and *khuluq*). The equilibrium in the distribution of these qualities in the two principals of a match, which *ᶜUmar al-Nuᶜmān* takes for granted, is spelt out in a painstaking fashion in Mahfouz's account of what happens to Dunyazād.

Mahfouz's Nūr al-Dīn appears in *The Two Viziers* and *Qamar al-Zamān* in the garb of *Nūr al-Dīn and Maryam*. He is a merchant and son of a merchant who marries the sister of the Queen, *ukht al-sulṭāna* (as in the latter), who should have been queen in her own right. But the story of his marriage to Dunyazād is the adventure of Nūr al-Dīn's son (as in the former), the plot of whose story is constructed around a game played by two demons and unravelled by the playing out of the consequences of this game. Sakhrabūṭ and Zarambāḥa, Mahfouz's two 'evil' genies, bring Nūr al-Dīn and Dunyazād together for a night of passion, just as the two anonymous genies in the *Nights* do for Ḥasan Badr al-Dīn,[6] son of Nūr al-Dīn, and his cousin Sitt al-Ḥusn, daughter of Shams al-Dīn, or Maymūna and Dahnāsh do for Qamar al-Zamān and Budūr only to separate them and leave them trapped in longing and uncertainty. Both pairs do find their way to reunion. The trajectories of the two reunions are, however, divergent. The intention of the matchmakers seems to set the narratives off in opposite directions.

Mahfouz's Dunyazād becomes pregnant and returns to her father's house. Her mother aborts her unborn child when no trace of the bridegroom is found. The affair is hushed up, for '[i]f the Sultan gets to know your story', Shahrazād explains to her sister, 'his doubts will once more be awakened and he will revert to his low opinion of our sex and will perhaps send me to the executioner and himself go back to his previous behaviour'.[7] It is, however, impossible for Dunyazād to hide forever. She, being sought after by many powerful and wealthy men, is soon promised to Karam al-Aaṣīl, the *ḥāra*'s millionaire. In the aftermath of a war with the Byzantine armies over one of the border towns (*aḥad al-thughūr*),[8] the treasure is depleted and Shahrayār seeks a loan from the millionaire to make ends meet. The millionaire agrees on condition that Dunyazād be given to him as a new addition to his already crowded harem. Shahrayār has no choice but to accept. Dunyazād tries to postpone the inevitable by pretending to be ill. She is able to put off the wedding but not the signing of the marriage contract. When she realises she will soon be exposed, she decides to run away from home and commit suicide.

In the meantime, Nūr al-Dīn, initially a student of ᶜAbdallāh al-Balkhī following the Sufi way, now abandons his religious calling and looks for his partner of the one-night-stand. He confides in the reincarnation of al-Bulṭī, now a madman residing on a peninsula outside the city, and when he finds inadequate consolation and reassurance, he also confides in two merchants he meets one night. One of them is Shahrayār in disguise.The Sulṭān orders a search for Nūr al-Dīn's beloved. Dunyazād, who at this point in the story arrives at the peninsula determined to throw herself into the river there, meets the madman and discovers the identity of her lover. She finds her way to Nūr al-Dīn's shop and they decide to present their case to the Sulṭān. The Sulṭān, upon hearing their story, is inclined to let them marry if it had not been for one technicality – Dunyazād is still legally married to al-Aṣīl. At this critical juncture, news reaches Shahrayār that the madman has assassinated the millionaire. What could be more opportune than al-Aṣīl's death for the happy ending of 'Nūr al-Dīn and Dunyazād'? They marry with the blessings of the Sulṭān.

The happy ending of the story, which on the surface points to Shahrayār's rehabilitation from cruel despotism and, more importantly, the beginning of the democratisation of the *Sulṭana*, cannot mask an ambivalence towards the outcome of the desired political process. For one thing, this is not really the end of the story, and for another, the question 'are Nūr al-Dīn and Dunyazād really compatible?' plagues Mahfouz's narrative. Before Nūr al-Dīn meets Dunyazād, he is intent on marrying his social equal, Ḥusniyya al-Jamālī, daughter of another merchant. His change of heart is sudden, brought on by the orchestrated encounter he has with Dunyazād. Their matchmakers' joke is intended for the consumption of the followers of convention oblivious to its occasional absurdity, of those who 'have an intellect but . . . live the life of imbeciles'.[9] That Dunyazād should find a compatible suitor only in the circle of the super rich and powerful is stupidity itself.[10] Among those who compete over her, such as, al-Ṭāhir, governor of the quarter, and al-Aṣīl the millionaire, none is worthy (*kufʾ*) of the sister of the sulṭān's wife.[11] Nūr al-Dīn, a perfume seller, is 'of all males . . . most suited to my young girl', according to Zarambāḥa, 'and she of all females is most suited to him'.[12] What makes them perfect for each other, at least according to their matchmakers, is their beauty; '[h]er beauty is in truth greater than life itself'[13] and '[h]e is a paragon of handsomeness'.[14] The distance that separates them, in the estimate of Sakhrabūṭ and Zarambāḥa, is not geography but rather conventional notions of class, '[t]hey live in the same city but are as divided as the sky and the earth'.[15] Mahfouz reverses the *Nights*' formula here, for geography is what keeps the two young lovers in *The Two Viziers* and *Qamar al-Zamān* apart, not class. The importance of Nūr al-Dīn's background (*ᶜaṣl*), sidestepped in Mahfouz, is underscored by the clarity of the origin and geneaology (*ḥasab wa nasab*) in the *Nights*.

SOCIAL CLIMBING

In what Hamori calls 'comic romance',[16] Jaᶜfar tells Hārūn al-Rashīd the story of *The Two Viziers* in an attempt to ransom his slave, Rayḥān, who has a hand in the murder of an innocent woman in *The Three Apples*. The *Nights* story begins with a fight between two brothers who share the post of vizier in Cairo. Shams al-Dīn, the older brother, and Nūr al-Dīn, the younger sibling, are so close that they even discuss plans to marry two sisters on the same day and have their children marry each other.[17] The conversation, however, turns sour at this point, for Nūr al-Dīn takes the thread of his brother's daydreaming too far. He is not content with nodding in agreement, but asks about the conditions of the projected marriage of their children, 'But what dowry will you require from my son for your daughter?', a question that leads to a quarrel so injurious to both that the parting of their way is inevitable.

> The elder brother replied, 'I will take at least three thousand dinars, three orchards, and three farms in addition to an amount specified in the contract.' Nur al-Din replied, 'Brother Shams al-Din, why such an excessive dowry? Are we not brothers, and is not each of us a vizier who knows his obligations? It behoves you to offer your daughter to my son without a dowry, for the male is worthier than the female . . .' Shams al-Din said, 'Enough of your comments. Damn you for comparing your son to my daughter and thinking that he is worthier than she; by God, you lack understanding and wisdom. You say that we are partners in the vizierate, without realizing that I let you share it with me, only in order to spare your feelings by letting you assist me. By God, I will never marry my daughter to your son, not even for her weight in gold. I will never marry her to your son and have him for a son-in-law, not even if I suffer death.' When Nur al-Din heard his brother's words, he became very angry and asked, 'Will you indeed not marry your daughter to my son?' Shams al-Din replied, 'No, I will never consent to that, for he is not worth even a paring of her nail. Were I not on the eve of a journey, I would make an example of you, but when I come back, I will show you how I will vindicate my honour.' Nur al-Din's anger grew so great that he was beside himself with rage, but he hid what he felt, while the brother sulked, and the two spent the night far apart, each full of wrath against the other.[18]

I quote this long passage in full because it provides the reason for the break-up of the family and sets up the legal framework for the eventual marriage of the yet-to-be-born Ḥasan and Sitt al-Ḥusn. There is an asymmetry in the status of the two brothers at the outset, for even though Nūr al-Dīn is the handsome one he is not necessarily as accomplished as his older brother, especially if what Shams al-Dīn says of letting him share the vizierate is true. On the morrow Shams al-Dīn goes on an errand with the King and Nūr al-Dīn sets out on his own. He travels all the way to Basra where he is taken in by the vizier there, marries his daughter and becomes vizier himself. He is now his brother's true equal. Alas, he languishes in exile and dies young, leaving his son to fend for himself. Ḥasan mourns for his father for two months and abandons his duties as vizier. His king becomes impatient (and should we be surprised?) and appoints a new vizier who confiscates his properties and gets ready to capture him and put him to death. Ḥasan gets away in time and hides in his father's tomb. He meets a Jewish merchant who gives him a thousand dinars owed to his father. He puts the gold in a pouch and wraps it around his waist then falls asleep. He has no idea he has holed up in the demons' enclave. Two demons, though ignorant of his relationship with Sitt al-Ḥusn, cook up a plan to unite them, for they are of equal beauty.

Alas, her father, Vizier Shams al-Dīn has irked the King by refusing him as his daughter's suitor, especially because he has just had news of his brother and nephew, and the King has spitefully ordered that she be married to his hunchback groom that very night. Maymūna and Dahnāsh lock the hunchback up in a restroom and send Ḥasan to Sitt al-Ḥusn as the bridesgroom. As in the tale Mahfouz tells of Nūr al-Dīn and Dunyazād, the demons then take Ḥasan away, leaving him in Damascus. Nine months later Sitt al-Ḥusn gives birth to a son, ^{c}Ajīb, whose complaint about being laughed at for not knowing his father serves as catalyst for the final search for Ḥasan ten years later. Shams al-Dīn is finally granted permission from the King (who never takes him to task for what befell his hunchback groom?!) to take his family to Basra to find his brother's family. He finds his sister-in-law and decides to take her home to Cairo. And on their way they too find Ḥasan, who is now a cook in Damascus. Never mind how it happens, Ḥasan is reunited with Sitt al-Ḥusn and in time inherits Shams al-Dīn's vizierate.

Clearly Ja^{c}far must observe strict protocol in addressing al-Rashīd, whose authority he must fear in order to stay alive and whose temper he must appease in order to save his slave. He may get away with taking a jab at royal malice and abuse of power, and even foolishness – in this he is Mahfouz's intellectual interlocutor, alluding in many instances to his king's unchecked license to inflict misery and take lives on whim. Al-Rashīd, there is no doubt in the narrative, is a good, just ruler – he does want to find the murderer, but where is justice or, for that matter, wisdom in his ordering Ja^{c}far to find the murderer within three days otherwise he would have him sent to the gallows? There is little difference between this kind of abuse of power, or is it foolishness?, and the type of punishment the king in *The Two Viziers* metes out on Sitt al-Ḥusn when her father turns down his offer of marriage. In this regard Mahfouz's Shahrayār is wiser;

at least he is motivated by the needs of the state, though at the expense of the nation. Mahfouz's nation-state has, it seems, departed from the world ruled by an omniscient, omnipresent Sulṭān vested in the status quo. Would Jaᶜfar dare tell his king a story of a vizier's son marrying a king's sister or daughter? It is perhaps safer not to transgress the boundaries between the two classes after all. But this alone is not sufficient explanation for the pattern or outcome of the story. Jaᶜfar is a fictitious name given to a character and, above all, a storyteller in the *Nights* and the stories he tells willy-nilly adhere, respond to and occasionally subvert the operative paradigms of both narrative and knowledge. The love story of Ḥasan and Sitt al-Ḥusn in *The Two Viziers* is like *ᶜAzīz and ᶜAzīza* and *Tāj al-Mulūk* in *ᶜUmar al-Nuᶜmān*. It is the catalyst of family reunion and mechanism of narrative coherence that is entirely dependent on the transformation of 'romance' into 'epic'. It necessarily moulds itself in the familiar pattern of legitimate proper love.

Parental consent is secured at the outset. The conditions over which the brothers Shams al-Dīn and Nūr al-Dīn fall out become binding for a marriage contract between their son and daughter. On the morning of his daughter's wedding, Shams al-Dīn storms into Sitt al-Ḥusn's chambers determined to kill her if she has indeed consummated her marriage to the hunchback only to find out that his nephew has become his son-in-law. After an initial misunderstanding – Shams al-Dīn's conviction that his daughter has become pregnant with the hunchback's child – and confrontation – Sitt al-Ḥusn's and her father's argument over whether the hunchback is the husband she knows – Sitt al-Ḥusn leads Shams al-Dīn to the pieces of clothing Ḥasan has left behind. A close examination reveals Ḥasan's true identity. That the fantastic event is the fulfilment of a promise two brothers made to each other is confirmed by the actualisation of the details of their earlier daydream. There can be no stronger proof and vindication of the marriage than the coincidence that the brothers indeed married on the same night and that their respective wives conceived at the same time. It should not surprise us then that when Shams al-Dīn reports to the king what has happened, the king happily approves the match, conveniently forgetting that Shams al-Dīn's commitment to the tacit agreement he has with his brother, in hindsight, was what made him angry in the first instance. It is true that the anticipated family reunion has to wait for another ten years, when ᶜAjīb is old enough to feel the shame of being fatherless, before Shams al-Dīn finally embarks on a search-and-rescue mission, but the postponement, which makes room for a dazzling display of drama, comic relief and narrative dexterity, cannot detract from the assured finale. The ending is forecast in the beginning, and the beginning sets the trajectory of the story in motion all the way to the end. There will be no surprises in a story that fits the paradigm in which it has been cast. Surprises can be anticipated, in an expected way, in stories that play havoc with the paradigm. Class hopping in a class-conscious text, and the *Nights* is as guilty as *Layālī* in this regard, is a form of transgression that, unless legitimate, comes with an exacting price tag.

What is then to be expected of Nūr al-Dīn and Dunyazād's marriage? The signs do not bode well. Their eventual marriage is pervaded by a sense of scandal associated with a clandestine affair that, admittedly, is not of their own design. The scandal nevertheless prevails in the long run. The absence of a legal framework, which becomes noticeable when 'Nūr al-Dīn and Dunyazād' is juxtaposed to *The Two Viziers*, is the consequence of breach of social hierarchy and predicts the abortion. Mahfouz's narrative of nation does not condemn the affair explicitly, but rather writes into the story a kind of uncertainty. Dunyazād drops out of sight while Nūr al-Dīn uses his influence as the Sulṭān's brother-in-law to serve his friends until he, together with those around him, succumbs to the allure of Anīs al-Jalīs. Does the extra-marital affair, a form of betrayal in *Nights*' paradigmatic love story, lead to his personal ruin and the downfall of his family? The novel is silent on this, though not of his fate: he remains a retail merchant who has a marginal role in the running of the nation-state. In this he resembles the protagonist of *Nūr al-Dīn and Maryam*, who too marries into a royal family. There, the marriage of a merchant to a princess is similarly sanctioned by Hārūn al-Rashīd. The propriety and legality of this marriage of unequals are seemingly premised on the Islamicisation of Maryam. As this tale of love unfolds on the pages of the *Nights*' text, however, doubts lurk beneath the surface, menacing the happy ending of the tale.

A man marrying a woman of a social status beneath his own in the *Nights* never raises any disproving brow. Plentiful are enduring love stories of a man and his slave-girl who either find a happy ending against all odds, or perish in longing. The protagonists of these stories all seem to benefit from the devotion of their slave-girls. Shahrayār's marriage to his vizier's daughter is similarly beneficial to the king and his kingdom. *Nūr al-Dīn and Maryam* can read like a moving story of one man's love for his slave-girl. This may be the case if one overlooks the ways in which the story is set up. It begins with Nūr al-Dīn's violation of the rules of love. One day he goes off with the sons of other merchants, parties all night long, gets drunk and makes love to a courtesan. When he returns home, he slaps his father on the face when chastised and absconds with a thousand dinars. He then uses this money to buy Maryam who, it turns out, is a Byzantine princess captured into slavery while on pilgrimage. When her father's vizier 'rescues' her and takes her home, she runs away with Nūr al-Dīn every time he comes after her. When her father the king in a moment of anger forces her to marry the vizier, she conspires with Nūr al-Dīn to run away again. This time she drugs the vizier and kills her brothers in combat– she is skilled in martial arts – when they pursue her with their father. The king finally appeals to al-Rashīd for help. Al-Rashīd has the two culprits brought before him and when he hears their story and Maryam's refusal to go home, for she is now a Muslim and cannot live among the infidels let alone marry one, he is so moved that he arranges and stages their wedding ceremony and banquet, in fact, he even has the messenger beheaded. Endowed with gifts from the Sulṭān, Nūr al-Dīn returns to his family with his bride and together they live happily ever after in the *Nights*' style.

Perhaps one should here venture a question like 'happily ever after for whom'? Nūr al-Dīn is the obvious beneficiary of the marriage. He finds a more than worthy mate, wealth beyond his imagination, and his way to a family reunion. Could the same be said of Maryam? She seems to have found personal happiness with Nūr al-Dīn, a new family and comes to be integrated into a new community, but at what cost? She gives up her royal flesh and blood, marries a man clearly beneath in every way and becomes a commoner in a community not her own. More importantly, the nation from which she comes falls apart as a result of her improper conduct. The story of the downfall of her father's kingdom is the flipside of *ᶜUmar al-Nuᶜmān*. In this story of a Christian kingdom 'erotic romance' does not cohere with 'patrimonial romance' thanks to Maryam's actions, which are tantamount to ultimate betrayal from the perspective of her 'original' community. Whether telling the story of the rise of a Muslim 'nation', 'self', or the demise of a Christian 'nation', the *Nights* makes no distinction between 'self' and 'other' except in one crucial way: Muslims are inevitably triumphant. The rise and fall of both 'nations' follows an identical blueprint summed up in the paradigmatic love story. In such a story, the 'other' is cast in the image of the 'self'. The storyteller's assertion of the happy ending only draws our attention to the interrupted genealogy of both families. There will be no 'legitimate' heir to the Christian kingdom when the king eventually dies. His daughter has killed all his three sons and has not brought home a substitute heir. Do Nūr al-Din and Maryam have children?

The same question may be asked of Nūr al-Dīn and Dunyazād. And, what becomes of Shāhzamān's kingdom? Will it come to the same fateful end as that of Maryam's home community?

SEXUAL MISCONDUCT

But is not Nur al-Din's marital infidelity an echo of *Qamar al-Zamān*? *Qamar al-Zamān* arguably finishes the tale begun in *The Two Viziers* and *Nūr al-Dīn and Maryam* in Mahfouz's telling of 'Nūr al-Dīn and Dunyazād'. Hamori shows us that it is possible to look at the embedded misogyny of *Qamar al-Zamān* and come to the conclusion that, where there is tension between 'erotic romance' and 'patrimonial romance', 'patrimonial romance' will be triumphant. Women in *Qamar al-Zamān* are in charge. Budūr and Ḥayāt al-Nufūs, the two princesses Qamar al-Zamān marries, are like Maryam. They are beautiful, intelligent, brave, powerful and, more importantly, stand to inherit their fathers' kingdoms. Qamar al-Zamān, despite his blue blood, comes across as passive and occasionally foolish. In the famous scene of his first encounter with Budūr, Budūr is more aggressive in expressing her passion. Later, when Qamar al-Zamān wanders off with a precious stone he finds on Budūr following the giant bird that snatches it, Budūr follows his trails, disguised as her husband, and rules Ḥayāt al-Nufūs' kingdom; in fact, she marries her as Qamar al-Zamān first, and when she is reunited with her husband, she tacitly decides for her husband to take a second wife. Their sons are known by their names rather than their husband's: Al-Amjad is referred to as 'son of Budūr' and al-As'ad as 'son of Ḥayāt al-Nufūs'. When their sons grow up, Budūr and Ḥayāt al-Nufūs fall in love each with the son of the other and take action in expressing their desire. This is one story in which 'patrimonial romance' seemingly parts its way with 'erotic romance'. How quickly has Budūr forgotten her love for Qamar al-Zamān! Has Ḥayāt al-Nufūs ever loved Qamar al-Zamān at all? Even in the second part of the story, in which the 'betrayed' sons supposedly find their way back to a throne after their father casts them out, no love story of the type we see in *The Two Viziers* and *Nūr al-Dīn and Maryam* is visible. This is not to say that al-Amjad and al-Asᶜad do not get married; they do, but in a poignantly different way. Al-Amjad marries Bustān, daughter of the Magian responsible for kidnapping and holding al-Asᶜad hostage for years, who is in fact in love with al-Asᶜad. Al-Asᶜad himself marries Queen Marjāna with whom he is not known to be in love. Nevertheless, all the male kings come together at the end of the story, and each kingdom seems to cohere again. Qamar al-Zamān finally returns with his father and al-Amjad and al-As^cad with their maternal grandfathers, each to inherit a kingdom. 'Patrimonial romance', notwithstanding the lacklustre performance of 'erotic romance', can stand on its own. The failure of 'erotic romance' – premised on allowing women to have power – does not necessarily affect the outcome of 'patrimonial romance'. I am not entirely persuaded.

There is something that defies the necessarily imperial logic of a narrative that combines 'patrimonial romance' and 'erotic romance' – the presence of which is strongly felt – to tell the story of kings, queens and their kingdoms. Would it not be more logical, at least within the convention of narratives of nations or what we call epics, for the five kingdoms to amalgamate into one large kingdom? Would it not make more sense for Qamar al-Zamān to inherit three kingdoms then divide them between his sons, who will also acquire two more new kingdoms? Of these two kingdoms one may ask a further question: what is the fate of ᶜMadīnat al-Majūs, of which al-Amjad is king for a while, and of Marjāna's kingdom? The ending is simply too wilfully tidy in that it does not account for the untidy details. The narrative, albeit too hasty in arriving at an epical ending, is not oblivious to the consequences of the defeat of 'erotic romance'. *Qamar al-Zaman* reads like another, though longer, version of the story of Maryam in *Nūr al-Dīn and Maryam*. In the shadow of transgressions occurring in 'erotic romance', 'patrimonial romance' comes to read like a romance aspiring to be epic that fails to make the transformation. The story is less about the political and social consequences of allowing women to retain power or of men marrying women superior to them in Mahfouz's novel but more about a nation-state rising out of the ashes of an empire. 'Nūr al-Dīn and Dunyazād' is but a piece, perhaps two, in the mosaic of a 'homeland' that has yet to be. Nūr al-Dīn's ascent is parallel to Dunyazād's descent.

Dunyazād in Mahfouz's novel belongs to the 'kingly ruling class', in good company with Shahrayār and Sharhazād, who must cede the throne in order to allow a new form of political structure – a democratic, modern nation-state – to come into being. She looks more like a reincarnation of Maryam, even of Budūr or Ḥayāt al-Nufūs on occasion, than of Sitt al-Ḥusn, but she has nothing of their courage and determination. Like them, she is, and must be, written out of a queenly destiny. Her life story now mirrors that of Shahrazād in one poignant aspect: she too will be 'abandoned' by her husband. The parallel, disrupted here, does not lead to an untwining of the fates of Shahrazād and Dunyazād; rather, their destinies remain interdependent. Dunyazād's story now complements Shahrazād's and provides an example of what happens when the code of paradigmatic love is flagrantly flouted. The absence of love between Shahrayār and Shahrazād is only a first symptom of much deeper malaise. Dunyazād's story, read against the story Dandān tells, is a cautionary tale of all the things any 'erotic romance' should not do in order not to endanger 'patrimonial romance'. *Qamar al-Zamān* may look like *^{c}Umar al-Nu^{c}mān* at first glance, but is in fact cast in the latter's counter image, its evil twin, so to speak. The patterns of these two *Nights*' stories are not exact duplicates. *^{c}Umar al-Nu^{c}mān* has an additional layer not accorded to *Qamar al-Zamān*. In the latter, the story of ^{c}Umar al-Nu^{c}mān's family and that of Tāj al-Mulūk are collapsed into one. This tripartite story begins like *Tāj al-Mulūk* and ends vaguely like *^{c}Umar al-Nu^{c}mān*. In the first part of the story, Prince Qamar al-Zamān, like Tāj al-Mulūk, refuses all entreaties to marry until he meets Budūr. In the second part, Qamar al-Zamān is ^{c}Umar al-Nu^{c}mān-like, marrying two women and sowing the seeds for future trouble. The third part, which similarly follows an enframed love story, overlaps with the ending of *^{c}Umar al-Nu^{c}mān* but diverges in a significant way. The ^{c}Umar al-Nu^{c}mān family is reunited, cohering into an 'empire', and it seems that they together will defeat their enemies, while Qamar al-Zamān's family disperse in three kingdoms. How would King Shāhrimān, also the name of Tāj al-Mulūk's father, feel as he returns to his kingdom with his long lost son without the rest of the family, his daughters-in-law and grandsons? The condition for the kingdom with which the story begins remains unchanged. Is the kingdom to stay heirless? This less-than-hoped-for outcome may be explicable in terms of the curious workings of 'unrequited' love.

The eclipse of Qamar al-Zamān and Budūr's love, Daniel Beaumont explains, is attributable to temporarily distinguished desire. Desire, in this Freudian/Lacanian interpretation, is as narcissistic as love, often stirred by the subject finding in or with the object what he or she lacks. The precious jewel symbolises this lack in Qamar al-Zamān and when he takes it away from Budūr he is freed of his desire,[19] and she of bondage to this desire. This explains only one incident of the eruption and extinction of desire or the ebb and flow of love in this cycle of stories. Parts of this story may inadvertently reveal something about the nature and motivational function of desire and love, but perhaps these are ultimately facile metaphors of the workings of power and the principles of 'national' coherence. The trajectory of desire and love here falls into a pattern that is diametrically opposed to that of *ᶜUmar al-Nuᶜmān*. The Qamar al-Zamān and Budūr episode is a false set-up. It lures us into the kind of symmetry *ᶜUmar al-Nuᶜmān* has accustomed us to only to play games with our expectations. Lovers come in couples, not triads or quads. Three is always too much of a crowd. ᶜUmar al-Nuᶜmān's dalliance with more than one partner outside a legitimate framework brings his kingdom to the brink of destruction. ᶜAzīz's womanising results in his castration. Bringing a third party into a couple is a form of betrayal of love; it violates the one cardinal rule of love: exclusive devotion of the lover to the beloved that is loyalty. The triangulation of Qamar al-Zamān, Budūr and Ḥayāt al-Nufūs forecasts the trouble ahead. Their union, however, is the crystallisation of various narrative strands steered by ominous signs of impropriety.

The story brims with impropriety, ranging from aggressive expression of passion, to homosexuality and incest. Budūr, for example, caresses every inch of a sleeping Qamar al-Zamān before they are wed. She dallies with Ḥayāt al-Nufūs, kissing her on the mouth, embracing her and 'playing' with her. There is more than a hint of lesbian sex in the Arabic use of mutually responsive Form VI of the verbs for playing (*laᶜibatā*), embracing (*taᶜānaqatā*) and kissing (*tabāwasatā*) – in this order – followed by their sleeping until the call for the dawn prayer (*nāmalā ila qarībi l-ādhān*).[20] In the rather comic scene of Qamar al-Zamān's reunion with Budūr the reference to male homosexuality is clear: Qamar al-Zamān, who does not recognise Budūr disguised as him and, consents, though reluctantly, to have sex with his own double, and Budūr reveals herself only when they are already in the process of making love. Is Budūr and Ḥayāt al-Nufūs's incestual desire for each other's sons the playing out of a hint dropped early in the narrative? How are King Shāhrimān's feeling for and behaviour around his son to be qualified? The night he sends Qamar al-Zamān to be imprisoned in a tower cell for disobeying his wish three times and insulting him in public, he is sleepless, tossing and turning and shedding bitter tears. He, the story goes, 'could not sleep every night unless he has put his arm under Qamar al-Zamān's neck (*kulla laylatin lam yajiʾ lahu n-nawmu illā idhā waḍaᶜa dhirāᶜahu taḥta raqabati Qamari z-Zamān*)'.[21]

Proper love cannot prosper under these circumstances, when desire goes awry and breaks all rules of legitimacy. Betrayal (*ghadr*) necessarily follows impatience and weakness (*jazaᶜ*). Both Qamar al-Zamān and Budūr go mad when they are separated the first time. Budūr and Ḥayāt al-Nufūs strike out in anger when their wishes are ungratified. To cover up their disloyalty to Qamar al-Zamān, they resort to a second act of betrayal and,

Potiphar-like, they accuse al-Amjad and al-As^{c}ad of the very treacherous act they commit. Is it any wonder that al-Amjad and al-As^{c}ad do not find love? *Qamar al-Zamān* is the story of what can go wrong when the code of paradigmatic love is violated. This code is not imported from *^{c}Umar al-Nu^{c}mān*; rather, it is encrypted in its own enframed story of *Ni^{c}ma and Nu^{c}m*. This story of love is the exact opposite of *^{c}Azīz and ^{c}Azīza*. It is about the happy ending a devoted couple will as a matter of course achieve thanks to their adherence to proper conduct in love. Ni^{c}matallāh grows up with Nu^{c}m, a slave-girl his father buys. They are inseparable. Their love for each other is so obvious that his parents consent to their marriage. Their marriage does not dim their desire for each other and they remain consistently devoted to each other. This devotion becomes even stronger when they are separated. Al-Ḥajjāj, governor of their hometown Kufa, abducts and sends her to Damascus intended as a gift for his caliph ^{c}Abd al-Malik b. Marwān. In the caliphal palace she falls ill, as Mahfouz's Dunyazād pretends to do, pining for Ni^{c}ma, postponing her 'marriage' to the caliph. In the meantime, Ni^{c}ma falls ill too, longing for Nu^{c}m. A well-travelled Persian physician his father summons makes an accurate diagnosis and takes him to Damascus knowing that his reunion with Nu^{c}m will cure him. Indeed it does. The reunion, however, takes some manoeuvring. Ni^{c}ma disguises himself as a physician and sneaks into the caliphal palace and sends Nu^{c}m a revelatory note. They then present the case to the caliph's sister in charge of Nu^{c}m, who convinces her brother that it is kingly of him to let them go home. He does.

The overlapping in the pattern and theme between the first part of the frame tale and enframed tale cannot be missed. Union followed by separation then reunion, love sickness during separation and recovery at reunion, and the centrality of a third party (Marzūwān in the frame tale and the Persian physician in the enframed tale) in effecting the reunion are some of the obvious indicators. *Ni^{c}ma and Nu^{c}m* should have been the mechanism of transformation in a similar way as the cycle of love stories embedded in *Umar al-Nu^{c}mān* is, but it is not. Perhaps the symptomatic difference in love sickness is key. Madness in the frame tale is not duplicated in the enframed tale. Madness, as I shall explore fully in *Politics of Nostalgia in the Arabic Novel*, signals that all is not well and signifies the deviation of the frame tale from the enframed one. 'Erotic romance' cannot guide 'patrimonial romance' and romance stops short of turning into epic. Qamar al-Zamān departs with Marzūwān and leaves signs of his death, leading his father to perpetual mourning. Shāhrimān's kingdom is practically the house of sorrows (*bayt al-aḥzān*) he erects in memory of his son. Qamar al-Zamān's kingdom, inherited from Ḥayāt al-Nufūs's father, similarly becomes the house of sorrows he erects in memory of his innocent sons when he discovers that he has ordered them killed prematurely. More significantly, the departures of future kings, Qamar al-Zamān, al-Amjad and al-Asᶜad, do not lead to their hoped-for heroic transformation. None slays a dragon, reunites with his beloved, and goes home to restore their kingdoms. The less-than-epical ending of the story makes sense. Despite the epical bluff at the end of the story – the clamorous royal arrivals of Marjāna, Qamar al-Zamān and his father Shāhrimān, al-Malik al-Ghayūr, father of Budūr, and Armānūs, father of Ḥayāt al-Nufūs, who gather at the gates of the City of Magians, where al-Amjad has been vizier, for a seeming reunion – they in the end disperse, breaking up the 'family' that should have been at the core of an empire. The empire as a matter of course does not cohere.

AFFAIRS OF THE STATE

That kingdom should give way to a nation-state is a matter taken for granted in any imagination of nation. In this kind of imagination, narrative of kingdom must be formulated as romance and that of nation-state epic. The twining of the two narratives, however, does link inextricably the two different formulations of community, making the fate and shape of one relevant to the other. The nation-state's health is inevitably contaminated by the rampant infections of an empire huffing and puffing its last breath but refusing to give up the ghost. There are inescapable dangers in reviving then reformulating paradigms belonging to the past for the purpose of the present or future. Patriarchy and social hierarchy, two phenomena interrogated in 'Nūr al-Dīn and Dunyazād', are in effect major stumbling blocks in the formation of the nation-state. In a gendered nationalist discourse that revives a patriarchal story of the inevitable fall of a kingdom that privileges women, the femininised nation (Dunyazād) is not allowed to overcome the tyranny of the masculinised state. In a class-conscious text that resurrects cautionary tales about class hopping, democratisation of the state (Nūr al-Dīn) is undermined. Nūr al-Dīn's marital infidelity, a drop in the ocean of betrayals recurring in the world he inhabits, is symptomatic of what ails the process of transformation from kingdom to nation-state. Where power is contested, betrayal is a premise not consequence. No one is immune.

The rampage of sexual desire in 'Mughāmarāt ᶜUjr al-Ḥallāq', 'Anīs al-Jalīs' and 'Qūt al-Qulūb' is, in a sense, about the political ambition of the powerless and its collision with the will of the powerful. In these three chapters, Mahfouz reorganises the bits and pieces he picks and chooses from four cycles of stories from the *Nights*, *The Hunchback*, *Nūr al-Dīn and Anīs al-Jalīs*, *Ghānim Ibn Ayyūb and Qūt al-Qulūb* and *The Seven Viziers* (or *Wiles of Women*) to set the stage for the transformation of kingdom into nation-state. Most of the stories contained in these cycles, albeit told to one king or another, are about merchants, tailors, barbers, butchers, beggars, cobblers, eunuchs, slave-girls, and wives with roaming eyes. These stories are rewritten in the middle chapters of the novel in such a way that questions the status quo. They, more importantly, expose the corruption of those in charge and pave the way for a radical change of personnel.

ᶜUjr's adventures, or rather misadventures, are but some examples of what can go wrong when power falls in the wrong hands. Mishandling of power comes in the form of allegories about desire going out of control. ᶜUjr borrows from the *Nights*' barber in *The Hunchback* his ability to tell stories – he is more of a storyteller (*rāwiya*) than a barber (*ḥallāq*) in Mahfouz's novel,[22] and from *The Hunchback* the frame tale, and the enframed story of the young merchant from Mosul. ᶜUjr, husband to Fattūḥa and father to the good ᶜAlāʾ al-Dīn, whose story will be told later as part of the rise of middle class to power, is a man ruled by his sexual appetite. His adventures begin when he meets up with the governor Yūsuf al-Ṭāhir's sister, Jullanār, who invites him to her 'pleasure palace' outside the governor's mansion for an evening of fun. Like the young merchant from Mosul in the *Nights* story, which the Jewish doctor tells the king of China in order to save the lives of those accused of killing his royal clown the hunchback, he is not content with his affair with Jullanār especially when he meets her equally beautiful but younger sister Zahrayār and begins an affair with her. Alas, when he awakes in the morning he finds Zahrayār's dead body next to him. Before he runs away, he does not forget to pick up an expensive diamond necklace and put it in his pocket. This first adventure comes to an end when he can no longer enjoy his time with Jullanār at the scene of the crime, and when Jullanār disappears.

He then sets his sight first on Ḥusniyya al-Jamālī, then on Qamar al-ᶜAṭṭār. He moves in for the kill, when on one occasion at the quarter's café the mob beats up Shahrayār's clown, the hunchback Shamlūl, and puts him in a temporary coma. Unlike the hapless characters in the *Nights* cycle who send the hunchback's body on a fool's errand, hoping to escape punishment for a crime they did not commit, ᶜUjr is full of malice. He hides, in fact, imprisons Shamlūl in his house with the help of his wife Fattūḥa and blackmails Ḥasan al-ᶜAṭṭār into agreeing to let him take Qamar as his second wife, as well as extorting large sums of money from those who took part in the beating. His wife exposes his ploy when she hears the news of his second marriage. He is captured by the mob and taken to the governor who is intent on letting him go, on account of ᶜUjr's friendship with Nūr al-Dīn, the royal brother-in-law, until he discovers his sister's diamond necklace in his pocket. He swiftly changes his mind and sentences ᶜUjr to be beheaded for murder. Dandān suddenly arrives with an order from Shahrayār to retry the culprit. In the new trial, it transpires that both the governor and his private secretary have known about the immoral lifestyle of Jullanār and Zahrayār and, more importantly, that Jullanār has murdered Zahrayār out of jealousy. Unlike the ending of the *Nights*' tale, which tells of the governor's discovery of one sister murdering another, the murderer dying of remorse, and his marrying their youngest sister to the youth, Mahfouz's tale ends with the dismissal of al-Ṭāhir and his private secretary Ḥusām al-Faqī, the flogging of the members of the café, and the confiscation of ᶜUjr's properties.

That some governors cannot be trusted with power is a recurring theme in the *Nights* too. *Nūr al-Dīn and Anīs al-Jalīs* is as much about enduring love as about the rivalry of two viziers, the good al-Faḍl Ibn Khāqān and evil al-Muᶜīn Ibn Ṣāwī. King Muḥammad Ibn Sulaymān al-Zaynī of Basra asks Ibn Khāqān to buy him a talented, beautiful slave-girl for ten thousand dinars. Ibn Khāqān obliges. Alas, when he takes Anīs al-Jalīs home for a rest, she falls in love with his son Nūr al-Dīn. The king promptly forgets about the entire affair and the young lovers are able to marry. Ibn Khāqān dies and Nūr al-Dīn squanders the family fortune and is forced to sell Anīs al-Jalīs in the slave market. When he realises that Ibn Ṣāwī intends foul play, he runs away with his beloved to Baghdad. There he persuades Hārūn al-Rashīd's gardener to let them stay at the royal gardens and to join in their merry making. Al-Rashīd spies the activities and goes to investigate with his vizier Jaᶜfar and guard Masrūr. He hears Nūr al-Dīn's story and decides to appoint him king of Basra instead of al-Zaynī. He sends the order with Nūr al-Dīn. At Ibn Ṣāwī's instigation, al-Zaynī arrests Nūr al-Dīn and orders his execution. Jaᶜfar arrives in Basra in time to rescue Nūr al-Dīn. He makes him king and three days later Nūr al-Dīn asks Jaᶜfar to take him to al-Rashīd. Jaᶜfar orders al-Zaynī and Ibn Ṣāwī to accompany them. In Baghdad, al-Rashīd has Masrūr behead Ibn Ṣāwī and lets Nūr al-Dīn remain in Baghdad when the latter expresses his disinterest in kingship. Al-Rashīd, in a typical *Nights*' fashion, saves the day again.

Mahfouz's 'Anīs al-Jalīs' tells a rather different story, even as it makes use of the characters in its pre-text. Sulaymān al-Zaynī is now governor of the *ḥāra*, with al-Faḍl Ibn Khāqān as his private secretary and al-Mu'īn Ibn Ṣāwī his chamberlain. Anīs al-Jalīs, however, is Zarambāḥa masquerading as the lead character of 'the story of the woman and her five suitors' taken from *The Seven Viziers*. This *Nights*' story, the vernacular version of the famous *Sindbādnāmeh* (Arabic; *Sindbād al-Ḥakīm*), is one of the stories on the wiles of women the seven vizier exchange with the royal concubine who, upon failing to seduce the prince, accuses him of impropriety before the king. The prince cannot defend himself as he is gagged by a prophecy: during this trying period of his life he must be silent for seven days otherwise he will die. Storytelling in this cycle of stories is clearly for the purpose of postponing death and saving life. The particular story the sixth sagacious vizier tells his king is about a beautiful adulterous woman whose young lover, a servant, is arrested during a street brawl when her husband is away. When she turns to the governor, the judge, the vizier and the king in person to petition for his freedom, they invite her to their houses. She turns around and invites them to her house at roughly the same time. She then goes to a carpenter to have him make a cupboard with four compartments. When he also asks her to pay him by bestowing her favours upon him, she asks him to make the cupboard with five compartments and promises that he will receive his payment when he delivers the cupboard on an agreed date. On that day, the carpenter arrives first with the delivery only to hear a knock on the door before he is paid. Pretending that her husband is at the door, she hides the carpenter in one compartment, locks him in, and receives her other guests one by one and similarly locks them in the remaining compartments. She extorts a release note from the judge, gets her young lover out of prison and runs away with him, leaving her prisoners in the cupboard for days until the hullabaloo they make alerts the neighbours. When they are rescued in their state of undress, they are all scandalised for their less than impeccable mores.

Mahfouz indeed concludes his tale of desire gone mad with a similar plot. 'Anīs al-Jalīs', however, begins more like 'the story of the Christian merchant' in *The Hunchback* about a young man who, having spent all his money on his beloved, attempts stealing from the chief of police and has his right hand cut off for punishment. Anīs al-Jalīs appears in the *ḥāra* inexplicably and takes up residence in a red house (*al-dār al-ḥamrā'*). Her charms make men tremble with desire and her liberality turns her house into the Mecca of the rich and powerful. The wealthy of the *ḥāra*, starting with al-Ṭāhir, the forcibly retired governor, and ending with al-Faqī, al-ᶜAṭṭār, Jalīl al-Bazzāz, like the Christian merchant in the *Nights* story, exhaust their resources and end up penniless. Worse, when al-Faqī sees al-Ṭāhir at the door, he kills him in jealousy and eventually loses his head. Bayyūmī al-Armal, chief of police, falls for her wiles too when he is asked to investigate. He helps himself to the government treasury and is beheaded too when he is found out. The new trinity of power in the *ḥāra*, al-Zaynī, al-Faḍl and al-Muᶜīn, together with Nūr al-Dīn, Dandān and even Shahrayār, all are unable to escape the tight grip of sexual desire Anīs al-Jalīs rouses in them. They end up like the five suitors in the *Nights*' tale, in a cupboard, until ᶜAbdallāh the madman frees them, and lets them slip away in the darkness of the night. The wisdom in not exposing them, as the madman tells his alter ego ᶜAbdallāh the seaman, is that the community will always need a leader: 'I was sorry that morning should come and the citizens should not find a sultan or a vizier or a governor or a private secretary or a chief of police. They would have been taken by the strongest of the wicked'.[23] The simultaneous need for leadership and the corruptibility of power have presented a paradoxical challenge to humanity since time immemorial. In a situation where one cannot live with or without leadership, how is power to be handled? Mahfouz prescribes a two-pronged approach implicit in his palimpsestic narrative: humanising power by exposing humanity's vulnerability towards its corruptive influence, and by replacing the familiar paradigm of power embedded in extant modes of narration with an alternative one.

The culpability of man, especially in abusing power, is most readily manifest in the ways the powerful protect themselves and their own. Even the most benign from among the ruling elite abuse power on occasions. The lure of sexual desire, an allegory of the wayward trajectory of power, is Hydra-like, and paves multifarious paths for those seduced by its dazzling glory. The elite's infatuation with Anīs al-Jalīs in Mahfouz's tale is the manifestation of one of the many heads of the Hydra. 'Qūt al-Qulūb' is yet another. Like its *Nights*' precursor, it tells of a conspiracy to murder a favoured royal concubine. In the *Nights*' story of *Ghānim Ibn Ayyūb*, the eponymous protagonist witnesses Qūt al-Qulūb, doped, being buried alive by three black eunuchs one night while on a commercial trip to Baghdad. He rescues her and they fall in love. Their relationship, however, remains Platonic. She, being the caliph's consort, is forbidden to him. She does tell him her story. Queen Zubayda, jealous of al-Rashīd's affection for Qūt al-Qulūb, orders her eunuchs to get rid of the rival. She even stages a wake to deceive her husband. Al-Rashīd of course finds out, retrieves Qūt al-Qulūb, but exiles her from his affections, thinking that she has made love to Ghānim. He also sends words to his governor in Damascus, one Muḥammad Ibn Sulaymān al-Zaynī, to arrest Ghānim as soon he as turns up in his home town and to confiscate all his properties. In the meantime Ghānim falls ill, pining for Qūt al-Qulūb. He languishes away in the hospital (Māristān) he is taken to. Al-Rashīd finds out the truth from his banished concubine one night, and the just ruler that he is in the *Nights*, he orders Ghānim found. Qūt al-Qulūb begins her search and eventually finds him in the house of the hospital orderly who has taken him in. Lo and behold, his mother and sister turn up at the same time. All four come before the caliph and he restores Ghānim's properties to him, gives him Qūt al-Qulūb, and himself marries Ghānim's sister, Fitna. Zubyada, of course, goes unpunished.

In Mahfouz's reformulation of the story, there is an attempt at rectifying the kind of justice usually meted out in the *Nights* by al-Rashīd. Rajab the porter, like Ghānim Ibn Ayyūb, witnesses a number of slaves burying a box in the cemetery at night. He sneaks in afterwards to inspect the box, and finds a female body. He leaves the body and runs away. Alas, he runs into Saḥlūl the wholesale merchant outside the cemetery. After a few moments of reflection, he decides to report the crime to al-Mu^{c}īn, chief of police. When he does, al-Mu^{c}īn arrests him rather than look for the real culprit. The body belongs to Qūt al-Qulūb, the governor al-Zaynī's favourite slave-girl, with whose recovery al-Mu^{c}īn is charged. Saḥlūl is called in as al-Mu^{c}īn's witness. When he arrives, he pronounces that Qūt al-Qulūb is still alive. The doctor, al-Mahīnī, is summoned and he successfully manages to revive her. When she awakens and sees al-Mu^{c}īn in front of her, she announces that he is the real culprit. Al-Mu^{c}īn angrily blurts out that al-Zaynī's wife, Jamīla, is his accomplice. A confused al-Zaynī decides to let go of al-Mu^{c}īn and Jamīla, as well as Qūt al-Qulūb, who now feels unsafe at home. The scandal would have been hushed up if Shahrayār had not heard Qūt al-Qulūb's sad songs on one of his nocturnal journeys. When he finds out the truth, he is at first tempted to have al-Mu^{c}īn and Jamīla executed, but in the end decides to only dismiss al-Zaynī and al-Mu^{c}īn from their posts and confiscate their properties, remembering that they are among the best men of the city. But he has Jamīla and al-Mu^{c}īn flogged as punishment for conspiracy to commit murder.

In what may be called a 'cabinet reshuffle' – in the aftermath of al-Zaynī and al-Mu^{c}īn's dismissal, al-Faḍl is promoted to governor,

Haykal al-Za^c^faranī private secretary and Darwīsh ʻUmrān the chief of police – there is acknowledgement that humanity, despite its good intentions, is fallible and often irresponsible in power. This recognition is seen in Shahrayār's willingness to pardon al-Zaynī at Qūt al-Qulūb's behest. Al-Zaynī may have kept his head, but his irresponsibility cost him his position and wealth. This, at least, is better justice than what we read in the *Nights*' tale of ʻa morally random universe' ruled by al-Rashīd where the culprit gets away scot-free (but to punish Zubayda for a fictitious crime would be historically implausible). This subtle subversive engagement with a familiar paradigm of knowledge invested in the figure of political authority is both inspired by the *Nights* stories Mahfouz rewrites in these middle chapters and dictated by the aspirations of the nation-state. The authority figure in *The Merchant and the Genie*, *The Fisherman and the Demon*, *The Porter and the Three Ladies*, *The Three Apples*, *The Hunchback*, *Nūr al-Dīn and Anīs al-Jalīs*, *Ghānim Ibn Ayyūb and Qūt al-Qulūb* and *The Seven Viziers* is cast in the image of a simultaneous historical and mythical Hārūn al-Rashīd. These stories, unlike *^c^Umar al-Nu^c^mān* and *Qamar al-Zamān* concern themselves understandably first and foremost with the running of an empire rather than the rise of one. The kingdom, after all, already exists. The real or mock historical, geographical and systemic settings of these stories say as much.

It is not the function of kings in these stories to marry and produce heirs, but rather to ensure that the machinery of the kingdom is well oiled and running smoothly. Justice, however one may wish to define it, is this machinery that needs constant oiling. The qualities bestowed upon *Nights*' al-Rashīd are reflections, or refractions, of the tenets listed and elaborated in a wide variety of *adab* works intended as compendia for the education of a cultured Muslim. Tough, decisive, caring, kind, generous, and forgiving are some of these qualities we see in *Nights*' al-Rashīd. The one distinguishing mark of a ruler, however, is his ability to spread justice in his kingdom, and dispel injustice. These stories are as much about the qualifications of a good (*ṣāliḥ*) ruler as the harmony this ruler can bring to the community he governs. In the stories where he plays the ultimate arbitrator of injustice – *ẓulm* – that is often manifest in forms of betrayal, ʻerotic romance' conveniently serves as an allegory of either loyalty that is rewarded or betrayal that is punished as I have already shown. Mahfouz's novel takes up the responsibility of educating the king bequeathed by *adab* and expands its remit to include all members of the nation-state. The health of the nation-state cannot depend on the ruler handling power justly alone.

Rather, the responsibility for power now resides in every member of the community, from those in government to each individual who has a stake in seeing justice done and harmony prevail. Qualifications of a good ruler necessarily transfer to each individual who is expected, as we find *The Fisherman and the Demon*, both to be good and to do good, to be able to handle power reasonably and responsibly. This education in the responsibility of power is effected through stories of educating desire, source of chaos and injustice and motor driving betrayal into love, symbol of reason.

EDUCATION OF THE NATION

The beginning of the turning point in Mahfouz's narrative of nation may be located in his reformulation of *Nights*' *ᶜAlāᵓ al-Dīn Abū al-Shāmāt*, in which only one strand of the *Nights*' cycle, of the same title, is recast in the process of its integration into *The Hunchback*. ᶜAlāᵓ al-Dīn is ᶜUjr's son, a barber by virtue of being the son of one, not the son of a merchant in the *Nights* pre-text. He is identified by ᶜAbdallāh al-Balkhī as a worthy disciple, his piety obvious to all around him, and comes to be favoured by the Shaykh. In fact, al-Balkhī marries his only daughter, Zubayda, to him. The names ᶜAlāᵓ al-Dīn, identified as one who has moles on his cheeks, and Zubayda, his first wife, points to the *Nights* cycle, but the intertextual engagement does not become fully visible until later, when in the following chapter of the novel, a 'false caliph' retries the case of ᶜAlāᵓ al-Dīn, who is executed for a crime he did not commit. In 'the Sultan', water-carrier Ibrāhīm al-Saqqā' stages ᶜAlāᵓ al-Dīn's trial, accidentally attended by an insomniac Shahrayār making one of his nocturnal rounds, and exposes the role of Ḥabaẓlam (or Ḥubbẓulm) Baẓaẓa in the plot against the barber. Like his namesake in the *Nights*, Ḥabaẓlam Baẓaẓa is the governor's son and competes with ᶜAlāᵓ al-Dīn for the love of a woman.

In the *Nights*, his mother conspires with a thief, Ahmad Qamāqim, behind the governor's back to steal Hārūn al-Rashīd's dress, rosary, dagger, kerchief, signet-ring and a lanthorn of pearls and to place them in ᶜAlāᵓ al-Dīn's house, when Ḥabaẓlam loses his bid for a slave-girl to ᶜAlāᵓ al-Dīn. ᶜAlāᵓ al-Dīn, a royal boon companion, suddenly loses favour with the Caliph and is sentenced to hang. His friend, an honourable thief Aḥmad al-Danaf, thankfully comes to his help. He rescues ᶜAlāᵓ a-Dīn from the gallows, uncovers the plot, albeit almost twenty years later, exposes the mischief-makers and restores his place among the Caliph's entourage. In *Layālī*, Ḥabaẓlam is the chief of police, Darwīsh ᶜUmrān's son, who is desirous of having Zubayda for his wife. When he fails in his endeavours, he and his father, in concert with al-Muᶜīn, the now dismissed corrupt governor, hash a plot against ᶜAlāᵓ al-Dīn. They steal a jewel from the house of the governor al-Faḍl and put it in ᶜAlāᵓ al-Dīn's, together with forged letters pointing to the barber's membership in opposition groups, the Shiᶜites and the Kharajites, a membership considered betrayal to the Sulṭān. Mahfouz's ᶜAlāᵓ al-Dīn is not as fortunate as his *Nights* counterpart. He is swiftly tried and sentenced to death by the governor whose jewel he allegedly stole. His death, as opposed to the survival and redemption of his *Nights*' namesake, bespeaks the lack of faith in the kind of justice that depends on the king's magnanimity. That a moral ruler is at the helm of the state does not necessarily entail that justice will pervade in the nation-state. Here, Mahfouz turns the *Nights*' paradigm on its head yet again. If the charismatic al-Rashīd, by his mere presence in the *Nights*, ensures 'perfect' justice, the world of *Layālī* is hauntingly 'imperfect'.

Shahrayār is himself of dubious qualifications as king. This is how Fāḍil Sanᶜān assesses him: 'Sometimes . . . he repents of his repentance, and for sure he is not the most deserving of the Muslims to be in sovereign power'.[24] He comes face to face with this realisation during his attendance of the mock trial of his officers mounted by the false caliph. He is, it seems, kept in the dark about the corruption of his supposedly instrument of justice. The chief of police, Darwīsh ᶜUmrān, unlike his *Nights* counterpart, charismatic Governor Khālid, is the lead conspirator. Governor al-Faḍl does not bring the guilty parties to justice when he finds out the truth, notwithstanding belatedly. His private secretary, Haykal al-Zaᶜfarānī, similarly prefers to sit on the truth rather than 'right the wrong'. Fear of consequences is their excuse. Alas, this fear internalised by his officers is in turn a vote of no confidence in the king. After all, who dares expect justice from a formerly blood-thirsty tyrant? Shahrayār's experience in the alternative world staged by Ibrāhīm the water-carrier serves as a reminder of the injustices lived by his subjects, especially the poor. It also marks his exit from power games. Before he does, however, he makes sure he appoints the right people instead. The new governor, ᶜAbbās al-Khalījī, private secretary, Sāmī Shukrī, and chief of police, Khalīl Fāris, all 'came to their positions following bitter experiences that toppled those who had transgressed',[25] according to Sakhrabūṭ and Zarambāḥa, 'no depravity is to be expected from them in the near future'.[26] This could have been the happy ending of the novel – there are now responsible people running the *ḥāra*, but it is not. The nation-state imagined here is a democracy struggling to take shape and impose itself on the ordering of the world. All ought to be free to take part in the political process. However, only those who pass the test of power will be qualified to lead.

The following two chapters of the novel, 'Ṭāqiyat al-Ikhtifāʾ' and 'Maᶜrūf al-Iskāfī', are understandably a chequered history of the middle and working classes' foray into power. While Fāḍil Sanᶜān, a member of the middle class, fails miserably, Maᶜrūf al-Iskāfī passes the test with flying colours. Given a cap of invisibility, Fāḍil is not able to resist the lure of power to transgress all bounds of propriety and legality, and commits a series of acts the likes of which he has been denouncing all along, from stealing to bullying and raping. He is finally exposed when he lets his powers get to his head, his cap taken away by the very genie who gave it to him. Maᶜrūf, whose biography comes vaguely close to that of his namesake in the *Nights*, is a cobbler married to a shrew. Both prosper on the basis of a bluff. The *Nights* good-hearted labourer is whisked away by a genie to a faraway kingdom, pretends to be a rich merchant, lives extravagantly on borrowed money, marries a princess for it, then finds Solomon's ring and saves the day. Mahfouz's cobbler, on the hand, brags in the *ḥāra* that he owns Solomon's ring and when his bluff is called a genie saves his face. He prospers, borrowing and taking gifts from those who covet the powers of his ring, and comes to be one of the richest men in town. The genie, either Sakhrabūṭ or Zarambāḥa, has favoured him for a reason. They want ᶜAbdallāh al-Balkhī and the madman killed. Here, Maᶜrūf pauses, reminds himself of the fates of Fāḍil, his father Sanᶜān al-Jamālī, and al-Bulṭī, and turns the genie(s) down. He is exposed, arrested and put in jail. Nothing bad, however, happens to him. Shahrayār frees him at the eleventh hour and appoints him the governor of the *ḥāra* and, at the suggestion of Maᶜrūf, Nūr al-Dīn private secretary and the madman chief of police.

NARRATION OF NATION

There is something touching, from the perspective of the kind of nation-states familiar to us today, about seeing persons we know intimately in positions of power and responsibility. It will, at least, be possible to work with them; they are, whatever happens, from our midst, not imposed from outside. The nation-state that is the *ḥāra* has finally cohered and been set on the right path, its leaders and guardians having risen up through their own ranks. The exit of Shahrayār, premised on the education and training of the citizens in the responsibility of power, is then natural and ought to be expected. His continued role in the appointment of the officers of the state is, at this juncture, an indication that the hope-for-democracy is not yet achieved. The coming together of nation and state, forced from above, may yet prove untenable. For political authority and justice remain the privileges of a select few. More significantly, power being what it is; responsible political authority will always be a process of taming the desire it inspires and a protracted resistance to its allure. Shahrayār's abandonment of his kingdom and palace at the end of the novel is, seen in this light, a noble attempt at transcending the kind of desire located in worldly powers, in political authority, in territorial control. That he is unable to curb his curiosity about what lies beyond the doors to his hard-earned paradise is a poignant statement on the hold political authority has on community and power on humanity. Narratives of nation can rarely free themselves of the question of political authority, especially where it has been the culprit in the faltering of the state – where imagining of nation and national allegory intersect and overlap in an interrogation of political authority and the nature of power. But what is at stake in Mahfouz's novel is not merely the question of political authority but also of the legitimacy of the novel in Arab culture, its cultural power. The tight grip of desire on Shahrayār and the narrative, not letting go even after the successful transformation of the paradigm of knowledge from kingship to nationhood, is suggestive.

Even as Mahfouz forcefully links the novel to pre-modern Arabic storytelling, thus inventing a 'native' genealogy for this new literary genre imported from an 'alien' culture, a culture that inadvertently ruptured its continuity, this genre remains precariously perched on a conflictual two-fork desire: to simultaneously cohere with its invented past and to generate new narrative. But how can one 'love' so dark a past and so hegemonic a new source of inspiration? How can the modernised Shahrazād love the now changed but still haunted Shahrayār? And without this love, how can Shahrayār hope to procreate? Will he be able to procreate, when he forgets his past completely, as his new wife in heaven tells him? But that is impossible, as Mahfouz's narrative demonstrates, for the past is the source of the present. After all, even though his novel begins where Shahrazād's stories end, it is deeply entrenched in them. Love, as a symbol of cohesion is, then, understandably absent in contemporary Arabic narrative. The principal objective of love, *wiṣāl*, has not occurred yet – the modern Arab is neither fully reconciled with his past nor integrated in the present – for mistrust looms ominously in the background. The flip side of *wiṣāl*, *hijrān*, is therefore prevalent. Abandonment, both of and by the beloved, in this case becomes a metaphor for alienation and its consequent wandering. Shahrayār's exit from his new found heaven echoes the story of the modern Arabic novel: this initially alien genre, despite efforts to create a link for it with pre-modern Arabic narrative, has not come home yet. Like Shahrayār who has exiled himself from his past – his palace and kingdom – modern Arabic narrative remains outside the world of Shahrazād, the narrative of which has been brought to a close. The triangulation of desire's trajectory in the Arabic novel, as it moves back and forth between nation-state, the community it imagines, modernity, the state it wills, and tradition, the authenticity it seeks, tells a story not only of the rise and faltering of the nation-state, but also of the status of modernity and the shape of tradition haunted by the novel's quest for power.

The selection of and the ways in which the *Nights* stories have been rewritten are part of the 'vision of the world' Mahfouz speaks of in the interview with *Fuṣūl*, a vision inspired by the famous corpus of pre-modern Arabic storytelling. He explains,

> I discovered on this mature second reading, that the *Nights* has managed to signify a world in its entirety, expressing its mentality, beliefs, imaginings and dreams. I discovered that it was indeed a unique work to be ranked among the great works of humanity.[27]

This vision is 'modernised' and employed by Mahfouz in the novel to delineate a new vision that is at once optimistic and pessimistic, political and philosophical, grounded in history and looking forward to the future, real and fantastic. It is paradoxically caught between the two poles of these dualities, both here and there, neither here nor there. *Layālī* is at one level, according to Mahfouz, a concoction of themes he picked out from the *Nights* and wove into a cohesive novelistic world,[28] and at another, an experiment in form that brings together, as *Nights* does, divergent modes of expression.[29] The fantastic, the staple feature of the *Nights*, comes to cohabit with realism in the world of the novel. Here, the various forms of betrayal, marital or political, more often than not inexorably linked to a breach of the code of appropriate sexual conduct exemplified by the paradigmatic love story in the *Nights*', simultaneously tells the story of the emergence of the nation-state of Mahfouz's imagining and betrays the text's anxiety about the trajectory of its own narrative.

In the contemporary analysis of the *Nights* frame tale, critics and scholars have focused on one aspect of love portrayed in this corpus of stories, that of desire. In *Reading for the Plot: Design and Intention in Narrative*, Peter Brooks takes this aspect of the *Nights* and thus links narrative to desire.

> In *The Thousand and One Nights*, Shahrazad's storytelling takes a desire that has gone off the rails – the Sultan's desire, derailed by his wife's infidelity, become sadistic and discontinuous, so that the mistress of the night must have her head chopped off in the morning – and cures it by prolonging it, precisely by narrativising it. Desire becomes reinvested in the telling of and the listening to stories, it is reconstituted as metonymy – over a thousand and one nights – until the sultan can resume a normal erotic state, marrying Shahrazad, who thus fulfils her name as 'savior of the city'. Narration, in this allegory, is seen to be life-giving in that it arouses and sustains desire, ensuring that the terminus it both delays and beckons toward will offer what we might call a lucid repose, desire both come to rest and set in perspective.[30]

Brook's analysis may ring true in our assessment of the narration and narrative of the frame tale as well as other tales of the *Nights*, and perhaps even of the contemporary Arabic novel. Desire, however, represents only the initial step in engendering of the genre and genealogy of pre-modern Arabic storytelling in general. Shahrazād's tales are born out of her desire to save her people and Shahrayār's desire for her body. What sustained the continuity of these tales, however, is Shahrazād's loyalty and endurance (staying power), and I would add, legitimacy, which are translated into love in the stories of, for instance, *^{c}Umar al-Nu^{c}mān*, *Tāj al-Mulūk* and *^{c}Azīz and ^{c}Azīza*. This love in turn ensures the cohesion of the genre and genealogy of this corpus of tales, from whatever origin they may be (Indian, Persian or indigenous), as it does the lineage and, therefore, kingdom of both Tāj al-Mulūk and ^{c}Umar al-Nu^{c}mān. Desire drives narration and gives birth to narrative, but love makes a home for them. The absence of love in Mahfouz's novel is a profound statement of doubt of the legitimacy of both the nation-state and the novel.

NOTES

1. This is Bulaq's rendition; Muḥammad Qiṭṭa al-^{c}Adawī (ed.), *Alfa layla wa layla*, 2 vols (Bulaq: 1252 AH), vol. 1, pp. 54–73. It appears as 'the Story of Shams al-Dīn Muḥammad the Vizier of Cairo and Nūr al-Dīn the Vizier of

Basra' in W. H. Macnaghten, *Alf Layla wa-Layla: the Alif Laila or Book of the Thousand Nights and One Night, Commonly Known as ʿThe Arabian Nights' Entertainment'*, 4 vols (Calcutta, 1839–42), vol. I, pp. 148–95.

2. Rendered as 'the Story of the Two Viziers and Anīs al-Jalīs' in Bulaq, vol. I, pp. 106–25 and Macnaghten, vol. I, pp. 278–320.
3. Bulaq, vol. 1, pp. 405–55; Macnaghten, vol. 4, pp. 346–52.
4. Andras Hamori, 'The Magian and the Whore: Readings of Qamar al-Zamān', *The 1001 Nights: Critical Essays and Annotated Bibliography, Mundus Arabicus 3* (Cambridge: Cambridge University Press, 1983), pp. 25–40, 25.
5. Hamori, 'The Magian and the Whore', p. 25. See also, Danie Beaumont, *Slave of Desire: Sex, Love and Death in the 1001 Nights* (Madison, NJ: Fairleigh Dickinson University Press, 2002), especially pp. 66–85.
6. Bulaq; Badr al-Dīn Ḥasan in Macnaghten.
7. Denys Johnson-Davies, *Arabian Nights and Days* (New York, NY: Doubleday, 1995), pp. 82–3.
8. Najīb Maḥfūẓ, *Layālī alf layla* (Cairo: Maktabat Miṣr, n.d.), p. 102.
9. Maḥfūẓ, *Layālī*, p. 93; Johnson-Davies, *Arabian Nights*, p. 78.
10. Maḥfūẓ, *Layālī*, p. 93; Johnson-Davies, *Arabian Nights*, p. 79.
11. Maḥfūẓ, *Layālī*, p. 93; Johnson-Davies, *Arabian Nights*, p. 79.
12. Maḥfūẓ, *Layālī*, p. 93; Johnson-Davies, *Arabian Nights*, p. 78.
13. Maḥfūẓ, *Layālī*, p. 92; Johnson-Davies, *Arabian Nights*, p. 78.
14. Maḥfūẓ, *Layālī*, p. 93; Johnson-Davies, *Arabian Nights*, p. 79.
15. Maḥfūẓ, *Layālī*, p. 93; Johnson-Davies, *Arabian Nights*, p. 79.
16. See Andras Hamori, 'A comic romance from the *Thousand and One Nights*: The Tale of Two Viziers', *Arabica* 30 (1983), pp. 38–56.
17. *The Arabian Nights*, tr. Husain Haddawy based on the text of the fourteenth-century Syrian manuscript edited by Muhsin Mahdi (New York, NY: Norton, 1990), pp. 157–8.
18. Ibid. p. 158.
19. Beaumont, *Slave of Desire*, pp. 81–5.
20. Macnaghten, vol. 1, p. 885.
21. Macnaghten, vol. 1, p. 818.
22. Maḥfūẓ, *Layālī*, p. 127.
23. Maḥfūẓ, *Layālī*, p. 174; Johnson-Davies, *Arabian Nights*, p. 145.
24. Maḥfūẓ, *Layālī*, p. 190; Johnson-Davies, *Arabian Nights*, p. 159.
25. Johnson-Davies, *Arabian Nights*, p. 179.
26. Ibid. p. 179.
27. *Fuṣūl*, 13: 2, p. 378.
28. Ibid. pp. 379–80
29. Ibid. p. 380.
30. Peter Brooks, *Reading for the Plot: Design and Intention in Narrative* (Cambridge, MA: Harvard University Press, 1984 [1996]), p. 60.

PART III

Desire: Arab Experiences of Modernity

Chapter Five

DECOLONISATION

'ALL THAT IS SOLID MELTS INTO AIR'

'A cold coming we had of it,
Just the worst time of the year
For a journey, and such a long journey:
The ways deep and the weather sharp,
The very dead of winter.'
And the camels galled, sore-footed, refractory,
Lying down in the melting snow.
There were times we regretted
The summer palaces on slopes, the terraces,
And the silken girls bringing sherbert.
Then the camel men cursing and grumbling
And running away, and wanting their liquor and women,
And the night-fires going out, and the lack of shelters,
And the cities hostile and the towns unfriendly
And the villages dirty and charging high prices:
A hard time we had of it.
At the end we preferred to travel all night,
Sleeping in snatches,
With the voices singing in our ears, saying
That this was all folly.

Then at dawn we came down to a temperate valley,
Wet, below the snow line, smelling of vegetation,
With a running stream and a water-mill beating the darkness,
And three trees on the low sky.
And an old white horse galloped away in the meadow.

Then we came to a tavern with vine-leaves over the lintel,
Six hands at an open door dicing for pieces of silver,
And feet kicking the empty wine-skins.
But there was no information, so we continued
And arrived at evening, not a moment too soon
Finding the place; it was (you may say) satisfactory.

All this was a long time ago, I remember,
And I would do it again, but set down
This set down
This: were we led all that way for
Birth or Death? There was a Birth, certainly,
We had evidence and no doubt. I had seen birth and death,
But had thought they were different; this birth and death.
We returned to our places, these Kingdoms,
But no longer at ease here, in the old dispensation,
With an alien people clutching their gods.
I should be glad of another death.

T. S. Eliot, 'The Journey of the Magi', 1927

I begin my exploration of the experience of modernity in the Arabic novel with T. S. Eliot because of his ubiquitous presence in an early form of poetic modernism that has continued to exert influence on Arab literary imaginary. I will not speak of *The Waste Land*, the landmark collection of poems and its titular poem that marked Eliot's own rise as one of the key architects of poetic modernism in the world. Instead I turn to 'The Journey of the Magi', a less glamorous poem written at a later but more critical stage in Eliot's life. This is not to deny the spread of the impulses, sensibilities and expressions of *The Waste Land* from English into Arabic, as well as other languages, and their leaving indelible marks on poetry and its criticism and, more importantly, poetics in these other languages. That the construction of a poem around a central symbol, return to ancient mythology, breaking away from strict 'traditional' metric schemes, and a turn to a more intimate language of conversation are all Eliot's contribution to modern Arabic poetry is a familiar argument today. Eliot inevitably figures prominently in discussions of, for example, Tammuzi poetry, which effected radical transformations in the composition and reception of poetry in the second half of the twentieth century. However, Eliot's presence in the Arab literary imaginary is not only symbolic of Western influence on

Arabic modernist poetics but also symptomatic of Arab experiences of modernity whether expressed in poetry or the novel.

There has been a great deal of focus on influence, on pursuing the threads of thought traceable to Eliot, whether as poet or critic, and quibbling over the minutiae of poetics or critical thought imprisoned in ideologised blind spots. Critics and historians of modern Arabic poetry may very often attribute the modernisation of Arabic poetry to the Western influence, as if Eliot was there himself, mapping the trajectories of modern Arabic poetics. His influence then becomes a source of contention, asserted or undermined dependent on the ways in which 'Western' influence is further divided, politicised and theorised. Those who follow more closely the 'quarrels' between the groups of poets clustered around the two Beiruti avant-garde literary journals at the time, Suhayl Idrīs's *Al-ādāb* and Yūsuf al-Khāl's *Shi*ᶜ*r*, may explain and justify modern Arabic poetics in terms of ideological conflicts or different sources of influence. The *Al-ādāb* group is linked to Arab nationalism and Anglophone influence. *Shi*ᶜ*r* is, on the other hand, deemed the platform for Anṭūn Saᶜāda's Syrian National Party, its agenda shaped by a vision of political and cultural coherence as well as the singularity of Greater Syria that had more affinity with Mediterranean Europe than Muslim Asia. Its poetics, it is often argued, are inspired by Francophone pretensions, influenced more by Baudelaire, Mallarmé and Valéry and less by Eliot, as if Eliot was not himself a beneficiary of French *symbolisme*. Modernity, as an experience of the present seen as markedly different from the past; modernism, as an aesthetic movement firmly grounded in the experience of here and now; and modernisation, as a process of radical cultural transformation, in all cases are identified with the West, with colonisation and Westernisation. The modern is then contrasted to the East and grappled with as the 'other'. It may be embraced wholeheartedly as welcome cultural transformation, or tolerated dubiously as unavoidable influence, or rejected unequivocally as part of an imperialist conspiracy to destroy an ideal(ised) Muslim community founded on and legitimated by tradition, and to disrupt the natural flow of its 'cultural heritage' (*turāth*) and history (*tārikh*).

However, cultural and identity politics surrounding a poem go beyond facile post-colonial posturing grounded in polarised categories, such as 'East' and 'West', 'past' and 'present', 'master' and 'slave', and 'coloniser' and 'colonised' prevalent in discourses on modernity, modernism and modernisation. I want to move away from the debates of Western influence defined by such stringent polarities and regard a literary text, a poem or a novel, not only as a palimpsest fashioned from and on 'other' texts, but also as site of the confluence of multiple, overlapping political and cultural forces, ideological responses, literary aspirations, poetic sensibilities and personal muses and demons, all shaped by the experience of radically and rapidly transforming, and transformed, reality and ways of life. Rather than thinking of modernity as a phenomenon that may be defined as and imprisoned in a conceptual category inherent in the language we use, such as Western influence or Westernisation, I prefer to think of it as an experience of the present, whose tumultuousness is captured in but not confined to the literary vision and expression. By shifting the site of inquiry to that of experience, I wish to rethink the relation between politics and aesthetics in a modernist literary text. Eliot, whose presence in modern Arabic poetry is indisputable, is an ideal entry into the kind of cultural, political and identitarian negotiations behind and beyond a literary text that show up in the text, giving it shape and colouring its surface, for modern Arabic poetry has simultaneously internalised Eliot and transcended him. It is possible to tease out from Eliot's poem I have quoted above a convenient blueprint for the kind of cultural and identity politics behind modernism pervaded by the early generation of Arab modernists. It can, in addition, provide an explanation for the signature themes and motifs pervasive in modernist Arabic writings.

THE JOURNEY IN ELIOT'S POETIC VISION

'The Journey of the Magi', the first poem in *Ash-Wednesday* (1930), is considered 'the poem of a convert'. Written at the time of Eliot's formal conversion from Catholicism to the Anglican Communion and his becoming a British citizen in 1927, it marks Eliot's return to 'an ostensibly religious subject since his student days', and 'takes it as its theme the painful necessity of rebirth which is itself a form of "Death", creating weariness and suffering – as well as a sense of alienation among men . . .'.[1] It gives a teleological hint of the kind of religious conversion that we will find expression in *Ash-Wednesday*, widely regarded as a 'conversion poem,' or as John Kwan-Terry puts it, poetry of 'verification' that points to both the desire and possibility for transcending the personal, and more particularly, personal experience of sequential time, to reach for the absolute.[2] It begins with renunciation of love, signalling his readiness for death, a necessary step required for rebirth, and is cast in the form of a journey from initial death to rebirth, from being trapped in time to existing in the realm of eternal possibilities. It is the existence of this longed for eternal realm that makes possible the ordering of the chaos of history, the random movements of time, and gives meaning to human life. In 'The Journey of the Magi', Eliot 'creates a devotional language out of his own preoccupations'[3] that is saturated with 'Biblical references as well as passages which are strongly reminiscent of Anglo-Catholic liturgy, just as much of its imagery and symbolism derived from his reading of Dante'.[4] 'Eliot evokes the tone of "religious verse" without any faith being articulated or convictions expressed. Belief falls away, and what we find is the expression of an unattached religious sensibility – the instinct for belief'.[5] The renunciation here, though finite, does not lead to the kind of clarity of faith expressed in the later poems of *Ash-Wednesday*. Kwan-Terry argues,

> The narrator of the . . . poem only calls it 'satisfactory'. While the birth offers potential significance for the world of time, as the narrator ought to see when he enters the 'temperate valley' with all its pregnant symbols of what can be at the child's birth, the narrator does not manage to fully break out of the nether world of the temporal time and unregenerate realm: he returns to his kingdom, but 'no longer at ease . . . in the old dispensation/With an alien people clutching their gods.'[6]

In his assessment of 'The Journey of the Magi', Kwan-Terry concludes as follows:

> In considering 'The Journey of the Magi,' we need to consider how the content of the poem clashes with the – at least – initial form of this poem. The creative repetition of Andrewes' sermon [quoted in the first five lines of the poem] is itself a form of recovery of the meaningful from the past. But how successful can this specific tactic be when weighed against the Magus not fully letting go of the old historical realm, and failing to be 'born again' into regenerate history? In presenting eternal history as the way out of the nether world of the sequential, one does encounter some problems. This journey to the goal of full significance is not without its attendant pains and stresses.
>
> The perpetual possibility of the this-worldly plane connecting with the other-worldly plane eludes Eliot in the actual realm. But the business of the poet that he would be is to keep the frontiers of practical verification of Absolute Truth open. The poetry as much as temporal experience will always hope to transcend itself . . .[7]

This impulse of the poem, the perpetual desire to transcend itself, is precisely that which distinguishes Eliot's poetry, according to Marc Manganaro. More importantly, '[w]hat makes much of Eliot's poetry, and especially *The Waste Land*, so compelling is the textual, and densely textured, momentum toward what is not of the text, and the necessary circling back to what is'.[8]

Whether we think in terms of Kwan-Terry's 'this-worldly sequential time' and 'other-worldly eternal realm' or of Manganaro's 'of-the-text' and 'not-of-the-text', the tension between the two structurally opposed realms is conspicuous, the circular movement between the two poles visible, and the absence of resolution evident. This makes sense, for the experience of the global cultural transformation that accompanied advances in the sciences and massive technologisation spread around the world by the machinery of empire between the eighteenth and twentieth centuries, is both disorienting and alienating for, as Marshall Berman puts it in Marx's words, 'all that is solid melts into air'[9] in this very experience of the present, or modern experience. In this kind of topsy-turvy world, desire for transcendence, for coherence, understandably becomes the dominant theme in modernist expressions. In these expressions, this coherence becomes the object of desire that drives a journey of search, narrativised as journey from death to rebirth in Eliot. Modernity in turn becomes the narrative trope Fredric Jameson theorises,[10] on which the trajectories of anxiety-ridden utopian modernist expressions are hung and played out. A schism between what is being escaped, 'here' and 'now', and what is desired, 'then' and 'there', becomes palpable. Analysts of Eliot's poetry during the interwar period, particularly of *Ash-Wednesday* and *Ariel Poems*, for example, do not hesitate to link Eliot's metaphysical aspirations to the sense of civilisational crisis acutely felt by his generation during and between the two world wars. '[T]he rhetorical strategies of integration [in Eliot's works] is basically nostalgic,' Manganaro asserts, 'as the author strives to reunite what an overdeveloped civilization has torn asunder'.[11] The polarity of 'now' and 'then' and 'here' and 'there', as that which structures Eliot's discourse on modernity, let us say, may in this case be aligned with 'primitivist Christian community' at one end and 'modern liberalism' at the other.[12]

The schism, it is possible to say, is between the modern empire and what it represents now and here, that is being destroyed by its very own modernisation, especially during the two world wars; and an alternative imagining of community that harks back at a 'simpler' life, perhaps less fraught with contradictions and crises from a particularized perspective, such as that of a clearly, if not rigidly, defined religious community, located in 'then' and 'there'. This imagined community is paradoxically justified as founded in the present with deep roots in the past, a past crystallised in the tradition bequeathed by the ancients to the modern, regardless of the quarrels in which they may be seen as embroiled. The modern, located in 'now' and 'here', and the traditional, situated in 'then' and 'there', are here rhetorical categories the polarisation of which makes possible the discourses on modernity to regard modernity as simultaneously rupture and continuity in history, as a civilisational process moving circularly along time that promulgates cultural change legitimated by what is articulated as tradition. Eliot's 'The Journey of the Magi' exhibits the almost universal impulse to be simultaneously in 'now' and 'then', 'here' and 'there', perceived in its intertextual strategies, its textual construction of a world grounded in a tradition of its own making. The shuttling back and forth between 'past' and 'present' in the historical process internalised in his text is understandably cast in the form of a journey, from night to day, winter to summer, enclosed human settlements (city, town and village) to open countryside (temperate valley), folly to wisdom, and death to birth.

There is a role for the cultural other, the Magi, to play in Eliot's utopian vision. This role is, however, not easily detectable. The Magi, a traveller from the East, though innocuously integrated into the background of the poem, silent and a still part of the landscape, cuts not only a peculiar figure but also figure of speech. The silencing of the other in Eliot does not entirely erase its traces, its presence, or its role in the movement of the poem. The foreignness of the Magi, whether taken literally as the Biblical wise man of the 'East' or a more contemporary 'Easterner', is betrayed by signifiers, such as 'camels' and 'camel men'; for what are camels doing, 'lying down in the melting snow' amidst 'the summer palaces on slopes' and 'terraces' in 'hostile cities', 'unfriendly towns' and 'dirty villages'? If the 'camels' in the first part of the poem signify a decayed civilisation inhabited by men 'wanting their liquor and women', the 'old white horse' in the second part of the poem, as juxtaposed to the 'camels', signals the opening up of the landscape to a new way of life, the possible birth out of the death of winter. These images of the 'camel' frame the journey from death to birth, of rebirth, which is arguably a symbolic one allegorised as travel from one place to another premised on a certain return, 'We returned to our places, these Kingdoms', though 'no longer at ease here, in the old dispensation'. The divergent landscapes are metaphors for, in this case, spiritual stations attained through acceptance or rejection of the real cultural context in which they are firmly grounded. Leaving and returning to the same place, 'our places', rather frame a journey from 'folly' to wisdom whereby transformation is not of place but of the sense of place. To be then returned to the same place is necessarily problematic, for it now suddenly comes across as littered '[w]ith an alien people clutching their gods', as home of alienation where one is pushed to 'be glad for another death'. The role of cultural other in effecting such a journey of rebirth haunts Eliot's poetic landscape.

There is, of course, no compelling reason to think of these 'alien people' as the 'Orientals', in fact, they may be more appropriately interpreted as those who hold faiths or ideologies different from that of the poem's protagonist. What is afoot here is rather 'orientalising' as mechanism of 'othering' whereby the undesirable is stigmatised then rejected. European modernity is, in part, assimilation and transcendence of the East, the 'Oriental Renaissance' Raymond Schwab theorises as lying at the heart of the modern in Western culture.[13] The occasional suppression of the 'Orient' in discourses on modernity in the West is part of the process of othering that accentuates the authenticity of a civilisational 'breakthrough', of a cultural transformation. 'Orientalism' is, as John M. Ganim cogently postulates in *Medievalism and Orientalism* (2005), the other face of 'Medievalism' – a narrative category that makes possible speaking of 'the modern' as progress, as departure from 'backwardness' and arrival in modernity. Alterity, or cultural difference between 'past' and 'present', comes in the guise of a foreign figure passing from 'there' through 'here', and in his passage transforms 'here' to 'there', 'familiar' to 'alien'. It is, it seems, impossible to speak of cultural transformation without turning to the cultural other, or putting the burden of change on his shoulders. Absenting the 'other' in Eliot, and perhaps in a majority of imperial and post-imperial Western discourses on modernity, is a ploy through which linear continuity of metropolitan history is maintained.

THE SEVEN VOYAGES OF SINDBĀD

I have necessarily summed up Eliot's poetic vision through the prism of Arabic poetics, for my purpose is not to shed more light on Eliot, or even to trace the diffusion of his vision and poetics in Arabic poetry, which have already been analysed and theorised extensively, but is rather to look at the ways in which Eliot is adopted, transformed then redeployed in the Arab literary imaginary, which ostensibly pays homage to Eliot, to the role the cultural other plays in Arab modernity. The location of Eliot in the imperial metropolis and the Tammuzi poets in the periphery makes this marked difference in their respective attitudes and management of the cultural other inevitable. The colonial intrusion is such that discounting the role of the other in its history in Arab culture, say, leaves a glaring gap in its linear history. Yet incorporating it necessarily destroys the linearity of history. All this makes it impossible to regard and speak of modernisation in the Arab context as a self-propagated unilateral cultural transformation. The Arab discourses on the most recent modernity in Arab culture produced in the margin of the Western empires, unlike those on the ninth-century modernity that took shape in the centre of the Islamic empire, must willy-nilly acknowledge openly, explicitly and unequivocally the 'other' in its making, whether the Western ways of life are willingly, or even hesitantly adopted and adapted, or eventually condemned, given up and thrown out. The space given to the 'other' in Arabic discourses interestingly opens the cultural and literary landscape to a variety of mappings with unpredictably exciting trajectories. If birth of the new in Eliot's poem is a matter of rebirth, of recycling the decaying familiar into a 'satisfactory' different place, of defining the present along the lines of a redefined past, where 'now' and 'then' merge into 'here' and 'there', the birth of the modern in Arab literary imaginary follows a path that forks into at least two trajectories where 'now' and 'then' do not always correspond to 'here' and 'there'. What do such trajectories tell us about the Arab experiences of modernity?

These experiences are expressed, like Eliot's 'The Journey of the Magi', as the meeting of 'individual talent' with 'tradition' and the ability of the 'individual talent' to forge something new and unique out of 'tradition', and in the form of a journey from dystopia to Utopia. These contradictory impulses and the utopian fantasies underpinning Eliot's poetic vision find sympathy in the Arab expressions of a complex experience of modernity in the twentieth century that overlaps with but diverges from the kind of experience of modernity Eliot expresses. More importantly, their intersection with discourses on the modernisation of Arabic literature has much to tell us about the ways in which diverse and divergent forces converge to give direction and substance to any process of forward-looking cultural transformation, of modernisation, and to pave the way for revolutionary poetic visions and new trajectories of poetic expressions in the development of modern Arabic literature. In all this the figure of the Magi is central; experiences of modernity are expressed through his journeys. Eliot's Magi, an understated cultural other, is adopted but transformed in the Arab literary imaginary into a highly visible insider-outsider, a Sindbād who is at once

Odysseus, Ulysses and Faust. The appearance of Sindbād and the persistence of his endless journeying in the Arabic literary imaginary is both an expression of Arab experiences of the West, absorbing its expressions of modernity, as well as of its own modernity that is, as I shall explain, invested in but at the same time goes beyond the experience of the nation-state, which is itself a product of modernity.

The nation-state, like Eliot's modernist poetics, is justified as founded in the present with deep roots in the past.[14] The nation-state in al-Sayyāb's 'Song of the Rain' that I discussed in Chapter 1, Khalīl Ḥāwī's poems and Mahfouz's novels that I will look at closely in this chapter, exhibits the almost universal impulse to be simultaneously in 'now' and 'then', 'here' and 'there' perceived too in its intertextual strategies, its textual construction of a world grounded in a textual tradition of each text's own making. However, even though modernity, like nation-state, is everywhere, the experience of it is multiple; modernity is irreducible to a single cultural logic. There is no singular response to the most recent wave of modernity as experience of the kind of present overwhelmed by technology and its attendant rationalism, speedy exchange of information, spread of print capital, facility of travel of people, goods and arts, rise of the middle class, women's increasing participation in public life, and familiar worlds torn asunder by wars, unrests and revolutions, to name but a few manifestations. Modernity, in this sense, may be spoken of only in the plural, as 'alternative modernities', or even 'other modernities'.

There is, this said, a consistent impulse pulsating underneath any drive towards modernity, whether emanating from the metropolis or periphery of the empire: that of imagining community structured by a profound disappointment in empire, and by a utopianism manifesting in, as the 2006 'Modernism' exhibition at the Victoria and Albert Museum goes to show, a radical transformation of both public and private spaces, as well as the material culture intended to fill these spaces that would in the long run constitute the actualisation of this imagined community. The Arab nation-state, imagined in Arabic literary texts and print capital, in this sense, is not unlike Eliot's 'religious community', conceived in his poetry and criticism, a very modern artefact, one of the many articulations of a utopian fantasy that is turned off by the very empire it is nostalgic for. Nationalism, as a way of imagining political community, is by the same token utterly modern, a modern experience that carves out a space for individual voice even as it invests its future in the destiny of the collective. Modernity has always been considered a fundamental part of the nationalist project, from the early European experience beginning in the sixteenth century to the anti- and post-colonial movements in the rest of the world in the twentieth century. Paradoxically, nationalism may have in hindsight proven inadequate as a framework for the analysis of modernity, as Neil Lazarus argues persuasively in *Nationalism and Cultural Practice in the Postcolonial World* (1999). Arab modernity is necessarily the totality of the experience of the nation-state, the West and more.

Any exploration of Arab modernity is at risk of getting lost in the trajectories of desire born out of the investment and disappointment in the above-mentioned three overlapping clusters of experiences, and focusing on two does not reduce the risk, for both the 'West' and the 'more', experienced as modernity, are at once vague and chaotically multiple. I have found it productive to begin by pursuing a line of inquiry that is informed by and situated in tracking the transformations of Eliot's poetic vision, structured around the figure of the Magi and his journey, in the Arab literary imaginary. Eliot's Magi is transformed into Sindbād in both Arabic poetry and novel, and his voyages into a vision of the modern world constructed around the 'Seven Voyages of Sindbād', which are lifted out of the *Thousand and One Nights* only to be completely distorted then expanded into eight. Mahfouz's Sindbād in *Layālī alf layla* provides a glimpse of what has become of Eliot's Magi in Arab literary imaginary and opens up his novel to the vision of modernity that would find fuller expression in Arabic poetics. *Layālī* situates the Arab experiences of modernity in the nation-state, which revolutionises the way we know the world. Our experience of political authority is key to our knowledge of the modern. Modernity is in one essential respect the reordering of political authority and society.

MODERN KNOWLEDGE

In Mahfouz's tale of the rise of the Egyptian nation-state Sindbād is conspicuously absent in the events leading up to the abdication of Shahrayār and the installation of Maᶜrūf al-Iskāfī to the governorship of the *ḥāra*. He returns after the nation-state has taken shape and is set on the right path only to tell the tales of his voyages to Shahrayār, sending the Sulṭān on a journey of discovery of his own, then to leave again at the end of the novel. The story of his travels abroad, of his seven voyages, intriguingly frames the journey of the transformation of political authority, of Shahrayār, that is the novel; in fact, the wisdom Sindbād gains from his travels, as the story unfolds, overlaps with and confirms the knowledge learned through the process of internal strife. The twin(n)ing of the two journeys, Sindbād's sea voyages and the quarter's adventures in political authority, is unmistakable even during his first encounter with his friends in the Café of Emirs upon his return. When he postpones telling his tales of wonder at the behest of ᶜAbd al-Qādir al-Mahīnī, '"You have seen many worlds," said the doctor Abdul Qadir al-Maheeni, "What did you see, Sindbad?"',[15] he is instead told of what has happened in the quarter:

> 'Many have died and have had their fill of death,' answered Hasan al-Attar, 'and many have been born and have not had their fill of life. People have fallen down from the heights, and other people have risen up from the depths; some have grown rich after being hungry, while others are begging after having been of high rank. Some of the finest and the worst of jinn have arrived in our city, and the latest news is that Maᶜrouf the cobbler has been appointed to govern our quarter.'[16]

Upon hearing this, Sindbād exclaims, 'I had reckoned that wonders would be restricted to my travels. Now I am truly amazed!'[17] That the two journeys are two sides of the same coin comes across even more clearly in the way Sindbād tells Shahrayār of his travels.

Mahfouz's novel, I have already explained, does not only make ideological statements about political authority but also provides diagnosis and prognosis of the nation-state. The Egyptian nation-state, say, emerges and begins to take shape against a background of the receding political structures buttressed by religion and kingship, which continue to cast long shadows over the nation-state. In his analysis of the nation-state and its future, Mahfouz plays with the paradigm of knowledge inherent in the *Nights*' love stories. Survival of the nation often depends on the resolution of stories of love in happy endings. Mahfouz's reformulation of the *Nights*' frame tale and love stories is informed by but wary of their inherent paradigm of knowledge, or their genre ideology; it disrupts this paradigm. As the marriages dissolve in separation or death, the imagined community falls short of cohesions and the legitimacy of the political authority is brought into question. However, all is not lost. There are important lessons to be learned from the journeys Shahrayār and Sindbād undertake in the novel. Shahrayār is now a benevolent king rather like the famous ᶜAbbasid Hārūn al-Rashīd, who tours the city at night and inspects his subjects. In his nocturnal wanderings he comes to understand the incompatibility of wisdom and power, as the heart-breaking story of humanity's yearning and search for and failure in finding the utopian 'state of fantasy' unfolds. More importantly, he now sees that the transformation of power from despotism to something more akin to democracy must be grounded in knowledge gained from 'experience of power'. 'Knowledge is not gained by numerous narratives', al-Balkhī says to his former pupil when Sindbād offers to recount his adventures to his old tutor, 'but through following knowledge and using it'.[18] The transformation of power from tyranny to democracy is neatly summarised by Sindbād as a journey from 'folly' to wisdom, which is narrated by Mahfouz as two parallel journeys, one of Sindbād and the other of Shahrayār. The lessons both learn from their respective journeys are mutually confirming.

> The first thing I have learned, Your Majesty, is that man may be deceived by illusion so that he think it is the truth, and that there is no safety for us unless we dwell on solid land (first voyage) . . . I also learned, Your Majesty, that sleep is not permissible if wakefulness is necessary, and that while there is life, there is no reason to despair (second voyage) . . . I also learned, Your Majesty, that food is nourishment when taken in moderation but is a danger when taken gluttonously – and this is also true of the carnal appetites (third voyage) . . . I learned too, Your Majesty, that to continue with worn-out traditions is foolishly dangerous (fourth voyage) . . . I also learned, Your Majesty, that freedom is the life of the spirit and that Paradise itself is no avail to man if he has lost his freedom (fifth voyage) . . . I learned too, Your Majesty, that man may be afforded a miracle, but it is not sufficient that he should use it and appropriate it; he must also approach it with guidance from the light of God that shines in his heart (seventh voyage).[19]

These vague statements may be interpreted as a discourse on power. Truth about power is necessarily derived from on-ground experience: vigilance in curtailing power's abusive tendencies leads to optimism; naked desire for power is dangerous; power must guarantee freedom; and political authority must be tempered with wisdom. Sindbād's story, it seems, is integrated into the story of the education of Shahrayār, and his voyages, short of seven and shorn of details at the request of Mahfouz's Shahrayār – 'People have told me of your travels, and I would like to hear from you what you learned from them, whether you have gained from them any useful knowledge – but don't repeat anything unless it is necessary'[20] – are recast in order to serve as 'mirror' journeys of Shahrayār's transformation. Sindbād, now a secondary character, is subordinated to the plot revolving around the main protagonist, and once this is done his stories lose their previous characteristics. Instead, they take on the characteristics of the new role in which they are now cast. The travels of *Nights*' Sindbād – theme, trope and genre rolled up in one – are subordinated to a thematic structure, journey, at Mahfouz's hand and reduced from its sacred transcendental vision to a secular political process.

The transformation of the Sindbād cycle in Mahfouz is, it goes without saying, premised on our familiarity with the *Nights*' version.[21] Both the protagonist and his story look familiar and unfamiliar at the same time. At the outset, the seven voyages of Sindbād in Mahfouz's text are cast in the form of one journey that preserves on the surface the fairly universal premise and structure of a journey of adventure and transformation. A crisis precipitates departure, followed by adventure and ending with return upon resolution of crisis, all of which lead to a transformation of, in the immediate context of Mahfouz, the individual and the community. Sindbād, a porter at the beginning of Mahfouz's novel, decides to go out to sea because,

> I am fed up with lanes and alleys. I am also fed up with carrying furniture around, with no hope of seeing anything new. Over there is another life: the river joins up with the sea and the sea penetrates deeply into the unknown, and the unknown brings forth islands and mountains, living creatures and angles and devils. It is a magical call that cannot be resisted. I said to myself, 'Try your luck, Sindbad, and throw yourself into the arms of the invisible.'[22]

He returns as a sailor who has acquired both wealth and knowledge, or as Shahrayār puts it to him, 'You have seen such wonders of the world as no human eye has seen, and you have learned many lessons, so rejoice in what God has bestowed upon you in the way of wealth and wisdom.'[23] His transformation from a poor innocent porter to a rich wise sailor, he discovers when he comes face to face with Shahrayār, echoes Shahrayār's transformation from a vengeful bloodthirsty tyrant to a soul-searching troubled elder and, more importantly, the community's reincarnation into a nation-state.

This journey of the transformation of political authority is cast in a narrative paradigm specific to medieval Arabic-Islamic culture: the well-known genre of *al-faraj ba^cd al-shidda* framing the *Nights*' 'Seven Voyages of Sindbād'. *Faraj*, literally openness, refers to a state of emotional and material relief after a period of hardship, *shidda*, which means tightness. The pieces collected in the numerous compendia under the general rubric of *al-faraj ba^cd al-shidda*, whether in classical[24] or vernacular[25] Arabic, tell the stories of hardship followed by relief in a three-partite journey consisting of departure, danger and survival, premised on a trinity of faith in God (*imān*), patience as well as endurance (*ṣabr*), and the will to survive under duress. Inherent in this narrative pattern is an Islamic paradigm of knowledge that informs both the structure of the story and its narrative movements and, more significantly, speaks to the function of storytelling in this culture. The *Nights*' frame tale, as well as a majority of the enframed tales, exhibits the same narrative patterning. In the frame tale Shahrayār and Shāhzamān, as well as their kingdoms, clearly fall on hard times when the betrayal of their respective wives unleashes the 'gynocidal' wrath of the two kings. The kingdoms are thrown into crisis not only because women are being killed on a nightly basis, but also because 'gynocide' will result in the discontinuity of the kingdom. Who will bear the heirs to the kingdom when the virgins are all killed on their wedding night? Shahrazād resolves the crisis when she is able to postpone her death for one thousand and one nights, during which period she bears Shahrayār three sons. She saves Shahrayār's kingdom by first putting a stop to 'gynocide' then making sure that the genealogy of the kingly family is not interrupted. That this kingdom is saved is true also of Mahfouz's re-mapping of the world of the *Nights*'. There is, however, a twist. The nation-state is heir to the kingdom rife with violence and bloodshed and its rise is told in a novel that is cast in, albeit with distortions, the paradigm of the *al-faraj ba^cd al-shidda* genre, a journey of political adventure punctuated by political assassination and crisis in government. The seeming relief at the end of the story is overshadowed by a sense of lack of resolution. The two protagonists of the journey, Shahrayār and Sindbād, feeling a vague sense of unhappiness and dissatisfaction, leave home and are seemingly doomed to wander forever. *Faraj* is, under the circumstances, a temporary respite that will be followed by yet another episode of *shidda*. The journey, it seems, must never end.

The open-endedness of the Mahfouzian journey in *Layālī* emulates as well as subverts another Arabic-Islamic paradigm of knowledge implicit in the *Nights*' Sindbād cycle that is, at least on the surface, deferred to and imitated. The 'journey in search of knowledge', I have already pointed out, lies at the centre of the novel, driving its narrative and giving structure to the text. The merging of the Porter and Sailor, despite its initial de-familiarising effect, does not really distort the *Nights*' narrative pattern in any significant way, for the role of the Porter is given to Shahrayār. In fact, it emulates the ways in which search for knowledge functions as trope and narrative structure in the *Nights*' and other forms of pre-modern Arabic storytelling. The title of the Sindbād cycle in the *Nights* is *Ḥikāyat as-Sindbād al-Baḥri maᶜa s-Sindbād al-Ḥammāl* (the story of Sindbad the Sailor and Sindbad the Porter). Like the *Nights* in general and many of its stories, there are two stories, one framing another, a feature not duplicated in any contemporary reformulation of the story. The story of the Porter frames the story of the Sailor. Sindbād the Porter, a poor labourer making do with carrying heavy loads for rich people, chances upon Sindbād the Sailor's opulent palace one day and in a moment of exhaustion and weakness complains of the injustice of fate by reciting a poem aloud outside the gates. Sindbād the Sailor hears the recitation and invites the Porter to the feast he is giving in his house. He then tells him a story and sends him home with 100 gold dinars. For seven consecutive nights, the Sailor tells the Porter a story and sends him home with 100 gold dinars. By the end of this cycle of stories, not only did the Porter become rich but also good friends with the Sailor. The Porter, the listener, reaps the benefits of storytelling. This is true of the *Nights*' frame tale and Mahfouz's novel: Shahrayār is the beneficiary of both Shahrazād's tales in the *Nights* and Sindbād's stories in Mahfouz.

This narrative paradigm may be traced to the Qurᵓān, to its stories of the prophets. These stories, which showcase the miracles performed by the prophets, their gifts from God as proof of their prophecy, are inevitably about the prophets whose endurance is tested but whose patience, indeed their faith in God and their mission, ensure their survival and triumph. These are the precursors of the *al-faraj baᶜd al-shidda* genre, as al-Tanūkhī tacitly asserts by beginning his collection of stories with them in *Kitāb al-faraj baᶜd al-shidda*.[26] The purpose of telling these stories is clearly to teach that the faithful are the guaranteed winners. The beneficiaries are clearly the Muslims who had at the time fallen upon hard times. The story of Joseph in *Sūrat Yūsuf* epitomises the *al-faraj baᶜd al-shidda* paradigm of both narrative and knowledge. *Sūrat Yūsuf*, the only chapter in the Qurᵓān that consists of a story in its entirety,[27] tells the story of Joseph's 'exile' or departure from home – thanks to his brothers' jealousy and betrayal – then various ordeals he has to survive while exiled in Egypt, including Mrs Potiphar's failed attempt at seduction, her accusation of his improper behaviour, and his imprisonment. However, he survives. His faith and endurance turn 'duress' into 'triumph', poverty into wealth, powerlessness into power, separation into family reunion, and exile into homecoming. This journey from crisis to resolution interestingly overlaps with the paradigm of the 'journey in search of knowledge'. In fact, the latter frames the former.

The *Sūra* begins as follows (verses 1 and 2): 'Alif Lam Ra. Those are the signs of the Manifest Book. We have sent It down as an Arabic Koran; haply you will understand (*la^{c}allakum ta^{c}qilūn*)', which is immediately followed by 'We will relate to thee the fairest of stories (*naḥnu naquṣṣu ^{c}alayka aḥsana l-qaṣaṣ*) in that We have revealed to thee this Koran, though before it thou was one of the heedless (*kunta lamina l-ghāfilīn*).'[28] The end of the *Sūra* (verses 102–11), once the story is told, takes us back to the lesson implied in beginning:

> We sent not forth any before thee, but men We revealed to of the people living in the cities. Have they not journeyed in the land? Have they not beheld how was the end of those before them? Surely the abode of the world to come is better for those that are godfearing. What, do you not understand (*afalā ta^{c}qilūn*)? Till, when the Messengers despaired, deeming they were counted liars, Our help came to them and whosoever We willed was delivered. Our might will never be turned back from the people of the sinners. In their stories is surely a lesson to men possess of minds (*laqad kāna fī qaṣaṣihim ^{c}ibratan li ulī l-albāb*); it is not a tale forged, but a confirmation of what is before it, and a distinguishing of every thing, and a guidance, and a mercy to a people who believe.[29]

Knowledge in this context is, of course, knowledge of God, therefore, faith in Allāh. The last verses of the *Sūra* (102–11) define the knowledge to be learned – conveyed in the verb *ta^{c}qilūn*, *^{c}aql* being the instrument of knowledge at the core of the Islamic symbolic order, *^{c}ilm* – as the nature of Allah's power and mercy. The *Nights*' story of *Sindbād the Sailor* is an articulation of this article of faith. The horrors he encounters, the wonders he witnesses (referred to as *gharā$^{\supset}$ib wa ^{c}ajā$^{\supset}$ib* throughout the seven voyages), and the miracles he receives culminate in one resolution in Sindbād's last journey: God has shown him what calamities greed brings and he repents. His wilful escape in the seventh voyage, in which the only horror he experiences is the discovery that he is living in a community of non-Muslims, confirms his realisation that Islam is the ultimate goal for a

Muslim. He returns to Baghdad, settles down, and lives contently among the Muslims.

However, the 'journey in search of knowledge' is not only undertaken by the prophets (Joseph or Muḥammad) and Sindbād the Sailor, for they already know the content of this faith, but also by those who listen to the story; the 'you' in the *Sūra*. Sindbād the Porter in the *Nights*' story embodies the 'you' of *Sūrat Yūsuf*. He is given the task of listening to Sindbād the Sailor's stories. Sindbād the Sailor's narration is the knowledge Sindbād the Porter ought to learn and his reward. The Porter is poor at the beginning of the cycle but becomes rich by the end of the story. The only thing he does is listen to the Sailor's stories. The monetary reward makes no sense unless it is interpreted symbolically. This makes even more sense when the Sindbād cycle is read in the context of the frame tale of the *Nights*. The crux of the matter in the frame tale is a crisis that needs to be resolved. The resolution of this crisis is found in storytelling. And in the Sindbād cycle, the solution suggested is faith and patience. When the lesson is learned, the crisis in the frame tale is also resolved. Shahrayār spares Shahrazād, who embodies faith and patience, has a family with her, and harmony returns to their 'community'.

It is, then, quite poignant for Mahfouz to place the burden of listening on a reformed Shahrayār, but to a lesson on political authority instead of faith. Faith, as important as it is in framing the knowledge or wisdom to be gained and implemented, is no longer sufficient in spreading communal peace or ensuring individual happiness. The erosion of religious certainty, along with the re-mapping of the dynastic realm, is an essential part of the modern national imagining of community, as Anderson has persuasively argued. That faith, in the form of religion and its political efficacy, has been undermined by science and rationalism, which lie at the heart of modernity, is an idea already familiar in Mahfouz's infamous novel, *Awlād ḥāratinā* (1959). But perhaps the question Mahfouz is posing has little to do with religion as belief in God but rather as a paradigm of knowledge institutionalised by a particular form of religion and the consequent structures of power that allow for tyranny, abuse of individual rights and bloodshed to be rampant. The transformation of political authority from despotism into democracy must necessarily be brought about by a radical revolution within the paradigm of knowledge structuring the undesirable political authority. This revolution takes the form of a journey of discovery made up of two parts, one a journey within and the other without. This journey is, however, incomplete, for the nation-state is clearly imperfect and only taking its first tentative steps towards democracy. The Mahfouzian 'journey in search of knowledge', seen in this light, is understandably a story within story, a journey leading to another journey.

ALLURE OF THE MODERN

The open-endedness of the Mahfouzian journey is, however, not solely a statement about the process of political transformation, I have already hinted at the beginning of this chapter. It is rather a symptom of modernity, of which democracy is only one product. Modernity, in the final analysis, is like Mahfouz's prognosis of democratisation in Egypt, an open-ended process; it remains an incomplete project. As such, modernity opens up the 'journey' for a plurality of destinations, many of which are driven and informed by the lacuna created, as Eliot tells us, in the retreat into the background of the sense of wholeness and certainty that came with religion, religious world view and religious imaginings of community. 'The modern traveller', Jáo Elsner and Joan-Pau Rubiés, 'as questioner, is incapable of the spiritual fulfilment of the Arab Hajis in Burton's account',[30] just like Shahrayār and Sindbād in Mahfouz's novel, '[n]ontheless, he or she may carry the desire for a sacred vision – a spiritual desire deeply embedded in the European [in this case, Islamic] tradition'.[31] Spiritual fulfilment in the sense used by Elsner and Rubiés does not refer only to the kind of outcome derived from pilgrimage exemplified by the Islamic Haji Burton describes, but also the 'transcendental vision', by which they mean

> the sense of spiritual fulfilment with which the traveller achieves a kind of completion at the goal of his journey – as is perhaps most eloquently exemplified in the theme of the quest for the Holy Grail, which derives its power from allegory and which ends with the most virtuous of the knights attaining the direct vision of a miraculous spiritual mystery. By contrast, we define as open-ended travel that process the fulfilment of which is always deferred because its achievements are relativized by the very act of travelling.[32]

Modern travel writing is, by definition, a literature of disappointment, its disappointment brought on by a realisation of the impossibility of completeness, of wholeness, of perfection, and more importantly, of absolute knowledge. On the one hand, '[t]he scientific paradigm of travel as exploration, the process of accumulating empirical knowledge and of perfecting maps ever more minutely implies an infinitely open-ended future of improvement', and on the other, the 'past' the moderns inherit in the 'present' from the ancients comes in the shape of fragments, whereby desire for its once-upon-a-time availability in an ideal wholeness becomes a defining feature of modernity. This desire, at the core of religious awareness underlying the yearnings of both Shahrayār and Sindbād, also finds expression in 'the desire for authenticity in cultural encounters'.[33]

This desire for authenticity is, one may argue, one motive behind Shahrayār and Sindbād's continuous journeying, for the incorporation of Arabic-Islamic paradigms of narrative and knowledge cannot disguise the Western origin of modernity, and of the Arabic novel. The relegation of the Arabic-Islamic genre of the journey towards faith, in which knowledge and salvation are synonymous, to a supporting role in the process of the modernisation of political authority is an ambivalent admission to the ascendance of the novel, as a form of storytelling, of narrative and cultural discourse with epistemological and ontological implications, at the expense of traditional forms of knowledge, of transmission of knowledge and, consequently, ways of life. In its privileging of questioning, by sabotaging the message and disrupting the structure of the Arabic-Islamic journey, the novel allies itself with modernity and, at a certain level, with a Western form of world view and sense of self bequeathed by, as Susan Sontag would say, the romantics:

> The romantics construe the self as essentially a traveller – a questioning, homeless self whose standards derive from, whose citizenship is of, a place that does not exist at all or yet, or not longer exists; one consciously understood as an ideal, opposed to something real. It is understood that the journey is unending, and the destination, therefore, negotiable. To travel becomes the very condition of modern consciousness, of a modern view of the world – the acting out of longing or dismay.[34]

Here, the departure of Shahrayār and Sindbād becomes, in part, a statement of the novel's insistence on its own modernity, its commitment to the present. Is this interpretation not confirmed by the ways in which the novel rewrites the destiny of Shahrayār and Sindbād, who are condemned to a life of wandering, of homelessness? The fate of Shahrayār is particularly edifying; he seems doomed to lose one 'home' after another. His exit from his Shahrazād's palace puts him on a path to another queen, another palace, another kingdom, in fact, a paradise where he seems to find refuge from his past and happiness with a woman he loves. His happiness, however, does not last; for no sooner has he settled into his new life, a calling, in the form of a 'forbidden door', beckons him to open it and find out what is behind. He succumbs to the temptation and falls back down to earth and, for an instance, goes mad with disappointment and grief. He joins the line of grievers gathered on the green island weeping, like him, for their fall from heaven.

The story of the grievers into which Shahrayār is thrown in Mahfouz's novel is, as Chraïbi points out, a playful engagement with the 'forbidden door' motif found in the *Nights*' and other vernacular Arabic stories, except for the protagonist, who is now Shahrayār.[35] There is a detail that is perhaps worth noting. In Mahfouz's novel, the protagonist is given an acute consciousness of his past. Shahrayār's happiness is, if it were to last, dependent on forgetting his past. His wandering is, in fact, his attempt to erase his bloody past from his memory. He replies to the 'angelic young girl' at the gateway of paradise, 'A fugitive from his past', when he is asked, 'What is your trade?'[36] Later, in his conversation with his new queen, he is told that 'you will know true happiness when you forget the past completely'.[37] He is booted out of paradise and fated to live a life of mourning and, more important, of wandering, of trying to find a way back, because, it seems, 'the past has not yet been erased from your head',[38] as his queen tells him. It is at this juncture – Shahrayār stuck between struggling to obliterate the past and not being able to let go of it completely – that the intersection between his journey and that of Sindbād's acquires special significance. Shahrayār's inbound search, a journey to forget his past, is paralleled by Sindbād's outbound eighth voyage, a quest for knowledge that, as al-Mahīnī tries to tell him, eluded him in his earlier seven voyages. 'Go in peace', al-Mahīnī blesses Sindbād before he leaves, 'then return laden with diamonds and wisdom, but do not repeat the mistake'. When Sindbād does not understand as 'a confused look appeared in Sindbad's eyes and al-Maheeni said to him, "The roc had not previously flown with a man, and what did you do? You left it at the first opportunity, drawn by the sparkle of diamonds."' When Sindbād exclaims, 'I hardly believed I would make my escape', al-Maheeni replies, 'The roc flies from an unknown world to an unknown world, and it leaps from the peak of Waq to the peak of Qaf, so be not content with anything for it is the wish of the Sublime.'[39] The threshold of ideal community and of modernity, at this time, glimmers in the horizon but remains elusive, mirage like. The journey, undertaken at a crossroad of transformation, is a manifestation of a palpitating desire that seeks fulfilment.

Desire lies at the heart of travel, especially of modern travel, Elsner and Rubiés observe, '[b]ecause modernity is constituted in opposition to a past, for which there is [now] desire',[40] and because '[e]ven while there may exist ideologies of modernity which proclaim a complete rejection of the past as the key to progress, this rejection entails an awareness of this past and can only function in the wider context of an appropriation of tradition'.[41] Mahfouz's appropriation of tradition, of the travels of Sindbād as an allegory of the search for an ideal political community, is an Arab form of modernism, an expression of the very modernity of the Arabic novel. It is at the same time expressive of a parallel search for modernity. But the desire he inscribes into his novel as the heart of its narrative project and projection – the journey – is not necessarily heading towards a definitive destination. There are dangers lurking behind arrival and permanent settlement in an ideal political community, a Utopia. Utopia, I have discussed elsewhere,[42] is by definition totalitarian, tyrannical and oppressive because, for Utopia to be Utopia, absolute order must be maintained at all cost. There is no room for desire in Utopia because it is charged up with transgressive impulses and wanderlust. Desire must necessarily be educated, and fitted into the utopian straightjacket. With the domestication of desire, Utopia closes in on itself and in its isolation it becomes, so to speak, frozen in time and place. In other words, there is no life in Utopia: every one must live a regimented life like a robot. There can be no curiosity, no wonder, and no wandering, without which new knowledge may not be created and no stories will be told. What would, then, become of the Arabic novel?

Mahfouz's Sindbād must, seen from this perspective, go against the lesson he has learned from his first voyage, 'The first thing I have learned, Your Majesty, is that man may be deceived by illusion so that he think it is the truth, and that there is no safety for us unless we dwell on solid land',[43] and begin wandering again. The whale that is both the Garden of Eden and a sea monster the *Nights*' Sindbād straddles bespeaks the constant tension between Utopia and dystopia, heaven and hell, stability and mobility, love and desire. *Janna*, the name given to the Garden of Eden, has ambivalent connotations in *Nights*' Sindbād cycle. It is so called because it is covered with such lush greenery that earth is concealed. This concealment masks the flip side of the whale's identity, initially described as *janna* by Sindbād; it is a sea monster hiding behind the veil provided by its greenery as well as the sea. Arrival at the Garden of Eden is ever so sweet because it is always preceded by hardship, by the dangers on the way and by death. Settling permanently there, however, stifles curiosity, prevents adventure and stops life on its tracks. In the wake of his fifth voyage, Sindbād settles down at home and becomes even richer until, one day, he meets up with other merchants who have just returned from a journey abroad. Sindbād suddenly remembers the happiness he felt whenever he came from a sojourn abroad and the elation of seeing family and friends again. Nostalgia for those feelings would serve as the impulse behind his sixth voyage in the *Nights*. Sindbād must straddle two poles, must leave, come home and leave again, because running away in pursuit of desire, not love, is what makes storytelling possible and meaningful. Mahfouz's Sindbād, along with his Shahrayār, understandably succumb to desire, the very desire that rules dystopia as well as, in this case, the desire to be simultaneously in dystopia and Utopia, 'now' and 'then', 'here' and 'there'.

This story of the modern subject Mahfouz tells cryptically in *Layālī* gives us only a glimpse of the poetic vision underpinning Arab literary imaginary and the poetics of modernist Arabic writings. This poetic vision, and its attendant poetics are a creative amalgamation of Eliot's poetic vision and poetics, translated into Arabic in a way that came to be integrated into the 'native' pre-modern and modern Arabic poetic vision and poetics which, albeit varying from text to text, provide us with a blueprint of the detail ingredients that go into the shape of the literary text and the genre to which it belongs. The Arabic novel, squarely situated in the poetics of Arabic literary writings, having inherited not only the narrative paradigms of the pre-modern Arabic literary tradition but also classical Arabic poetics, as I shall show, now absorbs into it Eliot's poetics Arab writers have experienced in their encounter with the West. This encounter with the West, like that of nationalism, is equally part and parcel of the Arab experiences of modernity. It moreover adds complications to the 'journey in search of knowledge' at the heart of the experience of the nation-state. Mahfouz's *Layālī*, which alludes to this, is in a different sense a refashioning of the 'journey in search of knowledge' prompted by the meeting with the West into an encounter with the nation-state, for his narrative of the democratisation of political authority in Egypt is necessarily the extraction of one from diverse journeys in search of varieties of knowledge, all constructed around the figure of Sindbād, manifest in modernist Arabic poetry. Sindbād appeared as a key protagonist in Tammuzi poetry as early as the middle of the twentieth century, in the poetry of al-Sayyāb and Ṣalāh ᶜAbd al-Ṣabūr, for example, but finds fuller articulation in Khalīl Ḥāwī (1925–82),[44] whose poetic vision and poetics provide the broad canvas against which Sindbād in Mahfouz's novel, as well as the traveller in the Arabic novel, is painted. The various guises of Sindbād in the three poems discussed below tell the story of the modern subject Mahfouz only alludes to in *Layālī.*

INTELLECTUAL IN EXILE

Ḥāwī's Magi in *Al-majūs fī urūbbā* (1957; The Magi in Europe, 1988)[45] is, in one sense, Eliot's Magi, who embarks on a new journey from folly to wisdom in the wake of an overwhelming disillusion with Western civilisation. He is, in another sense, an allegorisation of the Eastern intellectual, like Ḥāwī and Mahfouz's Sindbād, who travels to the West in search of knowledge only to find himself stranded between East and West unable to return to his old home or build a new one. He is, unlike Eliot's Magi, acutely aware of his 'foreignness'. In fact, his foreignness is accentuated for a total effect of existential angst that pervades the poem. Much like Eliot's Magi, Ḥāwī's Magi, one of the 'Wisemen from the East, led by a star . . ./And when they saw the child, they knelt and worshipped him', is no longer sure of this faith. His journey, alas, does not lead to the kind of rebirth in Eliot's optimistic journey of religious renewal. Rather, it leads to a false prophet, Mephistopheles-like, who seems to have replaced the God behind Eliot's certainty.

> And we knelt in reverence to alchemy
> and to a magician
> who gathered paradise from the night of tombs –
> worshipped him, a God revealed in the cave.
> O God of the weary,
> God of the lost!
> O God escaping the blaze of the sun
> and the horror of certitude,
> who hides
> in the caves of the underworld
> from the land of civilization.[46]

The culmination of the Magi's journey in Ḥāwī's poem is the outcome not of Eliot's departure and arrival but of two separate sojourns. One takes place in the West and the other in the East, between which two worlds no visible movement is detected. The journey in the West does not lead to return to the East but is rather juxtaposed to another journey in the East. The West, presented as 'paradise on earth', is in fact a world where faith has gone missing.

> O magi from the East, have you come through
> the agony of the sea to the land of civilization
> to see what God
> is revealed anew in the cave?
> Here is the road, the star,
> the traveller's provisions.
> The venturous star led us
> across Paris. . . We tested the dwellings of thought,
> we shunned intellect on the Day of Masquerades
> and in Rome, the star was eclipsed by the embers of censers
> warm with the desires of priests.
> Then we lost it in London, were lost
> in the fog of coal, in a cipher of commerce.
> On Christmas Eve, no star
> no children's faith in a child and a stable.
> Midnight Christmas Eve – no breath –
> an emptying street, sad laughter
> and we descended the unholy corridors to the caves of the city.
> Eyes moved from door to door,
> eyes we questioned: Where is the stable?
> Beneath a red lantern we found a door inscribed:
> *Earthly Paradise! Here is no snake to seduce*
> *And no judge to throw stones.*
> *Here the roses have no thorns*
> *And the naked are innocent.*[47]

If this is the condition of the West, a state of civilisational degeneration, the East is no less problematic for the poem's protagonist. It is, even worse, a place that exists on borrowed identities.

> 'Take off these borrowed faces,
> skins stripped from the loathsome chameleon!'
> We neither take faces off nor put them on.
> We are from Beirut – born tragedies

with borrowed faces and minds.
Ideas are born whores in our red light district,
then pass through life protesting virginity.'
'Take off these borrowed faces!'[48]

Al-baḥḥār wa al-darwīsh (1953–7; The mariner and the dervish)[49] further exposes the East's 'borrowed faces' as a mask that conceals its true identity. This poem too follows the trails of those who went in 'search of knowledge' in the past only to arrive at a certain sense of futility at the end of the search. Ḥāwī's introduction to the poem gives the fateful ending away.

> He sailed with Ulysses into the unknown, with Faust he sacrificed his soul to achieve knowledge and finally he ended despairing of modern science. With Huxley he rejected it and set sail for the Ganges, the source of Sufism. He saw nothing but dead clay in the East and hot clay in the West, nothing but clay and clay.[50]

'The Mariner and the Dervish', like 'The Magi in Europe', is constructed around the juxtaposition of two seemingly opposing spheres, East and West, between which there is now traffic. The Mariner is here the Magi's pre- or reincarnate who returns home, to the East, after a disappointing sojourn in the West only to find himself homeless.

Homelessness experienced in the poem, it has been argued, is of a peculiar kind brought on by a profound intellectual disillusion with the civilisations of both East and West, each representing a world view and the tradition of thought behind it. The poem, Fuad Said Haddad explains,

> takes the form of an internal dialogue within the poet between two basic orientations, philosophical and mystic. The opening part constitutes a build up to the dialogue. The philosophical one is represented by a mariner, an adventurous wakeful mind bursting with vitality and hope. The mystic is represented by a dervish who transcended time and rested with the peace and tranquillity of grasping eternal truth.[51]

The Mariner's encounter with the Dervish is, more importantly, the meeting of the West, or Western culture in which the poet was educated, and the East, or the poet's native Eastern culture. While the West is a pile of ashes left behind by the vicissitudes of time,

and I see, what is this I see?
Death, ashes, flames
settling upon the western shore.
Gaze, you too shall see –
or can you not bear the sight –
that ghoul that boils in its froth.
The clay blobs furious.
The ports lie feverish in flames,
And lo – from time to time the earth is pregnant.
It writhes and suffers
occasional outbursts in the clay;
once Athens, now Rome,
it is the glow of fever rattling in a spent chest,
leaving in its place some blisters,
some ashes
from the refuse of time.[52]

the East is 'a land' content to be a forgotten 'dead earth' overrun with 'parasitic plants, old moss and thick ivy'.

Of which the storytellers speak:
a slothful tavern, legends, prayer, lore,
palm trees casting their tepid shade
swishing with languid murmuring,
a humid place that dulls the feeling
in his fervent nerves,
blots out all memory,
muffles the lure of distant ports.

Oh for the ascetic life
of the naked dervishes
twirling, dizzy in the 'circles of remembrance'
transcending life
circle upon circle
around the old dervish
mired in mud, motionless,
his feet striking deep roots
absorbing the ooze of the death earth.
In the folds of his skin

grow parasitic plants,
old moss and thick ivy;
unconscious, he will never awake.
All he takes from the teeming harvest
that clamors in his veins
is a mere rag
planting his elegant ostentation
on his old and tattered skin.
– Come, tell us of the treasures
that have nailed your eyes
to the hidden depths.[53]

It is, then, understandable that the Mariner takes to the sea again, to be away from the 'feverish clay' and 'dead clay' that beset him wherever he goes, and to throw his lot in with the sea, with the unknown, when all hope is lost, when 'the light in his eyes is dead, is dead', as he watches the 'lighthouses of the road have died to my eyes'.[54]

– Leave me. The lighthouses of the road
have died to my eyes
Let me go away
to where I do not know.
The distant ports will not lure me.
Some are feverish clay
some dead clay.
How often have I been burned by feverish clay?
How often have I died with dead clay?
The distant ports will not lure me.
Leave me to the sea, to the wind, to death
unfurling shrouds in blue
for those who drown.
A mariner in whose eyes
Lighthouses of the road died out:
that light in his eyes is dead, is dead.
Neither heroism will save him
nor the lowliness of prayer.[55]

The transformation of the Magi into Mariner is hope's decline into despair, despair's onslaught on hope, especially seen from the perspective of Eliot's 'The Journey of the Magi', where death is a prelude to a rebirth that is part of a spiritual awakening. Death, in Ḥāwī's poem, is the only way out of an ontological impasse brought on by an epistemological crisis that goes behind the facile opposition between the 'Western philosophical tradition' and the 'Eastern mystical tradition' Haddad speaks of. It is true, however, that faith is hopelessly lost in this poem. And Ḥāwī's protagonists, unlike Eliot's Magi, can no longer 'return to [their] places, these old kingdoms' to await rebirth, but must instead lose himself at sea in order to be spared the agony of returning and finding nothing but despair, 'death, ashes, flames' and 'feverish clay' and 'dead clay'. The Mariner suddenly acquires a name, Sindbād, a name bequeathed to him by an ancestor who, let us say, hanged up his sails and settled for a comfortable, happy life after seven successful voyages at sea, bringing home not only unequalled riches but also unheard of tales of wondrous adventures packed with wisdom and knowledge.

FRAGMENTATION OF SELFHOOD

But Ḥāwī's Sindbād is the reincarnation of the Biblical Magi in the form of the *Nights*' seafarer, Homer's Odysseus, or is it Dante's Ulysses?, and Goethe's Faust, who is, here, doomed to embark on a new journey of no foreseeable homecoming. Ḥāwī's Mariner is arguably cast, with poetic license, in his own image, an Eastern intellectual seeking knowledge in the West, who ends up 'not identify[ing] himself with neither culture but who, somehow, feels he belongs to both'.[56] The unravelling of the multiplicity of the wanderer's identity reaches a feverish pitch in *Wujūh al-Sindbād* (1958; The many faces of Sindbād).[57] Sindbād sports more than one face, as Ḥāwī tells us. The ancient seafarer may have given way to the modern traveller but, like a heart donor and recipient in a contemporary horror film of transplant gone awry, they come in and out of each other's life. 'The Many Faces of Sindbād' is in one sense the various levels of alienation a Lebanese newcomer to the West felt – and Ḥāwī wrote the series of four poems discussed here during his stay in Cambridge as a doctoral student. The signs of alienation range from the marks of loneliness visibly drawn on his face to the sense of being held prisoner on a train, locked up in boredom with a running fever, hidden behind masks, or engulfed in the darkness of the womb. The 'many faces of Sindbād' are, in another sense, only two. One is the wrinkled face of the ancient seafarer, its creases mapped by time and experience, and the other is the smooth face of the young adventurer haunted by his predecessor and anxious to keep the ancient face on his own mien and erase it completely at the same time. Despite the general sense of being stuck, this poem is alive with tangible mobility. Sindbād has put out to sea once more, but perhaps not completely without direction as the 'The Mariner and the Dervish' would have us believe. The movement in the poem is clearly of two trajectories, one following the footsteps of the protagonist between Cambridge and London and in London, and the other tracing the lines of history left on Sindbād's face.

The surface stillness intuited from the poem is, like the calm before a storm, a pause at a crossroads. It soon works itself up into a frenzied quest then quiets down again through the nine tableaux of the poem: (1) 'Two Faces', (2) 'A Prisoner on a Train', (3) 'Among the Gypsies', (4) 'After the Fever', (5) 'The Paradise of Boredom', (6) 'Masks, Female Demon and Waterloo Bridge', (7) 'In the Darkness of the Womb', (8) 'The Two Faces', and (9) 'The Eternal Face'. The journey begins with the protagonist's realisation of his multiple identities at a train station café remembering his goodbyes to his beloved, 'my face is woven from many faces,/the face of someone who will be lost'[58] and ends with his arrival at the possibility of a new life, of rebirth, of finding 'the Eternal Face'. His 'exile' in England, it seems, has initiated a journey of discovery and recovery; while he discovers London, say, he recovers the ancient Sindbād in himself. The journey West intersects with the journey into the past. The present is possible only upon successful completion of this two-fold journey of discovery and recovery. But of what? The third part of the poem, given the title 'Among the Gypsies', provides a clue. In his introduction to a later poem, *Jinniyyat al-shāṭī* (1961; The genie on the beach), Ḥāwī speaks of the gypsy as the symbol of the vitality of self and the Tree of Life:

> In gypsy tents, open to the winds, travelling with the winds, the self (*al-dhāt*) unveils the vitality of instinct (*fiṭra*) and original innocence. Vitality is the feasts of joy which issue from overflowing self and pour into it. Innocence is the state of the first man in the shade of the Tree of Life, before the sweetness and bitterness of knowledge in the Tree of Good and Evil tempted him. And so the sword of fire evicts his from Paradise.
>
> For this reason the self of the gypsy is the best symbol for both this unbridled vitality and for the Tree of Life, 'the apple of the fertile wild,' as well as for the ability of man in the state of innocence to coalesce with the elements of vitality in nature . . .

> The poet clothes the gypsy in wide, general descriptions that symbolize earth in its renewed vitality and in its eternal virginity.
>
> In the city the gypsy is incapable of understanding either the code (*al-sharīᶜa*) or the Tree of Knowledge . . .[59]

The participation of the protagonist's young self, as opposed to his ancient self, in a gypsy dance, a wedding lit by and taking place in fire while in London, is then a running away from the city and a turning to nature that will enable his eventual homecoming. As soon as he acquires a 'gypsy face', 'the face of someone who will be spitted out by the fervent whirlpool,/he will drop anchor at harbours,/and train stations',[60] but perhaps not before a fever catches up with him in (4) 'After the Fever',[61] and he finds himself walking the streets of London as a way of combating boredom brought on by long hours of sitting in museums and libraries reading pages of old books and seeing only frozen expressions on human faces in (5) 'Paradise of Boredom'.[62] The gypsy experience revitalises him, enabling him to resist the allure of a city overwhelmed by landmarks of modernity. It is practically drowned in the sounds of radios and rockets, charged with radiation, filled with the smoke from the coals burnt to run trains and boats, mired in banality and debauchery, and inhabited by people wearing masks in (6) 'Masks, Female Demon and Waterloo Bridge'.[63] The famous London fog, or smog?, as he approaches Waterloo Bridge towards the end of his wanderings, seems to set a trap for him, weaving around him a web of 'vipers, tentacles, claws and jaws',[64] but lets loose its grip on him[65] when the bridge collapses.[66] The protagonist falls not into the Thames but a womb in (7) 'In the Darkness of the Womb',[67] that is the earth.

> Lighten your footsteps,
> passers-by!
> We are not dead, just tired
> of dirty fogs,
> our face ragged, covered in darkness,
> riding vipers, tentacles
> and mysteries.
> We will have the womb of the earth, never the cursed air.
> Lighten your footsteps
> on our nerves,
> Passers-by!
> We are hiding

In the darkness of a quiet cellar
To wipe away our fever, to wake up, to sing,
And to hide away life from the path of time.
Lighten your footsteps,
o, passers-by![68]

When he emerges out of the cellar, the womb, the two unknown faces in (1) 'Two Faces' (*wajhān*) become known in (8) 'The Two Faces' (*al-wajhān*). The ancient seafarer becomes one with the young adventurer and this union, or is it reunion?, comes to be the first step towards an anticipated rebirth, almost Eliot-like in the final part of the poem, (9) 'The Eternal Face'.

You lived in a bend of a house,
and you were protected
because it was built on a rock.
Behind the door
In the silent corners
the waves dig, and the mutterings grow loud.
I see on your face traces
of the waves, of what they have erased and carved again.
I have just returned from a storm, my face
lost in the fever
and fell apart in the waves.
One of us died, so bury him!
Why do we knead fantasies
and put makeup on skulls?

***

Pile rubbles over rubbles
tighten them
and rest on my chest.
They will turn green again,
tomorrow they will grow in the limbs of a child
his life from you and from me
our blood in his, reviving
the singing fertility
his dream a memory of us
a rebirth of what we were and what he was.
Time will be defeated,

And will bark at his feet,
at our feet.[69]

'The Many Faces of Sindbād' is littered with signs of a journey of individuation in Freudian, Jungian or even Turnerian terms, in which departure, liminality and return make up the three stages in the variety of their staging, of the emergence of self, of self-knowledge, of individuality. The nine tableaux of the poem, even in the absence of a narrative that clearly maps its trajectories, evoke elliptically the required steps towards individuation. Departure, wandering, encounter with 'other', overcoming danger, surviving the 'belly of the whale', integration and rebirth, framed by the Tammuzi myth of regeneration, are easily detectable in the eyes keen for clues to a psychoanalytical reading. However, the development of the self, as the web of signs complexly woven in the poem shows, is far from straightforward. The integration of Sindbād's many faces, or 'borrowed' faces, into one is complicated by the ambiguity of the references to, let us say, their 'original' owners. The gathering of these symbolic figures – the Magi, Odysseus, Ulysses, Sindbād and Faust, who are themselves 'heroes' of their own 'allegories of travel' – points to a labyrinth of signification created by the ways in which various sets of signifier and signified overlap, interact and dance around the signs. The most immediately accessible layer of this densely textured labyrinth of signification is perhaps its engagement with post-colonial identity politics. It would not be too far fetched to think of these poems as an expression of a colonised subject's desire for selfhood, perhaps even along the lines of a recent post-colonial reading of al-Sayyāb.

DECOLONISATION OF THE SUBJECT

Terri DeYoung sees al-Sayyāb's gradual articulation of a poetic persona ambivalently carved out of a twined Arab Sindbād and Greek Odysseus as an allegory, through which al-Sayyāb tackles the complex process of an Iraqi subject's decolonisation, a process driven and shaped by an intensified attachment to the natal place. She locates the emergence of this subject, argued as caught between self and other, in the context of the revolutionary nation-building process sweeping across Iraq towards the end of 1950s and the beginning of 1960s and, more particularly, in the development of al-Sayyāb's own political engagement and poetic voice. 'Odysseus Returns as Sindbād', her chapter on the figure of the 'quester' in al-Sayyāb's poetry, also points to a new way of understanding al-Sayyāb's move from direct political involvement to metaphysical contemplation. 'The dramatization of the increasingly insistent imperatives of political involvement in the decade of the 1950s' to 'a growing introspection' in the 1960s is interpreted as a 'Quest for an Inner Landscape'.[70] Al-Sayyāb, according to DeYoung, 'at the end of his life seems to have found what many had found before him: that the figure of the aging quester makes an ideal vehicle for exploring the twists and turns of the human mind in mediation and, not the least, mediation on the final mystery of death'.[71]

This said, there is an insistent stream of post-colonial discourse in all al-Sayyāb's works that is directly relevant to the centrality of deterritorialisation of colonial Iraq and attendant national reterritorialisation as in decolonisation. These twin(n)ed processes are parts of 'an attempt to chart a path back to the primal unity of self with land/nation/other'.[72] The figures of Sindbād and Odysseus, as seafarers, exiles and questers in al-Sayyāb, are conveniently read as allegories of post-colonial discourses on identity premised on the idea that place, more particularly, place of birth, is crucial in the construction of subject, of self. Departure is then a form of exile that puts the subject at risk and return necessarily adumbrates reclaiming of both place and self and represents a first step towards a new cohesion. The location of the 'scene of primal integrated harmony between subject and landscape' in the past, more particularly in the poet's childhood, may be seen as a paradox, a nostalgic reconstruction of a pre-colonial past as well as disillusion in the revolutionary course of nation-building. There is an additional twin(n)ing in these post-colonial allegories (of the decolonisation of colonial subjects) of an external journey with an internal one. This additional twin(n)ing is, in a sense, an indication of al-Sayyāb's realisation that reclaiming the place alone is not sufficient for nation-building but that it must be accompanied by 'self-reappraisal focused on inward change rather than outer-directed activism'.[73] However, self-sacrifice, the paradigm of behaviour al-Sayyāb sought in his use of myth, has proven inadequate in the end. 'What al-Sayyāb discovered notably and early among his contemporaries, then', DeYoung argues, 'was that to *sacrifice* the self simply could not be enough, one had to emerge from that alienating nihilation armed with the patterns for constructing a re-formed self'.[74]

DeYoung identifies as a source of trouble for al-Sayyāb two 'alternate Odysseus': Dante and Tennyson's 'guileful Ulysses', 'master trickster and deceiver whose Trojan horse stratagem is indicative of a chronic pathological willingness to sacrifice honesty and heroic principles for the expediency of the moment'.[75] Dante's Ulysses, condemned to the eighth circle of hell in Canto 26 of *The Inferno*, has been persistently linked to the figure of colonial adventurer epitomised by Christopher Columbus.[76] Tennyson's Ulysses, though 'unreliable' and 'limited', is similarly given 'certain heroic characteristics' of a 'colonial administrator turning over the reins to a successor just before stepping on the boat to go home'.[77] The prominence of Ulysses at the expense of Sindbād and Odysseus in al-Sayyāb's journey of 'self-knowing', of the integration of self, nation and other premised on the cohesion of 'past' and 'present' and 'East' and 'West', problematises, even undermines the very quest that is its object. This journey of 'self-knowing', it seems, can only take place 'outside the orbit of European hegemony, where the colonial Ulysses is a foreign intruder without power to determine the parameters of the cultural discourses'.[78] And it must take place. There is, paradoxically, a price tag that comes with 'the glorious guest': it can exact 'a terrible price for other human beings'.[79] To seek 'self-knowledge' within the framework of revolutionary 'nation-building' is to tread on a path paved with blood.

It is clearly possible, in fact, prudent to speak of Ḥāwī's poetry as a form of political engagement with decolonisation[80] that places its stake in liberating the subject predicated on 'self-knowing', or liberating the self from other, and in 'nation-building'. Ḥāwī was a young contemporary of al-Sayyāb, and even more than al-Sayyāb in his later life (who eschewed at the time the internationalism that came with communism and opted for a more local Arab nationalism) was an ardent Arab nationalist despite his membership in Anṭūn Saᶜāda's 'Syrian National Party'. He was so committed to decolonisation and nation-building that even his death was a wilful, vociferous political act: he committed public suicide on 2 June 1982, the day the Israeli Army first crossed the border into Lebanon. '[H]is project as a poet', Adnan Haydar and Michael Beard sum up, 'was to speak for his people and his culture', the Greek Orthodox community into which he was born, Lebanon, and the Arab world.[81] In fact, he was able to create 'a series of saviour figures, cultural heroes who would be valid for the contemporary Arab world'[82] culminating in Lazarus. 'Lazarus 1962', the focal point of *Bayādir al-jūᶜ* (1965; The Threshing Floor of Hunger, 1984), 'is a reading of a specific moment of history in which the first wave of Arab revolutions in the twentieth century as well as the Mongol invasions of the thirteenth century are filtered through the story of Lazarus'.[83] More importantly, his contribution as a poet is inextricably linked to his political vision, according to Haydar and Beard:

> The creation of an archetypal Arab hero, even of a series of such heroes, does not in itself sum up Hawi's contribution as a poet. It may be more accurate to consider those heroes, with their sudden metamorphoses and simultaneous levels of identity, as a framework around which he has been able to develop two farther innovations. First, we notice Hawi's idiosyncratic style: those constantly shifting landscapes in which multiple figurative levels evolve on two or three fronts simultaneously, allowing him to exploit with startling efficiency the (also startling) evocative resources of the Arabic language. The second innovation may strike us as a paradoxical, that the surrealistic surface of Hawi's poetry is such an effect vehicle for political vision. But since the content of the political vision of 'Lazarus 1962' is a message of illusion versus realities, of paradox and ambiguity, it is perhaps articulated more directly in poetry than in paraphrase. Hawi's Lazarus is no simple representation of tyranny or corruption, but at once an embodiment of the *manaqib* or *virtues*, which an anti-colonial society requires, and also a fundamental derailment of that power, a process by which he comes to resemble the force he has opposed.[84]

These three features of Ḥāwī's poetry alone – the creation of cultural heroes, the alignment of twentieth-century Arab revolutions with thirteenth-century campaigns against the Mongol invasion, and the anticolonial discourse on power – place it among the post-colonial cultural discourses of the time. Ḥāwī's Magi is arguably a reclaiming of Eliot's Magi, a repossessing of a cultural, or even religious, symbol that has long been appropriated by the West. The Magi and Sindbād may all be considered a rewriting of the history of cultural exchange between East and West. They are now the original moulds in which 'Odysseus figures' (overlapping with al-Sayyāb's Odysseus and Ulysses) are 'updated and adapted to the non-Western world'.[85] And more significantly, their 'outward-turning' wandering, complemented by Lazarus's 'inward-turning' roaming, may be read as a post-colonial subject's two-fold journey in search of 'self-knowledge' and 'imagined political community' predicated on, as in al-Sayyāb's poetry, the integration of self, nation and other. This process of post-colonial 'becoming' is equally put at risk by the very presence of the West and the colonial legacy it has left behind.

There are some things to be said for such a straightforward post-colonial reading of Ḥāwī even in the context of a discussion of modernity. That the nation-state is essentially, perhaps even inexorably, part and parcel of the experience of modernity in the Arab world clearly goes without saying. But perhaps, more importantly, the metamorphosis of the subject into the exuberant modern self, its move from interiority to exteriority, may in this kind of reading be traced to a clear trajectory that shows the growing importance of the role of subject in knowing. Even in instances of total commitment to nation-building, the individual voice speaking of and for the project rings loud and comes to be the vehicle through which a multitude of national(ist) ideologies, programmes and experiences is expressed or simply manifest. To speak of modern Arabic literature only in terms of its decolonising impulses, agendas and achievements or disappointments is then to be reductive. Such a reading is pertinent, even indispensable in our understanding of literary texts as necessarily worldly and engaged in power politics. However, it also obfuscates and suppresses the 'multiplicity of possible meanings' Haydar and Beard see in Ḥāwī's poetry, and reduces Arabic literature to a mere national allegory and a single cultural logic, when this poetry is read only as the poet's 'attitude toward the social and political decadence of modern Arab civilization'[86] against the background of a derailed process of decolonisation.

Greek Odysseus, Elsner and Rubiés observe, has served as the 'allegorical model of the spiritual journey towards an inner vision' since Classical Antiquity in the European tradition.[87] He is a mythical figure al-Sayyāb could turn to naturally for a formulation of an inward journey of his own which, DeYoung points out, comes to be increasingly accentuated in al-Sayyāb's poems in the 1960s. However, Odysseus has been since the sixth century the centre of a tradition of contrasting readings, pagan, Christian or modern. The Odysseus created in these readings, according to Elsner and Rubiés

> might not have been recognized by Homer himself or by the bulk of ancient Greeks and Romans . . . In Greek tragedy, for instance, and in later Renaissance interpretations he serves as the morally ambivalent role of the model of worldly wisdom. The allegorical Odysseus – the inner traveller who may serve as the paradigm of the pilgrim in the later Christian medieval tradition – was a creation of religiously-minded philosophical readers in Hellenistic times which came into its full flowering in the late Antiquity. For Odysseus (and his numerous successors from Sir Perceval to John Bunyan's Christian in the Pilgrim's Progress of 1678) became the ideal model of a traveller whose journey brought inner as well as outer fulfilment, return to a

> spiritual plenitude lost in the travails of life, as well as success in the sense of worldly achievement.[88]

And it is this Janus-like Odysseus that is the hero of Ḥāwī's poetry, and more importantly, of Mahfouz's novels as well.

QUEST FOR COHESION IN AN APOCALYPTIC WORLD

'The wanderer, the loner, the exile, the restless and rootless and homeless individual', James MacFarlane explains in 'The Mind of Modernism',[89] 'were no longer the rejects of a self-confident society but rather those who, because they stood outside, were uniquely placed in an age when subjectivity was truth to speak with vision and authority'.[90] The subject's move to the centre of knowing the self and the world, of both ontology and epistemology, is a feature of modernity. This move began taking place in Europe in the nineteenth century when 'two of the most cherished beliefs of the liberal mind – that society at large not the individual was the real custodian of human values, and that "truth" once established was "absolute" – were repudiated and considered by Ibsen, for example, as of the "enemy of the people"'.[91] The passing of the 'custody of life's integrities from society to the individual – to an individual who necessarily commanded some unique perception of the things of life, who embodied some secret essence which alone gave the world its legitimization'[92] came hand in hand with the 'death of God' and the rejection of tradition, as well as parallel to and against the ascendance of science, rationalism and materialism. 'The individual', Frederick R. Karl asserts, 'for the first time might cohere as a whole, but he cohered at the expense of community and society . . . based on freedom, choice, liberation and expression of self'.[93]

The erosion of the 'absolute truth', of any kind of certainty in knowledge, whether in the form of God, tradition, science, rationalism or materialism, paradoxically opened up new, in fact, infinite vistas for the self to know as well as to cohere. It did so by ordering and reordering itself, albeit chaotically, as the lines and boundaries that came with certainty were erased. It paradoxically relativises. Knowledge is now made up of knowing not the whole but discrete or even disparate parts. It is, more importantly, contingent upon language, as well as upon the moment, the present instance in which knowing, or not knowing, happens; making the present, the very fleeting moment of an experience, an obsessive preoccupation of modernist expressions. And, more importantly, the coherence of the self is reduced to perpetual longing and the process of becoming to forever an incomplete project. The modern text becomes, among other things, a site on which desire for what is elusive or perceived as lost obsessively acts out the drama of loss and process of hoped for recovery. It is understandable then that the 'journey' comes to be such a pervasive modern theme and trope. The void left behind by the receding absolute comes to be the centre of self, both inside and outside, inviting the self to embark on voyages of discovery, journeys into the unknown. They take the form of 'spiritual autobiographies' in which the self searches for what is absent or lost, for its voice, and speaks in a new language that is teeming with 'new words and voices'.[94]

This new language develops out of and is required for new ways of reconciling familiar paradoxes, contrary and contradictory categories of knowledge: 'yes and no, life and death, man and woman, terror and bliss, crime and worship, god and devil lose their separate identity and merge'.[95] More importantly, and this is a staple feature of modernity, it is part of the attempt to reconcile 'two distinct ways of reconciling contradictions, ways which in themselves are also contrary'. The first is what may be termed as Hegelian synthesis of both/and, 'a higher unity which preserves the essence of the two conflicting elements whilst at the same time destroying them as separate entities'. And the second is what may be called Kierkegaard's either/or, which 'brings life's contraries into the most intimate relationship with each other, whilst at the same time preserving the validity of the contradiction between them'.[96] Ḥāwī's poetry partakes in the modern, as well as modernist sensibilities and ambivalences, and charts its unique trajectory of a subject's search for selfhood and knowledge against a background of simultaneously modern and post-colonial predicament, or apocalypse, when 'civilisation' is deemed corrupt, community in disarray, and the individual in mortal and moral danger thanks to the displacement of familiar orders or systems, which have yet to be replaced.

There is already a palpable sense of the apocalypse in Ḥāwī's poetry 'The Magi of the East' to 'The Mariner and the Dervish' and 'The Many Faces of Sindbād'. Signs of civilisational degeneration are everywhere in both the East and West. God is suffering death in the face of intellectual masquerades in Paris, church corruption in Rome and capitalist and industrial oppression in London. In the meantime, intellectual bankruptcy, moral hypocrisy and cultural dependency on the West plague the East. These signs make up a recipe for an apocalyptic vision akin to that of Nietzche's 'conviction that the history of man has arrived at a point of destiny, at the terminus of a long era of civilization, and that all human values must be subjected to total revision'.[97] In the absence of an alternative order, revision may be spoken of only as an unstable, open-ended process, in images, scenes and episodes, of the transformation of fundamental codes of culture Foucault discusses in relation to the emergence of the new unconscious at the heart of the modern. An image is a free-flowing signifier that cannot be pinned down to one signified. The cave, a recurring image in Ḥāwī's poetry, for example, is polyvalent and 'evades reduction into a particular univalent symbol', according to Haydar and Beard.[98] It may be 'a hungry mouth, a sterile womb, a religious supplicant empty of faith, a sound divested of meaning' in 'The Cave',[99] or the West, the East, a city, a sea, or paradise and hell in 'The Magi of the East'. 'The narrative motion' in Ḥāwī's poetry, for example 'The Cave', as Haydar and Beard describe it,

> resists the illusion of motion toward a goal, the inexorable unfolding of meaning . . . The polyvalent quality of the cave substitutes a narrative of a different kind, where the cave as a symbol resists sequential logic . . . the succession of the scenes [is] less a development . . . than a catalogue of possibilities which universalizes those scenes simply because they are not bound by anticipated narrative cause and effect.[100]

A symbol cast in scenes and episodes that transcend narrativisation resists identification and speaks in different voices. The 'you' and 'I' seemingly dichotomised in 'The Many Faces of Sindbād' may belong to the poet's alter ego, his young self before he left for Cambridge, and his exilic self. They may also belong to Sindbād, the young adventurer as he begins his voyages and the older, adventure-weary citizen of Baghdad. They are possibly the voices of the female statue the poet speaks of in his preface to the poem as a symbol of beauty, the voice of the statue from the past basking in her youthful beauty and the voice of time-ravaged old woman meditating on beauty, life and time. These 'six' voices engage in dialogues but in ways wholly unexpected because they are located in scenes and episodes constructed from images that refuse to be pinned down to unambiguously identifiable signs. One is never sure who is speaking, from where and to whom. Is the young poet speaking to his older self or is it the other way around? Is the poet speaking to Sindbād or is Sindbād speaking to him? Perhaps the speaking voice belongs to the female statue, but to the young beauty or the old hag, and is she speaking to the poet or Sindbād? In Ḥāwī's poetic world, like Eliot's, boundaries between dichotomised articulated categories of knowledge, such as 'self' and 'other', 'East' and 'West', 'female' and 'male, and 'past' and 'present' collapse and dissolve. Instead, they merge into each other and blur all distinctions. What remains, as expected in any apocalyptic vision, is a desire for renewed cohesion and coherence. The locus of this desire is inevitably a female 'you' or a 'she' who will be the mother giving birth to 'I' or the 'beloved', rebuilding 'I' from its ruins. 'The Many of Faces of Sindbād' poignantly ends with the reunion of two lovers, the traveller returning home to find his beloved waiting for him. Their reunion is expected to restore both to their former wholeness, integrating 'you' into 'I', 'past' into 'present' and 'exile' into 'home'.

NOTES

1. Peter Ackroyd, *T. S. Eliot* (London: Hamilton, 1984), p. 164.
2. John Kwan-Terry, 'Ash-Wednsday: a poetry of verification', in A. David Moody (ed.), *The Cambridge Companion to T. S. Eliot* (Cambridge: Cambridge University Press, 1994), pp. 134–9.
3. Ackroyd, *T. S. Eliot*, p. 165.
4. Ibid. pp. 164–5.
5. Ibid. p. 165.
6. Kwan-Terry, 'Ash-Wednesday', p. 140.
7. Ibid. p. 140.
8. Marc Manganaro, *Myth, Rhetoric, and the Voice of Authority: a Critique of Frazer, Eliot, Frye and Campbell* (New Haven, CT: Yale University Press, 1992), p. 81.
9. Marshall Berman, *All That is Solid Melts into Air: the Experience of Modernity* (New York, NY: Simon and Schuster, 1983).
10. Fredric Jameson theorises in *A Singular Modernity: Essay on the Ontology of the Present* (London: Verso, 2002) that whether the discourses are obviously narrative or merely structured by an invisible narrative, they are under the influence of what Michel Foucault would call pressures of power experienced, as it were, by the subject.
11. Manganaro, *Myth*, p. 98.
12. Ibid. p. 98.
13. Raymond Schwab, *The Oriental Renaissance: Europe's Rediscovery of India and the East, 1680–1880* (1950), tr. Gene Patterson-Black and Victor Reinking (New York, NY: Columbia University Press, 1984).
14. For a study of the relationship between past and present in Arabic modernist poetry in general, see Muhsin J. al-Musawi, *Arabic Poetry: Trajectories of Modernity and Tradition* (London: Routledge, 2006).

15. Najīb Maḥfūẓ, *Layālī alf layla* (Cairo: Maktabat Miṣr, 1979), p. 247; tr. Denys Johnson-Davies, *Arabian Nights and Days* (New York, NY: Doubleday, 1995), p. 208.
16. Maḥfūẓ p. 248; Johnson-Davies, pp. 208–9.
17. Maḥfūẓ, p. 248; Johnson-Davies, p. 209.
18. Maḥfūẓ, p. 249; Johnson-Davies, p. 210.
19. Maḥfūẓ, pp. 250–6; Johnson-Davies, pp. 211–15.
20. Maḥfūẓ, p. 250; Johnson-Davies, p. 210.
21. For the ways in which this is applicable to other rewritings of the cycle, see Wen-chin Ouyang, 'Whose story is it? Sindbad the Sailor in literature and film', *Middle Eastern Literatures* 7: 2 (July 2004), pp. 133–47.
22. Maḥfūẓ, p. 11; Johnson-Davies, p. 9.
23. Maḥfūẓ, p. 256; Johnson-Davies, p. 216.
24. For example Abū Bakr ᶜAbdallāh Ibn Abī al-Dunyā, *Al-faraj baᶜd al-shidda*, ed. Ḥasan ᶜAbd ᶜĀl (Ṭanṭā: Maktabat al-Ṣaḥāba, 1987), and Abū al-Muḥassin Ibn ᶜAlī al-Tanūkhī, *Kitāb al-faraj baᶜd al-shidda*, ed. ᶜAbbūd Shāljī (Beirut: Dār Ṣādir, 1979).
25. Hans Wehr (ed.), *Al-ḥikāyāt al-ᶜajība wa al-akhbār al-gharība* (Bibliotheca Islamica) (Wiesbaden: Franz Steiner Verlag, 1956), which includes many of the *Nights* stories.
26. A number of stories in al-Tanūkhī's compilation have been examined by Julia (Ashtiany) Bray: 'al-Tanūkhī's al-Faraj baᶜd al-Shidda as a Literary Source', in Alan Jones (ed.) *Arabicus Felix: Luminosus Britannicus: Essays in Honour of A. F. L. Beeston on His Eightieth Birthday* (Exeter: Ithaca, 1990), pp. 108–28, 'Isnāds and models of heroes: Abū Zubayd al-Ṭāᵓī, Tanūkhī's sundered lovers and Abū al-ᶜAnbas al-Ṣaymarī', *Arabic and Middle Eastern Literatures* 1: 1 (1998), pp. 7–30, and 'Figures in a landscape: the inhabitants of the Silver Village', in Stefan Leder (ed.), *Story-telling in the Framework of Non-fictional Arabic Literature* (Wiesbaden: Harrassowitz, 1998), pp. 79– 129; and Andras Hamori, 'Tinkers with the text: two variously related stories in the *Faraj Baᶜd al-Shidda*', in Stefan Leder (ed.) *Story-telling in the Framework of Non-fictional Arabic Literature* (Wiesbaden: Harrassowitz, 1998), pp. 61–78.
27. Mustansir Mir has looked at the literary dimensions of this Qurᵓanic story in 'The Qurᵓanic story of Joseph: plot, themes, and characters', *The Muslim World* 126: 1 (1986), pp. 1–15. However, he does not deal with the narrative paradigm implicit in the story.
28. A. J. Arberry, *The Koran Interpreted* (New York, NY: Macmillan, 1955), vol. I, p. 254.
29. Ibid. vol. I, p. 266.
30. Jao Elsner and Joan-Pau Rubiés, *Voyages and Visions: Towards a Cultural History of Travel* (London: Reaktion Books, 1999), p. 5.

31. Ibid. p. 5.
32. Ibid. p. 5.
33. Ibid. p. 6.
34. 'Model destinations', *Times Literary Supplement* (22 June 1984), pp. 699–700; quoted in Elsner and Rubiés, *Voyages and Visions*, p. 5.
35. Aboubakr Chraïbi, 'Les jinns penserus de Naguib Mahfouz', in F. Sangustin *et al.* (eds) *L'Orient en coeur, en honneur d'André Miquel* (Paris: Maisonneuve et Larose, 2001), pp. 171–83.
36. Maḥfūẓ, p. 265; Johnson-Davies, p. 224.
37. Maḥfūẓ, p. 268; Johnson-Davies, p. 227.
38. Maḥfūẓ, p. 268; Johnson-Davies, p. 227.
39. Maḥfūẓ, p. 262; Johnson-Davies, pp. 220–1.
40. Elsner and Rubiés, *Voyages and Visions*, p. 7.
41. Ibid. p. 7.
42. See Wen-chin Ouyang, 'Utopian fantasy or dystopian nightmare: trajectories of desire in classical Arabic and Chinese fiction', in Aboubakr Chraïbi, Frederic Bauden and Antonella Ghersetti (eds) *Le repertoire narrative arabe medieval: transmission et ouverture* (Geneva: Droz, 2008), pp. 323–51.
43. Maḥfūẓ, p. 250; Johnson-Davies, p. 211.
44. For his life, politics and work, see Iliyyā Ḥāwī, *Khālīl Ḥāwī*, 2 vols (Beirut: Dār al-Thaqāfa, 1984); ᶜAbd al-Majīd Ḥurr, *Khālīl Ḥāwī: shāᶜir al-ḥadātha wa al-rūmānsiyya* (Beirut: Dār al-Kutub al-ᶜIlmiyya, 1995); and Maḥmūd Shurayḥ, *Khālīl Ḥāwī wa-Anṭūn Saᶜāda* (Sweden: Dār Nilsin, 1995). For studies of his poetic techniques, see Marlé Hammond, 'From Phantasia to Paonomasia: image-evocation and the double entendre in Khālīl Ḥāwī's "The Mariner and the Dervish"', in Geert Jan van Gelder and Marlé Hammond (eds), *Takhyīl: The Imaginary in Classical Arabic Poetics* (Cambridge: Gibb Memorial Trust, 2008), pp. 274–86; and Yair Huri, '"My roads leads to the dark Bedouin girl": an aesthetic reading of Khālīl Ḥāwī's "The Flute and the Wind"', *Journal of Semitic Studies* L/2 (Autumn 2005), pp. 341–55.
45. Originally published in *Al-ādāb* 10 (October 1957), p. 12, then as part of *Nahr al-ramād* (Beirut: Dār al-Ṭalīᶜa, 1957). Translation by John Mikhail Asfour, in *When the Words Burn: an Anthology of Modern Arabic Poetry 1945–1987* (Ontario: Cormorant Books, 1988), pp. 155–6. Another translation by Diana Der Hovanessian and Lena Jayyusi may be found in Salma Khadra Jayyusi (ed.) *Modern Arabic Poetry: an Anthology* (New York, NY: Columbia University Press, 1987), pp. 258–60.
46. Reference is made to Ḥāwī, *Nahr al-ramād*, pp. 116–17; Asfour, *When the Words Burn*, pp. 155–6.
47. Ḥāwī, pp. 116–17; Asfour, pp. 155–6.
48. Ḥāwī, pp. 116–17; Asfour, pp. 155–6.
49. Or, 'The Sailor and the Dervish', tr. Issa J. Boullata, rev. Zahra Hussein

Ali, published as appendix to Ali, 'The Aesthetics of Transgression: Khalil Hawi's "The Sailor and the Dervish" and the European Grotesque', *Journal of Arabic Literature* 28 (1997), pp. 219–37; 235–7.

50. Ḥāwī, *Nahr al-ramād*, p. 9; tr. Adnan Haydar and Michael Beard (unpublished work).
51. Fuad Said Haddad, 'Introduction', *From the Vineyards of Lebanon: Poems by Khalil Hawi & Nadeem Naimy*, translated with a Preface and Introduction (Beirut: American University Press, 1991), pp. 13–29; 22.
52. Ḥāwī, *Nahr al-ramād*, pp. 15–16.
53. Ibid. pp. 12–14.
54. Ibid. pp. 17–19.
55. Ibid. pp. 17–19.
56. Haddad, *Poems by Khalil Hawi*, p. 23.
57. First published in *Al-ādāb* 1 (January 1958), p. 62, then as the third of four poems in *Al-nāy wa al-rīḥ* (Beirut: Dār al-ᶜAwda, 1972).
58. Ḥāwī, *Al-nāy wa al-rīḥ*, p. 53.
59. First published in *Al-ādāb* 7 (July 1961), pp. 4–5, then as the second poem in this collection of three poems, Khālīl Ḥāwī, *Bayādir al-jūᶜ* (Beirut: Dār al-Ādāb, 1965), p. 19. Translated by Adnan Haydar and Michael Beard in *Naked in Exile: Khalil Hawi's Threshing Floors of Hunger* (Washington, DC: Three Continents Press, 1984), p. 43.
60. Ḥāwī, *Bayādir al-jūᶜ*, p. 60.
61. Ibid. pp. 61–2.
62. Ibid. pp. 62–4.
63. Ibid. pp. 64–74.
64. Ibid. p. 70.
65. Ibid. p. 74.
66. Ibid. p. 73.
67. Ibid. pp. 74–6.
68. Ḥāwī, *Al-nāy wa al-rīḥ*, pp. 74–6.
69. Ibid. pp. 77–80.
70. Terri DeYoung, *Placing the Poet: Badr Shākir al-Sayyāb and Postcolonial Iraq* (Albany, NY: State University of New York Press, 1998), p. 97.
71. Ibid. pp. 97–8.
72. Ibid. p. 110.
73. Ibid. p. 99.
74. Ibid. p. 99.
75. Ibid. p. 105.
76. Ibid. p. 106.
77. Ibid. p. 109.
78. Ibid. p. 113.
79. Ibid. p. 117.

80. See also Hussein Khadim, *The Poetics of Anti-Colonialism in the Arabic Qaṣīdah* (Leiden: E. J. Brill, 2004).
81. Adnan Haydar and Michael Beard, *Naked in Exile*, p. 5.
82. Ibid. p. 8.
83. Ibid. p. 8.
84. Ibid. p. 9.
85. Ibid. p. 8.
86. Ibid. p. 28.
87. Elsner and Rubiés, *Voyages and Visions*, p. 8.
88. Ibid. p. 9.
89. 'The Mind of Modernism', a chapter he wrote for a guide to European Literature 1890–1930 given the title *Modernism*, eds Malcolm Bradbury and James McFarlane (London: Penguin Books, 1976), pp. 71–93.
90. Ibid. p. 82.
91. Ibid. p. 80.
92. Ibid. p. 82.
93. Frederick R. Karl, *Modern and Modernism: the Sovereignty of the Artist 1885–1925* (New York, NY: Macmillan, 1985), p. 42.
94. Ibid. p. xi.
95. Bradbury and McFarlane, *Modernism*, p. 87.
96. Ibid. p. 87.
97. Ibid. p. 79.
98. Haydar and Beard, *Naked in Exile*, p. 30.
99. Ibid. p. 30.
100. Ibid. p. 30.

Chapter 6

MODERNISATION

SPIRITUAL AUTOBIOGRAPHY

The twin(n)ed ontological and epistemological crisis begun in 'The Magi of the East', put through 'The Mariner and the Dervish', and complicated in 'The Many Faces of Sindbād' finds a fuller expression in *Al-Sindbād fī rḥilatihi al-thāmina* (1960; The eighth voyage of Sindbād).[1] The earlier three poems taken together give a sense of the ways in which disillusion and alienation attendant to degeneration of civilisation lead to homelessness, exile and wandering. All this is cast in an apocalyptic vision where humanity is steeped in hell on earth and doomed to perpetual yearning for paradise. The self is hopelessly lost and utterly 'stuck' in this loss. It is redeemable only through a journey across time and space, from 'present' to 'past' and back, and from 'East' to 'West' and back, and into the very depth of the self. This twofold journey of discovery and recovery that begins to take form in 'The Many Faces of Sindbād', where contours of a journey must be read into the nine tableaux made up of scenes and episodes that resist narrative coherence, comes to shape 'The Eighth Voyage of Sindbād'. Sindbād's eighth voyage, like the one detectable in 'The Many Faces of Sindbād' is born out of, driven and framed by desire. It is, on the one hand, symbolised by the siren of the Odyssey, or the she-demon lurking behind the darkness of the city, ready to distract the protagonist from his right path. It may also be the virginal beloved, on the other hand, waiting at home for his return so that they may begin rebuilding their abode from its ruins. This dichotomised desire rather than pushing the journey into divergent paths seems to give structure to it, mapping its now rather visible narrative trajectory and making possible the redemption that is the real object of desire.

There is a personalisation of the collective, a subjectivisation of the objective reality, and an individualisation of civilisational degeneration that require, in fact, demand purification. This purification impulse identified by Karl as a central desire in modernism[2] drives the intertwined processes of 'house-cleaning' and 'soul-cleansing' detailed in the poem. 'The Eighth Voyage of Sindbād' is, in a crucial sense, a 'spiritual autobiography' that charts the subject's development not necessarily into a social unit prescribed in 'pre-modern' autobiography but into a self in search of 'self-knowledge'. He goes on a journey within, into the recesses of the self, now that the journey without, from 'present' to 'past' and back and from the 'East' to the 'West' and back, has made such an itinerary urgent and inevitable. This itinerary, anticipated in 'The Many Faces of Sindbād', is predictably bifurcated by a gendered desire, in fact, a sexual desire that is given the responsibility of sin as well as the power of redemption. I will here focus instead on its other potential, what would be seen as a sinister force, on its divisive tendency, and the ways in which its resistance to education is transformed into the allure that lies at the heart of the modern.

'The Eighth Voyage of Sindbād', a long poem in ten tableaux, begins with an unspoken bifurcated desire.

> You have gone to sea,
> My home,
> And you and I have now become strangers.
> You were once the best of homes,
> Seasick and estranged,
> In a city,
> At night,
> Swallowed by the sorrow of its desert,
> I watch dust gather over your threshold,
> And I want to run away,
> To follow the soft light ahead,
> Not knowing where it would take me,
> Perhaps to a garden of serenity,
> And I board the train,
> Taking night with me.[3]

Tableau 1 is the very evocation of the love motif inscribed in the 'abode-in-ruins' prelude of the Arabic *qaṣīda*. There is clearly a twist here. In Ḥāwī's poem, what left the protagonist and the abode behind is not the 'beloved woman' but the 'beloved abode' that has, like Sindbād, taken to seafaring. Sindbād returns from his seven voyages to find himself estranged from his old house (*dār*), which has become a place of alienation, with dust piled up at the threshold of his room. The distance between him and his old home is magnified by their respective travels. He flees, throwing himself on a train in the middle of the night. The inward journey, here set up as the eighth voyage of Sindbād, is further complicated by the protagonist's bipolarisation, his body's having split from his 'soul' in a cave during his seven voyages. The desire for a home is informed by another desire, a desire for the body to return and reunite with the soul. There is, then, incentive for the protagonist to clean the house, so to speak, and make it seductive enough for the body to want to return, 'when it [the body] passes by, it [the house] will seduce him, claim him'.[4] The kind of desire implied in the word chosen to convey it, *tughwīhi*, makes the journey itself and its completion highly problematic, and the significance of the endeavour paradoxical. The verb *tughwī* and its noun *ghiwāya* imply the kind of desire that seduces, tempts and misguides one to stray from the right path and to sin. This type of desire, so rampant in the 'old house', is what demands 'house-cleaning' in the first place, as tableau 2 tells us, then what would be the point in re-injecting this very undesirable desire into the newly cleaned house? Perhaps the accompanying 'soul-cleansing' demands encountering, grappling with, resisting and conquering this sinful desire?

This sinful desire, *ghiwāya*, seems to haunt the 'old house'. It drives the protagonist out, step by step, from its central pavilion, *riwāq*, to the city and its alleys, and finally to the sea, where the protagonist gains a panoramic advantage to view the 'old house' from the 'shores of islands of ice' in tableaux 2, 3 and 4. The ice (*ṣaqīᶜ*) seems to dowse the fire of 'sinful desire' coursing through his veins,[5] the desire he has internalised from images drawn on the walls of his pavilion, relics from the past: the 'wall mural' of Moses carving the Ten Commandments in stone stands next to that of a soothsayer breeding snakes and mating with virgins in the Temple of Baal. These are complemented by the world painted in Abū al-ᶜAlāᵓ al-Ma'arrī's poetry as a wily woman who has not washed, the smell between her legs the 'bitter fruit' he finds both repulsive and desirable.[6] These images, 'a torrent of gas and poison', are interred in 'this blood, injected into and planted in his veins'. He sees on the steps of his house and in the dark alleys of the city in Lorca's 'blood wedding' and Dīk al-Jinn's 'sword play' as a confrontation between the serpent in the gypsy woman, who has absorbed those images, and the blind tiger in the 'jealous' man.[7] The child of this environment is one who is ‘ruined by his father’,[8] gets used to treachery[9] and finds himself in dire need of ‘soul-cleansing’ that must come hand in hand with ‘house-cleaning’. The soul, like the old house, is infested with ghosts, violence, dust, ruins, stench, refuse and darkness.[10] His sojourn in and vantage point gained on the ‘islands of ice’[11] paves the way for both ‘house-cleaning’ and ‘soul-cleansing’. As the ice puts out the fires of sinful desire, the desert that has been the old house transforms into fertile earth, winter into spring, and darkness into light.

Tableau 4 of the poem is a two-way liminal bridge. It is the exit of departure as well as the entry of return. It is the space where a Tammuzi rebirth takes place under glittering stars[12] and the shining sun.[13] The house rises from its ruins, as the earth turns green, the grass grows, the flowers blossom, and the fruits take form. It is as if an angel has injected into his frozen body ‘virginal wine and green embers’, ‘cleansed his blood of gas and poisons’ and ‘erased from the slate he carries on his chest the old stamps and drawings’.[14] The newly born child is necessarily ignorant, with ‘ignorance running in his veins’, ‘naked, unembarrassed by the morning’, feeling his ‘first heart-beat’ and seeing and hearing for the first time.[15] It is in this state of innocence that he hears ‘a call to love’.[16] The stirring of another desire, a longing for love, frames the inbound journey that retraces backward the steps of the previous outbound one. The new itinerary follows the footsteps of a woman, this time a ‘beautiful, brave, innocent’ woman *(ḥilwa jarīʾa barīʾa)* created from his rib (*shuqqat min ḍulūʿī*),[17] from the city streets to the cleaned house in tableaux 5 and 6. There, they are to celebrate his homecoming in a new setting that will not be abandoned by light to darkness, ‘The morning will not abandon us, at the end of the day’.[18]

There are two parallel rebirths here. The protagonist and his object of desire seem to play out the fertility rites of the Tammuzi myth at first sight. Tammuz dies every year, is taken to the netherworld and returns only when Ishtar finds him and negotiates his temporary release. During their absence the earth is plunged into darkness, drought and barrenness, but as soon as they return, the rain falls, vegetation grows, animals mate and life begins again. This mating ritual, squarely placed in the seasonal cycles of a calendar year, takes place in the shadow of equally ritualistic prostitution at the Temple of Baal where Ishtar, the great mother goddess, is worshipped. The metamorphosis of a more licentious Ishtar into a ‘beautiful, brave and innocent’ woman, even in the dizzying confluence of voices, images and symbols in the poem, may be read, on second thought, as the transformation of the protagonist's soul, the product of 'soul-cleansing' carried out in tandem with 'house-cleaning'. The poem, Ḥāwī explains in his preface, 'is a taking stock of what he [Sindbād] took pains in grappling with when he took on cleaning the hallways of his self until he came upon the illumination of rebirth (or regeneration) and found certainty'.[19] The journey experienced here is a seafaring adventure of a different kind:

> The tale told of Sindbād is that he sailed in the world of his self (*dhātihi*). He would come upon piles of old things and worn-out concepts. He threw them all into the sea. He did not feel sorry for his loss. He bared himself all the way until his nakedness allowed him to see his natural essence (*jawhar fiṭratihi*). He then returned, bringing to us a treasure unequalled even by the treasures he brought home during his earlier voyages.[20]

The kind of 'soul-cleansing' journey encountered here is like Eliot's in 'The Journey of the Magi', in which the rebirth sought after is that of the self, the soul. The journey is then that of the self or soul's search for ways to transcend the material world, whether in the form of worldly goods or sexual appetites, which are deemed the cause and effect of civilisational degeneration. Transcendence of the corrupt material world, then, must begin with separation, house from his owner and body from soul, and end with their reunion, reunification but only after purification. The 'call to love' the protagonist hears may be the home-maker, Odysseus' Penelope, summoning him to go home and put the house in order in her silent longing and loyal endurance, or his soul hailing his body to a reunion. As Īmīl Maᶜlūf sees, in his review of the poem for *Al-ādāb*, the poem is ultimately about the quest for the unity of the self amidst the contradictions pervading the universe. This unity of body and soul is achieved through redemption, or internal purification (*al-burʾ al-dākhilī*), that takes the form of a four-stage process: unconscious immersion in sin (*al-iktifāʾ bi l-ithm al-lā-waᶜy*), the soul's full awareness of sin (*itkifāʾ al-rūḥ bi waᶜy al-ithm*), the flashing of unifying love (*wamḍat al-ḥubb al-muwaḥḥid*), and perfect vision and bliss (*ruʾyā muktamila wa niᶜma*).[21] Another reviewer for *Al-ādāb*, Raʾīf ᶜAṭāyā, agrees with this reading, and similarly concludes that the poem represents the best of contemporary Arabic existential poetry that takes as its subject man's search for transcendence through redemption.[22]

THE ARCHITECT OF MODERNISATION

In narrowing the scope of the poem to this kind of existential angst, however, we are in danger of reducing the final four tableaux to tautology, whether we are looking at the original eight or the finalised ten tableaux. For by the time we reach the end of tableau 4 of the earlier version or tableau 6 of the later one, this existential reading is already a foregone conclusion. It is true that tableaux 7, 8, 9 and 10 seem to cover the same grounds. Tableau 7 sums up the transformation effected in tableaux 1 through to 6 as a process through which, between the darkness of yesterday and the warmth of today, the old ruins morph into a new house, a shelter for weary neighbours.[23] Tableau 8 takes us into the 'belly of the whale', 'the womb of the season (*raḥim al-faṣl*,[24] where cleansing takes place – the she-demon exorcised and poison let from blood, before the protagonist is born into the new season.[25] Tableau 9 then takes us through the process of rebuilding of the house, column by column, and of his soul, piece by piece. Out of the cold, dark and rotting old, spring will come, morning will dawn, olive groves and vineyards will flourish, and children will be born. Cleaning expectedly comes with cleansing, much like what we have already seen in the earlier six tableaux, and sin must be washed in the rivers Nile, Jordan and Euphrates,[26] or in the rain of his love.[27] It is then that life, the present, will grow out of the decay of yesterday, the past.[28] The poem ends with a very short tableau 10 that reaffirms this optimistic message of regeneration; the house will be rebuilt and his soul restored to his body.[29] There is, I think, more than meets the existentialist eye.

Ḥāwī drops enough hints along the way for us to spy the contours of another journey taking place in the poem. The first five lines of tableau 8 may read like a refrain straight out of tableau 1.

> I went on, I went after it
> Feeling it inside me, but not conscious of it.
> I wish I could clean my house, so that
> When it passes by, it will seduce it and claim it.
> I feel it inside me but am not conscious of it.[30]

'It' here may more readily be taken as the body that comes to be separated from the soul in tableau 1, when these lines are preceded by:

The day my body burst out of shrouds (*inshaqqat al-akfān ᶜan jismī*)
And the split (*al-shiqq*) flashed in the cave.[31]

It is clearly possible to read these two lines as a reference to Sindbād's good fortune in escaping being buried alive with his wife in the well in his *Nights*' fourth voyage. His escape is in a way the separation of his body from the shrouds that inhabit the collective tomb he is thrown into. The line that follows, 'I have been telling the same stories they have been telling about me'[32] seems to nudge the reading in this direction. The lines that come after, however, give it that slight twist that makes possible reading *shiqq* as also the body's split from the soul.

I concealed what words cannot express
And I went on, went after it
Feeling it inside me but not conscious of it.
How could I be led by it, knowing that
I will be led to nakedness and loss?
I wish I could clean the house so that
When it passes by, it will seduce it and claim it.
I feel it inside me but am not conscious of it.[33]

Stripped of this context, however, 'it' in the first five lines of tableau 8 loses the already ambivalent referent. They are followed not by a revisit to the murals spread across the walls of the central pavilion of the house, but by a night spent in solitude surrounded by darkness and silence. Silence? Silence is introduced, out of the blue here, not as the environment in which the wall murals are to be contemplated, but as a she-demon to be struggled with then overcome. The entire tableau is structured around two movements: light (of vision) breaking through darkness and, more importantly, spoken words (*alfāẓ*) breaking out of silence (*ṣamt*). Put differently, the new vision formed during 'house-cleaning' and 'soul-cleansing' is struggling to find articulation. This new vision is uniquely his. It is not found in stories customarily told and cannot be repeated (like the stories of Sindbād). The battle has not been fought in vain.

The well of drought gushed forth
A lighthouse appeared in my darkness
I see and experience the vision that knocks me out for a while
And I weep

Why is that I cannot live up to the prophecy
Two months, silence
My lips are dry
When, when will words come to my rescue?
I have long rebelled,
I have skinned the she-devil
Leaving her tails in my lands
I spitted poison and curses
And words gushed forth from my mouth
Like waterfall of wolves
Today, the vision sings in my blood
With the freshness of morning,
The tremors of lightning,
And the bird's talent to pick out the scent
Hidden in the heart of forests and winds
And to feel what is there
In the womb of the season
And sees him before he is born to the seasons
The vision pours forth, and what?
The time will come
When I shall say what I will say.[34]

The kind of rebuilding that takes place in tableau 9 is then not simply of the old house and the ancient soul but of poetry, of epic (*tabtanī al-malḥama*),[35] that is the responsibility of the poet in whose guise the protagonist returns in tableau 10.

My seven voyages are tales about
The she-demon, the devil, the cave
And unequaled stratagems
I repeat what they tell, and what? In vain!
I will never retrieve!
I lost my capital and trade
What stories did the waterfalls tell
To the well and dams
To a feather polishing its camouflaging skills,
Hiding avarice in the streams of expression
I lost my capital and trade
I have returned to you a poet

Prophecy on his tongue
Who says what he says
With the innate talent to sense what is in the womb of season
To see him before he is born to the seasons.[36]

I want to dwell a little on the original Arabic two-line refrain that ends the poem and begin to argue that, at another level, 'The Eighth Voyage of Sindbād' is a discourse on modernity in Arabic poetry. This discourse disguises itself in the form of a journey, of both poet and poetry, from present to past and back, from East to West and back. These two lines appear towards the end of tableau 8[37] and at the end of tableau 10.[38] Both tableaux are preoccupied more with verbal articulation of inner vision, of prophecy, and less with 'house-cleaning' or 'soul-cleansing' which have already been dealt with in the earlier tableaux. The difficulty in tableau 8 is overcome in tableau 10, clearly facilitated by the process of transformation detailed in the form of Tammuzi's death and rebirth in tableau 9. '*Tuḥissu ma fī raḥimi l-faṣl,/tarāhu qabla an yūlada fī l-fuṣūl*', read from the perspective of the Tammuzi myth, lend themselves to my initial translation of 'To sense what is in the womb of season,/to see it/him before it is born into the season'. However, the Arabic term for 'season', *faṣl*, like Ḥāwī's cave that Haydar and Beard speak of, comes with a wide semantic range and has multiple possible referents. It can mean division, partition, separation, or section, part, chapter, act of a play, movement of a symphony, article in a newspaper, class or grade in school, and season. In particular uses, as in *faṣl al-khiṭāb, al-qawl al-faṣl*, and *yawm al-faṣl*, the word *faṣl* denotes finality and decision, final decision. *Yawm al-faṣl*, in this sense of the word, means 'the day of decision' or 'the Day of Judgment', and *faṣl al-khiṭāb* 'conclusion' or 'the last word', like *al-qawl al-faṣl*. The possible, in fact, welcome shift in the referent from 'season' in the Tammuzi sense to 'the last word' allows us to read the poem as the poet-protagonist's journey within, in search of a new vision and without, in a strife for an expression appropriate to the new vision. Implicit in this journey is, it goes without saying, a discourse on modernity, on modernisation and modernism of contemporary Arabic poetry.

Modernisation of Arabic poetry, seen through the lenses of the poem and, more particularly, of tableau 9, may be achieved through the simultaneous processes of deconstruction and reconstruction: deconstruction of the past and construction of the present from the ashes of the deconstructed past. The movement of tableau 9 is framed by and pulled in two different directions by tableaux 8 and 10. The new vision is carved out of knowledge acquired through sight and touch (*ruʾyā yaqīni al-ʿayn wa l-lams*),[39] not from anecdotes sung by transmitters (*wa laysat khabaran yaḥdū bihi r-ruwāt*).[40] Arrival at this vision requires that the past be let go in order to make way for the present to grow out of its ruins.

I would not have welcomed
The sun, if I had not seen you bathe
In the morning
In the Nile, the River Jordan and Euphrates
Scrubbing off the stamp of sin.
Every body is a hill
That has turned into a gem under the sun
A fragrant shadow
An innocent lake
The crocodiles have left our lands
Our sea poured out of them and deepened
They left us some remains
Their skins were flayed
But no skins grew in their stead
Their present is in the decay of yesterday
Which is gone and will not return
Their names, burnt by the vision of my eye,
Into smoke that has no existence
Why, my Lord, has red smoke and fire
Pervaded the vision?
Were my hand a current of ice
That I may wipe clean the sins
From the decay of yesterday
And grow grapes and fruits
So that the crocodiles
The malice of muddied rivers
Will be lost in my sea.
And balm will grow out of my wound
On the mountain of Golgotha.
I fell in love, no, my love is rain
That will shower my land with green
And the firewood beyond
Will be burnt into smoke by the vision of my eye

It will no longer exist
A time will come when I will embrace
The earth, expose its chest
And erase its borders.[41]

The kind of discourse on modernity implicit in Ḥāwī's poem rings a familiar bell to those rehearsed in the debates on the directions of contemporary Arabic poetry, especially those surrounding the so-called 'free verse' movement including poetry of the Tammuzi persuasion. The revisionist impulse within the modernising trend, exemplified by Adonis in both his poetry and criticism, typically argues that what is modern in contemporary Arabic poetry is firmly grounded in classical Arabic poetry but in past instances of modernity that have thus far been obscured by convention or canonised tradition. The return to the past in the form of a creative process of deconstruction and reconstruction is undeniably inspired by the encounter with the West. The West does play a crucial role, especially in jolting Arabs into action, but it does not define Arab modernism or determine the trajectory of Arab modernisation. Ḥāwī's poetry says as much in its integration of, say, Odysseus and Faust into the Magi of the East and finally Sindbād, and in its opening up the textual space of poems to intertextuality of divergent kinds, to Babylonian and Christian mythology, Homer, al-Ma^{c}arrī, Dīk al-Jinn, Goethe, Eliot, and Lorca all at once. What makes contemporary Arabic poetry, and his poetry, modern is the ways in which it maps its own trajectory of modernisation in an intertextual labyrinth, the singularity of its articulation of a vision, a dream, constructed out of the ruins of what once was.

The modernist-moderniser here, put slightly differently, is a dreamer, a lover and a developer, Goethe's Faust in Marshall Berman's analysis. To realise his dream he must risk his soul, perhaps even sell it Faust-like to the devil, Mephistopheles. Ḥāwī's Mephisto appears in the guise of the 'false prophet' in 'Magi from the East', and as the she-demon in 'The Mariner and the Dervish', 'The Many Faces of Sindbād' and 'The Eighth Voyage of Sindbād' that must be encountered, resisted, grappled with and overcome. Success is not guaranteed. The she-demon, more than any other devil-incarnate, haunts his rebirth. The house cleaned and the soul cleansed, it seems, are never really free of danger. While the dream struggles to emerge as a vision, new love retreats and development falters. There is a price to be paid for development, for it is necessarily accompanied by destruction. Faust's Gretchen, for example, must die, and much of humanity is destroyed in the wake of his developmental projects. What would be the price of the kind of modernisation envisioned by Ḥāwī? Ḥāwī's she-demon appears more benign, a figure in the distance that casts long shadows, and less involved, unlike Mephisto who is at the centre of Faust's metamorphosis from dreamer to developer. She is rather Odysseus' siren whose seductive song promises happiness for the price of death. In Marxist use of Odysseus as an allegory of modern art, the stratagems used by Odysseus to escape death – tying himself to the mast and blocking the ears of the sailors rowing him away – paradoxically lead to the birth of modern nostalgia: enchantment, or the promise of happiness, is both within and out of reach. The taming of the she-demon into the virginal angel in Ḥāwī is then an expression of the will to master this paradox, to grasp that elusive enchantment that promised happiness.

Ḥāwī's she-demon (*al-ghūl*), however, cuts a peculiar paradoxical figure of another kind. She is situated in both the 'past' and 'present', the 'East' and 'West', and her enchantment represents the allure of both 'past' and 'present', 'East' and 'West', that is simultaneously coveted and resisted. The location of the poet-protagonist, as well as modern Arabic poetry, in 'now' and 'then', 'here' and 'there', is an attempt at mastering paradoxes, at reconciling what is articulated as contrasts and contradictions in a combination of Hegelian synthesis of both/and and Kierkedaardian formula of either/or. Mastery here, however, is only a matter of desire not reality. Modern Arabic poetry has internalised this desire, as torn between 'now' and 'then', 'here' and 'there', and finds expression in its grappling with this desire, gendered and further dichotomised into sexualised she-demon and virginal angel. The referents of the polarised demon and angel are, however, unclear and unpredictable. Is the West the she-demon or the angel? What of the East? Is the modern the siren? Or is it tradition? One can never be sure. What is visible is the affect of the attempt at mastery, of the grappling with the siren, on the Arabic novel and its narrative trajectories.

THE POLITICS OF DESIRE IN THE ARABIC NOVEL

The relentless pursuit of desire in the Arabic novel is simultaneously an essential requirement for and inevitable symptom of modernity. The desire for Utopia, let us say, is a necessary step towards imagining and implementing a plausible community that will allow for the emergence of the modern subject and structure its growth and move to the centre of knowing and being. The tight structure of 'Utopia', the imagined nation-state in the shadow of empire, paradoxically threatens the emergence of the modern subject and compromises its freedom of movement. The story of desire in the Arabic novel is, in yet another sense, the story of modern subject and its itineraries, as will be seen, of its rise in the complex interstices of the forces behind cultural transformation located at the crossroads of cultural exchange. As it negotiates these various, often contradictory, forces, it comes to be under their influence but strives to master them, especially the paradoxes they throw up, such as the seeming polarities of 'self' and 'other', 'here' and 'there', and 'then' and 'now'. These articulated categories of knowledge have their concrete manifestation in the way culture and, more particularly, cultural identity are constructed, felt, thought of and expressed. Each of these categories can, I have already alluded to earlier in this chapter, serve as an object of desire, privileging one category over another. But this is not the only possible scenario; in fact, a number of and on occasion all these categories play the role of the temptress, making the trajectories of desire, and necessarily the contours of the modern subject, unpredictable, illusive and all over the place. The contours of the modern subject may be blurred by the wayward movements of desire, but the persistence of desire in contemporary Arabic narrative tells the story of not only subject's will to know and cohere but also its wish to escape, perhaps even transcend, cohesion and coherence.

In telling this story of the modern subject, the Arabic novel explores one experience of modernity as a complex web of negotiated truces between contradictions woven by desire's uncontrollable multi-directional trajectories. Put differently, the Arabic novel tells a fantastic story of the modern subject's coming into being and taking centre stage in its insistent inscription of desire into its unfolding, giving it the function of the motor that drives the stories it tells. The pursuit of desire necessarily casts the stories it tells in the form of journeys. Travel, it goes without saying, comes to be the central trope of the Arabic novel as well. The modern Arab journey is, however, always moving towards at least two destinations: the 'past', or tradition, originating in the 'self', and the 'West' presented as the allure of the 'other'. Sindbād and Ulysses come to be one and the same wanderer in the Arab journey towards nationhood and modernity, towards home. Home, a space re-drawn and re-mapped by a new national imagining of community, is not wholly defined by the experience of the West, positively or negatively; for modernity in the Arab context is not synonymous with the West even though it cannot really do without it. Rather, it is shaped by a desire that drives, among others, 'the journey in search of knowledge', and that, in its wiliness, as will become clear, cannot be contained within 'self' or 'other,' 'here' or 'there', and 'then' and 'now'. Each of these articulated categories of knowledge would serve as an object of desire the movement towards which is complicated by the presence and influence of the others.

The consequent unpredictable multiple trajectories of desire are also an expression of the diversity of modernity as the experience of the present, of 'here' and 'now', always in the shadow of the past or future, of 'there' and 'then'. The Arab Magi, if one may use such an expression, is a traveller, just like Eliot's, but his journeys will acquire additional layers of complexity, just like Ḥāwī's and Mahfouz's. If Eliot's Magi shuttles back and forth between past and present, the Arab Magi is fated to wander not only from past to present and back, like Eliot's, but also from the East to the West and back, like Ḥāwī's and Mahfouz's. The Arabic novel has internalised this twofold desire and speaks of its aspirations in terms of its grappling with it. Shahrayār and Sindbād's open-ended journey in Mahfouz's *Layālī* is a grappling with this desire that is fuelled by nostalgia, by memories of what once was and dreams of what will be, for a new organisation of time and space. This nostalgia will make its mark on the text and narrative movements of the Arabic novel, for it must speak of the present, even future, by grappling with the past and, as we shall in what follows and saw in Chapter 4, in the language of the past.

I now turn to the nostalgic redeployment of the poetics of desire in *Qaṣr al-Shawq* (1957; Palace of Desire, 1990),[42] the second volume of Mahfouz's *Cairo Trilogy* (1956–7), in order to trace the continuity between an Arabic novel and an Arabic poem, especially the poetic vision and poetics operative beneath and behind the landscape of the Arabic novel, and to track the overlapping of these poetics with classical Arabic poetics, as well as poetics of pre-modern Arabic prose genres, particularly pre-modern Arabic travel writing, that is evoked, interred and reshaped in Mahfouz's novels. For poetics of desire, past and present, East and West, are at the heart of the story the Arabic novel tells of its search for form, inherent in its search for modernity as well as the expression of its experience of it. Modernity here is, as in Ḥāwī's poems, a 'siren' whose call simultaneously forewarns of an apocalypse and heralds a new world. The object of desire is cast in the form of a temptress, a beguiling woman in various disguises, the fall for whose allure will be the downfall of the Sindbād-like modern subject. Modernity, in the Arabic novel, is never simply the West; rather, it is like our experience of Ḥāwī's poetry, multiple, and may be the West, the East as present, or the myriad configurations of the overlapping of the two.

The Arabic novelistic temptress understandably comes from both East and West. There is, however, a reductive dichotomisation in critical assessment of the temptress in the Arabic novel, and facile reading of native women as allegories of the East, and their European counterparts as symbols of the West.

Native female protagonists like Haykal's Zaynab, the beautiful peasant woman in *Zaynab* (1913),[43] and Mahfouz's Ḥamīda, the sexy citizen of *Zuqāq al-midaqq* (1947; *Midaq Alley*, 1981), are two of the many memorable female characters embodying desire in the Arabic novel. They arguably represent two streams of allegorisation of Egypt. That these women, one from rural Egypt and another from an old Cairene quarter, should be both the subject and object of desire and fall victim to multifarious desires, of their own and of others competing for their body, is perhaps more noted than seeing them as necessarily a parallel and contrast to the Western woman who has, as an object of desire, lured Arab intellectuals away to the West only to leave them marooned in-between, neither here nor there, with nowhere to go. While Western women of the Arabic novel are read as the West and the modern, Zaynab and Ḥamīda are read as symbols of Egypt. *Zaynab* is an allegory of Egypt imprisoned in its traditional social structures, and *Midaq Alley* is a 'national allegory' in which Ḥamīda is arguably symbolic of Egypt and its predicament as it is pulled in all directions by and falls prey to competing forces – the British, the Monarchists, the Wafdists, the Communist, the Islamists, the Socialists, the Capitalists, among others. The famous, or infamous, Western women – Susie in Tawfīq al-Ḥakīm's *ᶜUṣfūr min al-sharq* (1938; Bird of the East, 1966),[44] Ann Hammond, Sheila Greenwood, Isabella Seymour, and particularly Jean Morris in al-Tayyib Salih's *Mawsim al-hijra ilā al-shamāl* (1967; Season of migration to the North, 1969),[45] and Janine Montreau in Suhayl Idrīs's *Al-ḥayy al-lātīnī* (1953; The Latin Quarter), on the other hand, represent the West and the modern that complicate post-colonial Arab identity politics.

The cultural discourses on post-colonial identity politics and modernisation, in their privileging of decolonisation, liberation and nation-building in the shadow of empire and imperialism, unavoidably cast the West as a site of contest where desire serves as both the will to seduce, tame, overcome and possess as well as the impulse to resist, reject, banish and destroy. Modernity has more often than not been equated with the Western aesthetics. What gets concealed and silenced are women like Ḥamīda, a 'traditional' woman from old Cairo seduced by new Cairo, and a variety of 'native' women 'Westernised' by virtue of their being citizens of a

'Westernised' metropolis, like Cairene Saniyya, the love object of Muḥsin in al-Ḥakīm's *ᶜAwdat al-rūḥ* (1933; Return of the Spirit, 1990);[46] or of their being partners of Westernised Arab men, such as Ḥusna Bint Maḥmūd, Muṣṭafā Saᶜīd's Sudanese wife in *Season of Migration to the North*. In fact, the Western women of the Arabic novel all have 'native' counterparts, just like Ḥusnā Bint Maḥmūd to Ann Hammond, Sheila Greenwood, Isabella Seymour and Jean Morris. Al-Ḥakīm's Susie in *Bird from the East*, for example, finds her match in Muḥsin's heartbreaker, Saniyya, in *The Return of the Spirit*, and Idrīs's Janine Montreau loses her love to a Lebanese rival in Hudā, a paradoxical Beiruti woman who is seemingly 'modern' but in reality 'traditional'.

These native women, whether they have been to the West or not, tell a different story of the Arab experience of modernity, as I shall show, in the ways they desire and inspire desire often but not always of the sexual kind. They do, on most occasions, play the twin(n)ed role of home-maker and home-wrecker, of siren, she-demon, whore and of angel, muse and goddess, wreaking fantastic havoc in the paths of their desiring and desired men. The intersecting trajectories of desire among Arab men and women in the Arabic novel at one level tell the story of the ways in which desire, as Freud and Lacan theorise, lies at the heart of and drives the modern subject. At another level, they also provide a blueprint for Arab modernity's complex psychic make-up, of which the impulse or will to decolonise, as is said of Muṣṭafā Saᶜīd's mission to counter-invade and counter-conquer through mastery of Western women, is only a part. It rather tells tales of the variety of Arab modernity's 'others' and 'alternatives', and of their aspiration or ambition to cohere in the identitarian labyrinth constructed out of imports from the West as well as relics of the past. The perceived role of the West in Arab modernity is, more to the point, complicated, renegotiated, redefined through the Arabic novel's remembrance and re-enactment of desire and its trajectories canonised in classical Arabic poetics, as well as the contemporary readings of these poetics.

The polarity of the feminised object of desire in Ḥāwī – the siren, she-demon home-wrecker and the angelic Penelope-like homemaker – gives a hint of the workings of desire in Arabic poetics. Desire, in its most readily expressible form, necessarily manifests itself as sexual desire made essential, as well as possible, by nature's self-perpetuating procreation entrusted to sexuality, to men and women's attraction to each other and their drive to satisfy this draw. Gendering desire, as required in its own engendering, in our expression and explanation of, let us say, nature's way of life, is problematic because it is based on 'othering', on distinction and separation requiring and occasionally leading to harmony and union. In the first draft of *Description of Egypt*,[47] Edward Lane remembers the moment he saw Alexandria for the first time in his life on 17 September 1825 after a long voyage, like this:

> As I approached the shore, I felt like an Eastern bridegroom, about to lift up the veil of his bride, and to see, for the first time, the features which were to charm, or disappoint, or disgust him. I was not visiting Egypt merely as a traveler, to examine its pyramids and temples and grottoes, and, after satisfying my curiosity, to quit it for other scenes and other pleasures: but I was about to throw myself entirely among strangers; to adopt their language, their customs and their dress; and, in associating almost exclusively with the natives, to prosecute the study of their literature. My feelings therefore, on that occasion, partook too much of anxiety to be pleasing.[48]

Arab novelists have applied similar gendering, feminising the West and masculinising the East, in speaking of cultural encounters. The unrequited love of Muḥsin for Susie in al-Ḥakīm is, among other things, an expression of the East's infatuation with the West. It is also a site on which the civilisational imbalance between the East and the West occasioned by colonisation that showcased the power of the West over the East is redressed. The East redeems itself, the narrative logic of *Bird of the East* goes to show, by asserting its own 'spiritual' superiority while acknowledging the West's technological advantage. The failed love affair between Suhayl Idrīs's alter ego and Janine Montreau in *The Latin Quarter*, on the other hand, serves as a vehicle for a comparison between the individual liberties of the culture in the West and their relative absence in that of the East. The comparison locates itself not in simplistic stereotyping of the Western woman as necessarily sexually licentious and morally loose but in the Eastern man's insecurity and inability to resist familial and social pressures. The failure of the central love affair is attributed not to Janine, who is fully committed to this love, but to the male protagonist who gives in to his mother's pressures and manipulations. Al-Ṭayyib Ṣāliḥ's violent tale of revenge, by now all too familiar to readers of Arabic and African fiction, is premised on feminising then mastering the West by a masculine East. Ann Hammond, Sheila Greenwood, Isabella Seymour and Jean Morris are, among other things, aspects of what Edward Said would call European 'Orientalism' that Muṣṭafā Saᶜīd attempts to purge less from European discourses on the East but more from Eastern discourses on culture and identity.

Whether we consider such gendering a universal impulse or a peculiar counter-colonial stratagem in the Arab context, the problems it poses are clear. The categories of thought that find expression in the twin(n)ed 'East' and 'West' mediated by sexual desire and set against a background of a another dichotomised pair – 'tradition' and 'modernity' – in contemporary Arabic cultural discourses on the features, direction and future of the Arabic novel, like that of poetry already discussed, are premised on difference; on thinking of the 'West' as the 'East's cultural other and 'modernity' as 'tradition's' historical other. Even though desire may bring about a union of two juxtaposed, perhaps even opposed categories, distinction and, on occasions, antagonism between the two poles of each pair of twin(n)ed categories cannot easily be erased. The relation between the 'West' as feminised object of desire and the 'East' as masculinised desiring subject in the Arabic novel is such that harmony and unity are far from self-evident. The certainty of union, expressed in the language of a bridegroom finally meeting his bride in Lane, is undermined in the Arabic novel. Susie rejects Muḥsin in *Bird of the East*, Suhayl abandons Janine Montreau in *The Latin Quarter*, and Muṣṭafā Saᶜīd murders Jean Morris in *Season of Migration to the North*. The marriage between 'East' and 'West', seen from the perspective of these novels, is a recipe for disaster if not tragedy. More importantly, 'modernisation' driven by 'Westernisation' is doomed to failure.

The love affair with the Western woman in the Arabic novel in particular tells only one side of the story of Arab encounter with modernity and modernisation. The figure of the Westernised woman in the Arabic novel, al-Ḥakīm's Saniyya, Idrīs's Hudā, Ṣāliḥ's Ḥusna Bint Maḥmūd, and Mahfouz's ᶜĀyda in the second part of *Cairo Trilogy*, supplements and complicates this story. ᶜĀyda, Kamāl's object of love in *Palace of Desire* is the epitome of desire that is the experience of modernity itself. She is the Arabic novel's equivalent of Ḥāwī's she-demon, who belongs to both East and West, past and present. She also puts at risk the idealised Eastern woman, such as Haykal's Zaynab, for she refuses to be transformed into an angelic, passive rural maiden, who represents a form of Egyptian 'authenticity'.[49] Rejecting both the West as the only site of modernity and source of modernisation and the East as the unadulterated 'primitivist religious community', she instead points to Cairo as a site of modernity, a modern Cairo that is located at the very heart of the East. More importantly, her story, or the story of Kamāl's initial infatuation with and final disappointment in her, is key to our understanding of the poetics of the Arabic novel, and the make up of a modernist text.

THE POETICS OF LOVE IN *PALACE OF DESIRE*

Mahfouz's *Cairo Trilogy* has been and continues to be under close scrutiny. There is a wealth of information on it; book reviews, translation reviews, critical assessments, literary analyses of perhaps the best-known Arabic novel in the world abound. It is rather overwhelming to even contemplate the list compiled by Ḥamdī Sakkūt in *Al-riwāya al-ᶜarabiyya: biblūgrāfiyā wa madkhal naqdī* (2000), let alone conduct a 'Google' search today, in 2011. There is, this said, a fairly universal agreement about what the novel is. The *Trilogy* is a representation of Cairo in the interwar period, and a critique of the contemporary political ideologies and social orthodoxies. It does this through the development of Kamāl, said to be Mahfouz's alter ego, from an impressionable child to a disillusioned intellectual, alienated from his surroundings and ineffectual in making changes. Mahfouz's Kamāl is an allegory of the Eastern intellectual at a time of national crisis that led to intellectual agonising. This allegory is located in the way Mahfouz portrays his relationship with ᶜĀyda. His disappointment in love is interpreted as a symptom of his failure to turn himself into an engaged, proactive and revolutionary public intellectual and to play a key role in nation-building. The idealised ᶜĀyda, like the iconised *Zaynab* in Haykal's eponymous novel, is symbolic of an intellectual Utopia that exists and must reside only in fantasy, in the world of ideals. An idealist like Kamāl, who hides himself behind the mask of a thinker (*mufakkir*), is doomed from the outset to slip through the cracks of socialisation and fall by the wayside of political activism. He thinks but does not act. He is, moreover, a hypocrite who lives by a double standard that is the parlance of his father. Like al-Sayyid ᶜAbd al-Jawād, he lives two sexual lives, but with a difference. His father allows himself limitless freedom in various self-indulgent extra-marital sexual liaisons but imposes his strict rule as a patriarch through tight control of the sexuality of the members of his family. Kamāl, like his father, turns to underground sex to satisfy his physical needs and drown his sorrows, albeit for only two months, but abstains from, or more aptly, cannot even contemplate marrying the real objects of his love, first ᶜĀyda and later her sister Budūr, for he is unable to reconcile between the 'loftiness' of love and the 'baseness' of desire. Kamāl is, to put it simply, like Ḥāwī's Sindbād, stuck, between ideal and reality, Utopia and dystopia.

The novel is interpreted through the prism of European realism, rather typical of readings of Mahfouz's novels wonderfully captured by Jūrj Ṭarābīshī:

> And the novelist Najīb Maḥfūẓ, as if giving in to the irresistible law of history, follows in the footsteps of Tawfīq al-Ḥakīm in experimenting with techniques. However, instead of being swept away by every trend in the world in his experiments, he quarantined himself in the laboratory of realism, wagering to derive infinite variations of the form by compounding or dissolving its chemical elements. From historical realism in *Kīfāḥ ṭība* to folk realism in *Zuqāq al-midaqq*, psychological realism in *Al-sarāb*, social realism in *Bidāya wa nihāya*, 'river'[50] realism in the *Trilogy*, new realism in *Al-liṣṣ wa l-kilāb*, symbolic realism in *Al-ṭarīq*, poetic realism in *Al-shaḥḥādh*, mythical realism in *Awlād ḥāratinā*, hallucinatory realism in *Tharthara fawq al-nīl*, multi-realism in *Mīrāmār*, surreal realism in *Taḥt al-miẓalla*, and fantastic realism in *Shahr al-ʿasal*, we see in Najīb Maḥfūẓ the face of Sisyphus who returns to climbing every time the rock rolls down the mountain. There is, however, a difference. Sisyphus of realism, unlike Sisyphus of the myth, intentionally lets the rock roll down the mountain when he reaches the summit, not for anything but to enjoy climbing to the summit again on another path.[51]

Here, Mahfouz's works are considered within the parameters set up by the Western novel of a certain mode, realism. Even the departures are contained in the broad category of this mode. The frame of reference is the West. Ṭarābīshī's description is, in a way, similar to statements to the effect that Mahfouz is, for example, the Balzac, Dickens, Tolstoy or Zola of the Arab world.[52] Perhaps it is inevitable that the case should be so. After all, the novel as a literary form did originate in the West and its maturity, at the hands of Mahfouz, is explicable in terms of its complete immersion in the Arabic language and culture. In other words, Mahfouz has domesticated a foreign genre by casting it in a native language and giving it a local content. The Arabic novel is, at its best, an Arab perfection of a Western form. There is, however, a quality in Mahfouz's writing that cast doubts on such a way of thinking about the Arabic novel.

In 'The Mahfouzian Sublime', Michael Beard situates the discussion of 'the quality of Maḥfūẓ's writing that strikes the Western reader as unfamiliar, eccentric, and well, strange' in the question of the novel as both 'a culture-specific form, a mode of story-telling that matches the concerns and ways of seeing of industrialized society' and on the other hand what we perceive as 'a neutral, flexible vision, nondistorting and infinitely exportable'.[53] Beard explains:

> The novel offers us the vista of two parallel streams of literary history. One is the European novel, the style that defines realism for us, whose major innovations we can trace back to Balzac – the emphasis on the relation of character and setting, the fascination with appearances and social roles, and the self-conscious manipulation of point of view – a tradition whose reversals in this century are founded on those patterns. The other stream is the more recent series of novelistic traditions that have grown up outside Europe or the United States – usually as part of the process of an awakening national identity – which conceive the novel as a tool for defining a national character and articulating national problems.[54]

Beard is referring to the national allegorical dimensions of the Arabic novel that has made it possible for Fredric Jameson to generalise that third world literature as necessarily national allegories. However, he is also alluding to the differing quality of Mahfouz's writing, what he calls 'sublime', that comes across even in translation. This 'sublime' is exactly what distinguishes the Arabic novel from any Western work of the same genre. The only problem is that the sublime aspects of Mahfouz's writing, as he shows in his discussion of *Al-marāyā*, are tangible but 'unclassifiable'. It is rather difficult, then, to speak in concrete terms of the identity markers of the Arabic novel, markers that allow us to articulate the distinctive features of the Arabic novel, especially at the level of form, and devise a critical language to speak of its unique aesthetics. I want to take Beard's discussion a step further and suggest that this sublime is classifiable. It is, for example, possible and promising to trace the aesthetics of *Palace of Desire* not only to the modernist poetics and politics of desire of East and West, but also classical Arabic poetics[55] and the cultural discourses on them in the first half of the twentieth century, the intersection of which tells the story of Cairo's very own 'local' modernity and its impact on Egyptian intellectuals.

The major events of *Palace of Desire* are, one may argue, the misadventures of the three male protagonists, al-Sayyid Aḥmad ᶜAbd al-Jawād, Yāsīn and Kamāl, in the sexual underworld of Cairo while a political resolution for Egypt's decolonisation and true independence is being worked out. The novel covers the period roughly between 1924, beginning five years after the 1919 revolution, when Saᶜd Zaghlūl formed the Wafd Government, and ending in 1927, the year in which he died. Nothing drastic happens at the political front; Zaghlūl is still negotiating with the Europeans. In the meantime, life returns to normal in the ᶜAbd al-Jawād household five years after Fahmī, the prodigal son, died in the violence of the 1919 revolution at the end of *Palace Walk*, the first part of the *Trilogy*. The daughters, Khadīja and ᶜĀʾisha, are settled in their married life, the divorced Yāsīn is contemplating getting married again, and the grown Kamāl makes a decision to enrol in the teachers training college in order to be able to pursue the study of and writing about literature and thought. Now, al-Sayyid Aḥmad enjoys spoiling his grandchildren every Friday, when his children and their spouses together with their children come for the weekly family reunion. Āmina, his wife, is her good old self again, serving him and his brood tirelessly. They are finally emerging from five years of mourning Fahmī. But how do the male members of the ᶜAbd al-Jawād family celebrate their return to life?

Al-Sayyid Aḥmad goes back to his secret libertine nocturnal lifestyle, this time forming a liaison with Zannūba, the young disciple of his former love, Zubayda. He sets her up in a boat (*ᶜawwāma*) on the Nile. Yāsīn marries a divorced Maryam, the love object of the departed Fahmī, falling out with Āmina, and moves to his own house in another part of old Cairo, Bayna al-Qaṣrayn. But Yāsīn is his father's son. While pursuing Maryam in marriage, he falls into an affair with her mother. He does marry her but throughout their short married life he carries on as usual, chasing after his prodigious sexual appetite in the nightlife of Cairo. He reconnects with Zannūba, now his father's lover, and brings her home for a tryst on a drunken night, only to be caught by Maryam at dawn. Divorce follows, so does marriage. Zannūba breaks up with al-Sayyid and marries Yāsīn. Marriage cannot put a damper on Yāsīn's enthusiasm for his extra-marital love life, but Zannūba seems to bear it stoically. She steadfastly makes a respectable home for herself and Yāsīn's children. As for Kamāl, he falls madly in love with ᶜĀyda, his school friend's sister, forsakes underground sex for a while, has his heart cruelly broken, and returns to his old double life. Kamāl, as it turns out, is also his father's son. He comes face to face with this reality when he runs into Yāsīn at a night party, and an intoxicated Yāsīn spills his father's beans.

The ᶜAbd al-Jawād family saga, as the *Trilogy* tends to be considered, reads like the ᶜUmar al-Nuᶜmān family saga discussed in Chapters 3 and 4; the improper sexual conduct of the male protagonists, bordering on incest on occasions, points to generational clashes at a time of national strife and crisis[56] and forecasts the disintegration of the family. Al-Sayyid Aḥmad closes down his shop (though perhaps more because of the changing economic circumstances), and suffers a debilitating heart attack at the end of this second part of the *Trilogy*. Yāsīn, as expected, barely manages to keep his lowly job thanks to his sexual scandals. The same may be said of Kamāl. His career as thinker/writer never takes off. Instead of pursuing a literary career, as he is often advised to do, he chooses to write lifeless summaries of Western philosophy for journals that very few people read, or find offensive when they do read them. And, the straw that finally breaks the camel's back is the fate of ᶜĀʾisha's husband and two sons: they perish in a typhoid epidemic. Practically every member of the family is cut down to size, forced to face dwindling fortunes and unhappy prospects as the curtains are drawn on the ᶜAbd al-Jawād family in the wake of Zaᶜd Zaghlūl's death.

Palace of Desire (1957) is sandwiched between two frenetic periods of political activism in the history of modern Egypt: the events leading up to the 1919 and 1952 revolutions, respectively in *Palace Walk* (1956) and *Sugar Street* (1957). The *Trilogy* looks back at the interwar period from the perspective of hindsight – Mahfouz completed the novel in April 1952, a few months short of the 23 July 1952 revolution.[57] Only from the postwar vantage point is the novel able to see the period between 1924 and 1927, in fact, the entire interwar period, as liminality, whereby the whole Egyptian nation lies in wait for something to happen, say, for the European nations to be done with their fights on their soil,[58] so that her destiny may unfold independently, away from European powers and interests.[59] *Palace of Desire* is a meditation on Egypt's powerlessness in effecting any political change in the period between 1924 and 1927. The absence of political resolution is, however, amply compensated for by the exuberance of eroticism. Eroticism is in turn seen as richness in characterisation[60] and critique of traditional forms of power and ways of life at a crisis point.[61] It is interpreted as symbolic of al-Sayyid Aḥmad's patriarchal hypocrisy, Yāsīn's frivolity, and Kamāl's idealism,[62] all contributing to the unravelling of a moral crisis engulfing the whole of Egyptian society.[63] No Mahfouz critic seems to have picked up on this juxtaposition between political inaction and love cornucopia, which serves as the central trope around which this novel is structured.[64] Eroticism, so central to the composition and feel of the *Trilogy*, ought to be related to the politicisation of classical love poetry and love stories current in the cultural discourses of the first half of the twentieth century.

In a series of articles on classical Arabic love poetry he published in the *Al-siyāsa* newspaper on a weekly basis in 1924,[65] Ṭāhā Ḥusayn, one of Mahfouz's acknowledged 'teachers',[66] proposed a radical re-reading of Umayyad love poetry and the stories about its famous 'authors', whom he terms '*al-ghazilūn*'.[67] Rather than looking for the historical persons, authenticating poems attributed to them and making moral judgments about a particular historical period, he suggested reading between the lines to find that 'special idea' (*fikra khāṣṣa*)[68] hidden in the poetry from that period, and in the stories 'fabricated' about the poets in a later period. The emergence of love poetry in Hijaz as an independent genre in the Umayyad period, when the centre of political, economic and cultural power had moved to Damascus, was responsive to the political marginalisation of Hijaz, changes in economic fortunes of the Arabian tribes, and penetration of Islamic teachings. While the rich, urban 'aristocrats' in Mecca and Medina, like ᶜUmar Ibn Abī Rabīᶜa, sought their outlet from the frustration of political inactivity in women, wine and music, the impoverished common class of Bedouins, their livelihood diminished by the imposition of alms tax and prohibition of looting, fell in love with unobtainable women and frequently went mad, like Jamīl Buthayna, Qays Laylā and Qays Lubnā. The poetic enterprise, Ḥusayn argued, was highly political. Umayyad love poetry ought not to be taken literally as 'realistic' representation of life and social mores of the time, but literarily as expressions of subversion. Indulgence in sex, wine and music is flouting political, social and moral authority of the Umayyads and Islam, and going mad and dying for love are similarly responsive to this authority and expressive of rebellion against it too. Love poetry, in both 'Casanovan' (*muḥaqqiqūn*) and 'Platonic' (*ᶜudhrī*) strands, was expressive of a profound sense of existential alienation caused by political marginalisation that came in the wake of a complete transformation of a way of life and its attendant world view. The political dimensions of Umayyad love poetry were obfuscated by the love stories (*qaṣaṣ gharāmī*, or *qiṣaṣ gharāmiyya*), so full of silliness (*sukhf*),[69] fabricated later then regurgitated unexamined in, for example, *Kitāb al-aghānī*. However, these 'silly' love stories could not erase completely references to the tension between the political elite and the poets, as well as political power and poetic expression.

I locate Mahfouz's exploration of powerlessness in this classical Arabic poetics of love and desire, and in the contemporary discourses on this poetics, which continue to have currency in today's Arabic scholarship, and look at the ways in which its overlap with Eliot and Ḥāwī's poetics gives shape to the novel and contemplates the experience of modernity in Cairo. I have already alluded to the parallel between the interwar period in the history of Egypt and the duration in *Palace of Desire*, which period may be characterised by political inactivity on the 'national' scale from the perspective of hindsight. The rise of the nation-state that would be Egypt had stalled, at least for now, for despite the declaration of her independence in 1922, she remained hostage to European powers with no real political authority or economic power. It would take a war and a revolution for her to finally achieve some sense of sovereignty. The experience of this quiet before the storm must have been frustrating and unsettling for Egyptian activists and intellectuals. Quoting a study by Muḥammad ᶜAwda on the relationship between intellectuals and revolution published in the *Al-jumhūriyya* newspaper (24 January 1963), Ghālī Shukrī speaks of the 1930s as witnessing the birth of a new generation of Egyptian intellectuals, to which Mahfouz belonged, in the shadow of political stagnation, when mass national liberation movements turned into a political cause fought over by the Palace, *Wafd* and the colonisers, or debated among various parties, each guided by its own ideology, which ranged from fascism to capitalism and communism. Paradoxically, this generation of intellectuals was also connected with the rest of the world in an unprecedented fashion, experiencing at the same time the most fundamental changes taking place around the globe.[70]

Egypt, it is palpably felt in Mahfouz's text, is powerless, existing in the margin of the international arena of war and power games, negotiating for self-mastery, while feeling the tidal waves of transformations of all kinds occurring in the global arena wash over her. This sense of powerlessness is conveyed less in the way Mahfouz portrays *Palace of Desire*'s three male protagonists as less than politically minded but more in the prominence he gives to their love life. This feature of *Palace of Desire* is poignant especially when it is read against *Palace Walk*, in which narrative is driven by Fahmī's participation in the 1919 revolution, and *Sugar Street*, which narrates the emergence of various political discourses in Egypt from communism (Aḥmad Shawkat) to Islamic fundamentalism (ᶜAbd al-Munᶜim) among the third generation of the ᶜAbd al-Jawād family. Little of political or national import happens in *Palace of Desire*. This second part of the *Trilogy* seems to be obsessed with love and sex. It reads more like the silly love adventures (*qiṣaṣ gharāmiyyaʾ*) Ṭāhā Ḥusayn dismisses as purposefully frivolous but of which Yāsīn is exclusively fond. It is arguably an extended essay on love and desire with a particular agenda. Mahfouz's decision to choose *shawq*, desire in Arabic, as the orthography of the quarter to which the title of his novel refers, over *shawk*, as it occasionally appeared on street signs, cannot be accidental.

The novel sets us up from the outset for following the trajectories of the three male protagonists' appetite for love and sex. It begins with a refrain, almost a duplicate of the first chapter of *Palace Walk*, as a reminder that we are still in the realm of the same story. But the gear shifts as early as chapter two, in which al-Sayyid Aḥamd, Yāsīn and Kamāl wake up in the morning with only thoughts of love. The father contemplates returning to the arms of Zubayda, the eldest son daydreams of the feel of Maryam in his embrace, and the youngest son eagerly anticipates a reunion with ᶜĀyda, the *maᶜbūd* (worshipped) whom he worships with every fibre of his being. Al-Sayyid Aḥmad's return to love after five years of abstinence brings to completion in *Palace of Desire* the triad of pleasure – wine, music and sex – in his other life, lived only away from his home. His reintegration into society, however, signals the beginning of his undoing. Yāsīn's decision to pursue Maryam will expose the purposelessness of his life; his life story is made up of extra-martial affairs and nights spent in pleasure houses surrounded by music and wine. Kamāl's infatuation with ᶜĀyda will begin the process of his unravelling. ᶜĀyda's marriage will push his sanity to the limit and make him ask questions about his idealism. How could he have been so wrong about ᶜĀyda and the nature of love and desire? How would he reconcile between ideal and reality? Could he trust his ability to know and understand? When he realises that ᶜĀyda has made fun of his boyish affections publicly and used them to ensnare a husband, he loses his mind and in turn resorts to the triad of pleasure for solace.

The undeniable poetic quality of Mahfouz's writing in this chapter, which Enany sees as 'drawn from the admitted autobiographical link between Kamāl and his creator',[71] is reminiscent and evocative of Umayyad love poetry. We read this particularly in the 'stream of consciousness' assigned to Yāsīn and Kamāl. Yāsīn's recollection of an encounter with Maryam is rendered in what reads like *ghazal sarīḥ*,[72] and Kamāl's contemplations of ᶜĀyda *ghazal udhrī*.[73] The novel is full of such poetically fashioned monologues, always consistently distributed between the two brothers. These introductory passages on the two brothers seal their fates in the novel. Yāsīn, like ᶜUmar Ibn Abī Rabīᶜa, will lose himself in the triad of sensual pleasure, and Kamāl, like Majnūn Laylā, will suffer not only the loss of love but also disillusion in love, and practically go mad. The love stories of the two brothers, framed by the love story of their father, are Mahfouz's re-politicisation of love poetry and politicisation of love stories from the classical tradition in the footsteps of Ṭāhā Ḥusayn. These love stories are modelled on the 'silly love stories' the ᶜAbbasids had woven around the highly political Umayyad love poetry. Mahfouz reconfigures these love stories in a way that would make them more appropriate to the purpose of love poetry, turning them into a 'national allegory' that chronicles the convulsive events taking place in Egypt and around the world but in the face of which Egyptians felt extremely helpless and hapless. In a world where the triad of pleasure (sex, wine and music) dominates, the triad of power (political authority, reason and justice) is pushed aside, refused entry to centre stage. The nation-state that is the imagined sovereign political community, the hoped for contours of which are found already in the works of al-Ṭahṭāwī and Mubārak, has yet to take concrete form on the site of Cairo, in fact, modern Cairo.

CAIRO MODERN

That Cairo is modern has already been documented in *Al-khiṭaṭ al-tawfīqīyya* and *Ḥadīth ᶜĪsā Ibn Hishām*. These two precursors of the Arabic novel not only remap Cairo spatially, as I have discussed in Chapters 1 and 2, but also communicate an experience of modernity particular to their time and place. *Ḥadīth ᶜĪsā Ibn Hishām* puts across an additional sense of alienation in the wake of the rapid and radical transformation of Cairo into an utterly unfamiliar metropolis. The protagonist, the resurrected Pasha, finds modern Cairo horrifyingly foreign, in its new spatial organisation, in the cultural and political institutions recently established, in the altered ways Cairenes dress, in the ethical codes informing the behaviour of its citizens, and in the ubiquitous presence of the West. This sense of space is necessarily accompanied by an equivalent alienating sense of time, a feeling that the present has become unrecognisably altered from the familiar, the past. The Pasha's induction into modern Cairo effectively drives him away and takes him to Paris in search of the source knowledge lying at the foundation of modern Cairo. Wanderlust is born out of this sense of alienation fundamental in the experience of modernity. The desire underlying *Ḥadīth ᶜĪsā Ibn Hishām*'s mobility, which has yet to be gendered, is already bifurcated, as in Ḥāwī's poems, one half pursuing a past exiled from present, and another chasing after a present, or utopian future, elsewhere. Even Mubārak's cartography of Cairo, *Al-khiṭaṭ al-tawfīqīyya*, has a twin, as I shall show in this chapter, a 'journey to the West', *ᶜAlam al-dīn*, through which the author-protagonist, ᶜAlam al-Dīn, and his son, Burhān al-Dīn, learn the ways of the West, beginning in modernised Egypt, then in Europe. Mahfouz's Kamāl, the main protagonist of his *Cairo Trilogy*, reprises the role of the native travelling in his homeland, whose itineraries would tell the story of an Arab intellectual's encounter with modernity experienced not in the West but in the very heart of Cairo, where the West has made herself indispensably present and permanently felt.

Modernity, despite the delayed actualisation of the nation-state, has arrived in Cairo, and its arrival marks the beginning of a process of soul-searching that is the hallmark of Arabic modernist writings. There is no need to travel to the West, for a generation of Egyptian intellectuals trained in various parts of the West has now come home to fashion Cairo into a cosmopolis.[74] Yaḥyā Ḥaqqī (1905/9–92), Tawfīq al-Ḥakīm, Ṭāha Ḥusayn, Ḥusayn Fawzī and Salāma Mūsā (1887–1958), to name a few of Mahfouz's acknowledged 'teachers', all Sindbāds come home, are now the key architects of cultural life in Egypt.[75] Cairo modern or cosmopolitan, however, is not exactly the West that Enany sees as the catalyst in Kamāl's 'secularization' accomplished via his unrequited love for ᶜĀyida, 'a one-way journey from Jamāliyya to Paris via ᶜAbbāsiyya',[76] or 'the ideal of modern Europe for whose sake Kamāl's generation rejected the past without succeeding, however, in attaining it'.[77] It is rather the West that has come to be intimately woven into the fabric of the East, of Egypt. ᶜĀyda is of dual personality. She is a gift the East seeks from the West,[78] a breath of fresh air from Paris,[79] a Parisian Egyptian who straddles two worlds. She reminds us of Aida, the heroine of Giuseppe Verdi's (1813–1901) opera commissioned by Ismail Pasha for Cairo Opera House and performed for the first time in Cairo on 24 December 1871.

Aida too is caught between two worlds. She is an Egyptian slave who is really an Ethiopian princess. Her story, cast in the form of a four-act melodrama, is a wartime love triangle. Egyptian princess Amneris is in love with warrior Radames, who loves Aida instead. He is assigned to lead the Egyptian army in the war against the Ethiopians led by Aida's father, king Amonasro. The initial Egyptian victory leads to treachery. A captured Amonasro plots revenge, so does Amneris for the ruin of Aida. While Amonasro uses Aida to find out from Radames where the Egyptian army will launch another attack on the Ethiopians, Amneris exposes Aida as traitor only to cause Radames' death sentence. Aida decides to die with Radames. Mahfouz's ᶜĀyda is clearly not Verdi's Aida despite surface resemblance – ᶜĀyda does die young after Ḥasan divorces her in the wake of the scandal of her family's fall from grace – for she does not have Aida's loyalty and willingness to die for her beloved. She rather plays her two 'lovers' against each other in order to entice one into marriage. But Aida, the opera, and ᶜĀyda, the character, have one thing in common: they both are 'local material' fashioned into Western forms, an opera and a Parisian Egyptian respectively, in the West. However, they are staged in modern Cairo. They are representations of Cairo modern or cosmopolitan. His unrequited love affair with ᶜĀyda is Kamāl's brush with not the West but a modernising East – and the very act of bringing the sexual underworld into light is a modern phenomenon – which has now come to straddle the line between East and West. In the end, he comes to be more like Aida and ᶜĀyda; he finds himself with more than one personality. ᶜĀyda is Kamāl's siren. Her call precipitates his death and rebirth.

Kamāl's crisis, which all Mahfouz's critics attribute to his disappointment in ᶜĀyda, pushes Kamāl to wander in the world of ideas between East and West. He is the 'Magi' in Eliot and Ḥāwī's poetry, an intellectual marooned in the ruins of a life altered beyond recognition by turbulent global and local events. His crisis is generated less by failure in love but more by the experience of an apocalypse. The world as he knows has fallen into smithereens, and the certainty of true knowledge, whether derived from religion or tradition, has been irrevocably eroded. The turmoil of political and intellectual life, caught between East and West and exacerbated by their tumultuous encounter, divides Kamāl's sense of self, as his polarised sex life goes to show, and prompts a quest for cohesion. Mafhouz's ᶜĀyda is Ḥāwī's she-demon, a creature of dual personality, who lures Kamāl, Ḥāwī's Eastern intellectual, away from home, from his familiar zone of comfort, to a journey in search of knowledge and into soul-searching, paralleled by a return journey, a process of 'house cleaning' and 'soul cleansing'. *Palace of Desire* is a part of Kamāl's 'spiritual autobiography', his coming to terms with temporary homelessness in uncertainty and his rebirth as a modern subject. It does this by novelising classical and modern Arabic poetics, crystallised by Tammuzi poets, including Ḥāwī, who belonged with Mahfouz to the same generation of Arab intellectuals, writers and artists. Mahfouz recasts ᶜUmar Ibn Abī Rabīᶜa and Majnūn Laylā in the roles of Sindbād, Odysseus, Ulysses and Faust, we may say, but gives them the flesh, bone and blood of an emerging Cairene intellectual who lives a full life with 'realistic' Cairene characters distributed among his family and friends in 'realistic' palaces, houses, shops, streets and alleys of both new and old Cairo.

Kamāl's unravelling and refashioning, or his coming of age, takes place against a background of the collapse of old values and the absence of viable alternatives. The convulsive events that have shaken the Egyptian intellectuals to the core pertain equally to the radical transformation of how the entire generation knew the world, lost faith in their inherited way of life, and would from now on struggle to find themselves again. Just as Darwin has dethroned God, Kamāl's discovery of his father's double life erodes the authority of patriarchy. God, it seems, is created in the image of al-Sayyid Aḥmad, tyrannical, unjust, oppressive, dictatorial and obedient to human instinctual desires (*al-jabarūt wa l-istibdād wa l-qahr wa l-diktātūriyya wa sāʾir al-gharāʾiz al-bashariyya*).[80] They both have now come down from their pedestal. The old ways of knowing based in religion and tradition are now bankrupt. However, al-Sayyid Aḥmad's tyranny, exposed as ignorance, is only one side of the coin. It must be complemented by his mother Āmina's tenderness in Kamal's imagined confrontation with his parents, for a picture of Kamāl's disillusion to be complete.

> Do you know what other consequences there were to loving you despite your tyranny? I loved another tyrant who was unfair to me for a long time, both to my face and behind my back. She oppressed me without ever loving me. In spite of all that, I worshipped her from the depths of my heart and still do. You're responsible for my love and torment as anyone else. I wonder if there's any truth to this idea. I'm not satisfied with it or overly enthusiastic about it. Whatever the reality of love may be, there's no doubt that it's attributable to causes more directly linked to the soul. Let's allow this to ride until we can study it later. In any case, Father, you're the one who made it easy for me to accept oppression through your continual tyranny.
>
> And, you Mother, don't stare at me with disapproval or ask me what I've done wrong when I've harmed no one. Ignorance is your crime, ignorance. . . ignorance. . . ignorance. My father's the manifestation of ignorant and you of ignorant tenderness. As long as I live, I'll remain the victim of these two opposites. It's your ignorance, too, that filled my spirit with legends. You're my link to the Stone Age. How miserable I am now as I try to liberate myself from your influence. And I'll be just as miserable in the future when I free myself from my father.
>
> I would have been better if you had spared me such exhausting effort. For this reason, I propose – with the darkness of this room as

> my witness – that the family be abolished, for it's nothing but a pit in which brackish water collects, and that fatherhood and motherhood cease. Indeed, grant me a nation with no history and a life without a past.[81]

However, no system of knowledge has emerged as a workable alternative that can serve as a foundation for individual conduct in a world that has yet to take shape. Yāsīn's aimlessness, his sisters' family's frivolity and his friends' social climbing, are but a few manifestations of the lack of direction among Kamāl's generation.

What kind of future awaits an individual without tradition, a nation without history, a present without past? These are the questions with which *Palace of Desire* ends. It is precisely at this juncture of such self-questioning that the modern subject is born; just as Kamāl decides to 'leave' his father's house (*al-hijra*)[82] he pledges to embark on a journey in search of knowledge, to study his soul through working out why and how tradition has had such a tight grip on him.[83] Paradoxically, *Palace of Desire* is Kamāl's journey in search not only of knowledge but also his self-mastery, the end of which begins his transformation. But we see the results only in the third part of the *Trilogy*. Kamāl in *Sugar Street* is the benevolent 'parent' to his nephews that he wished his father could have been for him. More important, as Ghālī Shukrī points out in *Al-muntamī*, his nephew Aḥmad Shawkat, Kamāl's intellectual heir and spiritual son, grows up to be a progressive intellectual actively engaged in fighting for Egypt's political liberation and cultural modernisation.[84]

ARCHITECTURE OF THE ARABIC NOVEL

Modernity may be at large, but the project of Egyptian modernisation remains incomplete in the *Trilogy*. The emergence of the questing modern subject against a background of chaos does not guarantee cohesion, neither for the individual nor for the nation. The desire for an individual without tradition, a nation without history, a present without past, may lead to political activism and national liberation of one form or another, but does not necessarily lead to a perfect community that is the subject of the national fantasies I have discussed in Chapters 3 and 4, or to the cohesion of the subject that has been up to now dependent on knowing the Truth based in religion and tradition. For one thing, it is not entirely possible to reject tradition, history or the past, for they are an essential part of both individual and community in the present, so ingrained in their sense of self. And, for another, the slippery ground of modernity, where knowledge of the world has been relativised thanks to Einstein's theory, split between subject and object tenuously connected by desire in Freud's psychology, and torn asunder by the two world wars, gives no assurances for any longed-for cohesion. Modern desire for liberation from the past is necessarily haunted by nostalgia; the modern is forever remembering and longing for the past it seeks to unload, for the fragmentary present proves no reasonable substitute for the solidity of the past. The modern subject is destined to wander, to forever quest for cohesion, so is the Eastern intellectual, Ḥāwī has already told us. The Eastern intellectual has the added responsibility of rebuilding the Eastern world from the debris left behind by the storm of change. This responsibility falls on Kamāl's shoulders in *Palace of Desire* and the *Trilogy* in general. Mahfouz's Kamāl, like Ḥāwī's Eastern intellectual, must become the architect of modernisation, who will always be nostalgic for a world lost in the tidal waves of modernity, as he travels in the world of ideas, of knowledge, in order to find the right formula for a new world. He will have numerous reincarnations. Sindbād and Shahrayār of *Layālī* are only two.

The Eastern intellectual's nostalgia is a desire of multiple itineraries. It is simultaneous longing for the discredited past, troubling present, and unpredictable future. It is also yearning to rebuild and build. It finds expression in the modernist text in a variety of ways, each dependent on the specialisation of the architect. While Ḥāwī expresses this complex desire in his search for modernist Arabic poetics, Mahfouz articulates it as the Arabic novel's longing for form, locatable in its interextuality. The story a modernist text tells of the Eastern modern subject is also an allegory for the Arabic novel's search for form. If modernism in Arabic poetry is, as Perry Meisel argues for the case of British literature and criticism after 1850 in *The Myth of the Modern* (1987), less a response to the decaying conditions of modern life but more an imaginative response to the impossibility of being original when coming of age too late in a literary and cultural tradition, modernism in the Arabic novel is equally an imaginative response to not only the pressure of the Western novelistic tradition but also its lateness. The Arabic novel injects into the form it has borrowed from the West ingredients extracted from both the West and Arabic literary and cultural heritage. It too is destined to wander between 'East' and 'West' and 'past' and 'present', and to strategically negotiate for a truce between the past and present, 'tradition' and the 'West'. It does so by at once demolishing, reviving and transforming 'tradition', as *Palace of Desire* does. *Palace of Desire* undermines the authority of tradition and rejects the powerful hold it has on the mind and heart of both individual and nation, but it also turns to classical poetics, albeit through the perspective of a contemporary interpretation, for material to fashion the literary imaginary that would be the architectural blueprint for the construction of the novel of a uniquely Arab variety. It is precisely its intertextuality with Umayyad love poetry and ᶜAbbasid love stories that gives it the 'sublime' Beard observes in Mahfouz's writings. A Mahfouzian novel, for that matter any Arabic novel, is necessarily of dual personality; it is at once East and West, old and new. It is this duality that would give the novel an identity split between East and West, and 'past' and 'present', just like Mahfouz's Kamāl and Ḥāwī's Sindbād, who will travel far and wide in search not only of knowledge but also form.

However, the itineraries of 'far and wide' target interiority not exteriority. Mahfouz's Kamāl, Sindbād and Shahrayār are not interested in the architectural monuments of Paris, or even Cairo, or in their attendant cultural institutions. They take no pleasure in recording the 'wonders' of Paris, London or modern Cairo. They rather turn inward, into the deep recesses of themselves, not to examine their sexuality, but to examine their 'psychic' and intellectual make-up, the paradigms of knowledge defining and structuring who they are, how they think, feel and conduct themselves in society. More importantly, they seek to fashion themselves into productive participants in building a modern nation through the process of recovering their built-in paradigms of knowledge and interrogating them with the hopes of finally transforming them. 'House cleaning' and 'soul cleansing' take on collective dimensions. They are not simply the details of an individual's spiritual autobiography, of coming of age, or finding enlightenment. They are rather metaphors for the entire process of cultural rejuvenation involving re-examining the habits of thought and conduct inherited from the past. Tradition comes to be both the 'homeland' and 'foreign country' on the other side of all itineraries of travel. An itinerant Arab intellectual travels in Paris, modern Cairo, and the 'cultural heritage' of the Arabs. As *Palace of Desire* lovingly recalls classical Arabic poetics, Kamāl's interrogation of tyrannical power structures and unenlightened paradigms of knowledge inherent in the cultural heritage of the Arabs is Mahfouz's gesture of loyalty towards Arabic cultural and literary tradition. Desire in classical Arabic poetics is transformed into nostalgia for tradition, the past, and what it will be, the future. But what is the future of tradition, of nostalgia? The journey has only just begun.

NOTES

1. Published in its initial form in *Al-ādāb* 5 (May 1960), pp. 19–21, and extensively reworked for the third collection of his poems, *Al-nāy wa al-rīḥ* (Beirut: Dār al-ᶜAwda, 1961).
2. Frederick R. Karl, *Modern and Modernism: the Sovereignty of the Artist 1885–1925* (New York, NY: Macmillan, 1985), pp. 162–9.
3. Khalīl Ḥāwī, *Al-nāy wa al-rīḥ* (Beirut: Dār al-ʻAwda, 1972), pp. 83–4.
4. Ibid. p. 86.
5. Ibid. p. 91.
6. Ibid. pp. 86–9.
7. Ibid. pp. 89–91.
8. Ibid. p. 92.
9. Ibid. pp. 94–5.
10. Ibid. pp. 95–9.
11. Ibid. p. 100.
12. Ibid. p. 101.
13. Ibid. p. 104.
14. Ibid. p. 101.
15. Ibid. p. 103.
16. Ibid. p. 103.
17. Ibid. p. 108.
18. Ibid. pp. 105–11.
19. Ibid. p. 81.
20. Ibid. p. 81.
21. Īmīl Maᶜlūf, 'Al-Sindbād fī riḥlatihi al-thāmina al-raᵓy al-awwal', *Al-ādāb* 8: 7 (July 1960), pp. 26–8; 26.
22. Raᵓīf ᶜAṭāyā, 'Al-Sindbād fī riḥlatihi al-thāmina al-raᵓy al-thānī', *Al-ādāb* 8: 7 (July 1960), pp. 28–31.
23. Ḥāwī, *Al-nāy wa al-rīḥ*, pp. 112–13.
24. Ibid. p. 118.
25. Ibid. pp. 114–18.
26. Ibid. p. 124.
27. Ibid. p. 125.
28. Ibid. pp. 118–26.
29. Ibid. pp. 126–7.
30. Ibid. p. 114.
31. Ibid. p. 85.
32. Ibid. p. 85.
33. Ibid. pp. 85–6.
34. Ibid. pp. 114–18.
35. Ibid. p. 119.

36. Ibid. pp. 126–7.
37. Ibid. p. 118.
38. Ibid. p. 127.
39. Ibid. p. 121.
40. Ibid. p. 122.
41. Ibid. pp. 122–6.
42. English translation by William M. Hutchins and Olive E. Kenny (New York, NY: Doubleday, 1990).
43. English translation by John Mohammed Grinsted (London: Darf, 1989).
44. English translation by R. Bayly Winder (Beirut: Khayyats, 1966).
45. English translation by Denys Johnson-Davis (London: Heinemann, 1969).
46. English translation by William M. Hutchins (Washington, DC: Three Continents Press, 1990).
47. This book has existed in manuscripts at various British libraries and was only published in 2000 by the American University Press. The published version was collated and edited by Jason Thompson (Cairo: American University in Cairo Press, 2000).
48. Quoted in Jason Thompson's 'Introduction' to Edward William Lane, *Description of Egypt*, to show the various stages of the development of the final version of the book. This quote appears only in the first draft and is not included in the final one, p. x.
49. For the ways in which rural Egypt is deployed as a hallmark of 'authenticity' in the Arabic novel, see Samah Selim, *The Novel and the Rural Imaginary in Egypt 1880–1985* (London: Routledge Curzon, 2004).
50. It is not clear what Ṭarābīshī means by the term 'river'. Perhaps he is referring to the French '*fleuve*', a narrative technique identified by Aḥmad Sayyid Muḥammad as '*insiyāb*', an image also borrowed from the flow of water, in Mahfouz's novels, especially the *Cairo Trilogy*.
51. Jūrj Ṭarābīshī, *Al-adab min al-dākhil* (Beirut: Dār al-Ṭalīᶜa, 1978), p. 177.
52. See, for example, the way Rajāᵓ al-Naqqāsh relates Maḥfūẓ to world famous novelists in 'Najīb Maḥfūẓ's global face' in *Fī ḥubb Najīb Maḥfūẓ* (Beirut: Dār al-Shurūq, 1995), pp. 55–62; 55. Mahfouz's novels are usually compared to what are perceived to be their Western precursors. Nādiya Badrān, for example, devotes a book to the comparison between Mahfouz's use of 'multiple points of view' in *Al-karnak*, *Afrāḥ al-qubba* and *Al-ᶜĀᵓish fī al-ḥaqīqa* to Western novelists, such as Henry James, Joseph Conrad, William Faulkner, Virginia Woolf, Thomas Mann, Albert Camus, James Joyce, Lawrence Durrell and André Gide (see Nādiya Badrān, *Najīb Maḥfūẓ wa ṣiyagh riwāya jadīda* (Cairo: Maktabat al-Anglū al-Miṣriyya, 1996)). The same may be said of Aḥmad Sayyid Muḥammad, who traces the use of '*fleuve*' in Mahfouz's novels to Balzac, Zola, Romain Rolland, Tolstoy and other Western novelists (see *Al-riwāya l-insiyābiyya wa taᵓthīruhā ᶜind al-riwāᵓiyyīn al-ᶜarab*

(Algiers: al-Muʾassasa al-Waṭaniyya li al-Kitāb, 1989)). There are also those who focus on a theme. Haim Gordon, for example, looks at existential themes in Mahfouz's writing (see *Naguib Mahfouz's Egypt: existential themes in his writings* (New York, NY: Greenwood Press, 1990)); Aḥmad Muḥammad ʿAṭiyya discusses the absurd and social realism (see *Maʿ Najīb Maḥfūẓ* (Cairo: Wizārat al-Thaqāfa, 1971)); Sylvia DuVerent observes Mahfouz's use of mythology and magical realism (see *The Observer and the Observed: Comments Concerning Six Novels by Naguib Mahfouz* (Toronto: DuVernet, 1989)); and Jamal Chehayed compares Mahfouz and Zola's 'conscience historique' (see *La Conscience historique dans les Rougon-Macquart d'Emile Zola et dans les romans de Nagib Mahfuz* (Damas: Èditions Universitaires; Paris: Maisonneuve et Larose, 1983)), all in the context of the Western novel. Even Nabīl Rāghib, who claims to intentionally deviate from what he calls 'the trend in the study of Mahfouz by comparing him with Western novelists' and devotes his attention to Mahfouz's departures from the norm in his early novels in *Qaḍiyyat al-shakl al-fannī ʿind Najīb Maḥfūẓ: dirāsa taḥlīliyya li uṣūlihā al-fikriyya wa al-jamāliyya* (Cairo: al-Hayʾa al-Miṣriyya al-ʿĀmma li al-Kitāb, 1975), is unable to break away from a 'Eurocentric' approach. Departures are inevitably conceived as centred on the Western novel; the Western novel is centrifugal to all departures.

53. Michael Beard, 'The Mahfouzian Sublime', in Beard and Haydar, *Naguib Mahfouz: From Regional Fame to Global Recognition* (Syracuse, NY: Syracuse University Press, 1993), pp. 95–105; 97.
54. Beard, 'The Mahfouzian Sublime', p. 96.
55. As Saʿīd Shawqī Muḥammad Sulaymān does, identifying seven instances in which Mahfouz quotes classical Arabic poetry in '*Qaṣr al-shawq*', in *Tawẓīf al-turāth fī riwāyāt Najīb Maḥfūẓ* (Cairo: Ītrāk li al-Nashr wa al-Tawzīʿ, 2000), p. 306.
56. See Rāghib, *Qaḍiyyat al-shakl al-fannī ʿinda Najīb Maḥfūẓ*, pp. 128–202; and Sulaymān al-Shaṭṭī, *Al-ramz wa al-ramziyya fī adab Najīb Maḥfūẓ* (Kuwait: al-Maṭbaʿa al-ʿAṣriyya, 1976), pp. 145–80.
57. Roger Allen, *The Arabic Novel: an Historical and Critical Introduction*, 2nd edn (Syracuse, NY: Syracuse University Press, 1995), p. 114.
58. As Rasheed El-Enany noted in his discussion of the *Trilogy* in *Naguib Mahfouz: The Pursuit of Meaning* (London: Routledge, 1993), pp. 71–90; 72.
59. For the views of Egyptian intellectuals on this period, see Ghālī Shukrī, *Al-muntamī: dirāsa fī adab Najīb Maḥfūẓ* (Cairo: Dār al-Maʿārif, 1965 [1969]), p. 34.
60. See, for example, ibid. pp. 106–36.
61. See Shukrī's wonderful study of the *Trilogy* in *Al-muntamī*, pp. 17–81.
62. See Enany, *Naguib Mahfouz*, pp. 71–90.

63. See Ghālī Shukrī, *Azmat al-jins fī al-qiṣṣa al-ᶜarabiyya* (Beirut: Dār al-Ādāb, 1962), pp. 81–126.
64. Sīzā Aḥmad Qāsim, who has written one of the most sophisticated analyses of the structure of the *Trilogy* misses this trope completely. She focuses on the organisation of time and space in the novel, and the perspective, both ideological and psychological, which give shape to the novel. See *Binā᾽ al-riwāya: dirāsa muqārana li-thulāthiyyat Najīb Maḥfūẓ* (Cairo: al-Hay᾽a al-Miṣriyya al-ᶜĀmma li al-Kitāb, 1984).
65. Mahfouz was an avid reader of these articles. See *Naguib Mahfouz at Sidi Gaber: Reflections of a Nobel Laureate 1994–2001, From Conversations with Mohamed Salmawy* (Cairo: American University in Cairo Press, 2001), p. 89.
66. *Asātidhatī li Najīb Maḥfūẓ* (My teachers by Naguib Mahfouz), a collection of interviews with Ibrāhīm ᶜAbd al-ᶜAzīz (Cairo: Mīrīt li al-Nashr wa al-Maᶜlūmāt, 2002), pp. 135–48.
67. These, together with all the articles on classical Arabic literature he wrote for *Al-siyāsa*, were published in three volumes under the title of *Ḥadīth al-ᶜarbiᶜā᾽* (Wednesday talk). It is one of Ḥusayn's most popular works and has gone through numerous reprints. References here are made to *Al-majmūᶜa al-kāmila li mu᾽allafāt al-duktūr Ṭāhā Ḥusayn* (Beirut: Dār al-Kitāb al-Lubnānī, 1973), vol. II, pp. 177–319.
68. Ibid. vol. II, p. 179.
69. Particularly in 'Al-ghazilūn: Qays Ibn al-Mulawwaḥ, aw Majnūn Banī ᶜĀmir, aw Majnūn Laylā' (pp. 177–87), and 'Al-ghazal wa l-ghazilūn: nash᾽atuhu wa asbābuhā – fann al-qaṣaṣ al-gharāmī' (pp. 188–96), in *Al-majmuᶜa al-kamila*, pp. 177–319.
70. Shukrī, *Al-muntamī*, p. 34.
71. Enany, *Pursuit of Meaning*, p. 85.
72. Maḥfūẓ, *Qaṣr*, p. 16.
73. Ibid. pp. 18–22.
74. See Shukrī, *Al-muntamī*, pp. 17–81.
75. See Ibrāhīm ᶜAbd al-ᶜAzīz, *Asātidhatī.*
76. Enany, *Pursuit of Meaning*, p. 87.
77. Enany, *Pursuit of Meaning*, p. 88.
78. Maḥfūẓ, *Qaṣr*, p. 18.
79. Ibid. p. 20.
80. Ibid. p. 385.
81. Maḥfūẓ, *Qaṣr*, pp. 384–6; Hutchins, *Palace*, pp. 373–4.
82. Maḥfūẓ, *Qaṣr*, p. 385.
83. Ibid. p. 385.
84. Shukrī, *Al-muntamī*, pp. 63–7.

Afterword

THE FUTURE IS A FOREIGN COUNTRY

> The past is everywhere. All around us lie features which, like ourselves and our thoughts, have more or less recognizable antecedents. Relics, histories, memories suffuse human experience. Each particular trace of the past ultimately perishes, but collectively they are immortal. Whether it is celebrated or rejected, attended to or ignored, the past is omnipresent.
>
> David Lowenthal, *The Past is a Foreign Country*, p. xv

Arabic cultural and literary heritage is everywhere in the Arabic novel. The past is an indispensable stitch in the fabric of the modern nation-state and a crucial ingredient in the recipe of Arab modernisation. The form of the Arabic novel takes shape in its imagining and allegorisation of nation, as well as in its narration of modernity and modernisation. Its narrative trajectories are bound by the territorial borders of the nation-state, and driven by the projects of modernisation expected to take place on this new geographical locus. In the present's mobilisation of the past, the past comes to be the site of competing discourses, evoked as a cultural heritage that must either be revivified in order to serve as the legitimating foundation for the future or transcended so that mistakes from the past will not be repeated. Cultural heritage is a paradox. Past forms of political authority and practices of power are interrogated as problematical, but traditional literary expressions are preserved lovingly and revived nostalgically to give the nation-state and its attendant modernity, as well as the novel that desires and imagines them, legitimacy and authenticity. The past is a construction site. It is where the present purges itself of the undesirable elements of the past and builds a future on the grounds of a cleansed tradition.

The omnipresence of the past in the Arabic novel 'that employs Arabic cultural and literary heritage' is a collective project that, as Lowenthal observes in *The Past is a Foreign Country*, gives the relics, histories and memories of the past immortality. The palpable nostalgia for the past is paradoxically expressive of the uncertainty of the future, for 'we can no more slip back to the past than leap forward to the future'.[1] Arabic novel's obsession with the past, of always deploying tradition in the service of present projects of nation-building and modernisation, speaks of and to a profound ambivalence towards both the nation-state and modernity. It tells two intertwined stories of the relationship between past and present in the stories it tells about nation-state and modernity. On the one hand, it insists on the relevance of the past to the present, for it is impossible to imagine the nation without roots in the immemorial past and infeasible to regard modernity as a historical rupture between past and present. On the other, it casts doubts on the role the past can play in the present. For nostalgia may potentially lock the present in the past and prevent the future from taking proper and desirable shape. Arab cultural and literary heritage may easily be transformed into the prison-house of tradition.

There is already a hint of the danger of tradition in stifling projects of nation-building and modernisation in the Arabic novel that employs tradition to imagine a political community and will a modern democratic nation-state into existence on its textual landscape, whether the imagining and will are located on the site of the nation-state or statelessness. Even in the moments of utmost optimism, of unadulterated love and unchecked desire, the past must always be simultaneously deconstructed and reconstructed anew for it to be appropriate to the present. The omnipresence of the past, we have seen, defines the present in terms of the past, and places an excessive burden on the present. How then is the burden of the past to be grappled, come to terms with and transcended? Or is the future forever imprisoned in the past? The Arabic novel, as I will show in *Politics of Nostalgia in the Arabic Novel*, continues its argument with the past in its interrogation of nostalgia and, more crucially, the ways in which tradition, recalled, revived and revised to give the nation and the novel a history in the immemorial past, can produce new forms of hegemony on top of old ones. Nostalgia at once imprisons the present in the past and distorts the past, making it impossible for the present and future to have the freedom they need to take their own shape. The only way forward is either madness or revolution, and the history of nation and novel inevitably takes the form of stories of tyranny and rebellion.

NOTE

1. David Lowenthal, *The Past is a Foreign Country* (Cambridge: Cambridge University Press, 1985), p. 4.

BIBLIOGRAPHY

^{c}Abbās, Iḥsān, *Badr Shākir al-Sayyāb: dirāsa fī ḥayātihi wa shi^{c}rihi* (Beirut: Dār al-Thaqāffa, 1969).

——'Al-mabnā al-ramzī fī qiṣaṣ Ghassān Kanafānī', 'Introduction' to Ghassān Kanafānī, *Al-a^{c}māl al-kāmila* (1972–3), vol. 1, pp. 11–27.

^{c}Abdallāh, Muḥammad Ḥasan, *Al-islāmiyya wa al-rūḥiyya fī adab Najīb Maḥfūẓ* (Kuwait: Maktabat al-Amal, 1972, 2001).

^{c}Abd al-Ghanī, Muṣṭafā, 'Khuṣuṣiyyat al-tanāṣṣ fī al-riwāya al-^{c}arabiyya: Majnūn al-ḥukm namūdajan taṭbīqīyyan', *Fuṣūl* 16: 4 (Spring 1998), pp. 270–89.

^{c}Abd al-Karīm, Muḥammad, *^{c}Alī Mubārak: ḥayātuhu wa maʾāthirhu* (Cairo: Maṭba^{c}at al-Risāla, n.d.).

^{c}Abd al-Ṣabūr, Ṣalāḥ, *Dīwān Ṣalāḥ ^{c}Abd al-Ṣabūr*, 2 vols (Beirut: Dar al-^{c}Awda, 1977).

Abū Ḥamdān, Samīr, *^{c}Alī Mubārak al-mufakkir wa al-mu^{c}ammir* (Beirut: al-Sharika al-^{c}Ālamiyya li al-Kitāb, 1993).

Abu-Lughod, Lila, *Dramas of Nationhood: the Politics of Television in Egypt* (Chicago, IL: University of Chicago Press, 2005).

Ackroyd, Peter, *T. S. Eliot* (London: Hamilton, 1984).

al-^{c}Adawī, Muḥammad Qiṭṭa (ed.), *Alfa layla wa layla*, 2 vols (Bulaq: 1252 AH) [= Bulaq text].

Al-^{c}Āfiya, Muḥammad, *Al-khitāb al-riwāʾī ^{c}inda Īmīl Ḥabībī* (al-Dār al-Bayḍā': Maṭa^{c}at al-Najāḥ al-Jadīda, 1997).

Aḥmad, ^{c}Abdallāh ^{c}Abd al-Muṭṭalib, *Al-Muwayliḥī al-Ṣaghīr: Ḥayātuhu wa adabuhu* (Cairo: al-Hay'a al-Miṣriyya al-^{c}Āmma li al-Kitāb, 1985).

^{c}Ālim, Maḥmūd Amīn, *Al-fikr al-^{c}arabī bayn al-khuṣusiyya wa al-kawniyya* (Cairo: Dār al-Mustaqbal al-^{c}Arabī, 1996).

Allen, Roger, *The Arabic Novel: an Historical and Critical Introduction*, 2nd edn (Syracuse, NY: Syracuse University Press, 1982, 1995).

——'Introduction', *A Period of Time* (Reading: Ithaca Press, 1992), pp. 1–97.

——'Mahfouz and the Arabic novel', in Michael Beard and Adnan Haydar (eds)

Naguib Mahfouz: From Regional Fame to Global Recognition (Syracuse, NY: Syracuse University Press, 1993).

——'Literary history and the Arabic novel', *World Literature Today* 75: 2 (Spring 2001), pp. 205–13.

Allen, Roger, Hilary Kilpatrick and Ed de Moor (eds) *Love and Sexuality in Modern Arabic Literature*, (London: Saqi Books, 1995).

Amanṣūr, Muḥamad, *Al-tajrīb al-riwāʾi ᶜind Najīb Maḥfūẓ* (Cairo: al-Majlis al-Aᶜlā li al-Thaqāfa, 2006).

Amīn, Aḥmad, *Zuᶜamāʾ al-iṣlāḥ fī al-ᶜaṣr al-ḥadīth* (Cairo: al-Nahḍa al-Miṣriyya, 1949).

Anderson, Bendedict, *Imagined Communities; Reflections on the Origin and Spread of Nationliasm* (London: Verso, 1991).

Appadurai, Arjun, *Modernity at Large: Cultural Dimensions of Globalization* (Minneapolis, MN: University of Minnesota Press, 1996).

Armstrong, J. A., *Nations Before Nationalism* (Chapell Hill, NC: University of North Carolina Press, 1982).

Asᶜad, Sāmiya, 'ᶜIndamā yaktub al-riwāʾī al-tārīkh', *Fuṣūl* 2: 2 (Spring 1982), pp. 67–73.

Asātidhatī li Najīb Maḥfūẓ, interviews with Ibrāhīm ᶜAbd al-ᶜAzīz (Cairo: Mīrīt li al-Nashr wa al-Maᶜlūmāt, 2002).

ᶜĀshūr, Raḍwā, *Al-Ṭarīq ilā al-khayma al-ukhrā: dirāsa fī aᶜmāl Ghassān Kanafānī* (Beirut: Dār al-Ādāb, 1977), pp. 59–91.

ᶜAṭāyā, Raʾīf, 'Al-Sindbād fī riḥlatihi al-thāmina al-raʾy al-thānī', *Al-ādāb* 8: 7 (July 1960), pp. 28–31.

ᶜAṭiyya, Aḥmad Muḥammad, *Maᶜ Najīb Maḥfūẓ* (Cairo: Wizārat al-Thaqāfa, 1971).

Audebert, C. F., 'Choice and responsibility in *Rijāl fī al-shams*', *Journal of Arabic Literature* 15 (1984), pp. 76–93.

ᶜAwaḍ, Yūsuf Nūr, *Fann al-maqāmāt bayn al-mashriq wa al-maghrib* (Beirut: Dār al-Qalam, 1979).

Ayubi, Nazih N., *Over-stating the Arab State: Politics and Society in the Middle East* (London: I.B. Tauris, 2001).

ᶜAzzūz, Muḥyi al-Dīn, *Al-lāmaᶜqūl wa falsafat al-Ghazzālī* (Tunis: al-Dār al-ᶜArabiyya li al-Kitāb, 1988).

Bachelard, Gaston, *Poetics of Space*, tr. Maria Jolas (Boston, MA: Beacon Press, 1964, 1969).

Badawī, Muḥammad, 'Mughāmarat al-shakl ᶜind riwāʾī al-sittīnāt', *Fuṣūl* 2: 2 (1982), pp. 125–42.

Badr, ᶜAbd al-Muḥsin Ṭāhā, *Ṭaṭawwur al-riwāya al-ᶜarabiyya al-ḥadītha* (Cairo: Dār al-Maᶜārif, 1973).

Badran, Margot, *Feminists, Islam and Nation: Gender and the Making of Modern Egypt* (Princeton, NJ: Princeton University Press, 1995).

Badrān, Nādiya, *Najīb Maḥfūẓ wa ṣiyagh riwāya jadīda* (Cairo: Maktabat al-Anglū al-Miṣriyya, 1996).

Bakhtin, Mikhail, *The Dialogic Imagination: Four Essays*, ed. Michael Holquist, tr. Caryl Morson and Michael Holquist (Austin, TX: Texas University Press, 1981).

Bammer, Angelia, 'Introduction', in A. Bammer (ed.), *Displacement: Cultural Identities in Questions* (Bloomington, IN: Indiana University Press, 1994), pp. xi–xx; xiii.

Baron, Beth, *The Women's Awakening in Egypt: Culture, Society, and the Press* (New Haven, CT: Yale University Press, 1994).

——*Egypt as Woman: Nationalism, Gender and Politics* (Berkeley, CA: University of California Press, 2005).

Beard, Michael, 'The Mahfouzian sublime', in Michael Beard and Adnan Haydar, *Naguib Mahfouz: From Regional Fame to Global Recognition* (Syracuse, NY: Syracuse University Press, 1993), pp. 95–105.

Beaucour, Fernand, Yves Laissus and Chantal Orgogozo, *The Discovery of Egypt*, tr. from French by Bambi Ballard (Paris: Flammarion, 1990).

Beaumont, Daniel, *Slave of Desire: Sex, Love and Death in the 1001 Nights* (Madison, WI: Fairleigh Dickinson University Press, 2002).

Bell, Joseph Norment, *Love Theory in Later Hanbalite Islam* (Albany, NY: State University of New York Press, 1979).

Benjamin,Walter, 'Theses on the Philosophy of History', in *Illuminations*, tr. Harry Zorn (London: Pimlico, 1968, 1999), pp. 245–55.

Berman, Marshall, *All That is Solid Melts into Air: the Experience of Modernity* (New York, NY: Simon and Schuster, 1983).

Blonsky, Marshall (ed.), *On Signs* (Baltimore, MD: Johns Hopkins University Press, 1985).

Bloom, Harold, *The Anxiety of Influence: a Theory of Poetry* (Oxford: Oxford University Press, 1975).

Booth, Marilyn, *May Her Likes Be Multiplied: Biography and Gender Politics in Egypt* (Berkeley, CA: University of California Press, 2001).

Boullata, Issa J., *Trends and Issues in Contemporary Arab Thought* (Albany, NY: State University of New York Press, 1990).

Boullata, Issa J. and Terri DeYoung (eds), *Tradition and Modernity in Arabic Literature*, (Fayetteville, AR: Arkansas University Press, 1997).

Bradbury, Malcolm, and James McFarlane (eds) *Modernism* (London: Penguin Books, 1976).

Breuilly, J., *Nationalism and the State* (New York, NY: St. Martin's Press, 1982).

Brooks, Peter, *Reading for the Plot: Design and Intention in Narrative* (Cambridge, MA: Harvard University Press, 1984, 1996).

Broton, Jerry, *Trading Territories: Mapping in Early Modern World* (London: Reaktion Books, 1997).

Bulaq: see al-ᶜAdawī.

Butler, Judith, 'Restaging the universal: hegemony and the limits of formalism', in Judith Butler, Ernesto Laclau and Slovaj Zizek (eds), *Contingency, Hegemony, Universality: Contemporary Dialogues on the Left* (London: Verso, 2000), pp. 11–43.

Cachia, Pierre, *An Overview of Modern Arabic Literature* (Edinburgh, Edinburgh University Press, 1990).

Campbell, Joseph, *The Hero with a Thousand Faces*, Bollington Series XVII (Princeton, NJ: Princeton University Press, 1973).

Chaterjee, Partha, *Nationalist Thought and the Colonial World: a Derivative Discourse?* (Minneapolis, MN: University of Minnesota Press, 1986).

——*The Nation and its Fragments: Colonial and Postcolonial Histories* (Princeton, NJ: Princeton University Press, 1993).

Chehayed, Jamal, *La Conscience historique dans les Rougon-Macquart d'Emile Zola et dans les romans de Nagib Mahfuz* (Damas: Éditions Universitaires; Paris: Maisonneuve et Larose, 1983.)

Chraïbi, Aboubakr, 'Les jinns penserus de Naguib Mahfouz', in F. Sangustin *et al.* (eds), *L'Orient en coeur, en honneur d'André Miquel* (Paris: Maisonneuve et Larose, 2001), pp. 171–83.

Clayton, Peter Arthur, *The Rediscovery of Ancient Egypt: Artists and Travellers in the 19th Century* (London: Thames and Hudson, 1982).

Coffin, Nancy, 'Reading inside and out: a look at Habībī's Pessoptimist', *Arab Studies Journal* 8: 2/9: 1 (Fall 2000/Spring 2001), pp. 25–46.

Crabbs, J. A., *The Writing of History in Nineteenth-century Egypt* (Cairo: American University Press/Detroit: Wayne State University Press, 1984).

Darrāj, Fayṣal, *Hiwār fī ᶜalāqāt al-thaqāfa wa al-siyāsa* (Damascus: Dāᵓirat al-Iᶜlām wa al-Thaqāfa, 1984),

——'al-riwāya wa al-tārīkh: al-Zaynī Barakāt', *Dalālāt al-ᶜalāqa al-riwāᵓiyya* (Nicosia: IBAL Publishing Institution, 1992), pp. 88–139.

——'Jamāl al-Ghīṭānī wa jamāliyyāt al-tajrīb al-riwāᵓī', *Naẓariyyāt al-riwāya wa al-riwāya al-ᶜarabiyya* (Beirut: al-Markaz al-Thaqāfī al-ᶜArabī, 1999), pp. 227–53.

Darwīsh, Maḥmūd, *Dhākira li al-nisyān*, original Arabic edn in *Al Karmel* 21–2 (1986), pp. 4–96; tr. Ibrahim Muhawi, *Memory for Forgetfulness* (Berkeley, CA: University of California Press, 1995).

——*Al-rasāᵓil: Maḥmūd Darwīsh wa Samīḥ al-Qāsim* (Beirut: Dār al-ᶜAwda, 1990).

Dawn, C. Ernest, *From Ottomanism to Arabism: Essays on the Origins of Arab Nationalism* (Urbana, IL: Illinois University Press, 1973).

——'The origins of Arab Nationalism', in Rashid Khalidi *et al.* (eds), *The Origins of Arab Nationalism* (New York, NY: Columbia University Press, 1991), pp. 3–30.

Delanoue, Gilbert, *Moralistes et Politiques Musulmans dans l'Egypte du XIXe Siècle (1798–1882)*, 2 vols (Cairo: IFAO, 1982).

DeYoung, Terri, 'A new reading of Badr Shākir al-Sayyāb's "Hymn of the Rain"', *Journal of Arabic Literature* 22 (1994), pp. 40–61.

——*Placing the Poet: Badr Shākir al-Sayyāb and Postcolonial Iraq* (Albany, NY: State University of New York Press, 1998).

Dupont, Anne-Laure, *Gurgi Zaydan (1861–1914): écrivain, réformiste et témoin de la renaissance arabe* (Damas: IFPO, Institut français du Proche-Orient, 2006).

DuVerent, Sylvia, *The Observer and the Observed: Comments Concerning Six Novels by Naguib Mahfouz* (Toronto: DuVernet, 1989).

Dykstra, Darrell Ivan, *A Biographical Study in Egyptian Modernisation: ᶜAlī Mubārak (1823/4–1893)*, Ph.D. dissertation, University of Michigan, 1977.

Elias, Norbert, *The Civilizing Process* (*Über den Prozess der Zivilisation*) [original German published in 1939], tr. Edmund Jephcott (Oxford: Blackwell, 1982, 1994, 2000).

Elsner, Jao and Joan-Pau Rubiés (eds), *Voyages and Visions: Towards a Cultural History of Travel* (London: Reaktion Books, 1999).

El-Enany, Rasheed, *Naguib Maḥfouz: The Pursuit of Meaning* (London: Routledge, 1993).

——*Arab Representations of the Occident: East-West Encounters in Arabic Fiction* (London: Routledge, 2006).

Encyclopedia of Arabic Literature, eds Julie Scott Meisai and Paul Starkey (London: Routledge, 1998).

The Encyclopaedia of Islam, 2nd edn, vol. II (Leiden: E. J. Brill; London: Luzac & Co., 1965).

Faraj, Alfrīd, *Dalīl al-mutafarrij al-dhakī ilā al-masraḥ* (1966), *Muᵓallafāt Alfrīd Faraj* (Cairo: al-Hayᵓa al-Miṣriyya li al-Kitāb, 1996), vol. 8.

——*Al-milāḥa fī biḥār ṣaᶜba* (Cairo: Dār al-Mustaqbal al-ᶜArabī, 1986), pp. 306–8.

Fishman, J. (ed.), *Language Problems of Developing Countries* (New York, NY: John Wiley & Sons, 1968).

Foucault, Michel, *Power/Knowledge: Selected Interviews and Other Writings 1972–1977*, ed. Colin Gordon, tr. Colin Gordon, Leo Marshall, John Mepham and Kate Soper (New York, NY: Pantheon Books, 1980).

Gaonkar, Dilip Parameshwar (ed.), *Alternative Modernities* (Durham, NC: Duke University Press, 2001).

Gellner, Ernest, *Nations and Nationalism* (Ithaca, NY: Cornell University Press, 1983).

Genette, Gerard, *Paratexts: Thresholds of Interpretation*, tr. Jane E. Lewin (Cambridge: Cambridge University Press, 1997).

——*Palimpsests: Literature in the Second Degree*, tr. Channa Newman and Claude Doubinsky (Lincoln, NE: University of Nebraska Press, 1997).

Gershoni, Israel, and James Jankowski, *Egypt, Islam and the Arabs: the Search for Egyptian Nationhood 1900–1930* (Oxford: Oxford University Press, 1986).
——*Redefining the Egyptian Nation 1930–1945* (Cambridge: Cambridge University Press, 1995).
——*Rethinking Nationlism in the Arab Middle East* (New York, NY: Columbia University Press, 1997).
Ghalyūn, Burhān, *Ightiyāl al-ᶜaql: miḥnat al-thaqāfa al-ᶜarabiyya bayn al-salfiyya wa al-tabaᶜiyya* (Beirut: Dār al-Tanwūr, 1985).
——*Mujtamaᶜ al-nukhba* (Beirut: Maᶜhad al-Inmāᵓ al-ᶜArabī, 1986), *Al-waᶜy al-dhātī* (al-Dār al-Bayḍāᵓ: Manshūrāt ᶜUyūn, 1987).
Al-Gharībī, Khālid, *Jadaliyyat al-aṣāla wa al-muᶜāṣara fi adab al-Masᶜadī* (Qayrawān: Ṣāmid, 1994).
Ghazoul, Ferial, *Nocturnal Poetics: the Arabian Nights in Comparative Perspective* (Cairo: American University Press, 1996).
al-Ghīṭānī, Jamāl, *Najīb Maḥfūẓ yatadhakkar* (Beirut: Dār al-Masīra, 1980).
——*Khiṭaṭ al-Ghīṭānī* (Beirut: Dār al-Masīra, 1981).
——'Mushkilat al-ibdāᶜ al-riwāᵓī ᶜind al-jīl al-sittīnīyāt wa al-sabᶜīnīyāt', *Fuṣūl* 2: 2 (Spring 1982), pp. 208–14.
——'Intertextual dialectics: an interview with Gamal al-Ghitany', *Alif* 4 (1984), pp. 71–82.
——*Muntahā al-ṭalab ilā turāth al-ᶜarab: dirāsa fī al-turāth* (Cairo: Dār al-Shurūq, 1997).
Gordon, David C., *Lebanon: the Fragmented Nation* (London: Croom Helm: 1980).
Gordon, Haim, *Naguib Mahfouz's Egypt: Existential Themes in his Writings* (New York, NY: Greenwood Press, 1990).
Greenfeld, Liah, *Nationalism: Five Roads to Modernity* (Cambridge, MA: Harvard University Press, 1992).
Grotzfeld, Heinz, 'Neglected conclusions of the Arabian Nights: gleanings in forgotten and overlooked recensions', *Journal of Arabic Literature* 14 (1983), pp. 73–87.
Habermas, Jürgen, *The Structural Transformation of the Public Sphere: an Inquiry into a Category of Bourgeois Society* (1962), tr. Thomas Burger and Frederick Lawrence (Cambridge, MA: MIT Press, 1989, 1991, 1994).
Ḥabībī, Īmīl (Emile Habiby), *Al-waqāᵓiᶜ al-gharība fī ikhtifāᵓ Saᶜīd Abī al-Naḥs al-mutashāᵓil* (Dār Shuhdā, n.d.); tr. Salma Khadra Jayyusi and Trevor LeGassick, *The Secret Life of Saeed the Pessoptimist* (London: Zed Books, 1985).
Haddad, Fuad Said, *From the Vineyards of Lebanon: Poems by Khalil Hawi & Nadeem Naimy* (Beirut: American University Press, 1991).
Ḥāfiẓ, Ṣabrī (Sabry Hafez), *The Genesis of Arabic Narrative Discourse* (London: Saqi Books, 1993).

——'Jadaliyyāt al-bunya al-sardiyya al-murakkaba fī layālī Shahrazād wa Najīb Maḥfūẓ', *Fuṣūl* 13: 2 (Summer 1994), pp. 20–69.

Hàmeen-Anttila, Jaako, *Maqama: a History of A Genre* (Wiesbaden: Harrassowitz Verlag, 2002).

Ḥammādī, Ṣabrī Muslim, *Athar al-turāth al-sha*ᶜ*bā fī al-riwāya al-*ᶜ*irāqiyya al-ḥadītha* (Beirut: al-Mussasa al-ᶜArabiyya li al-Dirāsāt wa al-Nashr, 1980).

Hammond, Marlé, 'From Phantasia to Paonomasia: image-evocation and the double entendre in Khālīl Ḥāwī's "The Mariner and the Dervish"', in Geert Jan van Gelder and Marlé Hammond (eds), *Takhyīl: the Imaginary in Classical Arabic Poetics* (Cambridge, Gibb Memorial Trust, 2008), pp. 274–86

Hamori, Andras, *On the Art of Medieval Arabic Literature* (Princeton, NJ: Princeton University Press, 1974).

——'The Magian and the Whore: Readings of Qamar al-Zaman', *The 1001 Nights: Critical Essays and Annotated Bibliography, Mundus Arabicus* 3 (Cambridge, MA: Dar Mahjar, 1983), pp. 25–40.

——'A Comic Romance from the *Thousand and One Nights*: The Tale of Two Viziers', *Arabica* 30 (1983), pp. 38–56.

Ḥanafī, Ḥasan, *Al-turāth wa al-tajdīd, mawqifunā min al-turāth al-qadīm* (Cairo: al-Markaz al-ᶜArabā li al-Baḥth wa al-Nashr, 1980).

——*Al-turāth wa al-tajdīd, mawqifunā min al-turāth al-gharbī: muqaddima fī* ᶜ*ilm al-istighrāb* (Cairo: al-Dār al-Faniyya li al-Nashr wa al-Tawzīᶜ, 1991).

Ḥanafī, Ḥasan, and Muḥammad ᶜĀbid al-Jābirī, *Ḥiwār al-mashriq wa al-maghrib* (Cairo: Maktabat Madbūlī, 1990).

Ḥasan, Muḥammad Rushdī, *Athar al-maqāma fī nash*ᵓ*at al-qiṣṣa al-miṣriyya al-ḥadītha* (Cairo: al-Hayᵓa al-Miṣriyya al-ᶜĀmma li al-Kitāb, 1974).

Al-Hawārī, Aḥmad Ibrāhīm, *Naqd al-mujtama*ᶜ *fī Ḥadīth* ᶜ*Īsā Ibn Hishām li al-Muwayliḥī* (Cairo: Dār al-Maᶜārif, 1986).

Ḥāwī, Iliyyā, *Badr Shākir al-Sayyāb*, 3 vols (Beirut: Dār al-Kitāb al-Lubnānī, 1973).

——*Khālīl Ḥāwī*, 2 vols (Beirut: Dār al-Thaqāfa, 1984).

Ḥāwī, Khalīl, *Nahr al-ramād* (Beirut: Dār al-Ṭalīᶜa, 1957).

——*Bayādir al-jū*ᶜ (Beirut: Dār al-Ādāb, 1965); tr. Adnan Haydar and Michael Beard as *Naked in Exile* (Washington, DC: Three Continents Press, 1984).

——*Al-nāy wa al-rīḥ* (Beirut: Dār al-ᶜAwda, 1972).

Haykal, Muḥammad Ḥusayn, *Zaynab* (1913), tr. John Mohammed Grinsted, *Zainab, the first Egyptian novel* (London: Darf, 1989).

Heath, Peter, 'Romance as genre in *The Thousand and One Nights*', Part I, *Journal of Arabic Literature* 18 (1987), pp. 1–21, and Part II, *Journal of Arabic Literature* 19 (1988), pp. 1–26.

Hobsbawm, E. J., *Nation and Nationalism since 1780: Programme, Myth, Reality* (Cambridge: Cambridge University Press, 1990).

Hobsbawm, Eric, and Terence Ranger, *The Invention of Tradition* (Cambridge: Cambridge University Press, 1983).

Hourani, Albert, *Arabic Thought in the Liberal Age, 1798–1939* (Oxford: Oxford University Press, 1962).

——*A History of the Arab Peoples* (Cambridge, MA: Belknap Press of Harvard University Press, 1991).

Hroch, Miroslav, *Social Preconditions of National Revival in Europe* (Cambridge: Cambridge University Press, 1985).

Huri, Yair, '"My Roads Leads to the Dark Bedouin Girl": an aesthetic reading of Khālīl Ḥāwī's "The Flute and the Wind"', *Journal of Semitic Studies* L/2 (Autumn 2005), pp. 341–55.

Ḥurr, ᶜAbd al-Majīd, *Khālīl Ḥāwī: shāᶜir al-ḥadātha wa al-rūmānsiyya* (Beirut: Dār al-Kutub al-ᶜIlmiyya, 1995).

Ibn Abī Ḥajla (d. 776/1375), *Dīwān al-ṣabāba* (Beirut: Dār wa Maktabat al-Hilāl, 1984).

Ibn ᶜArabī, Muḥyi al-Dīn, *Fuṣūṣ al-ḥikam* (Qum: Intisharāt Badyar, 1999 or 2000).

Ibn Dāwūd, Muḥammad (d. 297/910), *Kitāb al-zahra*, ed. Ibrāhīm al-Samarrāʾī (al-Zarqāʾ: Maktabat al-Manṣūr, 1985).

Ibn Ḥazm (d. 456/1064), *Ṭawq al-ḥamāma*, ed. Ṣalāḥ al-Dīn al-Qāsimī (Tunis: Dār Ibn Salāma, n.d.).

Ibn al-Jawzī (d. 597/1200), *Dhamm al-hawā*, ed. Muṣṭafā ᶜAbd al-Wāḥid and rev. Muḥammad al-Ghazālī (Cairo: Dār al-Kutub al-Ḥadītha, 1962).

Ibn al-Nadīm, *Al-fihrist*, ed. Riḍā (Cairo: Dār al-Masīra, 3rd edn 1988).

Ibn Qayyim al-Jawziyya (d. 751/1350), *Rawḍat al-muḥibbīn wa nuzhat al-mushtāqīn*, ed. Samīr Rabāb (Beriut: al-Maktaba al-ᶜAṣriyya, 2000).

Idrīs, Suhyal, *Al-ḥayy al-lātīnī* (Beirut: Dār al-Ādāb, 1953, 1995).

Idrīs, Yūsuf, *Al-farāfīr* (Cairo, 1964).

——'*Autumn of the Patriarch* . . . and our summer', *Islām bilā ḍifāf* (Cairo: al-Hayʾa al-Miṣriyya al-ᶜĀmma li al-Kitāb, 1989), pp. 127–37.

Ilie, Paul, *Literature and Inner Exile: Authoritarian Spain, 1939–75* (Baltimore, MD: Johns Hopkins University Press, 1980).

ᶜImāra, Muḥammad, *ᶜAlī Mubārak, muʾarrikh wa muhandis al-ᶜumrān* (Cairo: Dār al-Shurūq, 1988).

Irby, James E., 'Introduction', in Jorge Luis Borges, *Labyrinths: selected stories and other writings*, eds Donald A. Yates and James E. Irby (New York, NY: New Directions Books, 1964), pp. xv–xxiii; xix.

Al-Jābirī, Muḥammad ᶜĀbid, *Ishkāliyyat al-fikr al-ᶜarabī al-muᶜāṣir* (Beirut: Markaz Dirāsāt al-Waḥda al-ᶜArabiyya, 1989).

——*Al-turāth wa al-ḥadātha* (Beirut: Markaz Dirāsāt al-Waḥda al-ᶜArabiyya, 1991).

Jad, Ali B., *Form and Technique in the Egyptian Novel 1912–1971* (Reading: Ithaca Press, 1983).

Jarrar, Maher, 'A narration of "deterritorialization": Īmīl Ḥabībī's *The Pessoptimist*', *Middle Eastern Literatures* 5: 1 (2002), pp. 15–28.

Jibrīl, Muḥammad, *Najīb Maḥfūẓ: ṣadāqat jīlayn* (Cairo: Kitābāt Naqdiyya, 1993).

Kadhim, Hussein, *The Poetics of Anti-Colonialism in the Arabic Qaṣīdah* (Leiden: E. J. Brill, 2004).

Kanafānī, Ghassān, *Mā tabaqqā lakum* (Beirut: Muʾassasat al-Abḥāth al-ᶜArabiyya, 1966, 1986); tr. Hilary Kilpatrick, *All That is Left to You* (London: Heinemann, 1978).

Karl, Frederick R., *Modern and Modernism: the Sovereignty of the Artist 1885–1925* (New York, NY: Macmillan, 1985).

Kassab, Elizabeth Suzanne, *Contemporary Arab Thought: Cultural Critique in Comparative Perspective* (New York, NY: Columbia University Press, 2010).

Kenny, Lorne, 'ᶜAlī Mubārak: nineteenth century Egyptian educator and administrator', *Middle Eastern Journal* 31: 1 (Winter 1967), pp. 35–51.

Khalafallāh, Muḥammad Aḥmad, *ᶜAlī Mubārak wa āthāruhu* (Cairo: Anglo-Egyptian Library, 1957).

Khalidi, Rashid, Lisa Anderson, Muhammad Muslih and Reeva S. Simon (eds), *The Origins of Arab Nationalism* (New York, NY: Columbia University Press, 1991).

Khater, Akram F., 'Emile Habibi: the mirror of irony in Palestinian literature', *Journal of Arabic Literature* 24 (1993), pp. 75–94.

Khoury, Philip, *Urban Notables and Arab Nationalism: the Politics of Damascus 1860–1920* (Cambridge: Cambridge University Press, 1983).

Khūrī, Ilyās, 'Al-baṭal al-filasṭnī fī qiṣaṣ Ghassān Kanafānī', *Ghassān Kanafānī insānan wa-adīban wa-munāḍilan* (Beirut: Manshūrāt al-Ittiḥād, 1974), pp. 92–129.

——*Dirāsāt fī naqd al-shiᶜr* (Beirut: Dār Ibn Rushd, 1981).

Kilito, Abdelfattah, *Les Séances: Récits et code culturels chez Hamadhanî et Harîrî* (Paris: Sindbad, 1983).

——*Al-adab wa al-gharāba: dirāsāt bunyawiyya fī al-adab al-ᶜarabī* (Beirut: Dār al-Ṭalīᶜa, 1982).

——*Al-ghāʾib: dirāsa fī maqāma li al-Ḥarīrī* (al-Dār al-Bayḍāʾ, 1987).

Kilpatrick, Hilary, 'Tradition and innovation in the fiction of Ghassān Kanafānī', *Journal of Arabic Literature* 7 (1976), pp. 53–64.

Kurd ᶜAlī, Muḥammad, *Khiṭaṭ al-shām* (Beirut: Dār al-ᶜIlm li al-Malayīn, 1969–71).

Kwan-Terry, John, 'Ash-Wednsday: a poetry of verification', in A. David Moody (ed.) *The Cambridge Companion to T. S. Eliot* (Cambridge: Cambridge University Press, 1994).

Lane, Edward William, *An Account of the Manners and Customs of Modern Egyptians* (London: Charles Knight & Co., 1836).

——*Description of Egypt*, ed. Jason Thompson (Cairo: American University in Cairo Press, 2000).

Lazarus, Neil, *Nationalism and Cultural Practice in the Postcolonial* (Cambridge: Cambridge University Press, 1999).

Le Gassick, Trevor (ed.), *Critical Perspectives on Naguib Mahfouz* (Washington, DC: Three Continents Press, 1991).

Lowenthal, David, *The Past is a Foreign Country* (Cambridge: Cambridge University Press, 1985).

——*Possessed by the Past: the Heritage Crusade and the Spoils of History* (London: Viking, 1996).

Macnaghten, W. H. *Alf Layla wa-Layla: The Alif Laila or Book of the Thousand Nights and One Night, Commonly Known as "The Arabian Nights' Entertainment"; Now, for the First Time, Published Complete in the Original Arabic, from an Egyptian Manuscript Brought to India by the Later Major Turner Macan, editor of the Shah-Nameh*, 4 vols (Calcutta, 1839–42).

Madyanī, Muḥammad, *Ishkāliyyat ta'ṣīl al-masraḥ al-ᶜarabī* (Qarṭāj: al-Majmaᶜ al-Tūnisī li al-ᶜUlūm wa al-Ādāb wa al-Funūn, 1993).

Magrath, Douglas, 'A study of *Rijāl fī al-shams* by Ghassān Kanafānī', *Journal of Arabic Literature* 10 (1979), pp. 95–108.

Maḥfūẓ, Najīb (Naguib Mahfouz), *Qaṣr al-shawq* (Cairo: Maktabat Miṣr, n.d.); tr. William M. Hutchins and Olive E. Kenny, *Palace of Desire* (New York, NY: Doubleday, 1990).

——*Layālī alf layla* (Cairo: Maktabat Miṣr, n.d.); tr. Denys Johnson-Davies, *Arabian Nights and Days* (New York, NY: Doubleday, 1995).

Mahmoud, Fatma Moussa, *The Arabic Novel in Egypt* (Cairo: General Book Organisation, 1973).

Malti-Douglas, Fedwa, *Woman's Body, Woman's Word: Gender and Discourse in Arabo-Islamic Writing* (Princeton, NJ: Princeton University Press, 1991).

'Mahfouz's Dreams', in Michael Beard and Adnan Haydar (eds) *Naguib Mahfouz: From Regional Fame to Global Recognition* (Syracuse, NY: Syracuse University Press, 1993), pp. 126–43.

Maᶜlūf, Īmīl, 'Al-Sindbād fī riḥlatihi al-thāmina al-ra'y al-awwal', *Al-ādāb* 8: 7 (July 1960), pp. 26–8.

Manganaro, Marc, *Myth, Rhetoric, and the Voice of Authority: a Critique of Frazer, Eliot, Frye and Campbell* (New Haven, CT: Yale University Press, 1992).

Al-Maqrīzī, *Ighāthat al-umma bi kashf al-ghumma* (Cairo: Dār Taḥqīq al-Turāth, 2002); tr. Adel Allouche, *Mamluk Economics: a Study and Translation of al-Maqrīzī's Ighāthah* (Salt Lake City, UT: University of Utah Press, 1994).

——*Al-khiṭaṭ al-Maqrīziyya* (Beirut: Dār al-Kutub al-ᶜIlmiyya, 1998).

Mehrez, Samia, 'Irony in Joyce's *Ulysses* and Habibi's *Pessoptimist*', *Alif: Journal of Comparative Poetics* 4 (Spring 1984), pp. 33–54.

——*Egypt's Culture Wars: Politics and Practice* (Cairo: American University Press, 2010).

Meyer, Stefan G., *The Experimental Arabic Novel: Postcolonial Literary Modernism in the Levant* (Albany, NY: State University of New York Press, 2001).

Mitchell, Timothy, *Colonising Egypt* (Cambridge: Cambridge University Press, 1988, 1991).

Monroe, James T., *The Art of Badīᶜ az-Zamān al-Hamadhānī as Picaresque Narrative* (Beirut: American University of Beirut, 1983).

Moosa, Matti, *The Origins of Modern Arabic Fiction* (New York, NY: Three Continents Press, 1997).

Moretti, Franco, *Atlas of the European Novel: 1800–1900* (London: Verso, 1998).

Morrison, Toni, *Playing in the Dark: Whiteness and the Literary Imagination* (New York, NY: Vintage Books, 1993).

Mubārak, ᶜAlī, *Al-tawfīqiyya* (Cairo: Bulaq, 1886–9).

——*ᶜAlam al-Dīn* (Alexandria: Jarīdat al-Maḥrūsa, 1882).

Mubārak, Zakī, *Al-akhlāq ᶜind al-Ghazzālī* (Cairo: Dār al-Kitāb al-ᶜArabī, n.d.).

Muḥammad, Aḥmad Sayyid, *Al-riwāya l-insiyābiyya wa taʾthīruhā ᶜind al-riwāʾiyyīn al-ᶜarab* (Algiers: al-Muʾassasa al-Waṭaniyya li al-Kitāb, 1989).

Al-Mūsawī, Muḥsin J., *Al-riwāya al-ᶜarabiyya: al-nashʾa wa al-taḥawwul* (Cairo: al-Hayʾa al-Miṣriyya al-ᶜĀmma li al-Kitāb, 1988).

——*Thārāt Shahrazād: fann al-sard al-ᶜarabī al-ḥadīth* (Beirut: Dār al-Ādāb, 1993), p. 25.

——*The Postcolonial Arabic Novel: Debating Ambivalence* (Leiden: E. J. Brill, 2003).

——*Arabic Poetry: Trajectories of Modernity and Tradition* (London: Routledge, 2006).

Al-Muwayliḥī, Muḥammad, *Ḥadīth ᶜĪsā Ibn Hishām*, ed. Maḥmūd Ṭarshūna (Tunis: Dār al-Janūb li al-Nashr, 1984, 2000); tr. Roger Allen, *A Period of Time* (Reading: Ithaca Press, 1992).

Al-Nābulsī, Shākir, *Mabāhij al-ḥuriyya fī al-riwāya al-ᶜarabiyya* (Beirut: al-Muʾassasa al-ᶜArabiyya li al-Dirāsat wa al-Nashr, 1992).

Al-Najjār, Ḥusayn Fawzī, *ᶜAlī Mubārak Abū al-taᶜlīm* (Cairo: Dār al-Kitāb al-ᶜArabī, 1967).

Al-Najjar, Muḥammad Rajab, 'Qiṣaṣ al-ḥubb fī l-layālī: al-binā wa al-waẓā'if', *Fuṣūl*, 13: 1 (Spring 1994), pp. 251–68.

Al-Naqqāsh, Rajāʾ, *Fī ḥubb Najīb Maḥfūẓ* (Beirut: Dār al-Shurūq, 1995).

——*Najīb Maḥfūẓ: Ṣafaḥāt min mudhakkirātihi* (Cairo: Muʾassasat al-Ahrām, 1998).

Naṣrallāh, Ibrāhīm, *Barārī al-ḥummā* (Beirut: Dār al-Shurūq, 1992).

Newman, Daniel L. (tr.), *An Imam in Paris: Account of a Stay in France by an*

Egyptian Cleric (1826–1831) (*Takhlīṣ al-Ibrīz fī Talkhīṣ Bārīz aw al-Dīwān al-Nafīs bi-īwān Bārīs* by Rifāʿa Rāfiʿ al-Ṭahṭāwī) (London: Saqi, 2004).

Norman, D., *The Hero: Myth/Image/Symbol* (New York, NY: Doubleday Anchor Books, 1990).

Al-Nuṣayr, Yāsīn, 'Jadaliyyat al-qirāʾa al-thālitha', *Al-aqlām* 23: 3 (March 1988), pp. 22–39.

Omri, Mohamad-Salah, *Nationalism, Islam and World Literature: Sites of Confluence in the Writings of Maḥmūd al-Masʿadī* (London: Routledge, 2006).

Özkirimli, Umut, *Theories of Nationalism: a Critical Introduction* (Basingstoke: Macmillan, 2000).

Peden, Margaret Sayers, 'Translator's Introduction', *Selected Odes of Pablo Neruda* (Berkeley, CA: University of California Press, 1990).

Peled, Mattityahu, *Religion, My Own: the Literary Works of Najīb Maḥfūẓ* (New Brunswick, NJ: Transaction Books, 1983).

Pratt, Marie Louise, *Imperial Eyes: Travel Writing and Transculturation* (London: Routledge, 1992).

Qāsim, Sīzā Aḥmad, *Bināʾ al-riwāya: dirāsa muqārana li-thulāthiyyat Najīb Maḥfūẓ* (Cairo: al-Hayʾa al-Miṣriyya al-ʿĀmma li al-Kitāb, 1984).

Qaysūma (Guissouma), Manṣūr, *Al-riwāya al-ʿarabiyya: al-iskhāl wa al-tashakkul* (Tunis: Dār Saḥar, 1997).

Rāghib, Nabīl, *Qaḍiyyat al-shakl al-fannī ʿind Najīb Maḥfūẓ: dirāsa taḥlīliyya li uṣūlihā al-fikriyya wa al-jamāliyya* (Cairo: al-Hayʾa al-Miṣriyya al-ʿĀmma li al-Kitāb, 1975).

Rastegar, Kamran, *Literary Modernity between Middle East and Europe: Textual Transactions in 19th century Arabic, English and Persian Literatures* (London: Routledge, 2007).

Raymond, André, *Le Caire* (Paris: Librairie Arthème Fayrad, 1993); tr. Willard Wood, *Cairo: City of History* (Cairo: American University in Cairo Press, 2001).

Reynolds, Dwight F. (ed.), *Interpreting the Self: Autobiography in the Arabic Literary Tradition* (Berkeley, CA: University of California Press, 2001).

Rofel, Lisa, *Other Modernities: Gendered Yearnings in China after Socialism* (Berkeley, CA: University of California Press, 1999).

Rose, Jacqueline, *State of Fantasy* (Oxford: Clarendon Press, 1996).

Al-Saʿāfin, Ibrāhīm, *Taṭwwur al-riwāya al-ʿarabiyya al-ḥadītha fī bilād al-shām 1870–1967* (Baghdad: Dār al-Rashīd, 1980).

Said, Edward, *Reflections on Exile and Other Essays* (Cambridge, MA: Harvard University Press, 2000).

Saʿīd, Khālida, *Ḥarakiyyat al-ibdāʿ: dirāsa fī al-adab al-ʿarabī al-ḥadīth* (Beirut: Dār al-ʿAwad, 1979).

Sakkut, Hamdi, *The Egyptian Novel and Its Main Trends From 1913–1952* (Cairo: American University in Cairo Press, 1971).

Salem, Paul, *Bitter Legacy: Ideology and Politics in the Arab World* (Syracuse, NY: Syracuse University Press, 1994).
Ṣāliḥ, Ṣalāḥ, *Sardiyyāt al-riwāya al-ᶜarabiyya al-muᶜāṣira* (Cairo: al-Majlis al-Aᶜlā li al-Thaqāfa, 2003).
Al-Sayyāb, Badr Shākir, *Dīwān*, 2 vols (Beirut: Dār al-ᶜAwda, 1971).
Selim, Samah, *The Novel and the Rural Imaginary in Egypt 1880–1985* (London: RoutledgeCurzon, 2004).
Sessona, Anna Zambelli 'The Rewriting of *The Arabian Nights* by Īmīl Ḥabībī', *Middle Eastern Literatures* 5: 1 (2002), pp. 29–48.
Al-Shakᶜa, Muṣṭafā, *Badīᶜ al-Zamān al-Hamadhānī: Rāʾid al-qiṣṣa al-ᶜarabiyya wa al-maqāla al-ṣāḥāfiyya* (Beirut: Dār al-Rāʾid al-ᶜArabī, 1979).
Shaᶜrāna, al-Munṣif, *Azmat al-dhāt fī maqāmāt al-Hamadhānī* (Sūsa: Dār al-Maᶜārif li al-Ṭibāᶜa wa al-Nashr, 1996).
Al-Sharqāwī, Maḥmūd, *ᶜAlī Mubārak: ḥayātuhu wa daᶜwatuhu wa āthāruhu* (Cairo: Anglo-Egyptian Library, 1962).
Al-Shaṭṭī, Sulaymān, *Al-ramz wa al-ramziyya fī adab Najīb Maḥfūẓ* (Kuwait: al-Maṭbaᶜa al-ᶜAṣriyya, 1976).
Shukrī, Ghālī, *Al-muntamī: dirāsa fī adab Najīb Maḥfūẓ* (Cairo: Dār al-Maᶜārif, 1965, 1969).
——*Burj bābil: al-nqd wa al-ḥadāthat al-sharīda* (London: Riad el-Rayyes, 1989).
Shurayḥ, Maḥmūd, *Khālīl Ḥāwī wa-Anṭūn Saᶜāda* (Sweden: Dār Nilsin, 1995).
Siddiq, M., *Man Is A Cause: Political Consciousness and the Fiction of Ghassān Kanafānī* (Seattle, WA: Washington University Press, 1984).
——*Arab Culture and the Novel: Genre, Identity and Agency in Egyptian Fiction* (London: Routledge, 2007).
Smith, Anthony D., *Theories of Nationalism* (New York, NY: Holmes and Meier Publishers, 1983).
——*The Ethnic Origins of Nations* (Oxford: Blackwell, 1986).
——*Nationalism and Modernism: a Critical Survey of Recent Theories of Nations and Nationalism* (London: Routledge, 1998).
Smith, Steven G., *Gender Thinking* (Philadelphia, PA: Temple University Press, 1992).
Sulaymān, Saᶜīd Shawqī Muḥammad, *Tawẓīf al-turāth fī riwāyāt Najīb Maḥfūẓ* (Cairo: Ītrāk li al-Nashr wa al-Tawzīᶜ, 2000).
Suleiman, Yasir and Ibrahim Muhawi (eds) *Literature and Nation in the Middle East* (Edinburgh: Edinburgh University Press, 2006).
Sullamī, Muḥammad, *Fann al-maqāma bi al-maghrib fī al-ᶜaṣr al-ᶜalawī: dirāsa wa nuṣūṣ* (Rabat: al-ᶜUkāẓ, 1992).
Sulṭān, Jamīl, *Fann al-qiṣṣa wa al-maqāma* (Beirut: Dār al-Anwār, 1967).
Ṭāhā, Ibrāhīm, *The Palestinian Novel: a Study in Communication* (London: RoutledgeCurzon, 2002).

Ṭarābīshī, Jūrj, *Allāh fī riḥlat Najīb Maḥfūẓ al-ramziyya* (Beirut: Dār al-Talīʿa, 1973, 1978, 1980).

——*Al-adab min al-dākhil* (Beirut: Dār al-Ṭalīʿa, 1978).

——*Ramziyyat al-marʾa fī al-riwāya al-ʿarabiyya* (Beirut: Dār al-Ṭalīʿa li al-Ṭibāʿa wa al-Nashr, 1981).

——*ʿUqdat Ūdīb fī al-riwāya al-ʿarabiyya* (Beirut: Dār al-Ṭalīʿa li al-Ṭibāʿa wa al-Nashr, 1982).

——*Al-muthaqqafūn al-ʿarab wa al-turāth: al-taḥlīl al-nafsī li ʿuṣāb jamāʿī* (London: Riad El-Rayyes, 1991).

——*Madhbaḥat al-turāth fī al-thaqāfa al-ʿarabiyya al-muʿāṣira* (London: Riad El-Rayyes, 1993).

Ṭarshūna, Maḥmūd, 'Madrasat tawẓīf al-turāth fī al-riwāya al-ʿarabiyya al-muʿāṣira', *Fuṣūl* 17: 1 (Summer 1998), pp. 27–39.

Tawfīq, Ḥasan, *Shiʿr Badr Shākir al-Sayyāb: dirāsa faniyya wa fikriyya* (Beirut: al-Muʾassasa al-ʿArabiyya li al-Dirāsāt wa al-Nashr, 1979).

Thompson, Elizabeth, *Colonial Citizens: Republican Rights, Paternal Privilege, and Gender in French Syria and Lebanon* (New York, NY: Columbia University Press, 2001).

Tibi, Bassam, *Arab Nationalism: a Critical Enquiry*, tr. Marion Farouk-Sluglett and Peter Sluglett (New York, NY: St. Martin's Press, 1981, 1990).

Tīzīnī, al-Ṭayyib, *Mashrūʿ ruʾya jadīda li al-fikr al-ʿarabī fi al-ʿaṣr al-wasīt* (Damascus: Dār Dimashq, 1971).

——*Mashrūʿ ruʾya jadīda li al-fikr al-ʿarabī min al-ʿaṣr al-jāhilā ḥattā al-marḥala al-muʿāṣira*: vol. 1, *Min al-turāth ilā al-thawra: Ḥawl naẓariyya muqtaraḥa fī qaḍiyyat al-turāth al-ʿarabī* (Beirut: Dār Ibn Khaldūn, 1978); vol. 2, *Al-fikr al-ʿarabī fī bawākīrihi wa āfāqihi al-ūlā* (Damascus: Dār Dimashq, 1982).

Turki, Fawaz, *Soul in Exile: Lives of a Palestinian Revolutionary* (New York, NY: Monthly Review Press, 1988).

Al-ʿUsaylī, Thurayyā, *Al-masraḥ al-shiʿrī ʿind Ṣalāḥ ʿAbd al-Ṣabūr* (Cairo: al-Haʾya al-Miṣriyya al-ʿĀmma li al-Kitāb, 1995).

ʿUṣfūr, Jābir (Gaber Asfour), 'Aqniʿat al-shiʿr al-muʿāṣir: Mihyār al-Dimashqī', *Fuṣūl* 1: 4 (1981), pp. 123–48.

——*Zaman al-riwāya* (Damascus: Dār al-Madā, 1999).

——'*Ghiwāyat al-taḥdīth*', *Fuṣūl* 12: 1 (1993), pp. 9–21.

Wādī, Fārūq, *Thalāt ʿalāmāt fī al-riwāya al-filasṭīniyya: Ghassān Kanafānī, Imīl Ḥabībī, Jabrā Ibrāhīm Jabrā* (Acre: al-Aswār, 1985).

Yaqṭīn, Saʿīd, *Al-riwāya wa al-turāth al-sardī* (Beirut: al-Markaz al-Thaqāfī al-ʿArabī, 1992).

——*Taḥlīl al-khitāb al-riwāʾī* (Beirut: al-Markaz al-Thaqāfī al-ʿArabī, 1999).

——*Infitāḥ al-naṣṣ al-riwāʾī* (Beirut: al-Markaz al-Thaqāfī al-ʿArabī, 2001).

Zarāqiṭ, ʿAbd al-Majīd, *Najīb Maḥfūẓ wa al-riwāya al-ʿarabiyya: abḥāth*

al-mu'tamar al-thālith wa al-ʿishrīn li ittiḥād al-udabā' wa al-kuttāb (Cairo: Ittiḥād al-Kuttāb and al-Hay'a al-ʿĀmma li-Quṣūr al-Thaqāfa, 2006).
Zaydān, Jurjī, *Tarājim mashāhīr al-sharq fī al-qarn al-tāsiʿ ʿashr*, 2 vols (Cairo: Dār al-Hilāl, 1910).
Al-Zumurrulī, Fawzī, *Shiʿriyyat al-riwāya al-ʿarabiyya: baḥth fī ashkāl ta'ṣīl al-riwāya al-ʿarabiyya wa dalālatihā* (Tunis: Markaz al-Nashr al-Jāmiʿī, 2002).

INDEX